CLARE

THROUGH THE TWENTIETH CENTURY

CLARE

THROUGH THE TWENTIETH CENTURY

Portrait of a Cambridge College

THIRD MILLENNIUM PUBLISHING

Copyright © 2001 Clare College and Third Millennium Publishing Limited

First published in 2001 by Third Millennium Publishing Limited,
a subsidiary of Third Millennium Information Limited
Shawlands Court Newchapel Road
Lingfield Surrey RH7 6BL UK
www.tmiltd.com

ISBN 1 903942 03 9

Edited by Lindsey Shaw-Miller, Honeychurch Associates, Cambridge, UK

Designed by Pardoe Blacker Limited,
a subsidiary of Third Millennium Information Limited

Printed and bound in Slovenia

ENDPAPERS: Manuscript of *The Fear of the Lord* by Herbert Howells,
reproduced by kind permission of John Rutter.

LEFT: Lady Clare

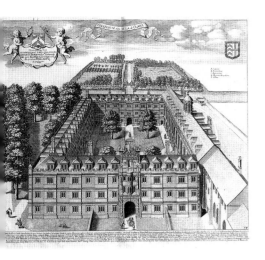

contents

8

RIGHT: *Freshmen 1945.*
David Attenborough is
on the back row, second
from left.

foreword

DAVID ATTENBOROUGH

It is difficult to know why Clare should have such a powerful hold on so many of us who, at some time, belonged to it. The nature of Oxbridge colleges is not easy to explain to those who have never attended them. Doubtless it is something to do with their size. Clare's, it seems to me, is almost ideal, generating a personal allegiance among its members that entities ten times as big cannot match.

I suspect that it also has something to do with Clare's sheer beauty – of Grumbold's Old Court (and personally, I would also include Gilbert Scott's Memorial Court since I had rooms there), of the bridge, of this particular stretch of the river and that incomparable riverside garden. And without any doubt, it is connected with the fact that the majority of us came to Clare at a time in our lives when we were most open to and appreciative of the wonders and excitements of the world.

Does it have anything to do with the fact that young scholars have been enrolling in our institution for nearly seven hundred years and that, for three hundred of them, have been sitting in the very rooms that we did? And have all these things added a unique facet to our characters that all of us who once belonged to Clare now share?

Whatever the answers, the fact remains that Clare has generated in us a love for it as an institution that has remained and often even grown throughout our lives. The evidence for that will be found in the following pages which are so full of perception, affection and delight.

editor's note

LINDSEY SHAW-MILLER

'For Clare is small; a better Cambridge, perhaps, for smallness is a lovable virtue.'

So wrote the reviewer of the last 'Clare Book', Mansfield Forbes' *Clare College 1326–1926*, in *Lady Clare Magazine* (Lent Term, 1928). Clare is, indeed, a precious jewel in the well-stocked Cambridge treasury. Unique in its architecture, strong in fellowship and spirit, conservative in its traditions, its progress has been made in sure, measured steps rather than impetuous strides. The clarity lent by these qualities, however, has not held Clare back from twentieth-century progress.

After the Second World War, all our institutions strove to regain solidity and security. In the progressive 1960s, however, not everyone would have been heartened that Clare felt like a college that would never change. By 1975, it was a college that would never be the same again: one of the first to admit women (1972), an increasing proportion of its students coming from state schools, powerful societies and academic excellence as its credentials. In the late twentieth century Clare has gone from strength to strength, and in 1999 was the first College in Cambridge to have sufficient confidence in the efficacy of its own procedures to allow the media to observe, uncensored, the admissions process.

I hope that, by direct and indirect means, this book reflects continuity and change at Clare in celebration of an astonishing century. It has been a great pleasure to work with contributors from such a wide range of experiences, viewpoints and interests, and to read all of the anecdotes sent in by members. Thanks to the enthusiastic response by members and Fellows, the book has grown to such an extent that, sadly, not everyone's reminiscences could be included. Yet every single communication has helped to set the tone, or direct attention to an aspect of the College we might otherwise have missed.

In addition to the contributors, I should like to thank Michelle Calvert and Jocelyn Poulton of the Development Office; Terry Moore; Tim Smiley (for directing my attention to Thomas Merton and John Berryman); Brian Smale-Adams, Adrian Travis and Nigel Weiss for stepping in to write much-needed pieces at very short notice; Tim Brown and, especially, John Rutter, for giving such care and attention to the CD through unforeseen and difficult circumstances; Dan Giles, Simon Blacker and Matthew Wilson of Third Millennium Publishing, and, of course, Julian Platt, without whom the book would never have been conceived in the first place. I should like to join with them in wishing the College a marvellous millennial century, its revelations tempered by the decorum and delicacy that is Clare.

a college for all seasons

PROFESSOR BOB HEPPLE QC

In 1900 Clare had 15 fellows, and 183 undergraduates drawn from a small number of public boarding schools and grammar schools. Only one in three of them would have expected to take an honours degree, the remainder leaving with ordinary degrees or no qualification at all. Although Clare was establishing "a modest presence in the Tripos list", it had a "more distinguished role in the playing fields and on the river."[1]

For the dons – only fairly recently (1879) allowed to marry – the tone was set by the Reverend Edward Atkinson, the last survivor of the Heads of Houses elected before the great reforms in the nineteenth-century university. He had taken his degree in 1842, been elected Master in 1856 and was to continue in office until his death, at the of age of 96, in 1915. His obituarist tells us that 'although a sound botanist of the old type', 'he never published anything' and that to him, Clare was, 'before all, a "religious foundation".' He opposed many of the great changes 'so long as opposition was possible.'[2]

It would be easy to make a comparison with the College in 2000, and to conclude that it has become not only much larger, but also more scholastic, more meritocratic, probably more democratic, and 'in the vanguard of reform.'[3] There are many obvious differences from the College of 1900. Just under half the undergraduate community now consists of women. The 440 undergraduates are drawn from a far wider range of schools. Academic standards are exceptionally high. Four out of five students achieve firsts or upper-second class honours – without any diminution of student participation on the playing fields and the river and in other extra-curricular activities, including an internationally renowned choir. There is a community of over 200 graduate students and a much expanded Fellowship of 66 men and women, most of them active in research as well as teaching, as well as 25 Life (retired) Fellows.

However, any comparison of this kind is bound to be superficial and pretty meaningless. As Christopher Brooke points out in volume IV of *A History of the University of Cambridge,*[4] as soon as we begin to look closer at questions such as the class background of students, the nature of the schools from which they come, and the aims of the University, we cannot make a comparison of any sophistication with an earlier age. It is perhaps more appropriate to characterize the College as a changing community, which reflects the wider University and the society in which it functions. This is not to suggest that the College is simply a mirror image of the outside world, or the passive recipient of changes decided by others. In some fields – such as the foundation of a graduate college (Clare Hall) in 1966, the admission of women in 1972, and broadening the range of schools from which we have recruited since the 1950s – the College has indeed been "in the vanguard." In some other areas we may have lagged behind. For example, our daughter foundation, Clare Hall, has been much more successful than we in breaking down hierarchies and enabling dons, most of whom are married, to reconcile working and family life.

RIGHT: *Punting on the Cam, September 2000, Clare Bridge.*

But overall, Clare is not an island – it is an integral part of a collegiate university whose fortunes are largely determined by political and social forces beyond our control.

Changing ideas of a university

We have inherited from our foundress, Elizabeth de Burgh, the medieval idea of a university as a democracy of masters (teachers), living together with scholars (students) in an educative community. Following the swinging days of student rebellion in the late 1960s, this democracy was broadened to allow for some student representation on the Council and the Finance Committee. In 1998 this representation was extended to the Governing Body. This is the Body which holds on trust the property of the corporation of Master, Fellows and scholars.

The idea of institutional autonomy embodied in collegial self-government and individual academic freedom accords well with liberal ideals. The assumption that education is ill-served by state interference continues to strike a deep chord in this country. A contrast is often drawn with continental Europe, where the revolutions of the late eighteenth and nineteenth centuries resulted in the incorporation of the universities in national bureaucratic systems. In reality, the ancient British universities have never been free from interfering rulers, patrons and benefactors – even Lady Clare reserved to herself during her life the interpretation and amendment of the statutes which she gave to the College in 1359, and she imposed many obligations of perpetual prayer and glorification of her family on the scholars.[5] Royal patronage – she was a granddaughter of Edward I and connected to the most powerful families in England – meant state interference.

In the twentieth century, as funding arrangements have changed, there has been increasing financial dependence of the University and the Colleges on the state. These developments are discussed by Brian Smale-Adams (pp. 90–104). The point of constitutional importance is that from 1919, when the University Grants Committee was established, until 1981, when government imposed cuts in resources and the UGC began to develop quality assessment, the

14

Oxbridge tradition of institutional autonomy was maintained, with the state being seen primarily as facilitator. But in the last two decades of the century the universities were subjected to extensive legislation, regulation and financial control. Whether this was because of expansion or a result of it is debatable. What is clear is that the consequences for institutions like Clare and for individual dons and students are profound.

By the end of the century the Colleges had lost their right to set fees for home and EC students, and they are now supplicants for a share of resources made available to the University by the Funding Council to replace the college fee. In the longer run the absorption of the Colleges into a centralized system of government financing will further undermine their autonomy, unless they increase their private endowments to an extent that would enable them to function without state support – at present an unrealistic prospect for most colleges. Systems of accountability between the University and the state, and between the Colleges and the University have become much tighter. Universities are expected to bid for limited resources for teaching and research. College Fellows (most of whom in Cambridge are University Teaching Officers) have to devote increasing amounts of time to applying for outside grants for their research, to supervise growing numbers of research students and to teach on graduate, as well as undergraduate courses. They are subjected to regular research assessment and teaching assessment exercises imposed by the Higher Education Funding Council. All of this at a time when average earnings of university staff have fallen behind the average for non-manual employees throughout the UK by 30%, and 18% behind the average for public sector, non-manual staff since 1981.[6]

Students, too, have felt the pinch. Following the Anderson report (1960), all home and (since 1973) EC undergraduates had their fees paid in full and were eligible for means-tested maintenance grants, so that ability to pay was no longer an obstacle to entering university. In the last decade of the century grants were replaced by loans, and since 1998 students have had to contribute up to one-quarter of their fees, depending on means. What the state gives, it can also take away.

A changing elite

Two hundred years ago Cambridge and Oxford were the only universities in England and Wales. This changed, with the emergence of the University of London and the great civic universities of the nineteenth century, the creation of the 'plateglass' universities in the era of expansion after the Robbins report (1963), and then the ending of the binary line between universities and polytechnics in 1992, which brought to 105 the number of universities. Nationally we have moved from an elite to a mass higher education system.

Cambridge and Oxford lost their monopoly of higher education but have remained pre-eminent in the changing national system. Their students and staff are part of a new elite with those of other so-called 'research' universities. In the ancient universities the student body has been transformed from an elite based on gender and social class to one based on academic merit. Until the Second World War only a privileged few entered university – less than one in 50 of the relevant age group in 1938, and for women less than one in 200. By 1948 the demand from returning ex-servicemen had reached its peak, and one in 25 of the 18-year-old population was entering university. Men outnumbered women by three to one nationally, and in Cambridge by ten to one. Social class differences were similarly striking: in 1945–54 less than 2% of all boys whose fathers were manual workers attended university

The periods of rapid expansion took place in the late 1960s, and again in the 1990s. In the early 1960s one in 18 of the 18-year-old age group went to university; by the late 1990s this was one in three, and in the first few decades of the twenty-first century this is likely to become one in two. The scale and effects of this expansion in Cambridge are discussed by Robin Matthews (pp. 36–42). I shall discuss three particular features of expansion in Cambridge and Clare relating to gender balance, social class, and internationalization of the Fellowship and graduate student body.

The gender revolution

The story of the admission of women to Clare has been told before,[7] but it is so important to the history of the College that I make no apology for a somewhat personal memoir.

It is a paradox that a college refounded in the fourteenth century by a remarkable woman took more than six centuries to open its doors to those of her gender. Her recent biographer remarks that 'one of the seals for Clare College depicts Elizabeth offering her statutes to her hall: a woman dictating the rules for academic males.'[8] It was not until the second half of the twentieth century that her example of female potential was revived. The opening of the professions and the extension of political democracy to women, and their changed economic and social status as a result of two world wars, inevitably led to the demand of the feminist movement inside and outside Cambridge for full educational equality. Here the Colleges were even more backward than the University, which, after half a century of struggles, finally admitted women to full membership only in 1948. But women remained few in number and segregated in Girton, Newnham and (from 1954) New Hall. If opportunities for women were to be expanded, there would either have to be a considerable enlargement of the women's colleges, or existing men's colleges would have to become co-residential.

As a Fellow from 1968, I was puzzled – as were most of the Fellows who had experience of mixed universities — by the arguments advanced against co-residence. However, thanks largely to the skill and subtlety of the Master, Eric Ashby, who had been persuaded to back the initiative of John Northam, the Governing Body resolved in April 1969, by a two-thirds majority, to declare an intention to make Clare co-residential. There was still the obstacle of a statute which barred membership of the College to women. This had been added as recently as 1926, to defeat any argument that the Sex Disqualification (Removal) Act of 1919 applied to colleges. So a statutory meeting was called a few weeks later to repeal this statute. There was much dismay when some retired Fellows, who had taken no part in the complex discussions over a period of three years, turned up to prevent the repeal. The disappointment was short-lived, because in May 1970 the necessary majority was secured, and Clare, along with Churchill and King's, became one of the first mixed colleges from 1972. This head-start enabled Clare to shoot to the top of the academic league tables for a few years, until other colleges followed suit and the advantages evened out.

In my capacity as Registrar (now called Tutor) for Admissions in the early years, I was not surprised by the enormous pool of female talent that had been opened up. The unquestioned success of Clare's lead was made possible by the undogmatic, rational and extremely fair way in which Charles Feinstein, and later Ken Riley, conducted admissions and tutorial matters, with the support of most of the alumni, and by the enthusiasm with which the Fellows, including those who had opposed the change, worked for its implementation. The educational and social character of the College was forever changed, from an exclusive male club into a mixed society in which women and men could work and socialize as equals.

That goal has been achieved in respect of our undergraduate population, roughly half of whom are female. Progress is being steadily made to complete this twentieth-century revolution so far as the graduate student body is concerned. There is a paucity of female research students, particularly in the sciences, but the proportion of women postgraduates in the university has increased from less than 20% in the early 1970s to over 40% in 1999. Clare has made special efforts to attract well-qualified women, who now make up 44% of its graduate body. An even more difficult problem in this and other former men's colleges has proved to be that of attracting women to the Fellowship. This is because of the relatively small number of women appointed to University posts (from which most Fellows are drawn). But by recruiting talented women who have not followed traditional career paths, we have been able to increase the proportion of women to over one-third of the teaching Fellows, higher than that in any other former men's college.

Full equality in practice is not simply a question of numbers, however. It involves removing obstacles to women's participation and creating an atmosphere in which both women and men can feel at home. One particularly complex phenomenon in the Faculties is the underachievement of women in some Tripos examinations, such as English and History. Clare can be expected to maintain the impetus for change where stubborn barriers in the University deny women substantive equality.

The persistence of class inequality

A more intractable problem for universities in general is that of the relatively narrow social class from which students are drawn. Most students and dons, in this as in other universities, still come from the higher-ranking socio-economic classes, but the great changes in occupational structure in the twentieth century make it difficult to define 'class' consistently and to measure the changes. Dr Bob Blackburn (a Fellow of Clare since 1966) has studied the changing inequalities in access to British universities in depth. Adopting a sophisticated technique which allows for consistent measurement of class inequalities over time, he reached the depressing conclusion in 1993 that 'there is a strong class differential among both men and women, and little has changed despite the large expansion of provision.'[9] In the period 1950–60, the growing number of places in higher education were largely taken up by children of managerial and professional par-

16

ents who could afford fees, and class inequalities were widening. In the 1960s and 1970s, policies of expansion based on academic ability and aptitude were followed by a decline in inequality. Inequality rose in the early 1980s as the provision of places failed to keep pace with increasing demand. Expansion in the 1990s made possible the narrowing of inequalities, but the replacement of grants by loans and the introduction of student contributions to fees will tend to favour inequality in future. The most likely outcome, believes Dr Blackburn, is that expansion will be achieved without much change in existing class inequalities.

No study has been made of the social backgrounds of Clare students. The top classes from which they were drawn in 1900 were obviously different from those of 2000. Assuming, perhaps erroneously, that Clare was not much different from Caius (for which some statistics are available),[10] then the sons of the landed gentry were still well-represented in 1900. But an image of pre-Second

World War Clare as a haven for idle Bertie Woosters or Sebastian Flytes would be a gross distortion. The sons of clergy, lawyers, physicians and the lower-ranking "trades" seem to have predominated. In the country at large, in every generation, the majority of university students have come from non-graduate homes; in Clare too, there have been many first-generation university students. A snapshot of the occupations of parents disclosed on the application forms of those given places by Clare in 2000, reflects the professionalization of the wider society. The strongest representation is from those whose parents are in business and finance (28%) and in education (27%), followed by medicine (11%), government and law (7%), and miscellaneous professions (10%). The occupations of parents of 12% of the Clare entrants might broadly be described as being in socio-economic groups IV (partly skilled) and V (unskilled), compared to the 10% in these occupations in all universities.[11] The remainder (5%) are retired or with no stated occupation.

These national and local statistics shed some light on the vexed question of admissions. Since the Anderson (1960) and Robbins (1963) Reports, national policy has been that students should be admitted solely on the basis of academic ability and aptitude. The Dearing Report (1997) advocated a more proactive approach to widening participation as a necessary and desirable objective of national policy over the next 20 years.[12] Here it is government that can call the tune by paying the piper. Preferential funding is given to those institutions which can demonstrate a commitment to widening participation, and have in place a participation strategy and mechanisms for reviewing progress. But even without this incentive, the experience with the admission of women showed us that by widening access one taps a large pool of talent which might otherwise be wasted. This raises standards and affords opportunities to individuals who can make the greatest contribution to society.

I feel that Lady Clare would have been sympathetic to this argument. Her statutes of 1359 provided that educational opportunities were to be extended to poor youth 'chosen from amongst the poorest that can be found.' So we can claim to be following her precepts in widening access to Clare. The dilemma is how to reconcile the uncontroversial criterion of 'academic ability and aptitude' with choosing from amongst the disadvantaged sections of society. Nationally, in 1993 the mean A-level score for candidates from the highest socio-economic groups

BELOW: *The sexcentenary celebrations, July 13th 1926, Princess Mary and Viscount Lascelles with the Master, Dr W.L. Mollison, 1924, and his successor, G.H.A. Wilson.*

form colleges, have on the whole had a very much stronger record of access to Cambridge than comprehensive schools. Many believe that the abolition of direct grant and (most) grammar schools in the 1970s was a major factor in the shift of applicants from state to independent schools. From 1970–80 applicants from state schools (mostly grammar schools) rose from 45% to 56%, and a further 15% came from direct grant schools. During the same period applications from independent schools fell from 40% to 29%. By 1986, however, the proportion from independent schools had risen to 56%.

The Colleges cannot cure the social inequalities in the school system. At best they can match in admissions the proportion of school leavers from state schools with three or more top A-level grades (about 65%). A great deal has been done over many years by Cambridge admissions tutors to this end. Considerable resources have been devoted to reach state-school applicants who have academic potential, including open days, school visits by tutors and students, sixth form conferences and publicity. Nearly every candidate is interviewed in order to assess their academic potential, as well as their likely contribution to college life and the wider society. When making offers, allowances are made for the educational and social background of candidates, while maintaining the standards that reflect the academic requirements for successful study at Cambridge. In the earlier part of the century, access was dominated by the system of scholarships and exhibitions. In the 1970s Clare was one of the colleges which began to use the alternative of conditional offers, based on projected A levels. The Colleges Entrance Examination was dropped in 1986 because of its adverse impact on those from state schools who did not have the same opportunities as those from independent schools to prepare for the examination. Other hurdles which have a disparate impact, such as the STEP examination, have been dropped (except in Mathematics). Initiatives such as these will continue in the twenty-first century. One of these is the Clare Partnership for schools in the London boroughs of Southwark and Tower Hamlets, an area in which the College established a Mission in the nineteenth century, and still supports a recent Clare graduate engaged in educational and youth projects at Bede House in Bermondsey.

As I noted earlier, comparisons can be misleading because of the changing nature of schools and the fluidity of the independent/state divide. But it is interesting to

FAR LEFT: *Graduands 2000, Old Court.*

achieving two or more A-levels was 17, for those from middle socio-economc groups 11, and those from the lowest socio-economic groups 8.[13] In Cambridge the norm for acceptance is three A-levels. Nearly 80% of applications and 98% of acceptances are from candidates with scores of 28–30. Obviously, those from the top socio-economic groups are most likely to get into Cambridge.

As is well known, there is a link between A-level scores and the kind of school at which the examinations were taken. The success of candidates from independent schools is not surprising. In the *Financial Times* ranking of schools in 1997, according to A-level performance, the first state school is a selective girls' school at 71st place, and the first English comprehensive lies outside the first 200 places. The division between 'state' and 'independent' schools is, of course, a crude one. There are important distinctions within the state sector: selective grammar, grant-maintained and church schools, and some sixth

18

observe that from 1929–38, 85% of students admitted by Clare came from public schools and only 15% from state schools. Three-quarters of those admitted came from just 12 major public boarding schools: Marlborough, Oundle, Rugby, Charterhouse, Repton, Uppingham, Shrewsbury, Wellington, Harrow. Haileybury, Fettes and Sedbergh.[14] In October 2000, the 139 matriculands came from 120 schools, 57% of them in the state sector and 43% independent. Sixty-five percent of those applying for admission in 2001 are from state schools and 35% from independent ones.

RIGHT: *Bob Hepple, the present Master.*

Internationalization

Another major change has been the internationalization of the Fellowship and the student body. Even in the decade before the Second World War, there was a fair sprinkling[15] of students from the USA, Australia and New Zealand, South Africa and India. But the enlargement of the graduate student population since the Second World War (discussed by Robin Matthews, pp. 41, 44–45) has been the main source of internationalization. Many of the graduates from other universities in this country and abroad were from schools or social backgrounds for whom entry at undergraduate level was not thought possible.

I would like to believe – as one who came to Clare as a mature graduate student from South Africa in 1964 – that the addition of a significant number of overseas students and Fellows has helped to make Clare a more cosmopolitan, multi-cultural community. Those of us who came from outside received a warm welcome. James Watson recalls, in his personal account of the discovery of the structure of DNA, that what led him in 1951 to come as an American postgraduate to Clare – 'an unexpectedly happy choice' – was the rosy outlook for foreign research students painted by Nick Hammond, then Senior Tutor, including the promise of rooms on R staircase.[16] For me, a flat and garden in Queen Edith's House, in which my wife and young children could enjoy the friendship of the families of Fellows and graduate students, while I worked in the Law Reading room on D staircase and met other graduates in the MCR (then just above), made this a specially happy period.

The College's strong connections with North America, dating back to Nicholas Ferrar and the Virginia Company in the seventeenth century, were cemented in the twentieth century by the Mellon Fellows to and from Yale, the Kellett Fellows from Columbia, the Duveen scholars from Smith College, and a regular stream of other American graduates. In 2000, Clare's graduate population mirrors that of the University, which has nearly 4,000 overseas students drawn from over 90 countries. The College has also become more diverse in reflecting the different British ethnic communities.

The future of the collegiate system

For nearly seven centuries the College has survived, and in the twentieth century flourished, by gradually adapting to the changing political, social and financial environment. There were times of great trauma – the two world wars – but, on the whole we have followed Ashby's advice that 'just as large mutations in genetics are harmful or lethal, so in universities large innovations create distress and massive resistance.'[17] The external and internal pressures for expansion, for greater democracy, and for the replacement of social and gender privilege by academic merit, have been absorbed gradually, and with relatively little pain. Clare has remained a remarkably congenial and happy community, in which changes have been achieved by rational argument, consensus and goodwill.

At various times in their long history the Colleges have been seen to stand for reaction and the state for progress.

LEFT: *Edward Atkinson,
Master of Clare
1856–1915.*

20

Within the University, some heads of departments have regarded the Colleges as an obstacle to effective, centralized management. There are many frustrations and delays in a system in which Colleges control admissions and provide individualized tuition and pastoral care, while the University lays down and examines the courses and provides lectures, libraries and laboratories. Why try to retain such a complex and seemingly irrational system in the twenty-first century?

The answer, I believe, is one that fits the spirit of the times. The collegiate system is better equipped than any form of mass higher education to overcome the inequalities of gender, class and origin, and to produce a new social identity and purpose for those who pass through it. The Colleges are better placed than single-subject departments to choose the students most likely to benefit, on the basis of all-round academic ability and potential to contribute to society. The intimacy of personalized tuition and pastoral care offered by the Colleges achieves the true purpose of education, by bringing out the best in every individual. The mingling of people drawn from different disciplines far exceeds anything which is possible in a hall of residence; the boundaries between the social and the academic become infinitely fluid. For the dons and graduate students, sharing commons provides the opportunity for each of us to see beyond our own specialism. James Watson recalls crossing Clare Bridge 'marvellously alive' on the morning after their discovery was confirmed, and reflecting 'that much of our success was due to the long uneventful periods when we walked among the Colleges.'[18] Colleagues in other disciplines talking casually over lunch or dinner can widen our intellectual horizons and social concerns, and stimulate new ideas in a way which purely departmental universities cannot.

Whatever the changes to which the College has to adapt in the twenty-first century, we can be confident that, with the support of its alumni, this will continue to be a vibrant community pursuing the purposes immortalized in Lady Clare's inspiring words of 1359: 'Through their study and teaching at the University the scholars should discover and acquire the precious pearl of learning so that it does not stay hidden under a bushel but is displayed abroad to enlighten those who walk in the dark paths of ignorance.'

September 2000

1 Christopher N.L. Brooke, *A History of the University of Cambridge*, Volume IV 1870–1990, (Cambridge University Press, 1993), p. 64.

2 *Lady Clare Magazine XIV/1*, Lent 1919, pp. 6–8.

3 Judith Judd, *The Independent*, May 2000.

4 Brooke, *op.cit.*, p. 240.

5 Frances A. Underhill, *For Her Good Estate: The Life of Elizabeth de Burgh* (Macmillan, 1999), p. 142.

6 *Independent Review of Higher Education Pay and Conditions*. Report of a Committee chaired by Sir Michael Bett (HMSO, 1999), p. 51.

7 See especially Eric Ashby, 'How ever did women get into Clare ?', *Clare Association Annual* 1986–87, p. 7.

8 Underhill, *op. cit.*, p. 132.

9 Robert M. Blackburn and Jennifer Jarman, 'Changing Inequalities in Access to British Universities', *Oxford Review of Education* 19 (1993), 197–215, at p. 211; see also C. Marsh and R.M. Blackburn 'Class differences in higher education', in R. Burrows and C. Marsh (eds) *Consumption and Class, Divisions and Change*, pp. 184–211.

10 Brooke, *op.cit*, Appendix 5, p. 601.

11 *Higher Education in the Learning Society*, Report of the National Committee of Inquiry into Higher Education (Chairman: Lord Dearing) (HMSO, 1997), p. 23.

12 *ibid.*, p.101.

13 *ibid.*, p. 103.

14 These statistics were compiled in 1993 by Mrs Suzy Johnston, then College Archivist.

15 Statistics of students admitted 1929–38, compiled by Mrs Johnston, show 26 from the USA, 24 from Australia, 13 from New Zealand, 10 from South Africa, 8 from India, 2 from Canada and one each from Barbados and China.

16 James D. Watson, *The Double Helix* (Weidenfeld and Nicolson, 1981), p. 87.

17 Eric Ashby, *Masters and Scholars: Reflections on the Rights and Responsibilities of Students* (Oxford University Press, 1970), p. 6.

18 Watson, *op.cit.*, p. 117.

SIEGFRIED SASSOON

There is no need to be exact about the date, but it is somewhere in the early part of June 1906, and about five o'clock in the morning. In broad daylight, under a quietly overclouded sky, a dozen young people are arranging themselves before the canopied fountain in the market-place at Cambridge. They have danced to the end of the Trinity Boat Club Ball and are about to corroborate the occasion by being photographed.

They are doing it in a good-natured unresisting sort of way, for it is a family party and they all take one another's presence as a matter of course, without any nonsense about wondering when they will meet again.

My cousin Alyce stifles a yawn and feels sure that the camera will catch her in the middle of the next one; my cousin Joan tells her brother Oliver to put his tie straight; the photographer emerges from black velvet obscurity, regards the group with a stabilizing simper, and removes the cap; for three seconds time holds its breath, and then relaxes us into animation again. A clock strikes five and the young people disappear in various directions, unaware that I shall have my eye on them more than thirty years afterwards. Scrutinizing that faded photograph now, I see myself surrounded by my cousins – the girls looking absent-mindedly amused and the men rather stolid and serious. There is that modest hero Malcolm, a stalwart Rowing Blue, destined to become an eminent surgeon. And his younger brother, who went into the Indian Army. And Oliver, who was to do well as an engineer. And my brother Hamo, whose engineering ambitions were sacrificed on the Gallipoli peninsula. And there am I, sitting on the ground in front, with a serenely vacant countenance which suggests that no plans for a practical career have as yet entered my head. Behind that head the jet of the drinking-fountain is just visible, as though the camera were hinting that my name would be written in water, which was what I myself sometimes foresaw.

It had been a jolly fine dance anyhow, I thought, picking up my cap and gown and taking my tired patent-leather feet across to my rooms, which were only about fifty yards from the fountain. And after all I wasn't quite nobody, for I'd got a whole column of blank verse (semi-facetious, in the manner of Browning) in the May Week Number of *The Granta*; it was a monologue by an anarchist who blew himself up when about to drop his bomb from a window on to a royal procession, and I had no notion why I had written it, except that I had wanted to follow up my exultant parody of Stephen Phillips, which had appeared in the previous week and had been about lovers alliteratively involved in a motor accident. And now I was back in my low-ceilinged room on the third floor, with *The Granta* lying on the writing-table, and *Atalanta in Calydon* open beside it, and the inappropriate daylight making it all look somehow as though time were playing a trick on me and I were seeing something which had happened before. The room looked too quiet to be quite real, and the reproductions of Rossetti and Burne-Jones were raptly remote from the dizzy waltzing I'd done in the Guildhall. Standing there for a moment, it was like changing from one of my selves to another. For a few hours I had been escaping from my everyday self, and here he was waiting up for me, telling me to get rid of my buttonhole and evening clothes, stop writing silly parodies, and do some real drudgery for those examinations which I didn't seem to have a ghost of a chance of getting through.

Perhaps for the first time, I had the sense of time slipping away from me, of not making serious use of my opportunities; and mixed up with this was the reiterated memory of a waltz tune which meant nothing but an allurement to forgetfulness and the pursuit of easy poetic emotion and idle pleasure. 'In three months I shall be twenty, and I don't seem to have done anything at Cambridge except buy books in vellum bindings,' I thought,

22

Siegfried Sassoon
Sir William
Rothenstein, 1921

Black chalk on paper
9" x 7.5"

while the clock watched me with its hands at half-past five and I overheard my thought as though it were a repetition of some previous experience.

It really seemed that in order to make a success of being up at Cambridge I needed to be three people at once. There was the swing-concerned person who so frequently spent his afternoon golfing at Mildenhall or Royston. There was he who sat up into the small hours composing high-principled poetry about nothing in particular. And – heaven help him – there was the one who ought to have been – and wasn't – advancing towards the acquisition of a University Degree. There was even a fluid fourth, who sprawled about in other people's rooms talking irrepressible nonsense or listening to someone playing Chopin scherzos on the pianola. The only thing these four had in common was that they neither smoked nor imbibed alcohol, and received £80 a term through the family solicitor.

They – or rather I – having come to the end of my first year, the College Tutor was only partly aware that my academic future was precarious. He had assumed from the start that I was fully capable of passing Tripos examinations, and for a time I had allowed myself to be influenced by his urgent optimism. My guardians were of opinion that after I left Cambridge the wisest thing for me to do would be to read for the Bar, and it was suggested that this would somehow coincide with my leanings toward literature. Since working for an ordinary degree would have meant more mathematics, I decided that anything would be better than that, and plunged blindly into the Law Tripos. Grappling with the Edicts of Gaius and Justinian, I memorized much information about the manumission of slaves, and other, to me, meaningless ancient Roman legal procedure. Dutifully I attended droning lectures, desperately scribbling fragments of what I overheard and seldom understanding what my notes were about when I perused them in private. Note-taking seemed to be physical rather than mental exercise. During my first term I submitted to my doom without realizing that nothing but a miracle could enable me to propitiate the examiners. The Lent term reduced me to blank despondency. Toiling at my textbooks, I discovered again and again that I had turned over two pages at once without noticing anything wrong. In the eyes of my Law coach, whom I attended twice a week, I became a manifest absurdity. He was a dark and dapper little LL.D. who had written a book about the

Hague Conference and wore a rich-red tie and a neatly waxed moustache. In after-years he became an important authority in the world of International Law. Precise and persistent, he took about half a dozen pupils at a time. The subjects he was teaching afforded him scant opportunities for humour, but on one occasion he caused a mild explosion of mirth – at my expense – by exclaiming: 'If I were to go out into the street and interrogate the first errand-boy I met he wouldn't know less than you do about Maine's International Law!'

This, I think, was the irrefutable remark which finally impelled me to call on the Senior Tutor of my College and announce my inability to learn any more Law. In my agitation I put it to him quite unashamedly that I was more interested in poetry than anything else. To my surprise and relief he responded sympathetically. For a few minutes he almost forgot that he was a Senior Tutor and revealed a warm admiration for Browning. I had entered his rooms in College a palpitating and self-ploughed candidate for my Tripos, and here we were, amicably enthusing over the glories of 'Abt Vogler' and 'Saul'. I could have embraced him when he declared that Law certainly allowed no scope at all for poetic imagination, and his proposal that I should transfer my attentions to the History Tripos was almost like receiving an honorary degree. So elated was I as I went out that I tripped and fell down the first flight of drumming wooden stairs, and landed with such a bump that the little man popped his head round the door to see what had happened.

'Dear me, what an impetuous fellow you are!' he exclaimed, as I arose, rubbing a bruised funny-bone. The Senior Tutor was a fussy, over-anxious man with a nervous stammer, which I used to catch when conversing with him. When we were together it was difficult to decide which was the jumpier and more jerky of the two. Continually twiddling his eyeglasses, he specialized in sudden darting movements which sometimes knocked things off tables, while I relied mainly on fidgeting with my fingers and feet. In fact, though favourably disposed toward one another, we were not unlike a couple of cats on hot bricks, and my exit from our crucial conference was quite characteristic. After this flying start I tackled the History Tripos with a spurt of unmethodical energy. I had found Law altogether too inhuman and arid, but History was bound to be much more lively and picturesque, and I got to work on the reign of Louis XI without any feeling of repugnance. The memoirs of Philip de Commines, in a seven-

24

Clare Bridge
John F. Greenwood,
1925

Linocut

teenth-century translation, made quite enjoyable reading, with their quaint literary flavour. But I soon discovered that I didn't retain much of them afterwards. I could only remember episodes which appealed to my visual imagination, such as the anecdote of Louis XI's scouts mistaking tall thistles for the spears of men-at-arms. Chastellains's memoirs, which I also had to read, brought me to a standstill, for they were in mediaeval French and no translation was available. The more I looked at Chastellain the less hopeful I felt of being able to get past him. He was incomprehensible, bulky, and ominously bound in black buckram. My main trouble as a student of history was that I wanted it to be more like Stanley Weyman's novels or

Shakespeare's plays. I had but a feeble grasp of constructive elements and political interworkings.

In fact it never consciously occurred to me that a prime minister in a richly furred robe was much the same as one who wore a frock-coat. I could only understand what history signified when it was being either dramatic or chronological. Dodging about in Thatcher and Schwill's *General History of Europe* I found little, except dates and names, which I could reproduce verbally to my History coach; he complained of my preoccupation with the career of Joan of Arc, about whom I was privately meditating a long poem in blank verse. 'You really must put in some solid work on the struggle between the

25

Empire and the Papacy,' he remarked. To which I duti-fully agreed, and spent most of the next day reading *The Earthly Paradise* in a punt. By reading I mean that my eyes moved from line to line while I overheard rather than 'took in' the beautifully monotonous word music of William Morris, which loitered through my mind as though it were one of the riverside sounds of that golden day in early summer. At that time I was finding much material for day-dreaming in the poems and pictures of the Preraphaelite Brotherhood. Through them I shared an imaginative existence which, as they had intended it to do, provided an ideal escape from commonplace actuali-ties. As ordinary human beings I didn't want to know too much about them, and had been rather sorry when my mother told me that Rossetti took chloral and suffered from insomnia, and that Morris had become an ardent Socialist in his later years. I preferred to think vaguely of them as a group of people with whom I could have been happy, and I wanted their world to resemble the one which they had created for me in their works. I imagined myself conversing with them to the music of citterns and citoles (though uncertain what those obsolete instru-ments would sound like), in arrassed rooms whose win-dows overlooked a river that flowed down to Camelot. Far away from factory chimneys, Rossetti would be reading me his latest sonnet, or Morris showing me the carp in his fish-pond, and my own poems would be being exquis-itely printed by the Kelmscott Press and bound in limp vellum with woven silk ties. Actually I had never met anyone, except myself, who wanted to be a poet, so I often sought companionship in the past, pretending that I had been at Cambridge with Tennyson, and having long talks with him and Edward Fitzgerald. At any moment they might come along the river-bank and get into my punt. Or else it would be Morris, arm-in-arm with Rossetti and the late Sir Edward Burne-Jones. As an offset to all this make-believe, I could claim that I had once met Mrs William Morris, who had been brought to see my mother when I was about six years old. I could remember a stately lady entering our nursery; but being shy, I refused to emerge from under the table, so I only viewed the origi-nal of Rossetti's picture, 'The Blessed Damozel', through the fringe of the table-cloth.

Anyway here I was, under a pollard willow, with a light breeze ruffling the bend of the river and bringing the scent of bean-fields, while Cambridge, a mile or two away, dozed in its academic afternoon. Successfully though I had

interposed *The Earthly Paradise* between myself and the struggle of the Empire and the Papacy, I couldn't evade the fact that I was due for the first part of my History Tripos in twelve months' time. And what would happen then, I asked myself, removing my eyes from the lulling stanzas of Pygmalion and the Image. Nothing, I was cer-tain, could possibly happen except an unqualified expo-sure of my ignorance and incompetence. I was well on my way to a fiasco of the first water, I thought, wondering whether a fiasco could also be of the deepest dye. The fact that I had been pouring out poems which seemed to me quite good made no difference to the fact that I should be chucked out of Cambridge at the end of my second year.

ABOVE: *Punting on the Cam, 2000.*

EDWARDIAN CLARE

MY FIRST DAY

I arrived at the Great Eastern station tired and worn. There were nine others – obviously 'freshers' like me – in the carriage all the way from Town; and the day was hot, as hot as an early October day can be – one of those days in which Summer seems to have realised it ought to have departed, and so tries to put all its superfluous heat into a few days, usually when it is not wanted. I fought – literally speaking – my way out of the station, and was pushed – figuratively speaking – into a hansom. I shouted my destination and we were off. My 'Varsity career was about to begin.

We drew up at Clare gates and not being a judge of distances gave the jehu 3/6, for which he seemed mightily pleased. I carried my dress-suit case in my hand and walked towards the Porter's Lodge. It was empty. I deposited my bag there and came out into the Court to look for somebody.

At that moment I saw somebody approaching. I walked towards him. 'I have left my bag at your lodge,' I remarked, 'can you tell somebody to take my boxes in.'

He eyed me gravely over his blue-tinted glasses. 'I see you are a Freshman,' he said. 'You have made a mistake!'

With these words he left me. I felt non-plussed. It was my first brick!

Fortunately at that moment one of the under-porters appeared and I sent him to assist the cabman, who was 'wrestling' with sundry trunks and packing cases.

I wandered across the court. Out of E staircase there appeared a portly form. He cut across the grass towards me.

'Ha, ha, how are you. I'm the Dean, ha, ha. What games are you going to play. Hockey and Tennis? Yes? Good! Come and see me some time. Cheerey oh!'

Another surprise! I had always imagined Deans and Dons to be synonymous with martinets and faddists. The idea of a sporting Don was new to me. So much the better!

I had scarcely recovered from my surprise when an immaculately attired form, smoking a cigarette with a delightful aroma, emerged from E staircase. He 'strolled' towards me.

'How are you?' he asked me, gently flicking the ash from his cigarette, and by the by, 'Who are you?'

I informed him. 'Ah yes, of course, you come from ___ School. Now would you like to be put for election to the Hawks Club? You would? Right! Again he strolled away. Another sporting don! Was it possible that all the dons in the College were 'sporting' – in the true sense of the word? I found later it was.

I turned round and saw a benevolent old gentleman standing on the top of the steps near the Hall. 'This must be the Master,' I thought to myself, 'I have heard he is old. I must introduce myself.'

I made my way to the steps, and, politely raising my hat, said 'The Master, I presume, may I introduce myself, I am Mr ___'

'I am delighted to make your acquaintance,' he answered, 'but I am not the Master, leastways not in name. I'm the College butler, that's what I am, and my name is Phipps. I quite agree I more or less run the place, and if I went I don't know what would happen.' 'Yes,' he continued, 'the Master is over ninety years old, and a fine hale and hearty gentleman he is. I'm not the Master, leastways, not yet!'

I was charmed. What a delightful personality! Were all the college servants like him?

'The Senior Tutor would like to see you, Sir,' put a stop to my musings, and I made my way to his room which had been pointed out to me. I knocked at his door and was bidden to enter. I found him surrounded with papers and books of all descriptions.

'Good afternoon, Mr ee, ee – let me see – Mr ee – I have really forgotten your name.'

I told him. 'Oh yes, of course, how stupid of me. You are going to take the ee ee – let me see – oh yes – the Natural Sciences Tripos. Is that right?'

1900 MAY BOAT

I nodded assent. 'Come up to-night after hall to arrange lectures. And now, Mr ___, what ee ee games do you play? I like all the men in this college to play games. We do not rely for our position in the University on work alone. Ha, ha!'

I informed him of my intention of playing Rugger for that term – 'and a very good game too, Mr ___,' – and we then talked of other things such as caps, gowns and fireworks! Shortly after I left, again surprised – although I was getting used to it by then – that even a senior tutor did not want you to work all day long! His last words were 'Introduce yourself to the – ee ee – tutor who keeps opposite. I am your tutor for exeats, etc. Good afternoon!'

I crossed the passage and knocked.

'Come in,' and I entered.

Again I found the sporting instinct rampant. After the usual formalities of introduction he asked ' of course you are going to row, Mr ___?'

I replied in the negative and his face fell. 'That is a pity as we want to get a lot of the first year to row.' I explained I had come to Clare to play Rugger and not to row.

'In any case I hope you will support the Boat Club, Mr ___ by running during the races, etc.'

I assented willingly, and after bidding him 'Adieu,' I came into the court again and walked towards the Porter's Lodge with the intention of fetching my suit-case. In this I was 'thwarted,' as at that moment I was seized by the arm.

'Have you just come up? Yes? Well, come up to my rooms and have some. tea. I always drink tea. It is the standing joke of the college. They say I have drunk 394.217 cups since I have been librarian of the college.

All this time I had been unable to get out a word, and by the time he had finished we had reached his room on F. There I had a most enjoyable tea and talked of many things and wondered how long it took him to cultivate his laugh!

After tea I left him. I had made up my mind to see the rest of the Dons on the following day. I wandered on to the bridge to collect my thoughts. I had been disillusioned.

Lady Clare Magazine Vol X/2, Lent Term 1911

HERODOTUS AT CLARE

And after this they brought me unto the city of the Elizabethidae; for all they that dwell therein say that they have one mother, even Elizabeth the daughter of Clare, who first colonized that place. And the name of the city they call Clare for none other reason than this. Now the children of Elizabeth be exceeding many, even so that some only who be rulers and the elder among the folk may have their habitation within the city; but the others dwell abroad in huts among the barbarians who inhabit the country round about. And I asked of them that brought me, wherefore then did not the rulers of the city make unto themselves other and larger dwellings? And they answered me that they did not know, but that some said that they were forbidden of an oracle.

Now this city lieth by the river that floweth through the country. And this river is not like the rivers of Hellas, for it floweth neither to the East, nor to the West, but stayeth still ever in the same place.

Now the approach to the city is on this wise. There be many and fair trees on both sides of the way, and beyond these also be gardens. But no man entereth therein, for they are accounted sacred of the elders. And after I had passed through these trees, I came to the bridge whereby men cross the river I have told you of. And of this bridge I will tell you: for about it there is much strife. The men of Clare indeed, hold that it is of all things the most beautiful in the land. Howbeit, nigh unto this city lieth an exceeding great temple, which a certain King builded for those that accounted themselves wise to worship therein. And these men cease not day and night, saying that there is nothing more beautiful than this. Now I hold that their's is a foolish saying, for a certain wise man, who had seen all the most beautiful temples in the world, did liken it to a table of which the legs are turned uppermost. They, on the other hand, say that he was a rude fellow.

And on this bridge there be many and great balls of stone, which no man is able to count. And many other things they told me concerning this bridge, which I will not set forth, for of a truth I do not think them worthy of belief. This, then, I learnt about the bridge.

And having passed over the bridge, and through a certain gate, they brought me unto the market place of that city: but no man bought nor sold therein, for these men think of no other thing, but only of how they may become more wise, and truly there is need thereof. And there is much grass in the place: albeit, men walk not thereon, save only the rulers and the priests. And all around the market be the dwelling places of the folk. And these be exceeding high, builded one upon another, even so that the streets of this city are, as it were, great staircases reaching unto heaven. And I saw there, also, certain of the citizens, that were in the uppermost dwellings, holding converse with a loud voice with those that were below in the market place. And I supposed it to be for this reason, that they were imprisoned there of the king; but they told me that this was not so. And on the north side of the market place groweth a tree, which surpasseth in size all that I ever yet beheld. And this tree hath not a trunk like unto other trees, but clingeth unto the walls of the city, spreading abroad to this side and to that, and entering into the chambers of the folk. And what manner of tree this may be I cannot tell, for it is neither silphium nor arbutus, and they be the only trees of which I have ever heard. And concerning this tree there is an oracle, which saith that as is the life of the tree so also shall the life of the city be, and so long as the tree flourisheth, so long also shall the city prosper.

And in the northern part of that side of the city which lieth toward the river dwelleth the great High Priests, one of exceeding great age and held in much reverence by the folk. And his dwellings be spread over one eighth part of the whole city. And on the south side of the city dwelleth the King, but his habitation is small; and over against him dwelleth also his chief counsellor, and nigh unto them likewise he whose duty it is to care for the worship of the gods. And whosoever willeth not to worship according to the law, him he constraineth within the gates at the going down of the sun so that he may not any more leave the city that day.

And I saw certain women, young and fair, passing to and fro within the market place: and I supposed that they were the ladies of the King's court; but they told me that this was not so, but that no women may dwell within this city, save only the wife of the High Priest and the wife of a certain wise man, of whom I will tell you hereafter: but that these women did but come and go to minister unto the folk, both making ready their beds and setting their houses in order. And there be men also who likewise do minister unto the people: and these they call in the language of that country Gyps, which name in the Greek tongue signifieth a vulture. And this, as it seemeth to me, they called them because in former times they did prey upon the folk.

And on the north side of the city standeth a hall, exceeding wide and high, wherein also is an image of the mother of the people. And herein do meet at sunset all the citizens, both they who dwell within the walls of the city and they who inhabit the huts without, and do eat strange food together. And me also they constrained to share in their feast; and many wondrous viands did they set before us at that feast, but this astonished me more than all the rest, namely a certain mighty and uncouth bird. For it seemed, in my opinion, to be void of breast, neither had it any wings save one only: but in lack thereof it had fourteen legs, and these full strong and sinewy. And at the end of the feast they brought me a dish stranger than all the rest. For to me it seemed to be mixed of meal and honey and grasshoppers pounded exceeding small. And when I had partaken thereof, sore trouble gat hold on my midward parts: but they mocked at my discomfiture and made merry upon me, and vowed that they would evermore call the name of this dish after my name. And this also they do unto this day.

Moreover, above this hall there be also certain strange dwellings which they told me were the habitations of rabbits. But I myself saw no rabbits herein, neither do I, of a truth, think that rabbits could live in such a place. Wherefore it seemeth to me that in saying such things they did but mock me.

And of the wise man of whom I told you formerly, they told me these things also. For of the doings of the people of this city he hath full knowledge, both of what men ever have done and of what they shall hereafter do. And he is held in great fear and reverence of the folk, both of the common sort and also of the elders. And of the worship of the gods moreover he hath exceeding great care, being likewise the cup-bearer of the King, having charge over all his drinking vessels, both of gold and of silver. But above all other things he cherisheth a certain table, whereat the elders to drink their wine. Upon this he bestoweth much labour, making it full smooth and bright, and verily I myself, looking on it, did see mine own image reflected therein, and at this I marvelled greatly.

And many strange customs have they in this city, for none of the men therein, have beards, save only the King and the great High Priest. And I wondered greatly at this saying, inasmuch as I saw much white hair round about the face of the wise man. But they told me that this was not a beard like other men's beards, but a fillet of the finest wool, such as they only wear, who have been devoted to the services of the gods. And many other strange things they do in this city, but none seemed to me more strange than this. For they told me that it was the purpose of certain among the folk to exercise their wits, and to bring forth, three times in the year, a book wherein men may read of the deeds that are done in that city. And of me also they demanded that I should bear a part therein, hearing that I had skill in these matters. And why they do these things, I know not, for full sore is the travail, both of them that write therein and of them that read.

Lady Clare Magazine Vol I/1, Lent Term 1902

A LEAF FROM ANOTHER TUTOR'S DIARY.

Strange how deceptive these dark mornings are. I really had considerable difficulty in meeting my class at the usual hour. Unfortunately several men were unusually prompt, and when I arrived they all seemed to be examining their watches with great attention. That reminds me my own watch had stopped this morning. Must have omitted to wind it up. My Gyp said that he had great difficulty in arousing me – he also mentioned that I was longer than usual in the Combination Room last night. Was not quite sure what he meant, so I looked at him. Personally I cannot see any connection between the two facts. In the course of my lecture Mr – Mr Mr – Strange! Now I forget that man's name. But no matter. One of my pupils discovered a slight error in my calculations. I passed the matter off – still felt somewhat annoyed. I must have been a little flurried. Took lunch at home – incidentally mentioned that I should not be sleeping in College again at present. My wife made no remark. Had soda water to lunch – no claret.

Took my usual exercise in he afternoon. Ran several times round back garden – without gown. On my way to College stopped for a moment to watch a football match – believe we were playing some Oxford College – not quite sure. Large crowd witnessing game. I cannot understand the man who watches football matches. These matches are a great expense and the dinners are often followed by breaches of discipline, particularly when champagne is partaken of. Cannot understand why men drink champagne. Spent remainder of the afternoon considering a very interesting mathematical problem – at least I intended to do so but must have fallen asleep. Woke up believing that I had squared the circle – very disappointing things dreams. Most unseemly noise occurred on the staircase at this moment. Went to the door but only saw Smith, who was walking downstairs. Said he thought noise proceeded from Court. Possibly – very strange how sound carries. The incident suggested an experiment, but thoughts interrupted by Robinson. Wanted an exeat – gave it him mechanically – seemed quite pleased. Went to Hall. Grace was read at most astonishing pace. Think scholars become more irreverent each year. Mentioned it to Dean. He said, 'Aah!' Took coffee in Combination Room. Went home early and retired at once. Recollected in bed why Robinson so pleased with 'exeat' – had occasion to gate him earlier in week – must mention matter when he returns. – Slept!

Lady Clare Magazine Vol III/1, Michaelmas Term 1903

MAY WEEK

It's not my fault that I have written this article on May Week; it's not even the fault of that mysterious individual who sits in an 'editorial chair, and perennially wields an editorial pen.' The times and the seasons alone are to be blamed: for it is owing to the appalling fact that this is May Term, and the shadow of the tripos examiner is already falling across my path, that I write on such a lugubrious subject.

Lugubrious? I hear the first year man ask in surprise, for he has no troubles (except a few paltry Mays) and an epoch of cricket, tennis and other forms of unmitigated slackness before him. But we who have had experience know that the much vaunted May Week is really a hollow fraud; it is a terminological inexactitude, it is at best a mere debauch in which we hide the awful apprehension of the Tripos list.

We don't like it, very few of our relations really do; we mutually bore each other tho' we may not say so.

To begin with our elderly parents and guardians desire to inspect the colleges – you know what that means; and so you spend three or four most delightful days in Trinity Great Court, and John's and King's Chapels, Clare Hall, the Peterhouse deer forest and various other charming and exhilarating spots. You are bound to display a certain historical knowledge of the places; you must assuredly point out Washington's cherry tree that grows in Christ's, and be careful to draw attention to the early Norman arches in Jesus New Court; you must, in fact, exert all your powers of patience and prevarication.

Then in the afternoon you row down to Ditton; this is very charming, and puts you in a good temper, especially after a morning of sight seeing, forty-nine stone (not counting a 'tea basket') in the stern, the temperature ninety in the shade, you at the oars, and the pretty girl in the bow. Charming! I repeat, – you meet many of your friends in the same predicament: they are all equally hot and equally bored, and are vowing fervently never to have people up for the May week again.

At last you may possibly reach Ditton and then until it is time to row back again your troubles are merely passive. All you've got to do now is to become a sort of assistant gyp, and participate in the manufacture and consumption of rather inferior tea. Don't grumble, however; enter into the work of tea making with all the energy that two miles of rowing have left in you: eat the sticky sandwich as if you liked it; gulp down the mild tea regardless of the various flora and fauna that have blown into it; blades of grass and small flies add new interest to the insipid meal. Remember only that by your action you are giving other people a little pleasure; for experience will show that tea making is the only part of the whole programme that the ladies really enjoy.

Poor dears! what else could they care for? The row down from Foster's alarms rather than amuses the fair creatures, and very few of them know anything about the races. It is true that the presence of other women is an attraction; it cannot be denied that Ditton affords an excellent opportunity for studying the subtleties of female clothing; but then church or even 'King's Parade' would do just as well, and so I am of the opinion that if it were not for tea making the annual pilgrimage to Ditton Corner would slowly come to an end. However, this is only a theory, and must be taken for what it is worth. Think the matter over and see if there is not truth in what I say.

To proceed: suddenly everyone moves to one side of the boat, your carefully balanced teacup upsets and you know that the races have begun. By and by your college boat appears, closely pursued by another; you are all excitement and then your excitement gives place to extreme irritation when you realise that you cannot get out and run. You are helpless, pent up in a wretched tub, surrounded by other tubs, and a momentary tantalising glimpse is all that you see of the races. Finally, you don't know whether to laugh or cry when the girl with the light blue hat, sitting in a neighbouring tub exclaims, 'And when our boat has bumped Clare it will go on and bump the boat in front of that again, won't it, Jack?' and 'Jack' who is too hot and bored to explain the true nature of a bumping race, says, 'Oh yes, of course.'

And thus the weary afternoon wears on, until the stampede back to Cambridge again. Oh that row back! how you hate it! On one side there's an idiot who splashes you every stroke he takes; ten to one there's a friend making predatory raids on your rudder; it is probable that you get stuck for fifteen minutes in a conglomeration of tubs and canoes. All the while you are tacitly raging, your sisters (or female friends) on the verge of screaming, and the people on the towpath in ecstacies.

I think that most fair-minded people will agree that I have drawn a perfectly unbiassed sketch (omitting sundry minor irritations) of a typical day in May week, and from what I have said it will be evident that May week is far otherwise than it is usually represented. There exists a mendacious literature on the subject which has always been a thorn in my eyes. Such titles as 'May Week and Maids' should be shunned. They represent Cambridge as a kind of Garden of Love where everyone falls under the spell of some beauty, and where life dwindles into a perpetual flirtation. In the language of the politicians this is a gross perversion of facts.

I don't believe anyone ever did, ever will, or ever could, fall in love during May week. I know that certain members of the College believe it possible, but I am ready to try the experiment any day they like, to prove my case. In the first place during the season in question, Cambridge resembles a house from which a wedding has just taken place. It is full of guests, jostling and elbowing each other at every turn; everyone is dressed in her or his best, and consequently everyone is hot and irritable. How can a man fall in love under such circumstances?

But, you will say, what about the River? I reply that either you are in a tub or a canada; if in a tub, then there are usually half-a-dozen chaperones; if in a canada you dare not fall in love lest the thing upset.

In effect, the heat, the worry, and above all the crowd, render the 'Varsity a most unsentimental place about the first week in June. Now in the words of the poet, we've 'had enough of this foolery,' and I must turn me to my books again.

Lady Clare Magazine Vol V/3, Easter Term 1906

'PHIPPS'

Members of College past and present will be sorry to hear of the retirement of 'Phipps' after so many years of faithful service as Fellows' butler. Below we reprint an article by kind permission of the Cambridge Chronicle and University Journal.

Today (February 23rd) 1916, the Clare College butler, Mr Henry Charles Phipps, will be the recipient of heartiest congratulations from the Master, Fellows, students and his colleagues and numerous other friends upon the completion of 50 years' service. He is known to thousands of old Clare Collegians throughout the world for his unfailing cheerfulness and courtesy. 'Phipps,' as he is best known in college life, has always manifested a great devotion for the college. He possesses an extraordinary memory, and ever retains a vivid recollection of old undergraduates, and, generally speaking, can give in accurate detail their many activities when in residence. Old boating men have carried away pleasant reminiscences of their training breakfasts at the college. Every guest or visitor has enthusiastically admired and commented upon the beautiful manner in which the College silver was kept, and in this and the tables and furniture of the Combination Room he has taken a great pride.

He has always appeared to be the 'father' of the servants, and has been a leading light in all their social gatherings. For a man of three score years and ten he is still very active and attentive to his duties, and recently remarked, 'I am best at work, it does me good.' In his early days he was a keen sportsman and gardener.

Mr Phipps is a Cambridge man, and first saw light on November 30th, 1845, in a cottage opposite Caius College Cricket Ground, Barton Road. When he was twenty years old, in 1866, he occupied the position of assistant butler under Mr Horrocks, and in 1868 was made gyp and bedmaker. On September 8th of the same year he married Elizabeth Francis Shirman. They have one son, who is a dispenser to a doctor at Woolwich. In June, 1879, he was appointed Fellows' butler, which position he has held nearly thirty-seven years. It has always been the custom for the butler to have rooms in College, a tradition, we believe, without precedent in any other college. Although Mrs Phipps is not officially employed by the College she has been a great helpmate in her husband's duties, and their combined services bear a record of 98 years.

Only sixty men were in residence at the College in his early days, but this number gradually grew, and in 1890 it reached about 200, an average number until the outbreak of war, but at present the numbers have fallen to 32.

Previous to 1870 the College Hall was very plain inside, having whitewashed walls and ceiling, with stone floor. Sir Digby Wyatt, who was Professor of Fine Arts at Fitzwilliam Museum, designed the ceiling, which is believed to be one of the most handsome in the University. In the following year the floor was re-laid with oak, and a year later the decoration of the walls was completed. The oak mantelpiece, which represents theology and science, was carved by Mr Phypers, sculptor, of London. The two pictures, the Duke of Newcastle and the Earl of Exeter were removed from the Combination Room to the Hall. All the other pictures that grace the wall have been presented since, including the portrait of the late Dr E. Atkinson, which was painted upon his jubilee, 1906.

Relating the many interesting incidents of his varied life, Mr Phipps had the honour of waiting on King Edward when he was Prince of Wales, on January 28, 1878. His Royal Highness's visit was on the occasion of the unveiling of the statue of his father, Prince Consort at the Fitzwilliam Museum. The Prince of Wales was afterwards entertained by Dr Atkinson, the Vice-Chancellor. The distinguished guest drove into the college courts in a carriage and pair. This was the only occasion that a carriage and horses have been seen in the College courts. The Prince of Wales walked through the Library and Combination Room downstairs to the dining hall. The function will always be remembered by the fact that the Royal guest was the first person to smoke in the hall, which broke the ice for all future functions. The turtle purchased for the soup on that occasion weighed about 120lbs, and the shell adorns the kitchen walls, bearing the Prince of Wales' feathers.

On speech days Mr Phipps assisted at the Senate House during the period of service of Mr Boning and Mr Sheldrick. He was present when the then Princess of Wales (now Queen Alexandra) and her two daughters were in attendance to watch the degree conferred upon her son, the Duke of Clarence.

In his early days Mr Phipps' principal pastimes were rowing and cricket. He figured a good deal in aquatic circles, and he rowed in the first Town Bumping Races about the year 1870. He rowed stroke of the College Servants' second boat for many years. One year in the races they rowed over the course with only seven oars without being bumped. It happened that one of the crew was taken ill. Another said, 'Let us tie the boat up to the bank,' but Phipps replied, 'No! let us row for our money.' The Church of England second boat was behind, stroked by the late organist of Clare, Mr W.C. Dewberry. At the start the C.E. quickly drew on them, and overlapped them at First Post Corner, but after this point the College Servants got clear and reached their post in safety.

Mr Phipps is the oldest member of the College Servants' Cricket and Boat Club. He held the office of second boat captain, and has been president, treasurer, and secretary for the club, holding the presidency in the year 1877–8, and afterwards was auditor for many years.

With regard to his cricket career Mr Phipps played for may years for the Clare servants against the gentlemen of the college, and in July, 1901, made the great score of 115, and was presented with a bat in recognition of his achievement. Two years later, when using the presentation bat, he again scored three figures, making 104.

Mr Phipps was always a prominent figure at the annual servants' gathering when all the Fellows of the College dined with them. This function has been held since 1868 until the commencement of the war. At the dinner the Senior Fellow occupied the chair, and each male servant was served with an old-fashioned churchwarden pipe, whether he was a smoker or not. For thirty or forty years he always had the pleasure of proposing the chief toast, and always gave the good old song 'Sarah's young man,' with much delight to the company. Since he has been in service at the college he has seen five cooks and six butlers.

His principle hobby has been gardening. For years he was a member of the Working Men's Cottage Gardeners' Society. He was a very successful exhibitor of flowers and vegetables, and won between 60 and 70 prize tickets. Mrs Phipps, too, won the competition for cooked potatoes nine years out of ten. Mr Phipps celebrated his 70th birthday on November 30 of last year. We congratulate Mr Phipps on his jubilee at the college.

THE LAST MEETING

SIEGFRIED SASSOON

I Because the night was falling warm and still
   Upon a golden day at April's end,
   I thought; I will go up the hill once more
   To find the face of him that I have lost,
   And speak with him before his ghost has flown
   Far from the earth that might not keep him long.

   So down the road I went, pausing to see
   How slow the dusk drew on, and how the folk
   Loitered about their doorways, well-content
   With the fine weather and the waxing year.
   The miller's house, that glimmered with grey walls,
   Turned me aside; and for a while I leaned
   Along the tottering rail beside the bridge
   To watch the dripping mill-wheel green with damp.
   The miller peered at me with shadowed eyes
   And pallid face; I could not hear his voice
   For sound of the weir's plunging. He was old.
   His days went round with the unhurrying wheel.

   Moving along the street, each side I saw
   The humble, kindly folk in lamp-lit rooms;
   Children at table; simple, homely wives;
   Strong, grizzled men; and soldiers back from war,
   Scaring the gaping elders with loud talk.

   Soon all the jumbled roofs were down the hill,
   And I was turning up the grassy lane
   That goes to the big, empty house that stands
   Above the town, half-hid by towering trees.
   I looked below and saw the glinting lights:
   I heard the treble cries of bustling life,
   And mirth, and scolding; and the grind of wheels.
   An engine whistled, piercing-shrill, and called
   High echoes from the sombre slopes afar;
   Then a long line of trucks began to move.
   It was quite still; the columned chestnuts stood
   Dark in their noble canopies of leaves.
   I thought: 'A little longer I'll delay,

   And then he'll be more glad to hear my feet,
   And with low laughter ask me why I'm late.
   The place will be too dim to show his eyes,
   But he will loom above me like a tree,
   With lifted arms and a body tall and strong.'

   There stood the empty house; a ghostly hulk
   Becalmed and huge, massed in the mantling dark,
   As builders left it when quick-shattering war
   Leapt upon France and called her men to fight.
   Lightly along the terraces I trod,
   Crunching the rubble till I found the door
   That gaped in twilight, framing inward gloom.
   An owl flew out from under the high eaves
   To vanish secretly among the firs,
   Where lofty boughs netted the gleam of stars.
   I stumbled in; the dusty floors were strewn
   With cumbering piles of planks and props and beams;
   Tall windows gapped the walls; the place was free
   To every searching gust and jousting gale;
   But now they slept; I was afraid to speak,
   And heavily the shadows crowded in.

   I called him, once; then listened: nothing moved:
   Only my thumping heart beat out the time.
   Whispering his name, I groped from room to room.

   Quite empty was that house; it could not hold
   His human ghost, remembered in the love
   That strove in vain to be companioned still.

II Blindly I sought the woods that I had known
   So beautiful with morning when I came
   Amazed with spring that wove the hazel twigs
   With misty raiment of awakening green.
   I found a holy dimness, and the peace
   Of sanctuary, austerely built of trees,
   And wonder stooping from the tranquil sky.

Ah! but there was no need to call his name.
He was beside me now, as swift as light.
I knew him crushed to earth in scentless flowers,
And lifted in the rapture of dark pines.
'For now,' he said, 'my spirit has more eyes
Than heaven has stars; and they are lit by love.
My body is the magic of the world,
And dawn and sunset flame with my spilt blood.
My breath is the great wind, and I am filled
With molten power and surge of the bright waves
That chant my doom along the ocean's edge.

'Look in the faces of the flowers and find
The innocence that shrives me: stoop to the stream
That you may share the wisdom of my peace.
For talking water travels undismayed.
The luminous willows lean to it with tales
Of the young earth; and swallows dip their wings
Where showering hawthorn strews the lanes of light.

'I can remember summer in one thought
Of wind-swept green, and deeps of melting blue,
And scent of limes in bloom; and I can hear
Distinct the early mower in the grass,
Whetting his blade along some morn of June.

'For I was born to the round world's delight,
And knowledge of enfolding motherhood,
Whose tenderness, that shines through constant toil,
Gathers the naked children to her knees.
In death I can remember how she came
To kiss me while I slept; still I can share
The glee of childhood; and the fleeting gloom
When all my flowers were washed with rain of tears.

'I triumph in the choruses of birds,
Bursting like April buds in gyres of song.
My meditations are the blaze of noon
On silent woods, where glory burns the leaves.
I have shared breathless vigils; I have slaked
The thirst of my desires in bounteous rain
Pouring and splashing downward through the dark.
Loud storm has roused me with its winking glare,
And voice of doom that crackles overhead.
I have been tired and watchful, craving rest,
Till the slow-footed hours have touched my brows
And laid me on the breast of sundering sleep.'

Falling Warrior, HENRY MOORE 1956–7, *Memorial Court*

III *I know that he is lost among the stars,*
    And may return no more but in their light.
    Though his hushed voice may call me in the stir
    Of whispering trees, I shall not understand.
    Men may not speak with stillness; and the joy
    Of brooks that leap and tumble down green hills
    Is faster than their feet; and all their thoughts
    Can win no meaning from the talk of birds.

    My heart is fooled with fancies, being wise;
    For fancy is the gleaming of wet flowers
    When the hid sun looks forth with golden stare.
    Thus, when I find new loveliness to praise,
    And things long-known shine out in sudden grace,
    Then will I think: 'He moves before me now.'
    So he will never come but in delight,
    And, as it was in life, his name shall be
    Wonder awaking in a summer dawn,
    And youth, that dying, touched my lips to song.

Flixécourt, May 1916

education, learning & research

ROBIN MATTHEWS

What is the purpose of the College?

Until recently, the Statutes of Clare were silent on this question. Some indication of an answer could be inferred indirectly from the Foundress's famous Preamble, though that does not have statutory force. Alternatively, a rather more direct answer can be inferred from the Statutes of the University, by which we are to some degree bound. The University Statutes state the purposes of the University with characteristic obliqueness, not in their opening chapter but later on, in the Statute relating to University Officers.[1] These people are there required 'to promote the interests of the University as a place of education, religion, learning, and research.' That famous phrase is not ancient; it is believed to have come into circulation first in the 1870s.[2] The wording is subtle. Potential controversy is avoided by not requiring individual University Officers actually to engage personally in all of these activities – or in any of them, for that matter.

Very recently, a new Statute (the so-called Commissioners' Statute) has imposed a 'mission statement' on all colleges. Fortunately, it says much the same thing as the famous old phrase, but it replaces explicit reference to religion by a mixture of Treasury-speak and political correctness. Its words are '...(b) to enable the College to provide education, to promote learning, and to engage in research efficiently and economically; (c) to apply the principles of justice and fairness.'

We can reasonably assume that the College has always tried to avoid being inefficient, uneconomical, unjust, or unfair. Moreover, the phrasing is not exclusive: there is no prohibition against engaging in other activities, including religion, provided that they are compatible with charity law. So I can still in good conscience structure my sketch around the old phrase. However, as the Dean has contributed a separate chapter on religion in the College, I shall leave that aside. I shall also pass over another pur-pose that is of necessity quite important in practice for Clare, as for many other colleges. That is the conservation of an ancient monument, which in conjunction with the buildings of the other Cambridge Colleges forms a significant part of England's architectural heritage.

Education

(i) Numbers

Perhaps the most obvious change in the contribution to education made by the College and the University during the last 100 years has been the increase in the number of its students. The number of Clare *undergraduates* has more than doubled since the beginning of the twentieth century. Moreover, they enter a much wider variety of occupations than formerly. The number of junior members (undergraduates and graduate students) has increased by much more; there were very few graduate students at the beginning of the century and not many in the inter-war period; at the time of writing there are 206.

This increase in the total number has been accompanied by a change in the nature of the constraint determining it. In recent decades the constraint has been in the number of places available. That in turn has been determined, in some years, by the government, in other years by the College's own view of the accommodation available or teaching capacity. We could have filled our places many times over. Excess demand for undergraduate places has been shown not only by the number of disappointed applicants but also by the successful applicants' very high A-level grades.

In the inter-war period, when there was no automatic state support to undergraduates, things were very different. The constraint was demand. There is an anecdote that when Thirkill took over in 1920 as Tutor, and hence became responsible for admissions, his predecessor said to him "You have 67 places to fill, and if you fill 60 you're

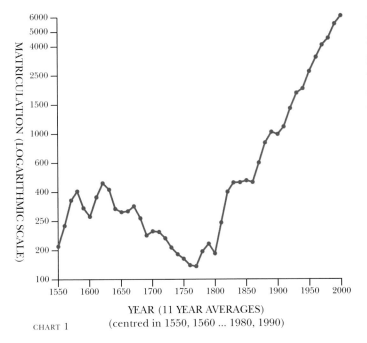

CHART 1

MATRICULATION (LOGARITHMIC SCALE)

YEAR (11 YEAR AVERAGES)
(centred in 1550, 1560 ... 1980, 1990)

doing very well" (I may have got the exact figures wrong, but that does not affect the point). The 60 would have been the number who (a) wanted to come to Clare (b) could afford it (c) were judged by Thirkill to be good chaps (d) were not so hopelessly lacking in academic ability as to be unlikely to be able to get a degree. Of these, (d) was not a very formidable hurdle. In the University as a whole, only two-thirds of undergraduates took Honours; the rest took the Ordinary Degree. Thirkill's achievement was to increase demand by building up relations with schools and choosing from them the applicants that were best by his standards (in which previous family connections with the College played a significant part). In this way both the number and the quality of the applicants were raised. The nepotistic element would nowadays be frowned on, but academic standards did become higher than they had been earlier. Of the 60 freshmen who came up in 1899, more than a third went down without any degree at all and only 20 took honours.[3]

When it comes to the second half of the twentieth century, there was a further increase in numbers, and the nature of the constraint on the numbers changed in the way already mentioned. On the face of it, the explanation for both these changes was financial. For many years after 1962, anyone from this country that a university was willing to admit to read for an undergraduate degree was automatically entitled to have fees and maintenance paid by the state. Latterly, it is true, support has changed to loans rather than grants, and has become subject to means tests. The present level of support may seem niggardly to students, but it remains more generous than it was before the Robbins Report. Developments in this century have to be seen against the background of what went before.

Chart 1 was kindly supplied to me by the University Registry. It is derived from data in a well-known source,[4] but as far as I know it has not previously been published in this form. I am grateful to the Registry for permission to print it.[5] What it shows is surprising. The rate of growth of numbers in the University, as measured by matriculations, has been constant, subject to some fluctuations, at a rate of about 1.8% a year (considerably higher than that of the total population) for over two centuries. This is notwithstanding what have appeared on the ground to be such huge changes in circumstances and attitudes. To judge by matriculations, Cambridge numbers seem to double every 40 or so years, regardless. Explanation purely in terms of events in the last 40 years is therefore not entirely plausible.

The Chart also shows, incidentally, that the well-known decline of Cambridge in the eighteenth century was quantitative as well as qualitative; that the decline began surprisingly early, even before the Civil War; and that the recovery began well before any major reforms in "unreformed Cambridge" had been put in place.

Was this constancy of the growth rate since about the time of the Industrial Revolution a coincidence? (Numbers in Oxford too seem to have risen over most parts of that period, though the average rate of increase was lower than in Cambridge.) Did it reflect merely the rise in income per head in the relevant social classes? Or was there some process at work more specific to the University? One conjecture could be that demand reacted on supply through accommodation: Colleges increased their numbers, the additional students had to go into lodgings, shortage of convenient lodgings put pressure on Colleges to add to their buildings, the shortage of lodgings was thereby relieved, and the cycle began again. Other explanations are possible. Moreover a separate explanation is obviously needed for the preceding period of decline. Study of the statistical material would be likely to raise issues that are not considered in the old-fashioned kind of College or University history, with its heavy emphasis on personalities. What is clear, however, and perhaps also significant for future government and University policy, is the Tolstoyan conclusion, that the steady growth of numbers in the last two centuries was not the result of any single act of will.

It is apparent from the data for the more recent years[6] that, whatever forces made for steady growth, they operated at the level of the University as a whole, not at the level of an individual college. A large part of the growth of Cambridge since World War II has come about from the establishment of new colleges. Between 1800 and 1954, by contrast, there were no additions to the number of recognized colleges and the expansion of the University came from expansion within existing colleges. The rate of growth of the number of junior members in Clare, as of most established colleges, was significantly lower after World War II than it had been in the nineteenth century and in the inter-war period.

In Clare, paradoxically, the fastest growth (in percentage terms, though not in absolute numbers) was *before* 1890 – I say paradoxically, because the College during that period added little to its buildings. Since then we have built Memorial Court and Thirkill Court, and we have developed the Colony, but the rate of growth of numbers has rather slowed down. The fast growth in numbers in the third quarter of the nineteenth century was at least partly due to known causes. Webb, the Master who died in

1855, was opposed to the College taking in more undergraduates than it could accommodate, but this policy was rapidly reversed after his death.[7] Much more of central Cambridge was taken up by dwellings then than it is now, and that no doubt made it easier to expand the supply of lodgings. Lodgings throughout the town will also have been vacated by the college buildings that had recently been put up, some of them very large, like St John's New Court and Trinity Whewell's Court.

(ii) Academic standards

From what has just been said, there has evidently been more to the explanation of the increase in numbers than the introduction of mandatory awards to students in 1962. But the latter surely *was* the reason for the rise in academic standards across the University – at least at the bottom. My own career as a university teacher began (not in Clare) before then, in 1949, and I well remember the tail that used to exist among the undergraduates I taught (and examined). In the case of Clare, a special source of improvement was given by the admission of women – not only because women had previously been under-represented in the University, but also because their admission gave Clare the reputation of being a go-ahead College and so attracted good men students as well. (Clare perhaps gained especially because the other two Colleges that first took this step were thought of as slightly special and therefore less attractive, Churchill because of its statutory science-orientation and King's because it had the reputation of being 'way-out'.)

A result was that over a period in the late 1970s, Clare, on average, ranked highest among the Colleges in Tripos results. An unfortunate concomitant was that Clare acquired the reputation of being extremely difficult to get into. Candidates whom we should have been very glad to take were put off from applying. So our ranking slipped a bit, while remaining perfectly respectable. Efforts are now being made to put this right, with some signs of success.

(iii) Subject-mix

In the nineteenth century Cambridge was strongly orientated towards Mathematics. The development of facilities for experimental science in the last quarter of the nineteenth century changed the position somewhat. New Arts Triposes were introduced as well, though at first they often had few takers. In the inter-war period and in the 1950s, Clare had the reputation of being more strongly

BELOW: *Clare Bridge on the occasion of the opening of Thirkill Court, 1955. Henry Thirkill is on the right, G.H.A. Wilson on the left.*

science-orientated even than the University as a whole. In talking to Fellows who were around in those days, I find some difference of opinion about whether this reputation entirely conformed to reality. But certainly the reputation was there. Thirkill seems to have thought that the Natural Sciences Tripos was the thing to do if you were up to it – if not, you might consider an Arts Tripos. Natural Sciences and Mathematics, and to a lesser extent Classics, were the subjects that commanded the most academic respect.

This was reflected in the composition of the Fellowship. A letter in the Spring 1937 issue of the *Lady Clare Magazine,* from a group of undergraduates, complained about this, in courteous and respectful terms:

'When one remembers that those taking History, Economics, English, Moral Sciences, Modern Languages, Law, Geography, and Anthropology must all go outside the College to be supervised, this reflects little credit on the educational facilities offered by the College. We say at once that we have no complaint about the supervisors in the above subjects; the grievance lies in the fact that science … has a quite disproportionate monopoly among the Fellows, while the humane subjects, in which the need for personal assistance and encouragement is far greater, are left to blossom in more catholic institutions.'

When John Northam became Senior Tutor in the late 1950s, he made a firm attempt to alter the situation. When I came in 1975, things had already changed. I found in existence an established convention that the Tutors would try to maintain a roughly 50-50 balance in their undergraduate admissions between arts and science, though this was not formally laid down. No doubt the advent of women students would have forced a change in the balance, if it had not already taken place. There has been a similar change in the composition of the Fellowship. The authors of that letter in 1937 would have been surprised to learn that by the end of the century, the College would have four teaching Fellows in Modern and Medieval languages, as well as two Professors. I was, incidentally, the first Master of Clare for over a century (probably much longer) not to have started his career as a mathematician or a scientist.

One change in subject-bias that took place mainly in my own time deserves special mention, even though, as far as Tripos numbers are concerned, it was more apparent than real. Already when Ashby was Master, Clare gained a reputation as a musical college, largely because of the inspiring lead of John Rutter. Ashby was himself a

Robin Matthews
Maggi Hambling, 1986

Oil on canvas
32" x 38"

keen amateur musician. He told me that when he first came to Clare, he used to join in the performance of chamber music with undergraduates; but as time went on, he had to give it up, because the students' standard had risen beyond his reach. When John Rutter stopped being Director of Music in order to become a whole-time composer, the College was fortunate to secure an equally inspiring successor, Tim Brown. Not only did the Choir go from strength to strength under his leadership, but also Clare gained a new reputation on the academic side. Nearly a quarter of all the entrance candidates seeking to read the Music Tripos in Cambridge give first preference to Clare, even though we are not able to accept a very large number.

(iv) Education for what?

Some broader questions remain. Some Old Clare men whose sons or daughters did not succeed in gaining admission to the College think we are only interested in admitting 'swots.' I would not accept this, but the charge does make me feel uneasy. It cannot be denied that the pressure on students to do well in their own disciplines is liable to have a narrowing effect on them. One occasion-

40

ally meets academics in all Cambridge colleges, alas, who think that their educational aim is merely to produce the academics of the next generation. While this may be a tenable objective in relation to graduate students doing the PhD, it cannot make sense in relation to undergraduates. For one thing, it would imply gross over-production in relation to demand, unless a large number of them went to seek their fortunes abroad.

'… When [knowledge of letters] has been found, it sends forth its students, who have tasted of its sweetness, fit and proper members in church and state, to rise to divers heights in accordance to the claims of their merits.' The words of the Foundress are still applicable, if we translate them into modern terms. Ideally, Triposes should be designed in such a way that good performance in them will be a suitable intellectual preparation for a variety of occupations. This ideal may not always be attained. But Cambridge recognizes it by making a point of referring to a seemingly vocational course like engineering as the Mechanical Sciences Tripos, the stress being on the underlying sciences. Hence while that Tripos is a good introduction to a career as an engineer, if someone who has read it then abandons engineering and goes on to work in accountancy or advertising (as quite often happens), their Cambridge education will not have been wasted – even apart from the gains through networking. Not surprisingly, most Clare undergraduates do not go on to academic careers, and many of them do not use in a vocational manner what they learnt in Cambridge.

Learning

Over most of the history of the University and the Colleges, 'learning' has featured prominently in discussions about objectives. It has now become unfashionable as an objective and is seldom referred to.

Learning means, I suppose, being well read and well informed on the present state of knowledge, including nowadays having the necessary access to electronic IT. Tripos candidates are supposed to display it, up to a point, as are their teachers and their examiners; so are professional practitioners, like barristers or physicians. Academics however are not much esteemed for learning, unless they *add* to the stock of knowledge, by means of research, though of course they will not do that successfully unless they are abreast with the current state of knowledge in their field.

However, learning used to be understood in a rather broader sense than this. It was at one time said that the ideal was 'knowing everything about something and something about everything.' The second part of this ideal has fallen out of vogue even more than the first. I regret this. Of course, the vast expansion of knowledge has made it impractical to be an Aristotle. None the less, specialization may be more or less exclusive.

Some might say: what is the point of broad learning, anyway? It dies with you. Certainly, little benefit would be had from the learning of a hermit, who never wrote anything and never talked to anybody. This is where an *institution* like a College is significant. It offers a way for the learned scholar *not* to be a hermit. Contact with a widely-read supervisor should help undergraduates to see their work in a light that is less narrow or less exclusively vocational. Contact with colleagues at lunch or dinner will have similar effect: even a research topic has often gained by being seen in the context of adjacent or not-so-closely adjacent disciplines. Disciplines and sub-disciplines are not a division imposed by nature, they are just a way of breaking things up that may be convenient. In the last resort all knowledge belongs to the same universe. Ideally, an unspecialized College facilitates this. In that respect it differs from one famous College in the University of London where, so I believe, it is not merely the economists who sit at the same table for lunch, it is the econometricians.

Those who have been members of Clare in recent decades are likely to think of Charles Parkin in this connection. He came from St John's to Clare in 1955 as the College's first Research Fellow in a non-scientific subject. He died at a comparatively early age in 1986. He wrote only one book (on Edmund Burke). He was not a University Teaching Officer. None the less he was a central figure in the College, and the College was central to his life. He was a bachelor and a resident Fellow. He was widely learned, not only in history and political science. One current Fellow remembers reading with him Eckermann's *Conversations with Goethe*. His range of interests extended in surprising directions. One was astronomy; another was photography. Without obtruding himself, he was glad to share these interests with other members of the College.

We must regretfully recognize that there are likely to be fewer Charles Parkins in future. Even apart from the increasing pressure to publish, there are fewer resident Fellows, and leisurely intellectual discourse over college dinner has less attraction for married Fellows, because spouses now usually have jobs and the evening is the only available family time.

However, all is not lost. An encouraging sign is the recent revival of the Dilettanti society, at the initiative of Sir Nicholas Barrington, Honorary Fellow. This also goes some way to meet the complaint that I used sometimes to hear from undergraduates, that they don't meet Fellows other than the ones in their own subject.

Research

This is a purpose that would have seemed strange, if not a little heretical, to the Foundress. The 'precious pearl of learning' was not something that she would have regarded as in need of improvement or supplementation. In her day even medicine, though it was an accepted field of study, was taught as if it depended on established authority.[8] This difference in attitudes reminds us that, shrewd and wise as she was, she was still a child of the Middle Ages.

A few members of the College have made particularly outstanding contributions to science and scholarship in the twentieth century. The list may not be as long as it would be, say, for Trinity, but it is at least as distinguished. I shall not attempt the invidious task of singling out names, suffice it to mention that the present Fellowship includes seven Fellows of the Royal Society and seven Fellows of the British Academy – a nice balance.

As to younger members of the College engaged in research, I have already mentioned that the number of our graduate students has risen proportionately by far more than the number of undergraduate students since World War II. We can be confident that many of the future staff of universities in this country, and many leaders in research in sciences and arts, will come from among those registered for the PhD. Students registered for Master's degrees did not exist before World War II (except for Law and Medicine). They are less likely to become researchers, though some will. Many of them will become professional practitioners of their subjects.

A remark here in parentheses. The rise in the number of our graduate students illustrates one interesting feature of the College's post-war history. The foundation of Clare Hall is something of which the College is justifiably proud. But it has not caused the development of Clare College itself to be very different from what it would have been anyway. One of the problems that was under discussion at the time when Clare Hall was founded was the need to improve facilities for the rapidly increasing number of graduate students. We now provide accommodation in College for all of our graduate students who want it, and we have witnessed lively development of the Middle Common Room as a social entity. Another problem was the need to increase the number of College Fellowships in order to bring in from the cold the many University Teaching Officers who had come to Cambridge from outside and had no college connection. Since then the number of Fellows of Clare has risen enormously, from the 12 to 15 of pre-war days, to its present figure of 91 (including, admittedly, an unusually large number of retired Fellows). I have never been a Fellow myself of such a small College as pre-war Clare (my previous Colleges, one in Cambridge, one in Oxford, were both large, so I cannot speak with personal experience of what it was like). A college with a very small number of Fellows must have permitted a degree of intimacy among the Fellowship that we cannot aspire to today; but I cannot help thinking that it must have been a little oppressive. They sat in order of seniority at dinner, so your neighbour was *always* the same man, for life – something that, happily, became impossible with increased numbers.

The third need that Clare Hall meets is something that Clare College has never done much: it provides for large numbers of visiting scholars. The existence of Clare Hall has perhaps discouraged us a little from accepting visiting scholars. If so, that is perhaps a pity. But probably we should not have gone far in that direction anyway. Clare Hall has done far more for visiting scholars than Clare College could ever have done.

The competition for the time and energy of academics between research and teaching is a delicate subject, but it cannot pass unmentioned. Government funds are apportioned between Universities in a way that rewards good research. For Cambridge, the amount of money involved is large. The Funding Councils also monitor the quality of teaching, but (at the time of writing) the outcome of their scrutiny has not been given any financial implications. This creates an obvious bias in incentives in favour of research at the expense of teaching. The bias is passed on from the University through faculties and departments to individuals. It reduces the amount of college teaching they want to do. It makes them less ready to take on college administrative duties. In some case it has made them unwilling to accept College Fellowships at all. It can also affect the choice of University appointments committees between candidates for vacancies; suitability for college teaching usually counts for little. All universities suffer

42

from this problem to some extent, but the traditional division of functions between University and Colleges has focussed it particularly sharply in Cambridge.

The reason why this policy has been adopted is not that governments have been particularly enamoured of the advancement of knowledge, compared with education. It has been simply a measurement bias. Governments have been enamoured of league tables. This his led them to emphasize what is quantifiable. They thought research was more easily measurable (however imperfectly) than the quality of teaching, so the bias went that way.

To do governments justice, the bias was not entirely their fault. It was consistent with the preferences of academics themselves. Eminence in research is the source of academics' self-esteem and of their reputation among their peers at home and abroad.

When the Research Assessment Exercise (RAE) was first introduced, it put such emphasis on the *number* of published papers that it led to absurd results. Papers proliferated. Too often they came to be about each other rather than about their ostensible subject. New journals multiplied. Keynes's dictum was forgotten that a book or a paper is not likely to be worth reading unless the author wanted to write it.

These results were so plainly ridiculous that a change was bound to be made. The RAE has now been amended so as to avoid its worst ill-effects. The bias in favour of research remains, but even this may be reduced or disappear if and when league tables for teaching are given financial consequences. However the task of producing meaningful league tables for teaching is still more difficult for universities than it is for schools, if only because universities are not even supposed to be non-selective in their intake. Is a university like Cambridge, that attracts very good students, to be given a plus mark, because students and their parents must be supposed to have taken trouble in a decision that is so important for them? Or is it to be given a minus point, because any good results it achieves are to be credited at least in part to the quality of the students, not to the quality of the provision that is made for them? The issue is complicated. It is easy to see how the introduction of teaching league tables might introduce distortions of its own.

All this sounds very gloomy. But a long view is needed. Ever since the beginning of its history, Cambridge, like Oxford, has felt the hand of monarchs or governments heavily on its shoulders – perhaps not so continuously as now, but more capriciously. Government's influence was often ignorant or politically vainglorious.

Reluctantly, however, we must also concede that it was sometimes useful or even necessary, however unwelcome at the time. Perhaps on balance our relation with the state is no worse now than it has been on average over the hundreds of years of our history.

1 Statute D.II.4.

2 Christopher N.L. Brooke, *A History of the University of Cambridge*, Vol. IV, 1870-1990 (Cambridge University Press, 1993) p. 103.

3 *Lady Clare Magazine*, Easter 1902.

4 J.R. Tanner, ed., *The Historical Register of the University of Cambridge 1910*, with five-yearly supplements up to 1986–90 (Cambridge University Press, 1910 and later).

5 Elisabeth Leedham-Green, *A Concise History of the University of Cambridge* (Cambridge University Press, 1996), (the annual figures are charted, not on a logarithmic scale, in Leedham-Green, Appendix 2).

6 (Brooke, *op. cit.*, Appendices 1 and 2).

7 Mansfield Forbes, *Clare College*, 1326–1926 (Cambridge University Press for the College, 1978), p. 198.

8 Damien R. Leader, *A History of the University of Cambridge*, Vol. I, *The University to 1546* (Cambridge University Press, 1988), p. 204.

JOHN NORTHAM

Everyone [who has resided in Clare] must have been struck ... with the ephemeral existence of all such bodies ... their short period of brilliance, their equally meteoric evanescence ... until some fierce vitality enables [them] to begin the cycle ... again'.[1]

Even with the exclusion of sports clubs and musical activities, it is a daunting task to attempt, across a century punctuated by three wars and by marked changes in social habits and circumstances, anything like a coherent account of the sheer variety, vitality and, in some instances, remarkable durability displayed by the College clubs and societies.

To judge by the paucity of comment in the *Magazine*, the Boer War seemed not to have impinged much on the clubs. There is one reference to the reappearance of T.H.Going long after he had been given up for dead; the note laconically mentions that he 'returned to complete his course and take his degree'.[2] By 1902 not only were long-established bodies like the Debating Society and the Dilettanti again active but, as the *Magazine* editorial points out, College energy was spilling out into the University at large, with Clare men occupying prominent posts in, for example, the Union and the Musical Club. A little-known society, the Clare College Association of Change Ringers, deserves a mention here: Joanne Garner, herself a current Master of Change Ringers, points out that a University society grew out of the Clare initiative, and that over the past fifty years Clare has provided it with no fewer than seven Masters.

Less surprising, perhaps, is that another activity, destined to prove long-lived, was theatrical. There were actors in the College long before there were Clare Actors – to the extent that the *Magazine* comments: 'If matters continue as they have commenced, the authorities will have to consider the question of histrionic scholarship, on account of the strides this art is making ... within the College'.[3] No fewer than eight Clare men were then playing prominent roles in ADC and Footlights productions. There are, however, only scanty references in the early years of club activity beyond the Debating Society, the Musical Society, the Patience Society and a Chess Club. To judge by the inordinate amount of coverage given to the Debating Society, it seems that it was regarded as the principal cultural body in the College, though the Dilettanti were briefly mentioned from time to time.

It was only after the Great War that the clubs and societies began to proliferate. The Debating Society, which had lapsed, was saved from extinction by the Amicie Communes (1916) who nursed it back to life after the War. The Dilettanti reappeared, and by 1920 the emergence or re-emergence was noted of the Musical, the Scientific and the Classical societies. There were some new foundations which, though they proved indeed evanescent, added a rather attractive tone of light-hearted eccentricity. The Cornwallis Club was started in 1922 by some ten men who happened to have dined in Hall beneath the portrait of their great patron. The Breakfast Club was founded in 1927 on nothing more substantial than a shared passion for that meal. There was nothing frivolous about the Peace Group, founded 1933–4 to contribute to the current debate about the League of Nations and disarmament, but having issued a Declaration it seems to have achieved its purpose and soon lapsed.

Other new societies were of a familiar subject-based kind: the Medical Society and the Clare Moot were started in 1922, the Economics Society, in response to the large numbers of men reading the subject, in 1924. But in addition to these, which may be called single-purpose bodies, there were one or two with different terms of reference. The self-styled Iliterate's Club (1921), 'a play-reading group,' helped keep alive something of the old theatrical tradition. The Falcons, founded soon after the

44

RIGHT: *Poster for* The
Skeleton Witness, *by
Leman Rede, performed
for the second and last
time in 1962.*

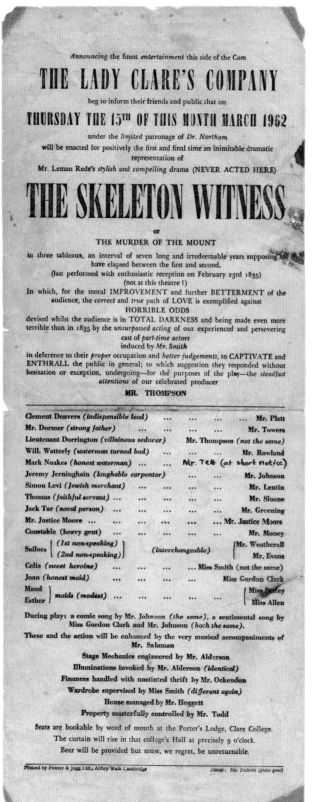

Great War, claimed for itself a social function: to be representative of the chief (mainly sporting) activities in the College, to further the interests of the College to the best of its ability, and to bring representatives of the Club into closer touch than hitherto. The aims may sound a little solemn but the Club survived for many years, bringing into amiable companionship men of different backgrounds and interests.

The Second World War was a great dislocator. For the majority on deferment from one or the other of the services there were heavy military demands to be met; in College there was fire-watching and fire-fighting instruction. In 1941–2 there seemed little time left save for work, the occasional game and the solace of companionship provided by participation in the Chapel choir under John Sidgwick, the organ scholar.

Many readers of these notes will have their own memories of returning to Clare after the war. I vividly recall the nervous wait for the Hall bell to ring for the first dinner; the delighted relief at meeting friends in the screens, at seeing, for the first time, my 'real' tutor as I thought him, Nick Hammond, strolling across the court with a student, chatting casually and showing not a sign of his arduous years with the Greek partisans; and then, in Hall, the satisfaction of spotting yet more familiar faces. That first meal in Hall felt like a family re-union, part of a deeply comforting stability that nobody, as it turned out, wanted to disturb by talking about the war. There was an overwhelming sense of wanting to be back to work, to make up for lost time, to explore the opportunities of civilized life again. The clubs and societies helped considerably.

As in the past, they ebbed and flowed. The Clarence Society, of uncertain date, came into being as a wining and dining club in memory of the Duke notoriously drowned in a vat of claret; I recall a Scottish meal of gargantuan proportions – broth, salmon, venison, haggis … athol brose. But I remember more warmly the opportunities for relaxed companionship that the new Society provided, and that the Falcons continued to offer. There were additions to the academically focused societies: the Clare lawyers were founded and a new Language Society was started by Paul Roubiczek in 1962. A discussion group, the Phoenix Society, was formed and, with many lapses, survived into the late sixties. A Film Society, still active today, was started in the sixties, as was a Graduate Society, perhaps the most significant innovation of them all. First mentioned in 1962, its emergence signalled a considerable increase in the number of research students, who by then constituted a quarter of the whole student body. The Society later opened membership to affiliated and fourth-year students and was allocated the old Music Room on E staircase for a Middle Combination Room. It meets regularly to hear invited speakers, dines regularly in Hall, and has developed its own social programme.

In recent years, however, circumstances have changed. The student body, like society at large, has developed a preference for informality, for inclusiveness in preference to what might be regarded, though wrongly, as a form of elitism. Elective clubs like the Falcons and the Clarence Society have ceased to exist. Subject-focused societies such as the Clare Lawyers, the Medical Society and the Modern Languages Society (as it became) seem to have turned into informal discussion groups. The participation of Fellows has been affected because of the pressures, unknown to their predecessors, that emanate from faculties and, in general terms, from society at large, where the claims of domestic life have challenged the claims of the corporate. Dining in Hall is no longer a requirement, and so there is no longer the general muster of students that made it easy to move on to an 8 o'clock meeting in some College room; students fill the Hall at lunchtime, and otherwise make use of the convenient running service in the Buttery that occupies what used to be the Old Court lavatory and bathroom in the basement.

Yet, as the 1899 *Magazine* comment pointed out, if societies wane they can also wax anew. And here I embark on a more expansive account of three bodies that hold out that promise. Two of them also demonstrate the extraordinary durability of some societies; to trace their history is to go back to the beginning of the century; the other is a more recent initiative.

Immediately after the war Oliver Stallybrass started an informal play-reading group. This was in the tradition of the earlier theatrical prominence of the College and of the later Iliterates, but on this occasion the initiative produced in 1950 a College Society, the Clare Actors, with Stallybrass as first Chairman, thus inaugurating a period of extraordinary activity both inside and beyond Clare. The Actors went public in their first year with a production, by Bernard Keeffe, of *The Devil's Disciple* in the ADC Theatre; it was an ambitious but successful undertaking, with students such as Guy Hutchings and David Humphreys in the cast, some of them already active in University theatre. And there were others whose energies were, at this stage,

directed outwards: Tony Church (1950) became known as Tony the Established Church in Cambridge theatrical circles and Gordon Gould, an affiliated student from the States, delighted the Cambridge audience with his comic talent in a production of *Love's Labours Lost* and a musical put on at the Arts Theatre called *Lady at the Wheel*. But the real achievement of the Clare Actors lay in the vitality and variety of their work in College.

The facilities were minimal, if one excepts the splendid setting of the Fellows' Garden. There was the Hall, where a rough and ready trestle of sorts would be erected over the hotplate between the doors; and foot-fidgeting by the cast could be attributed to the fact that the hotplate had not had time to cool. There was the Music Room on E which provided bare space, and there was the crypt, used as a bicycle store, without benefit of sets, heating or lighting other than candles. And yet by 1966 the *Magazine* reported three productions in the crypt, including a memorable *Endgame*, another, of *Entertaining Mr Sloan*, in the Music Room, and a production of *Much Ado About Nothing* in the Fellows' Garden that ran for nine performances and was seen by 1,750 customers. Alongside the Actors, the Dean, Maurice Wiles, was arranging performances in the Chapel of adaptations of the Book of Job and of Mystery plays. By 1967 the Magazine rated the Clare Actors as one of the most active groups in the whole University.

BELOW: *Paul Rogers' The Proctor's Dilemma at Clare, probably 1949. (second half of a Smoking Concert).*

Left to right: Dr John Parry (Bulldog); Bernard Keeffe (Proctor); Guy Hutchings (Bulldog); Angus Thomas (Herbert, the hero); John Hughes (Edward, an ordinary undergraduate); Shirley Walker (Amelia, the heroine); (behind her) Donald Heaton (Eugene, an athlete); David Galliford (Adonis, an athlete); Dennis McWilliam (William, a worker); Camille ("Pop") Prior (Producer); Bill Smyly (instigator and facilitator); Kenneth Mobbs (Municipal Director).

46

In that year they put on three productions a term, ranging from low-budget offerings in College to full-scale productions elsewhere of plays by Giles Cooper, N.F. Simpson, John Mortimer, and Pirandello. The May Week production in the Fellows' Garden, put on in collaboration with the ADC, was of *The Recruiting Officer* and won general acclaim. The collaboration with the ADC turned into something like an equal partnership. The range of productions grew even more impressive over the years: a series of Victorian melodramas in Hall, works by Molière, Chekhov, Whiting, Shaffer, Wilde, Pinter, Griffiths and, in May Week, of Shakespeare. On a smaller scale there was an adaptation of *Animal Farm*, a specially composed feminist play. In 1984 a piece written by a Clare student was chosen for performance in the Cambridge Festival and then was taken to Heidelberg. And so it went on. Given the vitality of the theatrical energy in Clare, it is perhaps no coincidence that Tony Church, after a long career on the acting staff at the Royal Shakespeare Company, should have later become Dean of the National Theatre Conservatory Centre at the Denver Centre for Performing Arts; nor that David Brierley, an immensely patient and capable stage-manager of many Cambridge productions, should have become General Manager of the Royal Shakespeare Company at Stratford and have retired with a CBE; and that David Cregan should have gone on to write his wisely-witty plays for the Royal Court Theatre.

This was, by any calculation, an astonishing record of creative energy. The hectic pace was not sustained. The

Actors have lost the crypt, now the JCR, and the Music Room, now the MCR, though the Latimer Room opposite offers a rudimentary stage. But the tradition is kept alive, principally through the May Week productions in the Fellows' Garden. Who knows, if the College were to erect a new building across Queen's Road . . . ?

The second society to merit special attention is the Dilettante Society, that outlived even the venerable Debating Society. Lyndon Bolton (1880) has recorded its foundation and early history. Bolton, impressed by what he had seen of the Science and Art Society at Caius decided to start something similar in Clare. He had been taken by his model's catholicity of membership, its amalgam not merely of sciences and arts but of the intelligentsia and active sportsmen, some of them Blues.

Bolton enlisted some friends to start the Dilettanti, as they were originally styled, with a membership of about forty; the Society was to meet fortnightly to discuss papers on, it was pointedly specified, any subjects other than politics or religion. By now, Bolton wrote, the Dons had begun to take notice, a detail that was to cause him some embarrassment. As Secretary, Bolton delivered the inaugural paper on the innocuous-seeming topic of The Ideal University, but he intended it to be a critical attack on the shortcomings of the teaching provided by the College at that time; he had not expected that one of the Dons, W. L. Mollison, Junior Tutor and later Master, would be in the audience. But in what became the true Dillettante style, his comments were not taken amiss and he survived.

So did the Dilettante Society, though like may other societies, it lapsed after a few years, but it was revived, though not, Bolton believed, on quite the original lines. For part of its subsequent history I shall use, with some necessary shortening and minor cuts, a splendid History of the Dilettante Society compiled in 1999 by Gagan Sood (1994).

The Dilettante Society made fitful appearances on the stage of College life after the end of the First World War, but it was not until the year of the General Strike, just as the College was celebrating its sexcentary, that the Society emerged in strength once more, and on this occasion to stay and blossom. This was a sign of the times, for throughout this period, the mid-1920s, there was a desire in Clare 'to see all the College clubs, societies and institutions in full bloom when we reached our sexcentary' . . . The decade following its resurrection [in 1926] was to be the most

BELOW: *Dilettanti 1928 (showing Harry Godwin, fifth from right, with Mansfield ('Manny') Forbes on his left), from* Lady Clare Magazine, *Lent Term, 1928.*

vigorous period of the Society's history, in all its manifestations, in which it flourished like it never had before and was never to after. And its guiding light during this period was Mansfield Forbes. In the words of his students ... Mansfield D Forbes, or 'Manny', was 'the modern founder, the Pitt cum Disraeli of our Empire,' 'the present and past inspiration of the Dilettante Society'. ... Though it might be an exaggeration to say 'the Dilettante was a one man show put together by Manny Forbes ...' his centrality to the existence and character of the Society of the time is unquestionable.

Forbes was elected to the College Fellowship in 1912, at the age of twenty-three, and 'of the body of fellows none made a more decisive impact'. Though his academic background was in history, he chose to lecture and teach English literature, then a new discipline, unsure of its status, and he did this with great effectiveness ... It is evident that many of the undergraduates with whom he came into contact were in thrall to him. They were touched by his kindness and friendship, and fascinated and excited by his eccentricities; to be acquainted with Manny Forbes was to gain entry into a world of intellectual effervescence, of carefree adventures and exploits.

Sir Harry Godwin remembers, 'When I had first been elected a fellow [Mansfield Forbes] had at once sought my help in the recreation of the college 'Dilettanti' society'. This was in the early twenties. Though the Society had been revived in the immediate postwar years, under the guidance of J.R. Wardale, a tutor of the College, the Society had to wait until Forbes himself 'ascended the shrine as patron saint' before it came to be an established and increasingly formative feature of College life. In this first decade of its new life, the Society was dynamic, self-conscious and bold.

Describing the Society, Sir Harry Godwin writes that it was ... 'a club mainly of undergraduates, united by enthusiastic curiosity about art, literature and philosophy, drawn without distinction of subjects being read or prowess in other circles, but united by a considerable tolerance, wit and good humour and a penchant for vigorous discussion and dinners of a somewhat mardi gras character'. The members ... venerated a certain, intentionally nebulous ideal, and had ... particular characteristics in common. Almost all members at this time took non-scientific Triposes. This predisposed them to a somewhat eclectic interest in the 'arts', a tendency the members (and the wider College community) were conscious of and cultivated. Indeed, at the revival of the society in 1926, the editor of the Lady Clare Magazine wrote, 'we look to our Dilettanti ... to show us what they can do to revive the beaux arts in the College.'

In the half-decade leading up to and the years following its Jubilee (1931–2), the Society was perhaps at its most healthy and vibrant ... In the Easter Term issue of the Magazine (1931), the Secretary reported that:

'The Society flourishes, and with Manny at its head is a force of great influence not only in Clare but in Cambridge'.

... The Society held a number of events beyond just their regular meetings. Each Michaelmas Term, a fancy dress party, the 'Annual Dilettante Devilment' ... The Annual Expedition during Easter Term [to] Clare Priory ... The Annual Dinner followed that same evening, rounding off the year in true Dilettante fashion ... But the mainstay of the Society remained the evenings when members would convene to listen to a paper ...

There were on average four such meetings a term, held, if possible, in 'Finella'. The house in the Backs, named after a Scottish queen, had been designed by a young architectural student called Raymond McGrath ... It provided an opportunity for Mansfield Forbes to express his consuming interest in the whole field of visual aesthetics, and offered ... a suitably stimulating environment for Dilettante Society meetings. Initially, most speakers were guests of the Society, but, with time, a greater proportion came to be chosen from amongst the members. Of those invited, there would often be Fellows, from Clare or other colleges, and sometimes also friends of members from outside the University. In describing one term's offerings, the Secretary wrote, 'The Dilettante Society ... has proved that its members are worthy inheritors of a great tradition'.

The confidence, however, proved to be short-lived ... Not long after the death of Mansfield Forbes in 1936, the Society experienced a dip in its fortunes, and there was a noticeable change in tone ... It appears that with the passing of Mansfield Forbes, the Dilettante Society lost the spirit which had sustained it for nearly a decade ... The decisive breach, however, came with the onset of war in 1939.

Following the prolonged absence enforced by the war, the Society had effectively vanished from the collective memory of the undergraduates coming up to Clare in the Michaelmas of 1945. So it fell to a senior member of the College, Nick Hammond, who had been an active member throughout the thirties and was now an Assistant Tutor, to reactivate the Society. In marked contrast to the illustrious days of its previous life, this Dilettante Society was a modest affair ... The Society met less frequently and it had a much smaller membership. It no longer wielded its former influence in College life. The traditions of the annual fancy dress party and the annual dinner were kept, though more formal than before and on a smaller scale. [There was] an increasing infusion of graduate students and fellows ... A contemporary remembers that there was no formal process for electing members [or officers] ... Though there is evidence that the Society was active at the turn of the sixties, not long after, there is no mention of it ... As Sir Harry

Godwin put it, the Society was 'no exception to the rule that such societies rise and fall and will not be compelled if the magic mood is absent'.

48

However, as the opening of this narrative reminds us, societies that wane can wax once more. Thanks to the initiatives of Nicholas Barrington, now Sir Nicholas and an Honorary Fellow, the Dilettante Society has started up again. It has a large membership, including students, graduate students and Fellows; it meets, in the old fashion, for the reading of papers and discussion. There are even signs of something like the old fondness for light-hearted conviviality on occasion. It is too early to judge whether the Society will develop a comparable sense of identity, but the signs are that the potent magic of the Dilettante tradition is once more at work.

The third, more recent, society has never aspired to a formal structure. The Picture Guild arose, in the early fifties, out of little more than the anguished longing of occupants of Memorial Court for something, anything, that might help counteract the uniform yellow paint – unkindly called Clare custard yellow – that covered every wall of every room. A small group of students, backed by Dr Michael Stoker, then an Assistant Tutor, decided to do something about the problem. Operating on a shoe-string they began to create the makings of a picture-lending

Still life of mushrooms on a plate William Nicholson.

library out of the limited range of cheap reproductions available at the time, using any old frames to be found in basements, attics and cupboards. The resulting pictures were hired out to students at a small charge. No doubt as a result of Michael Stoker's advocacy before the Governing Body, the College provided a small loan; with this and the income from rentals, the Picture Guild, as it styled itself, was able to replace its original stock with high-quality reproductions, newly-framed. The collection and the demand grew rapidly, until it became necessary to mount, at the beginning of the year, an exhibition of the Guild's stock so that students could ballot for their choice.

It was not long before the Guild developed the confidence to embark on live exhibitions from time to time. The first was of the work of a local artist, Gwen Raverat, grand-daughter of Charles Darwin and a noted Cambridge figure who could be seen, though severely handicapped, sitting in a wheelchair in the Backs indomitably painting in oil. The exhibition comprised the brilliant wood-cuts of her prime and it drew large attendances, attracted many sales and generated considerable good will towards the College and the Guild amongst admirers of her work. The good will proved crucial to the next stage of the Guild's development.

Encouraged by the success of this one-woman show, the Guild decided to become more adventurous and put on an exhibition of representative works by a range of artists. Accordingly a letter was written to Bryan Robertson, one of the Raverat circle, who had just left Cambridge to become Director of the Whitechapel Gallery. In response to the Guild's request for advice about how best to set about this ambitious undertaking, Bryan Robertson undertook to assemble a collection at his gallery, transport it to Clare and, after the exhibition, back to London at no cost to the Guild. There were studies by Henry Moore, works by Josef Herman, Lynn Chadwick, Ceri Richards, Prunella Clough, by the sculptor Bernard Meadows and many others.

Emboldened once more, the Guild decided to go in for purchasing works of art. It bought, out of its limited resources, augmented by a whip-around amongst students and Fellows, two paintings by Prunella Clough and a fine bronze by Bernard Meadows. Nicholas Barrington, a Guild member, arranged the next exhibition through family contacts with the Great Bardfield colony of artists and craftsmen who included, amongst others, Edward Bawden and John Aldridge.

Thereafter the Guild often found itself approached by artists asking to be shown – a memorable instance was an exhibition and live demonstration by Chinese calligraphic artist, Fang Chao Ling. It also invited the head of the Fine Arts Department at the Cambridge Technical College, John Bolam, to exhibit his own work and that of his students. Through the initiative of Mrs Doris Winny, the Guild was able to show graphics by Kokoshka, a collection that went on to be exhibited in Switzerland; and more recently Simon Franklin, the Russian scholar amongst the Fellows, procured an exhibition of the works of six Moscow artists, so extensive that it had to be shared with Emmanuel and Robinson Colleges. And having augmented its resources by selling some of its purchases to the College, and by renting to the College paintings to hang in much frequented rooms such as guest rooms and the Senior Tutor's room, the Guild gradually built up a respectable collection of its own.

Ambitious as ever, the Guild's thoughts turned towards large-scale sculpture. An exhibition was out of the question; the College possessed no suitable room and the Fellows' Garden was too vulnerable. And so it was decided to ask sculptors to lend a piece, for a reasonably long period, free of charge. The response proved breath-takingly generous. The first approach was to Barbara Hepworth, whose son happened to be at Trinity. She promptly loaned the Guild an elegant abstract in stone that was placed on a plinth in the perfect setting of the Scholars' garden – without charge. Her generosity was ill repaid; a nocturnal invasion of barbarians from without Clare's walls wrenched the piece from its pedestal and threw it into the shrubbery, bruising the beautifully worked stone, so that, as an angry Barbara Hepworth pointed out, the piece would have to be completely worked over to the detriment of its elegant proportions.

Because of this disaster, the Guild then approached Henry Moore with some trepidation, only to be reassured by what was to prove a customary invitation: 'Come and have a cup of tea and see what I've got.' What Clare got was a tall 'Standing Figure' in bronze, delivered, positioned and installed by Moore himself and his professional crew, on his preferred spot, the lawn in front of Memorial Court, free of charge, on extended loan. It was followed by a work by Anthony Caro, once an apprentice of Moore's but totally different in concept and in his chosen material. The front lawn is now impressively occupied by a magnificently monumental Barbara Hepworth

bronze on loan to the College from her trustees. It would be satisfying to think that the loan may have been encouraged by the Guild's activities.

The final coup in this area was the purchase of Moore's *Falling Warrior*, not directly by the Guild, but by a member of the Guild presuming on its standing with the artist: in response to a naïve plea: 'I want the College to own one of your pieces; I have no funds but I will try to raise the money!' came the usual invitation. The price named was so modest that it proved possible to raise the money in a few weeks by a whip-round amongst students and an appeal to Fellows, including Honorary Fellows and a final

BELOW: *Poster, 1956, exhibition of Bardfield artists.*

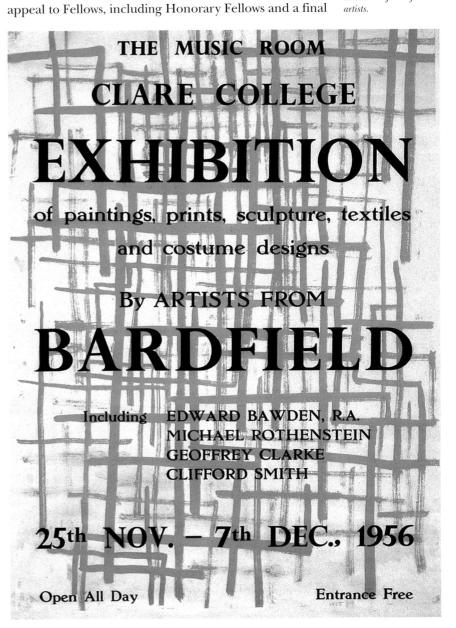

50

RIGHT:
*Two-forms – Divided
Circle*
Barbara Hepworth.

contribution from the College. So well does the piece suit its present location inside Memorial Court that the College has been informed, somewhat to its embarrassment, that it has been officially listed as a piece that may not be moved without planning permission.

In more recent years events have conspired against the Guild. The loss of the Music Room as an exhibition space was not fully compensated for by the Latimer Room which, because it must satisfy the demands of other activities, cannot be booked exclusively for week-long exhibitions; the comprehensive refurbishment of Memorial and Thirkill Courts has made storage a problem; the availability of cheap posters has diminished the need for a loan scheme, and the comings and goings of interested Fellows have broken an essential thread of continuity, so that the informal committee that constituted the Guild ceased to renew itself. And yet – and again one can refer back to the beginning of this brief chronicle – the Guild is once more stirring. Students have recently complained of the College's apparent disregard for art; though the Dean has helped provide works for the Buttery. One or two live wires have mounted shows in desperately unsuitable places and have been eager to assist the Guild's rebirth. An exhibition has been put on in the Latimer Room, not exactly by the Guild but with the benefit of its memory, of the powerful works of a Cambridge artist, the son of one of the Fellows, Dr J. Woodhouse, who is still, astonishingly, a schoolboy; and more recently an exhibition was mounted, in the old style, of paintings by Beryl Rankin, an artist from Northumberland. The Guild seems to be back in business.

If one may conjecture that the Guild's activities attracted the loan of the Hepworth bronze, one may also imagine that other gifts have been similarly inspired: the gift of a beautiful bronze by Paolo Negri from Oscar Weiss, himself a noted collector and father of Professor Nigel Weiss, a

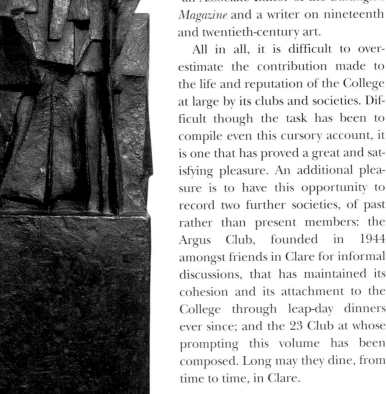

Fellow and sometime member of the Guild; the gift of the art collection of the late Royalton Kisch, the well-known Clare musician; the gift from Jim Ede, of Kettle's Yard fame, of two drawings by Gaudier Brzeska; a gift from his mother in memory of her son, John Davies, who died tragically young, of money to buy abstract work by Victor Pasmore. Besides these, the works purchased by the Guild itself may be considered permanent possessions of the College. Its contribution, direct and indirect, has been considerable. As with the Clare Actors, so with the Guild in respect to its influence on later careers in the outer world. It is small wonder that three student members of the Guild committee should have chosen to build their later careers around the experience: Mark Haworth-Booth went on to become Curator of Photography at the Victoria and Albert Museum, Duncan Robinson, sometime Director of the Mellon Centre for British Art at Yale, to become Director of the Fitzwilliam Museum, Richard Shone to become an Associate Editor of the *Burlington Magazine* and a writer on nineteenth and twentieth-century art.

All in all, it is difficult to over-estimate the contribution made to the life and reputation of the College at large by its clubs and societies. Difficult though the task has been to compile even this cursory account, it is one that has proved a great and satisfying pleasure. An additional pleasure is to have this opportunity to record two further societies, of past rather than present members: the Argus Club, founded in 1944 amongst friends in Clare for informal discussions, that has maintained its cohesion and its attachment to the College through leap-day dinners ever since; and the 23 Club at whose prompting this volume has been composed. Long may they dine, from time to time, in Clare.

1 *Lady Clare Magazine*, Lent Term 1899.
2 *ibid.*, Easter Term 1902.
3 *ibid.*, Easter Term 1904.

51

RIGHT: The Wall *by Paulo Negri, bronze, given in thanks by Oscar Weiss, father of Professor Nigel Weiss, on completion of Professor Weiss's PhD in 1962.*

the college arms

GORDON WRIGHT

The arms of Clare are the oldest in the University. They are known to have been used by our Foundress as her personal arms, and are derived from the first – and dynastically most important – of her three marriages. The three red chevrons, on a gold field, are for Clare, and the red cross, on a gold field, for de Burgh, her husband being heir to the earldom of Ulster. Normally when two coats are impaled in this way, the husband's arms hold the dexter position (the bearer's right side, the viewer's left). In Elizabeth's arms it is the *wife's* coat that holds the dexter position, reflecting the greater importance of her family.

BELOW: *Finishing touches are put to the coat of arms on the College gate in Trinity Lane, following its restoration in October 1969.*

In heraldic jargon, the College arms are, simply:

> Or, three chevrons gules, *impaling* Or, a cross gules,
> All within a bordure sable goutty d'or.

After the death of her third husband, Elizabeth adopted the black border with gold tears as a sign of mourning. Most current versions of the College arms show 12 tears, but the number is optional. Above the portrait of the Foundress, in our hall, is a shield with 19 tears; yet in a late Victorian window in the College chapel is one with as few as four tears. Other numbers are to be found on pieces of plate from various periods.

In modern times the shield has sometimes been surmounted with an earl's coronet, and a coronet has been a popular device on ties. This is anachronistic, because coronets were not granted to earls until 1444, well over a century after the Clare earldoms had become extinct.

The motto *Cave adsum*, sometimes found in the twentieth century, is applicable only to the Clare Boat Club.

from cambridge & clare

53

SIR HARRY GODWIN

Freshman

So great were the changes that accompanied my translation from school to university in the autumn of 1919 that the pallid phrase 'coming-up' is useless to describe them: the experience had more in common with falling over a cliff, nor, in retrospect does the experience seem less startling. It was, to begin with, my first experience of living away from home, and one entered a society where one made contacts with returned servicemen hardened by extreme experience of danger and hardship and where a majority of fellow students had been at preparatory and public school. This latter imbalance of schooling scarcely held, however, in the laboratories, for the Colleges were by now accustomed to taking many if not most of their scientists from the country's grammar and secondary schools, usually by way of scholarship awards. It was on these schools that the country had almost exclusively depended for its requirements in the technological parts of the services – navigation, wireless and artillery ranging and so forth: the important adaptation of the public schools took place later as the country accepted the inevitable expansion of science into every area of our existence, cultural or economic.

As undergraduate, now part of the population scrupulously referred to as the 'men', I found myself having to take responsibility for my own actions and decisions, whether to work or to play, to attend more lectures or more games or more politics or cinema or debates or theatre. The headiness of this new freedom has been expressed acutely and accurately by generations of university graduates looking back on this stage of their own lives. For me the indecisions were ironed out to a considerable extent by close financial constraint, that meant not only strict present limits on spending but a realization that my future depended on scholastic success, so that classes and reading were not to be trifled with – not that this was so much a burden as a very welcome opportunity to learn and expand.

The changes in my own lifestyle, I soon realized were coincident with a vast alteration in the customs and character of the College itself. So extensive had been the slaughter of the war and so horrifying the stresses of long sustained trench warfare, with its high saturation of artillery fire, that the returned service men who now thronged the college screens before going in to dinner in Hall were unlike any generation before or since. Their eyes were haunted, but they all displayed a kindness to one another and a gentleness to the schoolboy freshmen that were all-embracing: it was enough that you and they were still living for them to offer a friendship embracing everything they were possessed of; to be alive and alongside other friendly humans was all Elysium. They never spoke of their own experiences to those too young to have shared them but concentrated on rebuilding a structure of college society, and some few of them had indeed returned to College specifically to reconstruct Boat Club, athletics or other component as it used to be and as they remembered it. The Second World War had a totally different reaction upon the returning population, for in 1939–45 there was no more calling-up of subalterns at eighteen, straight from the school OTC to face a life-expectation in the trenches of two or three weeks. Instead all university men had one year before enrolment, there was far more selective employment in the services, and long spells of inactivity. Instead of long periods overseas away from home, the airforces might alternate strenuous warfare with recovery the same night on English soil. Moreover as we were all aware, the civilian population closely shared the direct dangers of warfare as they could not do in the first war. The return of men from service was altogether more gradual than after the First World War, and they entered college societies that had been far less scarified and diminished.

54

Sir Harry Godwin
Rupert Shepard, 1969

Black chalk on paper
17.25" x 12"

Although College and University retained for the most part their traditional structure, changes were at work here also, and a pre-war 'freshman's guide' would have been astray in many details. The custom of paying and returning visits, complete with engraved 'visiting cards' was almost extinct at undergraduate level, and the convention that only Egyptian or Turkish cigarettes were acceptable had been submerged in a great wave of cigarette smoking in which ninety-nine per cent of the population engaged and in which only the Virginian 'fag' was ever used. It was still possible to buy hand-made oriental cigarettes, the rice paper printed with one's college arms, and a parcel as small as a box of a hundred would be delivered by errand boy at one's rooms. In general, however, the ban against carrying one's own shopping was now inoperative, though the big grocery stores like Matthews, Brimley Wibley, Hallack & Bond, and Flack & Judge, with their enchantingly odorous cavernous ranges of counters, would send composite orders booked by a student or, on his behalf, by his bed-maker. A particularly striking reminder of changes in another direction was given me when, in my first May term, I commented to Miss Ranson, my ageing landlady, upon the sudden prevalence of pretty women and lovely dresses in the town. 'Ah', she said, 'but you should have seen the place before the Fellows were allowed to marry: we had some fine ladies about then!'. The time was within her easy recollection when college societies were entirely of unmarried dons, save for the Master who, in a separate establishment, constituted with his family a distinct and utterly superior layer of university society limited to 'Heads of Houses'. The University Act requiring all dons to be unmarried had been repealed in 1882, but the college bodies were very slow to change from their original organization as work places and homes for unmarried male scholars, and to accept the fact that many of their members were married men with wives and children who command some of the time formerly given to collegiate common-room life.

When college life was resumed after the First World War, Clare was indeed a small college restricted by its endowments to about a dozen Fellows, with an undergraduate population of roundabout 125 and with a single court which, although beautiful beyond all others in Cambridge, offered but scanty accommodation. Aside from lecture rooms, bursary, kitchen, rooms for resident dons, Hall and Chapel, there were available in the whole court only some thirty-five sets for undergraduates, many of these doubled. It followed that everyone spent at least one of his three student years in lodgings: only the needs of club secretaries, boat-captains and such others as needed to be near the notice-boards and porters' lodge, secured a longer foothold. The many lodgings were comfortable and close at hand, the rooms having the strong impress of black horsehair, polished mahogany, mantels with tasselated chenille hangings, a presiding black marble clock, window tables carrying an aspidistra (*ad astra*), and, in concession to the recent taste, a very elongated cane basket chair sprawling near the fire, at demonstrable risk of ignition. Occupants of the adjacent 'digs' might often be seen strolling in dressing gowns through the streets to enjoy a morning bath in college. A corresponding counter-flow, if it can be so called, could be seen at lunch or dinner time when some students in lodgings might order meals from college in their digs: they would be carried there in large deep-sided trays, insulated by heavy baize cloths, borne on the heads of skilful college porters.

Whether 'keeping' in digs or in college, one was expected to attend dinner in Hall on six nights a week where one's presence was pricked off by the buttery-clerk, Edgar, perforating a mounted attendance list: after the first day or two he had seldom to enquire a man's name, and failure to attend meant a summons to the tutor. No doubt regularity at Hall actively increased the coherence of the college as well as giving a guarantee of adequate nourishment for careless youth. The circumstances of dining were of course quite foreign to me. Food was ample and we were served at the vast oak tables by college servants, who, having dispensed the soup or fish, invariably enquired 'beef or mutton, sir?' The meat was carved with the greatest expedition at the hot-plate by senior gyps who brought their own cherished cutlery for the purpose and gained no little kudos from their expertise. We used the College's heavy Victorian silver at table and for ordinary drinks from the buttery likewise had the use of Georgian or Victorian tankards or silver beakers given by past generations of Clare men. Of the alumni whose portraits sloped darkly down from the walls, I had prior knowledge of only one, Marquis Cornwallis, and of that able and distinguished diplomat and soldier all I then recollected was the embarrassing footnote to my history lessons that he 'surrendered at Yorktown, with 80,000 men'.

The Hall itself was excellent late Jacobean, but its robust simplicity had been drenched and submerged in middle Victorian time by a plethora of applied carving and intricate variegated wall and ceiling decoration that left no

56

*View of Old Court
showing gateway with
oriel windows*
John F. Greenwood

Linocut

Cromwell's occupation of the town and commandeering of building material brought a stop for several years to the rebuilding of the court. It is thought that the Master consequentially had his Lodge on this staircase for it is still provided with a superb wooden staircase with massive newel posts, surmounted by fine finials supporting from each one to the next a long and neatly perforated oak plank, like fretwork performed by elephants. The staircase divided above into the steps leading to the two opposing sets of attic rooms, and between them was the window giving access to the leads of the roof. When unlocked, as it often was, it allowed one to contemplate at close quarters the magnificent square masonry chimneys on which so much of the aesthetic appeal of the building rests, the comfortable corners, the fragile heavy and uncommon Collyweston slates, only too susceptible to any careless treading but of exceptionally beautiful texture. I found subsequently that Mansfield Forbes shared my delight in the beauty of the Clare roof scenery, and when he came to edit the Book of Clare he introduced others to these generally overlooked prospects, so that there are illustrations by many high-grade photographers, by J.F. Greenwood (wood-engraving) and by Sydney W. Carline (pencil drawings), all showing the Clare roof-scapes. A sight that has never failed to move me by its calm beauty is that of the two stone cherubs that, one on either side of the entrance gateway, spread protecting wings towards the centre of the court and in the moonlight of the small hours wear the aspect of guardian angels.

It is only fair to remark that the attic rooms had more down-to-earth qualities. The rooms were heated by open fires fed from a scuttle on the hearth that was replenished from a wooden bin on the staircase landing, to which coal was carried by the sack-load. We bathed after games in a tin hip-bath before the fire in a canful of hot water carried up by the gyp from the kitchens across the court. Adequate enough for this and for toasting muffins, the heat of the living room fire scarcely penetrated to my bedroom beyond the intervening gyp-room, and in the harder winters the water in the hand-basin by my bed sometimes by morning carried ice over half-an-inch thick. In a mild season one would hear the sound of a rushing cataract of water, behind the wall alongside my bed: when curiosity impelled me to remove the covering panel, I found that a deep lead-lined wooden trough extended right through the thickness of the college, and in heavy rain it constituted a gutter draining all the roofing facing King's and

panel untouched: it all stood greatly in need of cleaning and restoration, but opportunity for these arrived only with time and changes of college circumstances.

There was really no doubt that the true colour of college life was to be gained only by residence in the Old Court at whatever level one might achieve this. I was lucky enough to be assigned share in a double attic set at the head of E staircase, in the centre of the College's southern front, that range of building just completed when carrying the water to down-pipes on the inside of the Clare courtyard. Whether we needed the water, or King's refused to take it, I never discovered, but I learned that the open gutter was liable to be a hazard when leaves choked its intake and locally flooded the roof-flats.

The communicating gyp room between the double living-room and my bedroom was haunted by mice so that food needed to be stored in tins. I managed to control their access to some extent by stacking bundles of fire-lighters over the mouseholes at floor level: unfortunately the naphthalene, whose crystals spattered the bundles of sticks, had a strong affinity for butter, whose virginity was readily compromised if it was left exposed.

The old-world limitations of life in E8 were also recognizable elsewhere in the old Court, quite unmistakably in its sewage disposal that was centred upon a short range of earth-closets situated right by the river's brim, so far in fact that a friend of mine kept his bicycle after dark at the foot of H staircase to diminish the fatigue of the journey.

From the river one could see the blocked-up, but quite recognizable, archways in the brickwork of the walls fronting the Cam: these were not *oubliettes* from the Master's Lodge, useful as these no doubt could have been, but sewers now no longer permitted to discharge directly into the river. This row of privies made use of a simple mechanical device to dispense a shot of suitably disin-fected earth into the waiting containers. This open air establishment, and early morning meeting-place, of course, was generally known as 'Lady Clare' (privily known, one might well say), a custom that allowed much pleasant gross humour at the expense of the ignorant. When I had told my own GP in the Midlands that I was coming to reside in Cambridge, he had told me that he himself was a native of the northern Fenland and that malaria was still endemic in those parts. Sure enough the river precincts of the Lady Clare swarmed with the malaria vector, the spotted-winged mosquito (*Anopoheles maculipen-nis*) taking full advantage of feeding opportunities. One unfortunate man of my year who had never been outside England in his life, duly went down with the disease, alongside the occasional ex-service men suffering recur-rences after an initial infection acquired overseas.

New Court

During my three years as research student I had lodgings near Parker's Piece where the nearness to the laboratories was a great convenience and the smallness of the rooms was compensated by the great kindness of my motherly landlady Mrs Howard. My bedroom on the first floor was the dimension of the hall below, so narrow that, whilst large enough to hold the single bed and the chest-cum-dressing table, side by side, there was barely room for drawers of the chest to open. Length was likewise cur-tailed and in bed in the summer one stretched one's feet luxuriously on the sill of the open window.

It was a great contrast moving to the Fellow's set of rooms in the Memorial Court. I bade farewell to the sad oleograph of the Cameron Highlander *Absent without Leave* who was now under arrest by the bedside of his dying father, and embraced the prospect for the first time of furnishing my own living quarters. The basic provision was indeed luxurious, with separate entrance hall, tele-phone, gyp-room and toilet, a well-proportioned sitting-room with built-in bookcase, cupboards and fire-place, large dining-room, bedroom and adjoining bathroom. Taking occasion of the visit by my former headmaster to his daughter in Cambridge, I was able to draw on Mr Clegg's experience and taste. On an excursion to the London shops I was introduced to the excitements of Heals and acquired dining-room furniture of 'limed' oak appropriate to the natural wood of the rooms, and this was followed by a visit to an old friend of Mr Clegg's in the Liverpool Street area. This was an Armenian carpet mer-chant, Mr Benlian. I was treated to a professional display of bargaining that ended, when agreement seemed unlikely, in my acquiring a few glowing Hamadan rugs that were to give continuing pleasure over many years. Railway posters done by Paul Henry and Medici prints took key positions on the walls, whilst leisure and service were provided by substantial plain hide-upholstered settee and chairs obtained at advantage from the midland town of origin: they remain serviceable if shabby fifty-seven years later. I claim a little indulgence in thus describing my first set of rooms since it was to be the centre of my col-lege life until after the end of the Second World War and became very familiar to generations of friends and stu-dents from Clare and elsewhere.

During 1914–18 the tremendous flow of war casualties had been met in the Cambridge region by the discharge of hospital trains at a large sidings next to the Long Road at the south side of the town. Thence the wounded suf-fered the uncomfortable transportation to the large tem-porary 'Eastern General' hospital that had been built on the Clare-King's playing field, the lovely cricket ground

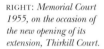

58

where now the University Library stands. The cessation of the War was followed by such acute housing shortages, that throughout the country 'squatters' took possession of any premises temporarily becoming vacant and this is what happened to the wooden huts of the Eastern General Hospital, which indeed suffered such occupation until the building of the University Library offered a reason for repossession of the site so strong that it could not reasonably be refused. In 1925 the families occupying the hospital site enlivened the scene beyond the Clare boundary fence by looped lines of coloured washing hung out to dry and air. The pictorial possibilities encouraged me to attempt to cut a colour wood-block of the scene from my sitting-room, but it was not very effective and I turned instead to representing the Real Tennis courts visible beyond the huts and framed by shapely trees. Here variation of the autumn sky in the hand printing of the blocks made an acceptable series of variants in the product. My interest in wood-block printing had been sustained by my friendship since undergraduate days with Frank Kendon of St John's who, after war service with the Friends' Ambulance, was now engaged under G. G. Coulton in research on mural paintings in English churches. In the book he afterwards published he ventured the conjecture that the medieval spread of printing and the associated black line wood-block illustration, were the likeliest means by which travelling artists promoted their craft of mural decoration. He readily learned the simple form of wood-block cutting that I had practised at school, and in return introduced me to the techniques of wood-block engraving with the burin upon the polished end-grain of box-wood, a process allowing reproduction of fine detail and only recently being superseded by half-tone printing in the commercial publishing trade.

RIGHT: *Memorial Court 1955, on the occasion of the new opening of its extension, Thirkill Court.*

Life in my new rooms was exceptionally comfortable and one came to accommodate to minor flaws in building design. The windows proved to be set too far below ceiling level, creating a heavy belt of shadow, a fault avoided in the later range of buildings. The set of the rectangular block transversely to the prevalent westerlies meant that the wind seemed to strive to get through the great archway and, failing that, rushed through windows, doors and crevices throughout the building so that no position remained in the bedroom where one had refuge from the blast on its way from the sitting-room, over one's legs to Queen's Road. Lt. Col. Barham, who provided the money for building one of the two corner staircases of the new court, laid down the requirement that there should be a yearly service on Armistice Day, held in the Memorial Gateway and at which should be sung either Kipling's 'Recessional' or the hymn 'The strife is o'er, the battle done'. Thus at 11 am on 11 November for many years the College held a religious service centred upon the placing of a wreath of Flanders' poppies beneath the bronze plaque of the names of the fallen that occupies the inside wall of the arch. In what I now think a priggish light-hearted way, I complained to Telfer that the line from 'Recessional' – 'Lest we forget, lest we forget' – seemed to have a hint of blackmail in it. Perhaps scenting blasphemy, even unintentional, the Dean promptly banned Kipling's hymn and henceforward our services had no choice.

In later years the service has ceased, which I find a matter for regret: perhaps I am too moved by the recollection of the deep hush that, on those earliest Armistice Days, fell across the whole landscape as the exploding maroon at eleven o'clock signalled the two minutes' silence, with all traffic along the Backs at a standstill as the multitudes of war dead were, in real reverence, for a while remembered by their survivors.

The purposes of the Fellows' sets in the Memorial Buildings were several. To begin with the statutes laid it down that the research and official Fellows had entitlement, subject to consent of the Council, to select vacant rooms for their occupation. The new buildings, of course, partly met the extreme limitation of space in the Old Court. It also went a long way towards solving the problem, becoming more serious now that fellows were more often married men, of finding fellows to pernoctate, to sleep in the new court and to be responsible for keeping order there. For a great many years and long after my marriage I fulfilled this duty as part of my obligation as a Fellow 'to best of my judgement and ability' to 'discharge the business of the College which may be entrusted to me'. Over a long period of time the pernoctation was shared by two of the Fellows: to begin with it was Raymond Priestly to whom every morning I waved from the bathroom across the archway space, but during the Second World War it was our close friend Dixon Boyd, Professor of Anatomy, with whom sharing was made simpler by the fact that he (and for some time his family) lived in our home as part of the wartime transfer of the London Hospital staff and students to Cambridge, when the severe demand for space led to such expedients as the dissection of cadavers at the top of the Sidgwick Museum of Geology.

I had enjoyed a term or so of ease in my comfortable rooms when I was slightly surprised to be reminded by the Tutor that it would be not unreasonable to undertake some supervision for the College: doubtless to soften the prospect, he told me that in the new academic year he had coming to college from Uppingham a particularly attractive student already addicted to botany and a well-informed field naturalist. Thus began a long and happy association as pupil and colleague with John Gilmour, who was to become in turn Assistant Director of the Royal Botanic Gardens at Kew, Director of the Royal Horticultural Society's Garden, Wisley, and, from 1951, Director of the University Botanic Garden in Cambridge.

The intention of supervision within individual subjects was a discharge of the all-over college responsibility for tuition that had progressively been assumed by the University system of organized lectures and practical work. As College supervisor one would see each allocated student in a class of two, three or four (more seldom singly) for an hour each week at which one discussed all the problems raised by the week's work, discussed the essay prepared for the class and already marked, and considered any general issues raised by oneself or the men. Especially one sought to fill in the gaps in botanical science left by the lectures, and to erase the errors or misconceptions that even professorial teaching can engender. Many men came up with very little knowledge of the old-fashioned principles of classification of flowering plants, although ability to use a flora was assumed; here was a gap one could help to fill and the Memorial Court provided at hand populations of suitable material for improvised field instruction, not least the great elms, afterwards alas victims of Dutch elm disease.

I always aimed to aggregate men of similar status or ability, and so to manage the class that they actively pursued

60

the logic of argument and evidence for themselves. It never worked better than in an *ad hoc* group consisting of three men respectively from Clare, Selwyn and Peterhouse, all quite first class. Of them the Clare man, G.C. Stevenson, became a plant pathologist employed for a long time in Mauritius; John Turner as Professor in Melbourne played a very considerable role over many years in the development of botany in Australia; and Nigel Balchin was the very able and esteemed author and playwright whose writings so perfectly reflected the manner and speech of this country in the years before and during the Second World War. In these classes no holds were barred and every subject under the sun was mentioned. John Turner and Nigel Balchin indeed developed a much cherished friendship with the family, and one which led us to informed detail of the intimacies of undergraduate life undreamed of by the average don. Nigel had attained his education at Dauntsey's School by way of a 'Kitchener'

RIGHT AND OPPOSITE:
Details of doorways in Memorial Court.

scholarship for sons of men wounded in the First World War, and to comply with a condition of studying agriculture, he found himself in his third year constructing experiments in field labour on the University Farm: thence he advanced to experimental and industrial psychology, the area which is so well illuminated in his writings and which *inter alia* let to the creation of the long-enduring and profitable invention of the selection of chocolates, 'Black Magic'. It is gratifying to consider my living-set on N staircase as background for the generation of such friendships, aside altogether from the instruction taken so much for granted.

We were separately paid for all College supervisions at rates generally agreed by the Colleges. It was hard work, especially as it involved careful marking beforehand of the essay preparations set for the week. Not less than fifteen or twenty minutes would be so spent for each man, and as I undertook eight or ten classes per week the total was formidable. Formidable even when the students were male. However I came under great pressure, hard to refuse as Demonstrator in the Botanical Department, also to supervise students for Newnham and Girton. I settled to take a weekly class of twelve or fifteen and this proved Herculean labour, for they were hideously conscientious. Each of the women students turned in two essays, and each essay was at least twice the average length of those of a male student. The marking alone took hours and when the class met me in the small lecture-room at the lab, it would *not* utter. It sat, poised to write down what I might impart, and resisted solidly all my efforts to get anyone to venture an idea or opinion: the give and take of controversy and argument on the validity of expressed opinion was not, it seemed, for them!

I guess that the essays must have provided me with plentiful subjects for exposition and amendment, for the demand for the class did not decline.

With the loss of their private garden beyond Queens' Road, the Fellows now made more use of the river garden, and on warm summer evenings took out the odd wooden 'cheeses' to play bowls on the lawn or improvised a form of soft-ball cricket that was, alas, rather destructive of the borders. To a botanist going along the avenue several times a day, it soon became evident that the trees of common lime, *Tilia europaea*, which composed it were very far from uniform. They consisted of three distinct populations of differing ages. The oldest and largest, planted when the avenue was constructed, had huge clear trunks and massive branches, attaining a great height, possibly ninety feet. In the intermediate age-generation the trees were smaller in size, both girth and height, and had clearly been planted in gaps opened up by local deaths of the older generation. The third generation was of trees, still at the original spacing, but much smaller than the older series, sickly and shedding their branches. Oddly enough the youngest were the weakest and gaps grew as they died and were not replaced. The key to this domestic problem in arboriculture was offered to me by our evening cricket games, where search for the tennis-ball showed that right along its length the north flank of the avenue was supported by a solid red brick wall standing up four or five feet from garden level. On the south-facing side the avenue stood next to King's Ditch and here the corresponding brick wall was far deeper, possibly eight or nine feet. Thus the two walls enclosed a raised causeway between the river bridge and the stone gateway fronting King's Pieces. The lime trees were thus planted inside a kind of giant window box whose soil had not been replenished for two centuries or more. The first generation of trees flourished admirably, but whenever age or disease made a gap in their regular rows, the replacements had to make what growth they might. The massive skeletal roots of the older trees were at hand to put their new feeding roots into the vacated plot and, facing such competition, the newcomers never reached the dimensions of their predecessors and many of them died early. As the avenue grew ragged again, further replanting made matters worse, and the condition of the third generation of limes was so poor that they have since been removed. Happily several of the noble giants of the first planting have been left and lend great dignity to the prospect of the avenue. Reconstruction of the history of the avenue would have been more difficult today for G.H.A. Wilson, Bursar when the Memorial Court building was in progress and, at a loss to dispose of the excavated sub-soil, ordered it to be dumped all alongside the north flank of the avenue, where it hid the retaining wall beneath a wide bank of gravel that has only been made fertile by much effort from the gardeners. The width and the lateral position of the bank have cost the avenue much of its former architectural quality of a narrow raised viaduct from the Old Court across the strip of low land liable to flood.

Along the north side of the river garden, shielding it alike from inclement wind and the gaze of the curious

along Garrett Hostel Lane, is a high wall of pleasantly weathered Cambridge brick. Then as now it supports on its southern face unusual flowering shrubs and climbers that luxuriate in the high midsummer temperatures, but on the opposite northern face it was backed in the 1920s by a closely set row of very tall elms that extended the full length of the garden, providing it with a notably impressive backbone. When one penetrated behind the wall, there was the Garrett Hostel ditch bordered and overhung by flourishing yews twenty or thirty feet tall and underspread with ivy. Beneath the heavy-foliaged yews and the tall columnar elms was a secluded gravel path where in the crepuscule one might come upon the Dean in quiet perambulation. At one point the exotic snowdrop-tree (*Halesia* sp.) had been planted, its pendant white blossoms suggesting to me that to reserve all the underplanting to white and preferably scented flowers would enhance the solemnity and dignity of the 'Dean's Walk'. This has in fact been most successfully accomplished, the effect even overriding the later felling of all the elms.

This dreadful excision was a consequence of the extensive spread of Dutch elm disease in the period before the Second World War, when, since coal was scarce in college, it was arranged that undergraduates might saw up the felled timber for their own use as fuel. In this way all evidence of the great line of elms disappeared. We were never again to see, as a result of an abnormally frost-free spring, the river garden so crowded with self-sown elm seedlings that the gardeners had to hoe through the flower beds to be rid of them.

Botanists may however comfort themselves that the river garden provides for them specimens of two fine exotic

trees, as it happens oddly similar in habit to one another. The longer-established is a swamp-cypress, *Taxodium distichum*, a native of the Everglades in Florida, in whose black swamps it produces its woody aerating roots that protrude into the air from the submerged root-system. Perched upon the drained river bank in the Clare garden, these structures are absent, but we can see its elegant habit, the larch-like foliage shed annually as feathery twiglets and the tiny round pollen-bearing cones falling in considerable number. Some years after introduction of the swamp-cypress, we planted in the wet centre of the garden a sapling of the dawn-cypress, *Metasequoia glyptostroboides*, a species known in ancient fossil state but regarded as extinct until rediscovered in 1945 by an expedition to a remote region of China. When introduced to the gardens and arboreta of many parts of temperate Europe and North America it has proved to grow with great vigour and this has been typical of the tree in the Clare garden, as of others planted elsewhere in Cambridge.

I have written in this Chapter primarily of the events and scenes associated with my earliest years in the Memorial Court. There were great changes to come, various colleges were to follow our example and build new courts across the Cam, the University was to create the Sidgwick Avenue centre for the Humanities and, most imposingly in every sense, Sir Giles Gilbert Scott entrusted by the University with the building of a new library, was to place it, almost to an inch, upon the axis of the Clare Memorial Court, and finally this court was itself greatly extended in those further episodes beyond that which initiated it in 1925. In the 1920s those manifold developments were only to be guessed at.

63

LEFT: *Memorial Court, September 2000.*

CLARE & THE GENERAL STRIKE

During the General Strike one hundred and fifty-seven undergraduates were absent on emergency service. The following list shows the varying nature of the work which they undertook in different parts of the country.

SPECIAL CONSTABLES (78)

K.A. Sinker	G.A. Emerson	J.W.J Rinkel	R.F.G. Lea
P.P.N. Fawcett	W.S. Scott	S. Cruikshank	C.G. Fraser
R.H. Smith	H. Sherlock	R.N.K. Granville	D.K. Whatley
H.G. Hammett	A.W. Hill	F.S. Winton	E.G. Benn
D. Howat	F.C.D. Wood	F.J. Sharman	E.H. Lyle
G.N. Bailey	C.B. Maloney	A.G. Stuart	W.R.S Bond
A.M. Dixon	G.T. Beckwith	J. Cherry	G.A. Mackintosh
F.T. Beilby	V.S. Hedges	J. Blair	D.H.V. Board
F.W.R. Leistikow	L.J. Batten	A.B. Carter	K. Pascall
G.V. Vane	H.D. Couzens	A.M. Russell	A.H. Service F.
W.L. Danger	J.D. Wilson	A.G. Adamson	W.H.T. Fisher
W.S. Thorbourn	V.D. Cory	A.H.G. Garratt	J.M. Bemrose
E.C. Harris	J.H.L. Gibbs	J. Leman	A.G. Trinder
B.X. Jessop	A.P. Welsh	G. Houldey	E.S. Kendall
J.P. Underhill	G.W.V. Sutton	B.E. Lester	G.S. Machin
W.O. Dickins	F.G. Maitland	J.E. Lumb	G.F. Millet
H.W. McGowan	R.H.P. Church	B.A. Hemelye	I.V. Mixon
J.L. le Farmer	H. Bailey	W.F. Pearce	R.D. Caesar
H.M. Crave	T.K.D. Pritchett	C.A. Black	A.G. de C. Ireland
–Trubshawe	W.K. Findlay		

UNDERGROUND AND TUBES (24)

K.W.J. Fison	C.J.T. Penroth	C. Nuttall	J.P. Nelson
G.Wynne-Davies	A.B. Banham	J. Prain	P. Lyne
R.M.L. Evans	B.W. Walter	C.W. Dupont	R. Reynolds
J.N. Jackaman	A.C.S. Clark	F.G. Wood-Smith	S.H. Ormerod
G.M. Mason	J.A. Hilton	J.B. Daltry	D.P. Bennett
W.C. Savage	A.W. Franklin	N.F. Marsh	D.W. Bawtree

TRANSPORT (18)

J.S. Paton	H.E. Wise	G.B. Herbert	F.H. Finlaison
D.H. Pirie	W.G. Airey	F.C. Clarke	B.C. Frankiss
C. Morriss	L.I.S. Campbell	P.G.B. Reynolds	P.H. Martin
A.B. Maconochie	T.F. Timmins	K. de C. Holroyd	E.S. Baker
D.B.H. Seymour	L.C. Rowe		

CAMBRIDGE UNDERGRADUATES WHO HAVE VOLUNTEERED TO WORK IN ONE OF THE
SPECIAL SERVICES GROUPS ASSEMBLED DURING THE GENERAL STRIKE.

DOCK WORKERS (16)

D.R. Freemantle	H.W. Kempthorne	G.B. Coghlan	J.M. Scott
G. Pyman	W.E. Preston	C.A. Wilson	E.G. Lloyd
A.R.A. Leeds	T.G.G. Cooper	J.S. Synge	G.M. Burton
F.D. Nicholson	C.K. Wrefford	O.M. Bullivant	A. Eckford

RAILWAYS (9)

J.F. Alcock	J.N. Crofton Atkins	H.F. Mander	J.B. Blakeborough
E.H. Holt	R. Wall	K.I.P. Barraclough	J.F. Pearson
A.H. Milward			

OMNIBUSES (5) TRAMS (3) MINES (2) "BRITISH GAZETTE" (2)

OMNIBUSES (5)	TRAMS (3)	MINES (2)	"BRITISH GAZETTE" (2)
A.W. Adeney	E.R. Arnold	F.S.V. Davies	T.E.B. Clarke
W.H. Dunbar	G. McConaghy	H.G. Best	T.P. Peatling
C.G.L. Francis	A.E.C. Harvey		
P.J.A. Innes			
J.P. Oliveira			

religion and college life[1]

JO BAILEY WELLS

The statutes that Lady Clare gave to the College in 1359 clearly state a dual function for the College, both religious and secular: 'to extend ... knowledge ... for the promotion of God's service, and for the welfare and advancement of the State'. These statutes provided for a Master and twenty Fellows, of whom six were to be in priest's orders. The latter as part of their duties were expected to lead the church offices and to ensure 'the attendance thereat of members of the Church *in statu pupillari*'.

The first reference to the office of Dean occurs in the College accounts for 1602. This used to be an elected office – as with other College offices such as Tutor, Bursar or Lecturer – which circulated between those Fellows who were in holy orders. Ever since the tenure of Henry W. Fulford (Dean 1884–1907), however, when the office has fallen vacant persons from outside the Fellowship have been elected to become both Dean and Fellow. Clare has a distinguished record of former Deans during the twentieth century, through whom the character of religion at Clare – so far as it is expressed in the formal life of the college – may be traced.

The story of 'religion' in Clare through the twentieth century is a fascinating one. It is marked by remarkable innovation within a traditional setting. Despite the rapid turnover of students, and the passing of ten Deans and sixteen Chaplains within the century, the character of worship and style of ministry have remained remarkably constant. Some might attribute this to the architecture of the Chapel, or to the Senior Tutor's choice intake of students, or the character of the Fellowship. Those who know the college best, however, would point to the influence of one particular Dean, C.F.D. Moule. Though Dean for only seven years, 1944–51, his active involvement with the Chapel continued for a further twenty-five years during his tenure as Lady Margaret Professor of Divinity. Even after he moved away from College, his support and

commitment to successive Deans, and to the work of the Chapel, continued – indeed *continues*, even in his nineties – through occasional visits to preach or pray and through his prodigious hand-written correspondence.

Compulsory Chapel

At the beginning of the century, compulsory chapel was still the order of the day – morning and evening, six days a week. It was the Dean's primary duty to lead these services, and to see that all took place decently and in order. This pattern was passed from Henry W.Fulford to Philip C.T. Crick (Dean 1909–20), in whose time the obligation was lifted (doubtless to the relief of all concerned).

Such habits brought to the office of Dean a certain responsibility for rigour and discipline in the college – such that even during William Telfer's time (1921–44), the Dean was a person to be feared as much as respected. One 'liturgical' responsibility which remained was that of Grace at meals, the duty of which fell to scholars until the 1970s. Since it was the habit of most Fellows to attend the second Hall each evening, it fell to the Dean to attend the first Hall, just to stand on the dais while Grace was read, in the (often vain) attempt to ensure that it was done with some gravity and sincerity.

'Telfer' (as he was known to colleagues, in the fashion of those times) looked austere, ascetic and rather forbidding. Acquaintance revealed a gentle, sensitive, pastoral character (and fine Church historian) with a twinkle in his eye and a highly developed sense of humour. It is said that the game amongst Fellows was to tell a good enough joke at the end of High Table so as to make it difficult for him to recover his gravity in time to say a post-prandial Grace (perhaps *Laus Deo! Deo Gratias!*). One story, from the archives of oral tradition, tells of him travelling in an ancient car with colleagues (probably Harry Godwin and the inevitable 'Manny' Forbes), when they were overtaken by a free-running back wheel which had come off. Instantly Will Telfer (nearly a running Blue) hopped out and sprinted after the errant wheel – 'so as to get it before the Boat Club could'!

Breakfast in E3

The pattern of Chapel life has changed little since the services became voluntary. On Sundays there has long been a morning Eucharist[2] – early enough for the keen to attend a service in a city Church of their choice – and an Evensong, usually with visiting preacher. During the week there has been the daily office of morning and evening prayer, now supplemented by a midweek eucharist and two further choral evensongs.

The Chapel fellowship has always been sustained after services with a meal – after Evensong, with dinner in Hall and after the morning Eucharist, with breakfast in E3. The days since Crick bellowed to the kitchen staff from his window across Old Court "hot breakfast for 30" are long passed, if not forgotten. Bacon & eggs have been replaced by rolls & marmalade, and the timing has drifted to a later hour, but this tradition has lasted the century. Charlie Moule inherited the practice from Will Telfer in 1944: he still recalls the occasion when Telfer (who remained at Clare, in the background, prior to becoming Master of Selwyn in 1947) brought an Italian newspaper with news of the death of Mussolini.

Post-war Remembrance

The building of Memorial Court was itself an act of Remembrance, and the names of the members of Clare who died in the Great War are engraved under the arch, as well as in the Antechapel.[3] One whole staircase was given by the Barham family in memory of Wilfred Saxby Barham (matriculated 1913; killed at Poperinghe, Flanders, 10 October 1915) on the condition that a service be held every Armistice Day (as it was then called) under the main archway of the building. Cambridge veterans and residents recall Will Telfer, and after him Charlie Moule, marching the choir across the Backs for this ritual at 11am. By the 1960s the practice was felt to have lost all meaning and, following the fiftieth anniversary of Armistice Day in 1968, was transferred to a service marking Rememberance Sunday in the Chapel. At the time of writing the practice of rememberance is growing more popular again: following the fiftieth anniversary of VE and VJ Day, there is a new generation of interest and concern.

It fell to Charlie Moule to design Chapel Services to celebrate the end of World War II, and to edit the Roll of Honour, superbly printed and bound in a book kept in a glass case in the Antechapel. Deans have guarded the key and turned the pages at regular intervals ever since – except, it is said, when John Robinson lost the key!

Chaplains

The College of the mid-forties was full of mature undergraduates, returned warriors, some with distinguished war records. Many were perhaps sighing for their old, traditional way of life after the years of exile. They were conformist and positive; many were religious. Relative to subsequent decades, they made life easy for 'the establishment'. In this climate, traditional Christianity was strong. Chapel was so full in those days that long disused benches were brought up from the crypt to augment the seating and the choir had to process in single file.

Although two Chaplains were appointed in the 1930s, A.C.H. Leeke (1935–38) and H.C. Blackburne (1939–40; never took up office), there was no tradition of chaplaincy established until the late 1940s. Charlie Moule was the sole priest in the College: until a Clare man, Arthur T. Howden, a CMS missionary invalided home from Persia on the

LEFT: *The Reverend Professor C.F.D. (Charlie) Moule, 1988.*

67

68

grounds of a 'horseshoe kidney', was allowed by the College to be a temporary Chaplain (at £100 per annum) in 1945–46. When Charlie Moule went to the Governing Body with a proposal for his replacement by Stanley W. Betts, a senior RAF Chaplain and former student of Charlie, the idea was ridiculed by the Bursar, 'Harrison': 'We don't even know what the Dean is for. What do we want with a Chaplain?'. The following year the Master, 'Thirks', took up the cause, and it went through (Harrison no doubt muttering, 'Oh well, we need only give him £150 or so').

In just two years, it is said, the new Chaplain Betts transformed the College. Despite the feudal character of the institution in those days, he had the capacity to get alongside junior and senior members alike. The Christian cause seemed to hum. CICCU (Cambridge Inter-Collegiate Christian Union) was strong and active, and so, then, was the SCM (Student Christian Movement) of which a promising young Christ's man, Maurice Wiles, was President. It is noteworthy that these student Christian groups in Clare have, on the whole, integrated well with the work of the Chapel and the Chaplain ever since. When Stanley Betts left after two years as Chaplain (1947–49) to become Vicar of Holy Trinity Church in Cambridge, the question was no longer, 'Shall we have a Chaplain?' but, 'Whom shall we have as Chaplain?' – and the habit of having a Chaplain as well as a Dean in Holy Orders spread to many of the other colleges. Charlie Moule subsequently became an unofficial Chaplain to the Chaplains, organising devotional and study sessions across the university.

'Liturgy coming to Life'[4]

John A.T. Robinson was appointed to the Deanship in 1951, when Charlie Moule became Lady Margaret Professor. The succeeding eight years saw unprecedented change in the forms of corporate worship in the Chapel, which in due course became highly influential for liturgi-

RIGHT AND OPPOSITE:
The menu, Charlie Moule's leaving meal.

CHARLES FRANCIS DIGBY MOULE
1944 TO 1988

Asparagus
–
Grilled Salmon
Hollandaise Sauce
–
Tournedos Rossini
New Potatoes
Mange Tout
–
Strawberries and Cream
–
Coffee and Petit Fours

divide. He maintained the Prayer Book service – convinced it was a necessary operative basis for Anglican unity – but he used it imaginatively. In due course a Communion Manual was printed for College use, which stressed the action as well as the words and which explained the service devotionally for newcomers. In due course this became a model for the liturgical innovations in the Church of England which led to the Alternative Service Book (1980) and Common Worship (2000).

Changes to the furniture of the Chapel also took place. With the Governing Body's concurrence, John Robinson made a clean sweep of the Victorian embellishments – the brass Communion rail and a large brass eagle lectern – as well as the solid altar against the east wall. (The Fellows' Butler had, allegedly, long since given up changing the frontal according to the liturgical season anyway, leaving the conscientious Dean to hoist it out of the case in the Antechapel and heave it on just before a service). Two fine wooden lecterns, in keeping with the original woodwork of the Chapel, were made to serve for reading and preaching, and an elegant, small, refectory-type table was acquired as an altar. Candlesticks were eventually designed also – to replace ponderous candlesticks too large for the new altar – and a new silver chalice and paten, to replace a chalice that was much too small given the new popularity of the Sunday morning Eucharist. (The vast Butler gold cup was – and still is – only brought out from the safe on special occasions). The Victorian brass went the way of all flesh – to the junk collection down the milkman's passage along the Trinity Hall wall – until Charlie Moule discovered that the Chaplain of the (then) St Luke's College of Education at Exeter would like it. When consulted, Master Eric Ashby replied, 'There aren't many things we can do without the Governing Body's leave: let's do it'. Without further ado, the said Chaplain arrived with a small truck and quietly carried it off.

The changes to the Chapel since John Robinson's time have been motivated more by expediency than theology. In 1969 the crypt below the Chapel was refurbished and made available as the Junior Common Room – a situation which established, for some, the distinction between Heaven and Hell. The organ was replaced in 1970 by R. von Beckerath of Hamburg. In 1976 the candleholders for the choir were added, a gift from Charlie Moule at the time of his retirement. And in 1992 the interior was redecorated, so far as possible to re-establish the original decorative scheme given to the Chapel in the 1760s.

cal reform in the Church of England as a whole. They were also hugely effective: the congregation doubled at Sunday morning Eucharist, such that Holy Communion came to occupy a central, creative position in the common life of the community. Robinson's concern was to enable the Christians at Clare – whatever their denominational or other 'party' loyalties – to *be* the Church in the College (as distinct from merely 'going to Chapel'), whilst at the same time enabling the Chapel to serve as the parish Church of every member of College.

John Robinson's preaching, teaching and example inspired many in the college. Chiefly through the service of Communion – which full communicants of any Christian denomination were invited to receive[5] – he managed to transcend the traditional catholic/evangelical split in the Chapel. Far from being a watery *via media*, this stressed the things that unite rather than the things that

70

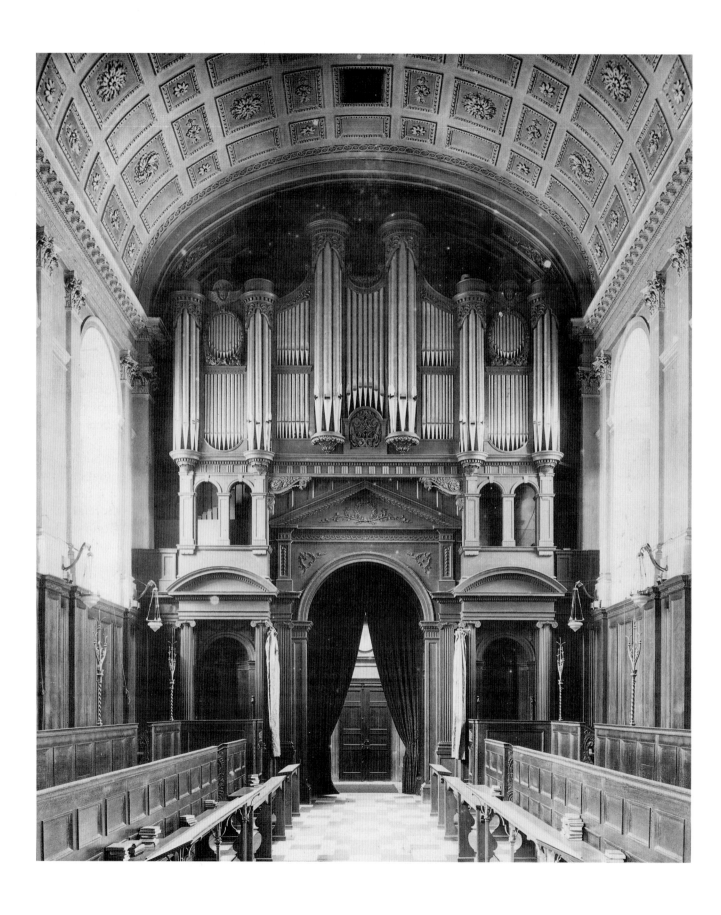

The Cambridge Pastorate

J. Denis Wakeling followed Stanley Betts as Chaplain 1950–52, after which a firm and fruitful link was established with the Cambridge Pastorate. This was a special ministry, attached to Holy Trinity Church, for students across the university. F.S. (Bill) Skelton (1952–59) was the first in a line of five chaplains to fulfil this dual role. He described the position to his successor, Christopher J.V. Drummond (1959–62) as 'the best job in the Church of England'.

This link furthered the work of Clare Chapel in serving the wider university. Just as the 'open table policy' at Sunday Eucharist prevented any narrow denominationalism within the College, so the Pastorate prevented any narrow 'Clare men only' empire developing beyond the College. The succession of Chaplains did what university Chaplains at their best have so frequently done: gained the confidence of a great number of students, many of whom never came near the Chapel, and helped them in very significant ways through all sorts of problems of personal development.

In this role, the Chaplains valued their detachment from the disciplinary and administrative side of College life: they were not Fellows, in order that they could better relate to students. Indeed, it would be more common to find such clergy at the College playing fields or in the College bar than at a meeting or even in the Chapel. Arriving back late from London with about 40 undergraduates, only to discover that the locks had been changed, John O.C. Alleyne (successor to Christopher Drummond, 1962) took pride in helping the group to climb back into College – and pacifying the Senior Tutor next morning.

It was a given that such Chaplains were young bachelors who lived 'in' – thus being available for those who might seek them out even during the night. (There is a story that when it was suggested in Trinity that the Chaplain be replaced by a professional counsellor, it was turned down on the grounds that a Chaplain offers four times the work for a quarter of the cost). The dark oak-panels of the first-floor set on A staircase (A2) have kept their counsel – and dispensed the occasional whisky – late into the night for generations.

Honest to God

1959 was a year of change in the life of Clare. Sir Henry Thirkill retired as Master, replaced by Sir Eric Ashby; John Robinson left to be Bishop of Woolwich, replaced by Maurice F. Wiles, and the Chaplain Bill Skelton went to Bermondsey as Rector, replaced by Christopher Drum-

mond. The Lady Margaret Professor provided the continuity – as ever – within a thriving Chapel community. The changing generations of Deans and Chaplains attribute their inspiration to him just as much as the countless Chapel-goers and students of Theology who passed under his gentle – but beady – eye. As the century ends, there are dozens of New Testament lecturers and professors, scattered across most continents of the world, who studied for their Ph.D. under 'Charlie'.

Perhaps more significant in 1959 were the changes in atmosphere within the College and the country. This was the first year when undergraduates had not had to face national service. The fifties were turning into the sixties: students were keen to 'kick over the traces'. Those who had suffered compulsory chapel at school no longer had the opportunity to react against the Church in the forces: the opportunity, rather, came at College. Across the University a greater resistance to formal religion was reported, which jolted the establishment in its complacency. Even in the relatively relaxed atmosphere of Clare Chapel some of the more harmless badges of rebellion became evident, in the resistance to members wearing surplices and in the cult of bare feet.

When John Robinson's *Honest to God* came out in 1963 – provoking a big stir nationally – it was naturally a topic of special interest in the College. For some it helped in the integration of life and faith. For others it reinforced, by way of reaction, the sense that a more firmly-defined profession of belief was vital. For others again, it sug-

BELOW: *The Chapel from the Organ Loft, 2000.*

OPPOSITE: *The chapel looking towards the Organ Loft in 1900.*

RIGHT: *The choir in procession.*

BELOW RIGHT: *The Reverend Dr Jo Bailey Wells, Dean 2000.*

gested that the strange, transcendent element of faith in God was too elusive to base one's life upon: one could live a life of service and compassion without commitment to the faith of the Church. It was both a symptom of and a catalyst towards the reduced size, but sustained liveliness, of Chapel attendance and involvement during the period.

From the religious perspective, the sixties are best characterized by the popularity of talks, discussions and debates: events which specifically addressed (and questioned) 'the big issues', but which took place aside from a specifically 'religious' context. Great St Mary's, the University Church, was frequently filled on Sunday nights for speaker events to which prominent public figures or Nobel prizewinners were invited. Maurice Wiles, and after him Mark Santer, organized many such events in College involving senior and junior members. Professor Brian Pippard is recalled, for example, arguing for the primary importance of human relations so long as they were not

LEFT: *The choir 2000.*

studied, through psychology or sociology, but appreciated through intuition. Then, he maintained, one could pursue the relatively useless discipline of the sciences for sheer aesthetic pleasure: for its beautiful problems and solutions. Julian R.P. Barker, successor to John Alleyne as Chaplain from 1966, organised discussion evenings each term with Dr Paul Roubiczek, another Clare Fellow. Paul was a Jew from Prague who escaped through Holland at the start of the war with nothing more than the clothes he was wearing. His remarkable story – of running an anti-Nazi press, of lecturing to German PoWs, of converting to the Christian faith, of teaching existential philosophy in Cambridge – fascinated wistful agnostics time after time. Late nights at his flat on Grange Road, drinking strong coffee and solving the meaning of life, were well spent.

The Bermondsey Link

The College's link with – and patronage of – the parish of St Mary's Rotherhithe goes back to Lady Clare. In practical terms this link, known for a long time as the 'College Mission', focused on a daughter church of the parish of Rotherhithe. Once or twice a year a team from Chapel went down to Bermondsey to serve this church: for instance, by visiting every home in the parish. Quite apart from any

work accomplished for the parish, this was of great value in deepening the fellowship and commitment of all who went.

The church was not flourishing, however, and severe structural cracks in the building led to its closure in the 1960s. Since then, the College link has been transferred to Bede House, an independent 'settlement' within the parish offering a diverse range of activities and resources for the people of the area. The link continues to offer a fruitful friendship – and healthy perspective – to both communities. It is common for undergraduates to help with children's holidays over the long vacation, and for a recent graduate to spend a year or more working for Bede House after leaving Clare. Groups from the various projects at Bede have also made visits to the College for days out.

Choral excellence

Until 1960, the Chapel choir drew boys from the town to provide the treble voices, in return for a penny or two each service. This was an uncomfortable situation: it took boys away from their local parishes, which was unfair to the town incumbents. Without a choir school, they received little training or support (or discipline!) – apart from an informal Sunday School which Charlie Moule ran for them faithfully, as well as an annual week of camping in Norfolk, assisted by a few stalwart undergraduates.

One Whitsuntide, when the boys were unavailable because of half-term, the choral scholars sang alone. They found themselves really free to sing, and it was quickly decided it would be far better without the boys, whatever limitations this would impose on the repertoire. And so the soprano line faded out, and it became a male-voice choir of undergraduates. John Rutter was one of the choral scholars of that period, who was encouraged to compose items for the choir.

It was the second of Clare's Fellows in Music, a young Australian, Peter Dennison, who began to put the choir on the map of excellence. It has never looked back. Once the College went mixed in 1972, there was a ready supply of female voices and John Rutter (Director of Music 1975–79) proved the potential of a good mixed-voice choir. The reputation of the Chapel for music – in particular, for music in the service of worship – has continued to grow. After John Rutter left, the College was consciously committed to the appointment of a full-time Director of Music (not so much an academic musician as someone who would help make music in the College), a role ably fulfilled by Tim Brown since 1979.

74

Women

Mark Santer took over the Deanship from Maurice Wiles in 1967, after the latter moved to a Chair at King's College, London. The College was in the midst of patient discussion as to whether to accept women.

Michael G.V. Roberts was appointed Chaplain in 1970, immediately prior to the decision. As ever, at interview he was specifically asked if he was engaged or likely to become so, since the position was not considered suitable to a married man. Very shortly afterwards he met his wife-to-be, and wondered if she might cost him his job. The climate was changing. Owing to the impending influx of women it was thought good to have a married Chaplain after all. They were to have moved into the A-staircase flat over the Chapel arch, but before long a baby was expected, which was a step too far for Old Court. As Christopher Drummond in a similar situation ten years earlier had discovered, it was probably the prospect of a pram in the College which was most feared!

The transition to co-education brought about a rise of talent and creativity in the community – evident in the Chapel as much as anywhere else. Arthur R. Peacocke followed Mark Santer as Dean in 1973. He recalls a highlight of his eleven years in the College when the choir performed a series of Bach Cantatas in the context of the worship for which they were originally intended, in the Lent of 1979 and 1982. These included the appropriate biblical readings and collects, with an address based on the cantata's theme, and with the congregation singing the final chorale in English after the choir had sung it in German. The intensity which filled the Chapel as the last chorale was sung together was unforgettable.

The line of Chaplains was maintained during these years by David G. Tennant (1975–76), Peter S.M. Judd (1976–81) and Alvyn L. Pettersen (1981–85).

Political Action

Whether or not the College has ever been quietist, it is now quietly proud of two recent Deans who raised the collective eyebrow.

Rowan D. Williams was Dean for just under two years, 1985–86, prior to moving to Oxford as Lady Margaret Professor (and from there to Wales, as Bishop of Monmouth and recently Archbishop). To those who knew him closely, he is remembered for his outstanding teaching and for the warmth with which he pastored the community. But to those who only knew *of* him, he is remembered as 'the red

Dean'. As a member of the Christian CND in Cambridge, he took part – the lead? – in a well-publicized protest one Ash Wednesday at the US airforce base of Alconbury. This involved a small group climbing over the barbed-wire perimeter fence (with the aid of a mattress) and holding a brief service of penitence – with imposition of ashes – on the runway. The group was quickly rounded up by gun-toting marines. They were arrested and detained for 12 hours at Alconbury, then Huntingdon Police Station. They were released quietly in the small hours – and never prosecuted. It was rumoured that no one could think what charge to press. Endangering aircraft? His detention left Clare Chapel without the Dean for the Ash Wednesday service that year.

Nicholas Sagovsky was Dean for eleven years, 1986–97. This Dean could indeed go red with anger and indignation at injustice. Countless individual students and staff – not to mention homeless individuals and other stricken people in the town – found in him a tireless advocate. The stand which attracted the local press, however, was the campaign in Cambridge during 1990 against the Poll Tax. For his personal refusal to pay, and for the sake of defending others unable to pay, he went to court.

The College itself took a principled stand – at least in the eyes of the established Church – when, before women could be ordained to the diaconate let alone the priesthood, it appointed a female Chaplain, Vivenne F. Faull, in 1985. The move was characteristic of the College's commitment to equal opportunities, to the value of lay ministry and to the ordination of women. It was another female Chaplain, Jane E.E. Charman, who succeeded her in 1990. Clare was also the first Cambridge College – three years after the first ordination of women to the priesthood in the Church of England – to appoint a female Dean, Jo Bailey Wells, in 1997.

Openness and Commitment

The nature of religion in the College is very different at the close of the twentieth century than it was at the beginning. Christian assumptions can no longer be made about College life or College members. Those of different faiths or no religious conviction rightly come to live and study at Clare College. The Dean – no longer assisted by a Chaplain[6] – now functions as a reference point for people of any faith as well as a pastor to the Christian community.

Nevertheless, the community still fosters the same distinctive feature of religion at Clare at the end of the twentieth century as depicted earlier: a community in which openness and commitment belong powerfully together. Such a community allows for difference and diversity – indeed, these are positively enjoyed and respected – without neglecting the need for and value of personal engagement and critical challenge.

The Chapel continues to be an integral part – even a defining part – of such a community, the running of which now owes more to the lively team of student Chapel Wardens than ever. The Sunday Morning Service, still a Eucharist, is now an intimate service in the round of the Antechapel, which tends to appeal to those with an established Christian commitment. The Sunday Evening Service has markedly grown in popularity in recent years – extra benches are regularly needed – and draws those, perhaps of varying Christian conviction but keen interest, who enjoy the combination of good music and thoughtful preaching. Finally, there are fortnightly late night services by candlelight of Compline, and Vigils for special occasions. In a secular and individualist age, these are valued increasingly for the time and space they provide, corporately, for reflection and contemplation. The Chapel continues to offer to all – in the midst of an essay crisis, during a frenetic eight-week term – a glimpse of eternity.

1 I am grateful to several former Deans and Chaplains who have offered their recollections for the writing of this chapter. I am particularly indebted to the Revd. Professor C.F.D. Moule for sharing his memories, despite his solemn advice that no-one depend on them.

2 The College archives contain a petition dating from 1870 or 1871 signed by 34 undergraduates requesting 'the Reverend the Master and the Reverend and Learned Fellows to restore to us the privilege of a weekly Celebration of the Holy Communion in our College Chapel'.

3 No list, inscribed or printed, is complete. In the course of his own research, Dr Gordon Wright has recently unearthed a printed supplementary list that had otherwise disappeared.

4 This is the title of John Robinson's book describing his liturgical experiment at Clare, published by Mowbray in 1960.

5 This freedom was regularized by the Upper Houses of the Convocations of Canterbury and York in January 1933, but it was not widely used.

6 Thanks to an anonymous benefaction in 1995 'to be used towards an award for a person who will assist the Dean in the work of the Chapel,' the post of Decanae Scholar has been established since 1997 for a period of ten years. The first (and current) incumbent is the Reverend Paul Swarup, a presbyter from the Church of North India, who assists the Dean in ministry whilst also pursuing a doctorate in Biblical Studies as a postgraduate member of the College.

the fellows' library

NIGEL WEISS

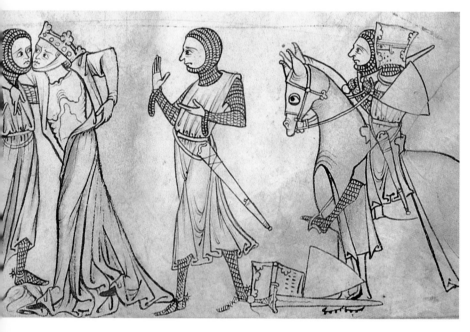

ABOVE: *Plate 1: Geoffrey of Monmouth's* Historia Regum Britanniae *with illustrations in the style of Matthew Paris.*

The Fellows' Library is virtually a fossil relic of our history. Situated between the Combination Room and the Master's Lodge, the Library is not easily accessible and is therefore unfamiliar to most members of the College. What it contains is a set of printed books assembled by a group of enlightened scholars in the seventeenth and eighteenth centuries, whose interest depends more on the coherence of the collection than on the rarity of individual items.

Our first recorded library was built between 1420 and 1430 but destroyed by a fire in 1521. A new building, with a library above the chapel, was completed by 1535 and furnished with upright bookcases (classes) in 1627. The present kitchen, with the Fellows' Library above it, was designed by Robert Grumbold and built between 1689 and 1693. (This arrangement, never too dry in summer and never too cold in winter, has proved extremely favourable for preserving books.) However, the woodwork, by James Essex, was not installed till 1729. The antiquary William Cole enthused over it in 1742 as follows: 'This Library also is the most elegant of any in the University, being a very large well-proportioned Room *à la moderne*, with the Books ranged all round it, not in Classes as in most of the rest of the Libraries in other Colleges.' This arrangement didn't last long. When the old chapel was demolished in 1763, ten classes, with their contents, were transferred from it to the Fellows' Library – and the elegant effect was ruined.

No manuscripts survived the ravages of the sixteenth century but, although all the early examples were lost or destroyed, the Library has since acquired about 30 manuscripts as gifts. The most notable group were presented by John Heaver, who died in 1670. These include a thirteenth-century manuscript of Geoffrey of Monmouth's *Historia Regum Britanniae* with the marvellous line drawing in the style of Matthew Paris that is illustrated in Plate 1. Another prized possession is an eleventh-century Anglo-Saxon manuscript of the *Dialogues of St Gregory*, with elaborate decorations.

The earliest printed books to enter the present collection were nine theological texts presented by Laurence Maptit (Master of Corpus) in 1557 and they bear traces of having been chained to a bookcase. In all, the Library possesses 35 *incunabula* (books printed before 1500) and about 400 books that were printed in England before 1640. There are some fine early bindings by Rood, Siberch and Spierinck. The collection was enlarged by donations from George Ruggle (284 volumes, many in Spanish and Italian) in 1620 and from Humphrey and Edmund Prideaux, who presented a fine group of early Hebrew printed books in 1730, while Charles Morgan, who died as Master in 1742, left a large collection of

LEFT: *Plate 2: Humming birds from John Gould's* Trochilidae, *Volume I, illustrated by Gould and Richter.*

78

BELOW: *Plate 3: Kestrel, from John Gould's* Birds of Great Britain.

books, including many on mathematical and physical topics, which now occupies much of the eastern wall of the room. At the end of the seventeenth century, Clare, as a Whig College, was a centre of enlightened thought. Morgan's own copy of the first edition of Newton's *Principia* is heavily annotated, and Richard Laughton (whose copy is also in the Library) was teaching the new physics to the students he attracted from across East Anglia. During this period many works were presented to the College or bought for the Library, but by the end of the eighteenth century Clare had sunk into intellectual decline and relatively few books were acquired. With a few notable exceptions, the present collection ceases at 1820.

When the Forbes Library was established for undergraduates in the 1930s the Fellows' Library remained where it was. Old photographs show a crowded room with bulky classes protruding into it and a showcase in the centre. This untidy arrangement continued until after the Second World War. Around 1950, the Librarian (E.T.C. Spooner) cleared out some of the piles of papers and unwanted books that had accumulated in the room. It was also agreed that the tall classes should be replaced by low cases that would make it possible to appreciate the open layout of the room. So the College commissioned Tim Swann to design and construct eight new bookcases for the Fellows' Library. These fine cases, made of dark diseased oak with bog-oak inlays, were installed by A.B. Pippard (later Sir Brian, Cavendish Professor of Physics and the first President of Clare Hall), who had succeeded Spooner as Librarian in 1954, and the old classes, dating from 1623, were carried across to the Forbes Library. (After the new Forbes-Mellon Library was built, the classes were eventually transferred to the University Library, on indefinite loan.) At the same time, books published after 1820 were culled and removed, while the fascinating collection of old maps was rebacked and restored by Charlotte Pippard.

The Library was now a magnificent room, visited from time to time by scholars who consulted the rare volumes in it and opened to visitors at special occasions. As the Fellowship grew during the 1960s and 70s there was a feeling that it ought to be possible to make better use of this splendid space. Charles Parkin, who was then the Librarian, proposed that College meetings, which were still held in the Combination Room, should be transferred to the Library, thereby freeing space for Fellows to sit in the Combination Room itself. The change was finally carried out in 1980, when a long table with chairs around it was placed by the windows in the Library. This arrangement, with leather-bound volumes all around the room, provided a sober background for meetings of the Governing Body and the Council. However, the Fellowship continued to grow and there was insufficient space for everyone to be seated. Consequently, Governing Body meetings are now held on the other side of Old Court, in the refurbished Latimer Room, while now the Library is used for meetings of the Council and smaller committees, as well as for occasional study and research.

The Collection does not remain completely static. If benefactors present books that complement those that we already have, their offers are gratefully accepted. Thus the Library has acquired a number of significant additions. The most generous and striking gift, however, was something very different. The Reverend Frank Innes Wane (who was admitted to Clare in 1907) assembled a remarkable collection of books about birds, and in 1954 he decided to present it to the College. The collection included some outstanding illustrated volumes dating from the eighteenth and nineteenth centuries and these are kept in the Fellows' Library. Notable among them are some volumes published by John Gould. Plates 2–4 display some exceptional images from these books. Plate 3, of a kestrel, is from his *Birds of Great Britain*, while the other two, of humming birds, are from the lavish volumes on the *Trochilidae*. With gifts like these, the Fellows' Library continues to develop.

RIGHT: *Plate 4: Eurynome hermits (Phaëthornis Eurynome) from John Gould's* Trochilidae, *Volume I, illustrated by Gould and Richter.*

A PHYSICIST FINDS POETRY...

TIM BOYD

One evening in 1964, while living on H staircase, I was supposed to be studying my physics. As pure displacement activity I instead went to the Old Court library and took out a volume of Gothic verse by "Monk" Lewis, *c.* 1790.

The book had been accessioned in 1923.

Forty one years later, the pages were still uncut.

1932: culture, cultivation and discussion in the dilettante

Editorial

A bon appétit, il ne faut point de sauce. Last year the College Boat Club celebrated the hundredth year since its foundation by a special ball; a special reunion dinner, preceded by a garden party; and the issue of a special Number of the College Magazine. The contagion of this activity of celebration is now responsible for expanding and modifying the College magazine once more, this time in commemoration of the Jubilee of the College Dilettante Society. A College Club has been defined as something which is held together by a common tie; the Dilettante has not even this, but, after the lapses and rejuvenations common to most indoor college clubs, it is still with us and shews all the evidences of a young and healthy organism, growing and asserting itself as confidently, and as much or more than most. In the festive atmosphere of jubilee it is only natural that the high peaks of Dilettante celebration should appear fully illuminated,

ABOVE: *Dilettante Jubilee Dinner, June 1932. Paul Mellon is at the right-hand edge of the third row, Geoffrey De Freitas, the first Mellon Fellow to go to Yale, is at the back. The poet, A. E. Houseman is third from the left of the third row and Thomas Merton third from right on the second row. Christopher Millett is second from left on the front row.*

but it is our aim in the pages of this issue to shew also the more substantial outcome of the cultivation and discussion of humane cultural and sociological subjects by Clare dilettanti during the past 50 years.

It would be difficult to find more praiseworthy examples of the practical results of Dilettantism than the work of two Clare men of, roughly, fifty years ago; Sir Archibald Flower and the late Cecil Sharp. Two illustrated articles describe respectively the Shakespeare Memorial Theatre at Stratford-on-Avon which owes its genesis largely to Sir Archibald Flower, and the late Cecil Sharp Memorial House recently opened and given over to the charge of the English Folk Dancing Society. A third article, also illustrated, deals with the opening ceremonies at the dedication of the Bourn windmill to the Cambridge Preservation Society. Not only is the part donor, Mr Forbes, the present and past inspiration of the Dilettante Society, but readers will discover how in this practical dilettantism he is supported, vocally and histrionically, by the mass of present Clare dilettanti who thought sufficiently of the occasion to make it replace their yearly pious pilgrimage to Clare, the home of the foundress of the college.

These major themes are supplemented by a vivid impression of the jubilee dinner, and a short history of the club by its president, Alastair Sharp. Wide as the scope of this account now is we confess we should still have wished to recall memorable members and momentous meetings: Mr H.D. Henderson, since editor of *The Nation*, discussing the causation of war; Dr C. Shearer illustrating genetics and inheritance with bananas for chromosomes; Dr E. Dingwall describing scientific investigation into the basis of psychical manifestations. Though limitations of space press on us here we can still herald notable achievements by post-war dilettanti, one such happily in an article, in which the dangers and difficulties of Arctic exploration are, characteristically, subjugated to the expression of the aspects more beautiful, amusing and enticing. We are able to print two very beautiful wood engravings by Raymond McGrath, who, when at Clare, so largely inspired the present format of this magazine and who is now most successfully practising modern architecture and decoration. The work of other dilettanti collaborators of the same period, C.F. Millett, J.F. Scott, and P. Mellon, also appears in this issue. Into further detail we will not go; this perambulatory index must not continue to point out each small and smaller item of the magazine, but must be content with having indicated the general geography of the number and the constructive forces which determined its form. To complete this task adequately we must stress the many American associations of the magazine. First, our frontispiece, which with its autograph message constitutes a singular honour, seeing that it was given us *ad hoc*. It was a very great gratification for Clare when, so soon after his election to an Honorary Fellowship, Mr Mellon returned to England in the highest of all capacities, as American Ambassador at the Court of St James. It is a particularly happy chance that other material in this number should set in such relief the American associations of Clare; associations which we think have been, and trust will ever be, of benefit on both sides. Mr Forbes, to whom these relations have always been a matter of the dearest concern, obtained for us the knowledge of yet another link, in the person of Sir Richard Saltonstall, founder of Watertown. The article hereinafter contained owes its *data* to the kindness of Professor S.E. Morison of Harvard. Lastly we should refer to the notices we print of the establishment of the Kellett Fellowships ensuring residence of Columbia men in Clare, and the interchange of men between Yale and Clare that commenced this Michaelmas term. It is very gratifying that a college with such abundant and close links with the early history of the United States (and indeed with her Declaration of Independence) should now be so effectively able to further Anglo-American friendship and to make towards what Dr Murray Butler has so concisely termed the new declaration of Interdependence.

Postcript

You will be entertained to hear that I am renooing acquaintance with Cartoon Films and taking over a permanent (?) job with Publicity Pictures Ltd. For the issuing of a series of full-length entertainment sound film cartoons of an exclusively Anglican flavour, an ambition realised after a year of yearnings. Actually the prospects are quite luminous ... The main problem we face is the fact that *there are only three of us at the moment to draw the films, which is not really enough in view of the work involved. Wherefore I would ask you if you come across any lad in the Dilettante or otherwise who might be a success at the job to get him into touch with me. Qualifications, ability to draw and to copy, perverted sense of humour, and entire lack of snobbishness, artistic or social.*

[Christopher Millett, in October
We must add that this will be the first British venture in Disney vein (alias 'first all-British synchronised full-length sound film cartoon (entertainment) in half tone,' etc.), and that these particular perversions will be liberated some time next January.]

81

Illustrations from Lady Clare Magazine, XXV/1, *1931–2, by Raymond McGrath and Christopher Millett*

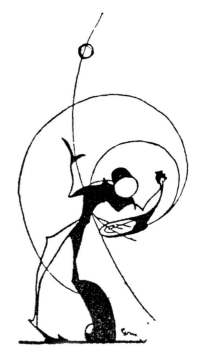

the house of dr dee

PETER ACKROYD

Peter Ackroyd gained a First in English at Clare (1968–71). His novels (Chatterton, First Light, English Music, Hawksmoor, The House of Dr Dee, The Last Testament of Oscar Wilde) have created a new genre, an historical, literary novel that has a dialogue with the present. Ackroyd is meticulously faithful to period detail, yet with a history whose dimension is essentially literary, just as Ackroyd himself, as a contemporary writer, is in dialogue with literary history. In addition to his novels, he has published innovative biographies of Charles Dickens, T.S. Eliot and William Blake, and a fascinating account of London.

The House of Dr Dee *explores the life of a sixteenth-century scientist, believed to be an alchemist, who was for a time court philosopher and 'conjuror' to Queen Elizabeth I. His house in Cloak Lane is left, in the late twentieth century, to a writer, who becomes engulfed by Dee's presence. In this extract, Dee describes his own upbringing and education at Cambridge, followed by a reported dialogue in which he describes the parameters of his intellectual world.*

'My parents were honest and of no little esteem among their neighbours, my father being agent to the estate of my lord Gravenar. I was the last of my mother's children and, since the others were much more advanced in years, I stayed pretty close to myself (as they say) and played in the fields next to our ancient house in east Acton. There is no telling the wonderful diversity of children's natures, the spirit itself being combined from so many contrary influences, but I myself was of a shy disposition and haughty mind: I played alone always, shunning fellows as I would shun flies, and when my father began to teach me I fell naturally into the company of old books. I learned my Latin and my Greek even before my tenth year, and had no little delight in reciting from memory the verses of Ovid or the sentences of Tully as I roamed among the lanes and hedges of our parish. I would preach Eliot's Dic-

tionary to the sheep and Lily's Grammar to the cows, and then run back to study Erasmus and Virgil at my own little table. Of course I shared my bed and my chamber with my two bothers (now both under the earth), but my parents understood my solitary disposition and gave me a chest, with lock and key, where I kept not only my apparel but also my texts. I had also a box of papers in my own writing, for my father had instructed me in the secretary hand, and there I concealed many verses and lessons of my own composition.

'I rose at five in the morning, my father calling out to me "Surgite! Surgite!" while I washed my face and hands very quickly. All of the household prayed together, and then he took me into his own chamber where I practised upon my lute: my father's care was always to increase my skill in music, and by daily exercise I grew more bold in singing and in playing upon instruments. At seven we came into the hall, where the table was already laden with meat and bread and ale (in those days called the angel's food) for our breakfast; after the meal was concluded I began my lessons in grammar, verse extempore, construction, translation and suchlike. Horace and Terence were my playfellows, though even then I had a true interest in the history of my own country, and from these early years I was the scholar and never the gamester.

'But soon enough it was time to rise into another sphere, and I was in November *anno* 1542 sent by my father to the University of Cambridge, there to begin with logic and so to proceed in the learning of good arts and sciences. I was then somewhat above fifteen years old, as being born *anno* 1527 July 13 –'

'Your birth,' Bartholomew Gray said very suddenly, 'is out of its place, and should have come at the beginning of your discourse. Ordering, as well as inventing, is true argument of a fine wit. Surely so premature a scholar should know that?'

I ignored the coxcomb, and continued with my theme. 'For the most part of these years I was so vehemently bent to studies that I inviolably kept this order – only to sleep four hours every night, to allow for meat and drink two hours every day, and of the other eighteen hours all (except the time of divine service) to be spent in my studies and learning. I had begun there with logic, and so I read Aristotle his *De sophisticis elenchis* and his *Topic* as well as his *Analytica Prioria* and *Analytica Posteriora*; but my thirst for knowledge was so great that I soon found myself bent towards other learning as towards a glorious light that could never be extinguished, no, nor even dimmed. I cared nothing at all for the lewd pastimes of my college fellows and found no comfort in banqueting and whoring, in dicing and in carding, in dancing and in bear-baiting, in bowling and in shooting, and other suchlike trifles of the town. Yet though I had nothing to do with dice or with primero, I did have a chess-board with a little bag of leather for my men: these I would advance from square to square, reminding myself of my own history up to that time. I knew then, as I picked up my ivory pieces and stroked them a little with my forefinger, that monarchs and bishops would be as nothing to one who could predict their movements.

'After seven years I had attained my Master of Arts and, presently leaving the university, I went to London in order to follow my studies philosophical and mathematical. I had heard by report of a poor studious gentleman, by name Ferdinand Griffen, who had for many years past been buried deep in his rare studies and who (it was said by those knowing my own course of learning) would teach me the use of the astrolabe and the astronomer's staff as a proper continuance of my exploits in geometry and arithmetic. He lived in a rambling tenement in the Bishop of London's rents, in a court near the waterside just by St Andrews' Hill – '

'I know it,' he said. 'By the glassworks on Addle Hill'.

'A little westward from there'. I refreshed myself by taking some more wine.

'I came to him on midsummer's day in the year 1549, and found him working among his globes and vessels with the nimbleness of an apprentice. He greeted me with bright words, having expected my coming after several learned letters had passed between us, and pretty soon he displayed to me certain rare and exquisitely made instruments upon which (as he told me) he had bestowed all his life and fortune – among which was one strong quadrant

William Butler unknown artist, early seventeenth century.

Oil on panel 21¾" x 17⅛"

William Butler was a Fellow of Clare 1564–81. He obtained a licence to practise medicine and styled himself 'Doctor'. He was well known in Cambridge for his skill and eccentricity. He attended Henry, Prince of Wales in his final illness in 1612.

of five-foot diameter, an excellent radius astronomicus which had its staff and cross very curiously divided in equal parts, a fair astrolabe and a great globe of metal. So it was that Ferdinand Griffen became my good master and with him I began my astronomical observations in earnest, all the time working with those very fine and very apt instruments which he taught me how to use carefully and circumspectly. We began observations, many to the hour and minute, of the heavenly influences and operations actual in this elemental portion of the world – '

At which point I broke off, fearing to say too much to one who was not practiced in these arts, and in my confusion

84

drank my fill of wine before continuing along another path. 'We were so close to the waterside that we would take our quadrant from his rambling lodgings down Water Lane to Blackfriars Stairs where, among the barges and the herring buses, we called out "Westward! Westward!" until one of the passing watermen noticed us. The wherry took us by the open fields beside Lambeth Marsh where, with the quadrant established upon firm earth, we would make various observations of the sun's progress. Sometimes, coming or going, we were close to falling into the Thames over head and ears with the cumbersomeness of the quadrant, but we always escaped on to dry ground. What instrument of the sun could be deluged with water? No, it could not be. There were sly citizens who were accustomed to call us sorcerers or magicians for all this measuring but it was all one to Ferdinand Griffen, and since that time I have taken my lesson from him in despising and condemning the ignorant multitude. On many other matters he also proved my good master, or should I say magus, with books, pamphlets, discourses, inventions and conclusions upon grave arts. You asked me if I raised the dead; no, I raise new life …' Again I broke off, fearing that I had fallen into too deep a vein, but Bartholomew Gray did nothing but pick at his teeth and call for more wine. 'Then,' I added, 'I went beyond the seas to speak and confer with some learned men'.

'Magicians,' he replied, now quite lost and wandering in his drink. 'Sorcerers'.

'They had nothing to do with what is vulgarly called magic'. I took more wine to consume the fire within me. 'Mine are wonderful sciences, greatly aiding our dim sight for the better view of God's power and goodness. I am by profession a scholar, sir, and not some magician or mountebank. Whose opinion was it but my own that the court sought for, relating to the great comet of 1577, after the judgement of certain so-called astronomers had unduly bred great fear and doubt? And who was it that prepared for our trades and voyages to Cathay and Muscovy with true charts and tables for our navigators? And who was it again that gave Euclid's propositions to the mechanics of this realm, from which they have derived inestimable benefit? I alone have achieved all these things. Is it the work of a mountebank?'

'Lord,' he said, drunken to the highest degree. 'I understand not one word of this'.

'But I understand. I have spent these last fifty years for good learning's sake – what a race have I run, so much done and so much suffered, for the attaining of wisdom! Do you recall that time when a certain image of wax, with a great pin stuck in the breast of it, was found in Lincoln's Inn field?' He seemed to shake his head, but I was now launched upon a tide of words. 'It was said then by malicious backbiters to be an image of my own making, and that I endeavoured by enchantment to destroy Queen Mary. All spiteful falsehoods, all brain-sick perjuries, and yet for many weeks I remained prisoner in the Tower while all the doors of my lodgings in London were sealed up and I was close to being overwhelmed by the circumstances of my grief, loss and discredit. Well well, I said to myself then, my unkind countrymen, my unnatural countrymen, my unthankful countrymen, I know you now and I know what I must do. In recent years they have said that I impoverish the earth, that I rob the man in the moon, and any such stuff as can be hurled upon me. But do you know what is worse still? That I must take a purse from one such as Nathaniel Cadman here, and provide mere shows and gewgaws'. I paused for a moment, but no one else had heard my complaint. 'So, Mr Gray. Now you know of the very great injuries, damages and indignities I have sustained. I ask you not to increase them'.

He seemed a little abashed, yet he drank some more wine and then with a high-pitched but not unpleasing voice began to sing out a verse from 'Fortune My Foe':

"The moon's my constant mistress,
And the lowly owl my morrow,
The flaming drake and night-crow make
Me music to my sorrow'.

'It is a fitting tune,' I said, 'to accompany me on my way. For now I must rise and leave you gentlemen – ' I looked across the board, where they lolled in various stages of drunkenness. 'I am tired now after my spectacle'.

'I sat amazed,' one of their number said, looking down into this cup, 'when the spheres came down amidst the brightness. And all revolved. It was well done. It was very well done'.

'I wish you good night,' I said again. 'I must return to my own proper sphere'. I bowed to Nathaniel Cadman, who could not raise his head from the table and sat like some poor shrunken thing. 'I wish all of you good night'.

I came out into New Fish Street, when a boy walked forward with a lantern. But I waved him away. It was a clear night, and the fixed stars were all I needed to light my path to Clerkenwell.

CAMBRIDGE DURING
THE EASTER VACATION

To the casual observer, that is, to the man keeping nights, staying up after the end of term offers no attraction; but to him who outstays his gyp's welcome, who outlasts the reign of sweeps and electric cleaners and arrives at solitude there is something very generous about our ancient city in the vac. which expresses itself practically in the shape of epoch-making sales at the more expensive shops; the porters, too, are at their best; let Galsworthy describe them: "Large man fresh faced small mouthed stood at his lodge door in frank and deferential attitude. His blue eyes rested on the travellers. 'I don't know you, sirs, but if you want to speak I shall be glad to hear the observations you have to make.'" There are stamps to buy; the telephone is at your immediate command you are welcome to be called at any hour you please. Matthew's entire establishment seems to halt, as the door is opened to let you in, and waits to hear your pleasure in groceries for the day. But my peculiar joy is Senate House Passage. Instead of zigzagging up it dodging avalanches of bicycles, instead of wondering whether to take the smooth path for adventure or the more difficult and nobbly way of safety, I now wander unconcernedly up the middle. Today on my bicycle I met, emerging at the top, two of the latest and most dangerous type of pram in line abreast. I begin to doubt … but, no, the streets of Cambridge are one long delight. One may bicycle all day and hit nothing.

During term I have lectures in Caius second court. To reach Clare again needs all the courage of a Serpentine swimmer: one's first wish is for a diving suit (in hard metal): one's second for a horizontal periscope to help get out of that gate of Horror. To-day I emerged without a falter.

It has, I must confess, its disadvantages. As one walks down the street on Sunday in grey flannel bags, one feels uncommonly like a Dutch peasant at Haarlem. Owners of small two-seaters, large limousines, and motor cyclists, look at you as if you had dressed up for their particular amusement and interest. By a process of elimination you have become one of the sights of the town.

Lady Clare Magazine XXI/3, Easter Term 1927

elected silence

THOMAS MERTON

Thomas Merton's life (1914–68) was a conflict between words and silence. Educated at Columbia University and Clare College (1932–33), he left teaching to become a Trappist monk in Kentucky in 1941. He deliberately chose a silent order, desiring anonymity and seclusion. His writing was encouraged, however, by the Abbot of Our Lady of Gethsemani. He began by publishing poems and then, in 1948, he published his autobiography, The Seven Storey Mountain, *which was a runaway success. After that he didn't cease to write, yet questioned the efficacy of living in a silent order while giving so many more words to the world. His edited journal,* The Intimate Merton, *shows him to have been a person of frequent doubts and questions; of his faith, his vocation and his community.*

The first extract comes from the European edition of his autobiography, which was edited by Evelyn Waugh and had a different title: Elected Silence. *It describes a little of his time at Clare; for him a wild, dark and shameful episode of drinking, vandalizing, overspending and unplanned paternity. These activities are not described in themselves, but there is a darkness to his memories of Cambridge; it was a place of temptation for him, perhaps because, while it intensified his intellectual nature, it was also an environment in which he felt excluded by class, 'colonial' and rough. It's as though he exaggerated that side of his identity in order to extinguish it.*

This extract is followed by poems from each stage of his life. Since his sudden, accidental death in 1968, there has been a flow of publications: letters, essays, photographs and most recently the journals. Their wide appeal has inspired the epithet 'a modern counterpart of Saint Augustine's Confessions.'

My freshman year went by very fast. It was a dizzy business that began in the dark, brief afternoons of the English autumn and ended after a short series of long summer evenings on the river. All those days and nights were without romance, horrible, everything that I did not want them to be.

At first it was confusing. It took me a month or two to find my level in this cloudy, semi-liquid medium in whose dregs I was ultimately destined to settle. There were my friends from Oakham. At first we clung together for protection, and used to spend much time in one another's rooms, although Andrew's digs were far away in the wilds beyond Addenbrooke's hospital. To get there I cycled through a mysterious world of new buildings dedicated to chemistry, and at the end of the journey drank tea and played *St. Louis Blues* on the piano. Dickens was much nearer. He was around the corner from my lodgings. You travelled through two or three courts of St. John's College and crossed the river. He was in the so-called New Building. His room directly overlooked the river and he and I and Andrew would eat breakfast there and throw bits of toast to the ducks while he told us all about Pavlov and conditioned reflexes.

As a year went on I drifted apart from them, especially from Andrew, who ended up as the leading man in the Footlights show that year. He was something of a singer. My crowd had no interest in singing and a certain amount of contempt, indeed, for the Footlights and all that it represented. I remember that I almost made friends with one or two serious and somewhat complicated young men who were reading modern languages with me and belonged to my own college, but their reticences bored me. And they, in their turn, were rather shocked by the two-handed heartiness with which I was grabbing at life.

In the room underneath mine, in my lodgings, was a round red-faced Yorkshireman who was a pacifist. He, too, was full of reticences. But on Armistice Day he got into some kind of a demonstration and all the rugger players and oarsmen threw eggs at him. I knew nothing about it until I saw the pictures in the evening paper.

I would not have been interested in making friends with him either – he was too tame and shy. But in any case the landlord took to coming into my room and calumniating the poor man while I listened patiently, knowing of no way to shut him up. Before the end of the year the landlord was much more disgusted with me than with any lodger he had ever had.

I think it was when I had become acquainted with some two hundred different people that I drifted into the crowd that had been gravitating around the nether pole of Cambridge life.

We were the ones who made all the noise when there was a "bump supper." We lived in the Lion Inn. We fought our way in and out of the Red Cow.

When it began to be spring, I was trying to row in the Clare fourth boat, although it nearly killed me. But at least, since we were supposed to be in training, I got up early for a few weeks and went to the College for breakfast, and went to bed without being too dizzy in the night time.

In these days I seem to remember there was a little sunlight. It fell through the ancient windows of Professor Bullough's room in Caius. It was a room with windows opening on the grass of two courts. It was below the level of those lawns and you had to go down a couple of steps to get into his sitting room. There he stood, a tall, thin, grey, somewhat ascetic scholar, placidly translating Dante to us, while ten or a dozen students, men and women, sat about in the chairs and followed in our Italian texts.

In the winter term we had begun with the *Inferno*, and had progressed slowly, taking each day part of a Canto. And now Dante and Virgil had come through the icy heart of hell, where the three-headed devil chewed the greatest traitors, and had climbed out to the peaceful sea at the foot of the seven-circled mountain of Purgatory. And now, in the Christian Lent, which I was observing without merit and without reason, for the sake of a sport which I had grown to detest, we were climbing from circle to circle of Purgatory.

I think the one great benefit I got out of Cambridge was this acquaintance with the genius of the greatest Catholic poet. I suppose it would have been too much to expect an application of his ideas to myself, in the moral order. I had done all that I could to make my heart untouchable by charity and had fortified it, as I hoped, impregnably in my own impenetrable selfishness.

At the same time, I could listen, and listen with gladness and a certain intentness, to the slow and majestic progress of the myths and symbols in which Dante was building up a whole poetic synthesis of scholastic philosophy and theology. And although not one of his ideas took firm root in my mind, which was both coarse and lazy, there remained in me a kind of armed neutrality in the presence of all these dogmas, which I tended to tolerate in so far as that was necessary to an understanding of the poem.

This, as I see it, was also a kind of grace: the greatest grace in the positive order that I got out of Cambridge.

The Flight into Egypt

Through every precinct of the wintry city
Squadroned iron resounds upon the streets;
Herod's police
Make shudder the dark steps of the tenements
At the business about to be done.

Neither look back upon Thy starry country,
Nor hear what rumours crowd across the dark
Where blood runs down these holy walls,
Nor frame a childish blessing with Thy hand
Towards that fiery spiral of exulting souls!

Go, Child of God, upon the singing desert,
Where, with eyes of flame,
The roaming lion keeps thy road from harm.

Thirty Poems, 1944

88

Untitled Poem

All theology is a kind of birthday
Each one who is born
Comes into the world as a question
For which old answers
Are not sufficient.

Birth is question and revelation.
The ground of birth is paradise
Yet we are born a thousand miles
Away from our home.
Paradise weeps in us
And we wander further away.
This the theology
Of our birthdays.

Obscure theology
On the steps of Cincinnati Station:
I am questioned by the cold December
Of 1941. One small snowflake
Melts on my eyelid like a guess
And is forgotten.
(Across the river my meaning has
*   taken flesh*
Is warm, cries for care
Across the river
Heaven is weeping.)

Heaven weeps without cause
Forever if I do not find
The question that seeks me

All the gates are shut
The monastery is cold
But everything here is certain:
Fire smoulders however
In the centre.

Fort Thomas Kentucky
In a year of war
Is like Bethlehem, obscure
But not so innocent.
And I too am a prisoner
In a theology of will
While north of me a question
Is weeping in the snow
Because I am (for the time being)
A man without doubts
Renouncing the luxury of questions.

Wisdom grows like a flower
Turns her innocent face
In sweet compassion
South and west
Wondering about the seasons
Sun rain and nuns
Not knowing.

I am stubborn
I build ten theories out of stone
In a stone wall Eden
An unknown flower loves me more
I do not know it
The fire in the centre
However is still there
And smoulders.

Heaven grows to a bird
With pretty wings
Her flight is like a question
Searching the south
For somebody.

Theology is sometimes sickness
A broken neck of questions
A helpless doubt
In an electric bed

The bird finds this doubt
Broken in the fever
And knows: 'You are my glory
And I your answer –
If you have a question.'

To sing is to begin a sentence
Like 'I want to get well.'
'I am not born for nothing
And neither are you:
Heaven never wept
Over nothing.'

'And the ground of loneliness
Is love. The ground of doubt:
Is it truth?'

So all theology
Is a kind of birthday
A way home to where we are

Epiphany and Eden
Where two lost questions
Make one orbit
In the middle of nothing.
Is this the answer?

No one ever got born
All by himself: It takes more than one.
Every birthday
Has its own theology.

Eighteen Poems, 1977

May Song

It is May we are lost
In sunlight and leaves
Briars and moss

Your blue skirt
Is wet with melted ice
And Sauterne

The sun dries us
You tell me last night's movie
One I never saw. The woods
Are sweet with the sound
Of your voice
And all birds sing
That we are lost
In this part of the wood
Where no special scenery
Deceives the eye
And nothing can ever be
Consistent

Lost, lost the words of poems sound
And in your listening heart
Are finally found
In this heaven let me lie down
Under the fragrant tent
Of your black hair

Under those long lashes
I am again found
By your wise and lasting look

As all the hair of the sky
Comes slowly down
To bury me forever
In warm love
Here in the wood
Where we eternally come home
To taste the creation of life
At that soft point
Where the heart somersaults
And flutters against
Your bird heart beating wings
At the warm edge of lips

It is May we are lost
In unexpected light
We drown in each other
Can you still breathe
Darling in despair
I clung to the round hull
Of your hips and cry
Lend me for God's love
Your lifeboat
Your saving body
Save me body for I die
In the ideal sun
Cool me for I am destroyed
By too much perfection

It is May
We weep for love
In the imperfect wood
In the land of bodies

O lonely little boat
Carry me away
Across the sea of wine

O small strong boat
Bring me
My child.

Eighteen Poems, 1977

aspects of clare's financial history

BRIAN SMALE-ADAMS

At the beginning of the twentieth century, Clare was one of seventeen colleges in Cambridge, an independent corporation governing itself under its own Royal Charter and Statutes. Provided it conformed to the financial provisions in its Statutes and to relevant points of law, it was not financially beholden – directly or indirectly – to any external entity. It had been generously endowed over the five-and-a-half, or so, centuries of its existence and held considerable investments in agricultural land and property. It had successfully weathered the severe agricultural recession of the 1870s and 1880s. The income from its investments, and from fees and rents paid by students, had enabled it, on its own, to pay its way.

The past century has seen a loss in the financial independence of the University and the Colleges arising from the increasing involvement of the state in their affairs. Where the University is concerned, this is a part of the price that has had to be paid for the growing excellence of its teaching and research: since the middle of the nineteenth century, it had become increasingly obvious that it would not be able to hold its own in the first rank of universities unless it received external financial support. A Royal Commission was set up in 1919 to investigate the University's needs and to recommend arrangements for state funding.

The Commission was required also to look into the finances of colleges and to recommend measures which they might be required to take to ensure that *they* could stand financially on their own feet. Among its recommendations were new accounting disciplines, which all colleges subsequently incorporated in revised statutes. Technically, colleges have retained their independence of direct state funding – but public funding of student fees and maintenance since the Second World War has given the State a lever, and this it has used, particularly since the early 1980s, progressively tightening the pinch on colleges' revenues from fees.

The end of the century finds both University and Colleges reacting strongly against bureaucratic interference, making determined efforts to attract new endowment, set on securing some measure of control over their own affairs.

Clare's economy, like that of most other colleges, is fairly simple. Money comes in from earnings on a portfolio of investments in stocks and shares, bonds, commercial property and farms, from rents and charges paid by students, and from government funding paid through the Higher Education Funding Council (HEFCE), in respect of almost all British and EC students, to cover the costs of their tuition and to make a contribution to some of the costs of running the establishment. This funding has taken the place of income from college fees, which were abolished during 1999–2000.

The investments of the College have been built up from endowments given or bequeathed over six and a half centuries. Some of these are held on behalf of named trust funds and some are held on general trust. The income earned on named trust funds must (with certain exceptions) be spent on restricted purposes, defined by donors at the time their gifts were made. Income earned on 'untied', or unrestricted, endowment may be spent by the College at its discretion – but only on collegiate and educational purposes.

Colleges' financial transactions are summarized annually in a form of accounts recommended by the 1919 Royal Commission. As has been said, one of the Commission's aims was to ensure that colleges were financially viable; another was to ensure as far as possible that they spent their income on proper purposes – and to these ends Statutory Commissioners worked with college bursars in drawing up the new accounting format. It is likely that they saw a *particular* vulnerability in the previous system: a temptation to maximize the 'bottom line', or

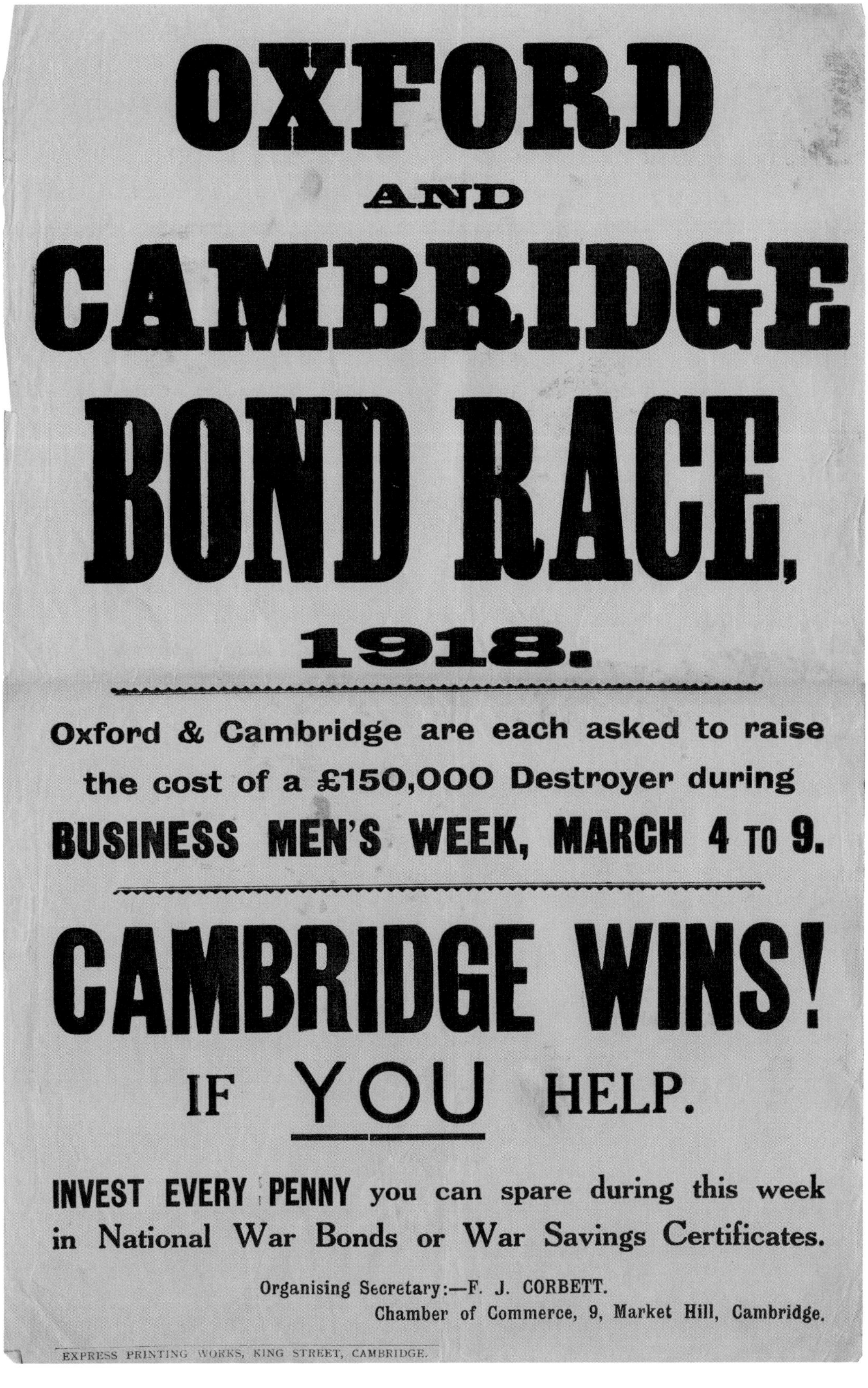

LEFT: *Poster: Oxford and Cambridge Bond Race, 1918.*

92

surplus; and a consequent reluctance to provide adequate reserve funds for scholarships, or for other future needs, particularly those relating to new building and the maintenance and repair of existing buildings. The key to their misgivings may well have lain in the fact that the surplus was commonly distributed among Fellows as an annual dividend!

The accounting format prescribed by the Royal and Statutory Commissioners in the 1920s was still in use in 2000. Much play is made of the charge that college accounts are opaque, designed for the convenience of devious bursars wishing to salt away hidden surpluses. (It is a common misconception in Cambridge that bursars are devious!) The alleged opaqueness of the accounts can, however, be exaggerated; understanding them does need a little patience and determination, it is true – but the intentions of the Commissioners are plain to see: the accounts are not intended as an indicator of profit performance, as a company's accounts would be; their purpose is rather to show *how* revenues received have been applied, and to reassure the University that it has received its due in University Contribution (a tax on college revenues introduced in the 1870s). That said, steps currently being taken to make the accounts more transparent can only be welcomed.

The Commission also recommended that a distinction be made between a college's corporate and general capital. Corporate capital was that which had been received originally in endowments of land and property from benefactors; general capital was that which had been built up from accumulated surpluses. Colleges had long been under an obligation to invest their capital only in land or property, or in government securities, and to obtain the approval of the Board of Agriculture (later the Ministry of Agriculture, Fisheries and Food – or MAFF) for any switches in investments.

To review a college's financial history in terms of its profit performance would not be appropriate or meaningful. Colleges are not *about* making profits so much as they are about maximizing revenues over the long term and spending them prudently and cost-effectively on the purposes for which colleges exist. Better and more interesting measures of historical performance are therefore growth in financial assets, and in the income they generate; growth in physical assets; and competence in managing internal, or domestic, revenues.

Clare is not – and has never been – one of the richer colleges, nor has it been one of the poorer. 'Somewhere in the middle' has defined its financial position for most of the past century.

Most of the College's wealth in 1900 was in agricultural land and related property, and in this it was typical. H.A.L. Fisher, once a Fellow of New College, Oxford, and then Vice Chancellor of Sheffield University, who went on to become President of the Board of Education, wrote in 1896, 'The College is a landlord; a steady-going, careful, impoverished landlord, vitally interested in wheat and barley, in roots and artificial grasses, in pig-sties and farm buildings, and all the paraphernalia of rural life.' And reading through the orders of the Clare Council in the 1890s and early 1900s, one can easily imagine the Bursar, in tweed suit and wellingtons, carrying a stout stick, walking across ploughed fields in the company of the College's land agent or a tenant farmer, deep in discussion of yields, soil quality, harvest prospects and like matters.[1]

Almost twenty College-owned farms are mentioned in the orders of the Council during the first ten years of the century, most of them in Lincolnshire, Cambridgeshire and Essex – and the Council's orders were predominantly concerned with farming matters: stables and gig houses, piggeries, cow houses and bullock sheds; granaries and turnip fallows; the making of farm roads; repairs to drains; the provision of fencing and gates and hedges; sales and purchases of farms and fields and strips of land; terminations and renewals of leases and tenancies – these were the stuff of Council orders in the early years of the century.

In 1900–01, the College ranked fifth out of seventeen colleges in Cambridge with 'untied' investment income of £10,709 – about £580,000 at today's prices (cf. £1,408,000 in the College's accounts for 1999–2000.) Prices were stable through the early years, 'untied' investment income rising to only £11,778 in 1910–11 and just about holding its own in real terms against its value at the start of the century. During the inflationary war years, 'untied' income continued to rise slowly in money terms, but it was not until 1930–1931 that it caught up with its real value in 1910. After 1930–31, it more than held its own against inflation until the outbreak of war in 1939, by which time it had risen to £26,998 (£800,000 a year at today's prices). This 'real' increase was a consequence in large part of a deliberate College policy (outlined below) to sell properties leased for long periods on fixed terms, and gilt-edged securities, and to invest the proceeds in commercial properties let at rack rents.

The First World War had a devastating effect on internal (domestic) revenue as undergraduates flocked to enlist: residents' dues fell from £2,419 in 1910–11 to only £487 in 1915–16, while internal revenue as a whole more than halved, falling from £4,719 in 1910–11 to £2,200 in 1915–16. Once the war was over, however, student numbers and associated revenues bounced back to higher than pre-war levels: internal revenue in 1920–1921 was £6,471.

In undergraduate numbers in 1900, Clare ranked sixth out of seventeen, having just gone through a period of rapid growth, from 70 undergraduates in 1870 to 183 in 1900 – twice the rate of growth of all other colleges taken together over the same period. Only about half the undergraduates would then have been reading for an honours degree; the remainder would have set their sights on an ordinary degree, or would not have intended taking a degree at all. Gordon Johnson writes: 'The University's educational role so far as its students were concerned was … conceived as being quite broad: to produce well-rounded citizens rather than to focus too narrowly on the training of the mind.'[2] He goes on to quote Noel Annan: 'It could easily accommodate the like of Sammy Woods, who resided "as a member of his college for twelve terms, playing rugger and cricket for Cambridge, while failing monotonously to pass the University entrance exam!"'[3]

Most Clare students in the years leading to the First World War would have been 'pensioners', generally drawn from the public schools, financially provided for by their parents. Specimen budgets drawn up in The Students' Handbook for the University for 1902, and quoted by Gordon Johnson, show that an undergraduate would have needed, overall, between £107. 5s. 0d. (equivalent to about £5,650 at today's prices) and £225 10s. 0d. (about £11,900 at today's prices) to make ends meet.

The equivalent overall cost in respect of a Home or EC arts or sciences undergraduate at Clare in 1999–2000 would be near the upper end of the range proposed in The Students' Handbook in 1902. It is difficult to make an exact comparison – and students themselves today pay only a part of the cost of their education, whereas in 1902 they would have had, usually, to find the full amount; but a rough comparison can be made. A Clare undergraduate *notionally* paying all costs due in his or her respect to the University and the College, (i.e. the appropriate *per capita* share of the sums now made available by the Higher Edu-

cation Funding Council) and incurring living costs equivalent to the maximum permitted loan under the Student Loans Scheme (£3,635 in 1999–2000) would incur an overall annual cost of around £10,300. (In fact, state subsidies mean that most students need themselves to pay only their own living costs together with a payment to the University in 1999–2000 of £1,025 – and both of these expenses are subject to parental means tests.)

Termly rents in Old Court in 1902 varied from £3. 0s. 0d. for an attic on B staircase (about £160 at today's prices) to £7. 0s. 0d. for ground or first floor rooms on E staircase (about £369 at today's prices). Dinner in Hall in 1911 cost 2s. 3d. (about £5.40 today). Rents were quite a lot higher in 1999–2000, ranging from £480 a term on B Staircase to £592 on E Staircase. The cost of dinner in 'formal hall' in 1999–2000 was £2.90 on most nights but £9.40 on the infrequent occasions of a meal in 'Superhall'. In addition, a small charge is made towards catering overhead costs.

There *was* a significant number of scholarships and exhibitions available in 1900 for the ablest students, but few of these would have met much more than one third of an undergraduate's needs. Clare's Statutes at the beginning of the century provided for up to 28 scholarships varying in value from £20 to £60 a year and for entrance scholarships carrying maximum emolument of £80 a year.

Council orders concerned with *domestic* financial matters centred, not surprisingly, on the routine life of the College: the stipends of College Officers, the wages of 'servants', the dividends of Fellows, repairs and improvements to buildings, tuition fees, room rents, meal charges and so on. Some carry the faint ring of an age gone by: 'that the payments charged to undergraduate members for electric light be henceforward as follows: during the Michaelmas and Lent Terms, for one lamp, of eight or sixteen candlepower, 10s; if of twenty-four candlepower, 15s; if of thirty-two candlepower, £1 a term.'[4] 'That in future enamelled in lieu of iron slop pails be provided to the Fellows and undergraduates for use on the various staircases.'[5]

'The committee … appointed to consider the question of providing the College with Telephone Communication beg leave to report as follows:

… they find that the telephone is in use in at least ten other colleges, the charge being £8. 0s. 0d. a term it was agreed that the Bursar's room, Mr Wardale's room, the Porters' Lodge and the Buttery be placed in communica-

94

tion with one another by a system of private telephone … and that Mr Mollison (the Master's) rooms be connected to the Porters' Lodge by electric bells.'[6]

There is little in the way of new building in the earliest years, although at a meeting of the Council in 1901 a new building is mooted on the site in the north-west corner of what is now Memorial Court, to comprise thirty-two sets of rooms and a porters lodge. 'During the discussion, considerable stress was laid upon the drawbacks and inconveniences associated with an isolated building so far removed from the existing College' – and it was agreed not to go ahead.[7]

It was not until the east range of the Memorial Court was opened in 1924 that a major addition to the accommodation available in Old Court was made.

The two main developments in the College's financial affairs between the wars were, first, the construction of Memorial Court and second, a progressive switch out of investments in farms and government securities and into commercial property.

The College had received two fairly substantial endowments for new building shortly before the First World War and had agreed, as a matter of policy, to give a high priority to providing additional undergraduate accommodation. These circumstances co-incided with a general wish to commemorate those Clare men who had died in the war.

On 17 March 1922, a tender from Coulson and Son of £44,734 (£1,150,000 at today's prices) was accepted by the Council for the construction of a new building, designed by the noted architect, Sir Giles Gilbert Scott, to be located to the west of Queens Road in what was then the Clare Fellows' Garden, set between the Fellows' Gardens of Trinity and King's. The cost was to be met from the two endowments and by donations invited from past Clare members – but bridging 'loans' from the Ministry of Agriculture, Fisheries and Food, made from monies held by the Ministry on the College's behalf, and from other College funds, enabled a prompt start to be made. The opening ceremony of the new court was performed by Lord Balfour, Chancellor of the University and the College Visitor, on 11 November 1924. Sir Harry Godwin, who had just become a Research Fellow (and was to become Professor of Botany in the University) was present, and recalled Balfour's address in words which have no financial relevance but convey rather charmingly a young man's plea-

sure in the occasion: 'I heard oratory in the grand manner and appreciated the quality and power in spoken English. The opening phrase was so soon elaborated and so qualified that as clause followed clause and ideas led from one to the next, I relinquished hope that the logic or grammar could ever withstand such pressure. At the time when all seemed lost, Balfour tied together the early gestures , summed up his theme and tossed it out to us, fully resolved and complete. It was an architectural performance to equal Gilbert Scott's own.'[8]

Plans put forward by Scott had envisaged an extension which would add 74 sets and make it possible for the College to house two-thirds of undergraduates in its two courts. On 13 July 1927, the Council agreed that work should start on the construction of north and south wings – and this continued in stages until the building was completed in 1934. It had cost an additional £73,000 (about £2,400,000 at today's prices) – bridged, again, by loans from the Ministry and from the College's general capital and funded primarily by a bequest and a continuing flow of small donations.

The other major financial development in the inter-war years was a shift in investment strategy, broadly speaking out of farms and government securities and into commercial property. This may have been occasioned by continuing financial difficulties experienced by farmers at the time; certainly, the College Council, in all the years from 1900 until the war, agreed a large number of rent abatements, which must have made a dent in College revenues. At all events, a committee of the College Council was set up on 4 November 1919 to 'consult with the College Agents in regard to the sale of some of the College's agricultural property.' Five farms were sold during 1919 and 1920 and another in 1925.

The prime advocate of the switch into commercial property was the Bursar of the time, W.J. Harrison, and, under his direction, purchases of freehold commercial properties were made in towns in many parts of the south of England: Eastbourne, Lewes, Kilburn, Yeovil, Frome, Rushden, Basingstoke, High Wycombe, Golders Green, Bishops Stortford, Great Dunmow, Watford, Leamington, Marylebone, Bournemouth, Boscombe, Slough, Bedford, Welling – all between 1932 and 1936. And two farms were bought during the same period. The effects are shown in a comparison of revenues from various sources in 1930–31 and 1940–41: farm rents went up from £1,877 to £4,223; rents from houses let on building leases from £1,609 to £2,893;

while interest from government securities went down, from £4,834 to £1,006. Rents from commercial property over the same ten years rose from £7,017 to £15,219.

On the domestic front, during the inter-war years, the charge to undergraduates for meals in Hall was raised in March 1919 to 2s. 6d., having last been increased (to 2s. 3d.) in 1909.

In May of the same year, the Council agreed that there should henceforth be an *inclusive* charge to undergraduates for room rent, furniture, attendance and shoe-blacking; and this was set at levels ranging from £7. 0s. 0d. (F10) to £16. 10s. 0d. per term (E3 and E4) – £150 to £360 a term at today's prices.

It was agreed at the meeting in May that charges for the conveyance of baggage to and from rooms in College should be 1s. 0d. (which would be £1.10 in today's money) and for removing undergraduates' belongings between lodgings and rooms in College 5s. 0d (£5.50 today) and that 'the sums so paid should be placed in the charge of the Head Porter, and distributed equally between the Head Porter, the Under Porter and Clark.' In a note attached to the orders of the meeting it was recommended, in respect of the aforesaid Clark, that he be employed henceforth almost entirely on boot cleaning 'for which he shall receive £90 annually (about £2,000 p.a. today.) and find his own materials.' His other specified duty would be the conveyance from time to time of undergraduates' baggage and belongings.

On 20 January 1922, a committee of the Council expressed the opinion that 'many servants, owing to the nature of their work, do not get sufficient free time for reasonable rest and recreation' and recommended that 'as far as practicable, each servant should get a half holiday each week.' Pension schemes for each of College Officers and College Servants were approved in July 1923.

On May 20 1926, Clark was 'relieved of his duty of moving furniture and luggage' and it was agreed that 'he receive a weekly wage of £2. 12s. 6d.' (reduced at a subsequent meeting to £2 10s. 0d.) – £3,500 a year today – 'for his services of boot-cleaning, porters lodge duty, window cleaning and waiting in Hall.'

It was agreed on 11 July 1929, that an area of 20.702 acres, forming part of the Trumpington Road Estate, should be purchased from Trinity College for the sum of £4,000 – to become the present College playing fields at the end of Bentley Road.

The cost to an undergraduate of dinner in Hall had been increased in April 1920 from 2s. 9d. to 3s. 0d. On 26 May 1933 it reverted – a sign of the depression – from 3s. 0d. to 2s. 9d. And, 'from out of the blue,' early in 1937, Brian Reddaway, who was then completing a teaching assignment in Melbourne, Australia, received a letter from Henry (later Sir Henry) Thirkill, then the Tutor, later Master of Clare:

We have had under consideration the question of electing someone to a Fellowship in Economics, with a view to providing for the Supervision of our men who are reading that subject. I have been authorized by the College to ask if you would be willing to accept an Official Fellowship and to act as the College Supervisor in Economics.

The stipend attached to an Official Fellowship is £350 (a year) and in addition a Fellow has free rooms in College and free Dinners in Hall. The payment for supervision is at the rate of £200 a year for twelve hours a week a term, rising by £40 a year every four years to a maximum of £320 a year.

Expansion

The Second World War was followed by a period of unprecedented expansion in higher education. This was based in part on a new and wider public interest, which found expression in the national politics of the time. Brooke writes: '… the island was full of anxious parents who wanted to see their offspring at university; and it was notorious that the opportunity to get there was less than in any other of the world's richer nations. So, for a time, university expansion was front-line political news and university funding grew at a rapid pace.'[9] Between 1953 and 1963, approval was given by the University Grants Committee, then under the chairmanship of Sir Keith (later Lord) Murray, for seven new universities. During the last two of these years, this expansion received further support from the Robbins Committee, which reported in 1963.

In the early 1960s, the government had accepted the recommendation of a committee chaired by Sir Colin Anderson that all students who qualified by achieving two passes in the A Level examinations and were accepted by a university should receive a grant – essentially that their university fees should be paid and that they should receive maintenance grants subject to a parental means test. The Robbins Committee took this further, recommending that university places should be found for all potential students who qualified.

96

Brooke writes that '… the euphoria which followed Robbins almost immediately received douches of cold water from the Treasury.'[10] But that was not before Cambridge had caught the expansionary mood. After 1945, eleven new departments came into being in the University and more than 250 University offices were approved.

There was general concern about the problems that so great a rate of expansion would bring to a collegiate university. In particular, there was anxiety about the large numbers of University Teaching Officers (UTOs) without College Fellowships, and research students and other graduate students who also were 'homeless'. The scale of those problems is illustrated in the following tables:

University Teaching Officers: 1928 – 1959[11]

	1928	1938	1951	1959
University Teaching Officers (UTOs)	372	446	690	866
UTOs without College Fellowships	109	170	318	414
% UTOs without College Fellowships	29	38	46	48

Research Students: 1929 – 1961[12]

	1929	1938	1951	1959	1961
Number of Research Students	204	231	760	916	1,114

In response to a problem which was not going to go away, most colleges, albeit with some misgivings, increased the size of their Fellowships and took in more graduate students. Corpus Christi College set up its own graduate centre at Leckhampton House, which provided attachments for some UTOs and accommodated most of the College's graduate students. With the help of a substantial gift from the Wolfson Foundation, the University established University (later Wolfson) College, which offered fellowships to some UTOs who had no college connections and provided places for both graduate and undergraduate students. Also in 1962, a new institution – Darwin College – was founded jointly by Trinity, St. John's and Caius Colleges. The initial intention was that the new College would be for Fellows only but, before it was established, it was decided to include graduate students also in the membership.

Clare, to its credit, conceived and gave birth to Clare Hall.

Considerations of cost and scarce accommodation made Clare reluctant to increase significantly the size of its own Fellowship – although the College did acknowledge a need for more teaching and tutorial fellows. Its newly-

elected Master in the early 1960s was Sir Eric (later Lord) Ashby (who took over from Sir Henry Thirkill in October 1958.) He had been Deputy Chairman under Lord Bridges of the Bridges Syndicate, which had been set up in the early 1960s to review relations between the University and the Colleges and so was particularly well-versed in the nature and extent of the problems facing the University.

The story of the founding of Clare Hall has been told in interesting detail by Richard Eden, Emeritus Professor of Energy Studies in the University and former Fellow of Clare, who was closely involved in the establishment of Clare Hall and went on to be a Fellow there. It is too long and complex a story to be done justice in this short chapter and it must suffice to say that the problems of the University and the Colleges, and alternative solutions to them, were debated earnestly in Clare's Governing Body, and outside it, in the years leading up to 1966. Richard Eden had, early in the story, proposed the setting up of a new society – an 'institute for advanced study' – and this was accepted in principle by the Governing Body on 11 January 1964.

It was at first intended that Clare Hall should have its own existence but remain a part of the College. On 3 July 1964 a Press announcement was drafted which began: 'Clare College has decided to promote *within the College* a new development to be known as Clare Hall. The intention is that Clare Hall shall make a contribution to meeting current Cambridge needs by providing a new graduate society for resident and visiting scholars …'

Land was acquired in Herschel Road as part of a tripartite exchange of sites between Clare College, St. John's College and the University. In mid-1964, Ralph Erskine was chosen as the architect of a new building; work on the

RIGHT: *Thirkill Court: bedroom and* (OPPOSITE) *sitting room in a set, 1955.*

building started in October 1966 and it was completed by the Spring of 1969. Clare Hall had become an Approved Society within the University, with Clare College as its Trustee, on 7 February 1966. It achieved its full independence when its own Royal Charter was sealed on 22 October 1984.

In addition to the gift of the land on which the first phase of Clare Hall was built, Clare College paid the professional fees involved in setting up the new foundation. 'In practice,' Richard Eden writes, 'these costs were small in comparison with the uncosted benefits provided by members of Clare College, particularly Ashby and Cooper (the Bursar), and by the Registrary and other officials in the University.'[13] Additionally, the College transferred the sum of £450,000 from its own endowment, and an additional £30,000 in land – about £4,650,000 in all at today's prices – to finance the first buildings and to provide income to meet early costs of operations. This imaginative gift – together with another, initiated by the late Paul Mellon (1929), the College's most generous benefactor in the twentieth century, paid from the Old Dominion Foundation[14] – $200,000 on each of two occasions – and

another, from the Ford Foundation – $175,000 over five years – set Clare Hall on the way to becoming the flourishing society that it is today.

In addition to its contributions to Clare Hall, the College, aided by many members, invested significantly during the second half of the century in increasing accommodation for graduate and undergraduate students, improving student library facilities and setting up an infrastructure and resources in information technology.

Soon after the end of the Second World War, the wish to commemorate those who had lost their lives coincided again with an intention to add to existing student accommodation. This led to an appeal to past members for funds to pay for a new building, to be erected on the south-west corner of the Memorial Court site. Sir Giles Gilbert Scott agreed to design the building, which was later named Thirkill Court after Sir Henry Thirkill, former Master of the College, who had recently retired. The new court was completed in 1955 and initially housed 44 undergraduates and a resident fellow. Donations amounting to just over £80,000 were made by past members towards the total cost of about £115,000 – about £1,750,000 at today's prices – the balance being drawn from the College's general capital and repaid over future years.

BELOW: *Braeside, 2000.*

Towards the end of the same decade, in 1958, two residential blocks, each comprising twenty bedsitting rooms and a flat, designed by the Cambridge architect David Roberts, were built on the Colony site at a cost of just under £100,000 (about £1,400,000 today) – which, again, was drawn from College funds. At the time, most students 'living out' were accommodated in houses let by the College to landladies and the two new 'lodging houses' were duly let, to Mrs Margaret Lawrie and Mrs A.K. Foyster in November 1959, at an annual rental of £1,460 – and took their place among the other lodging houses on the site – Castlebrae, Braeside, St. Andrew's, St. Giles, Etheldreda and 12–18 Castle Street, which the College had acquired earlier or at about the same time.

In 1964, a block of 32 flats in Chesterton Road, known as St. Regis, was bought to house graduate students, at a cost of £64,000 (about £750,000 today), while two years later the attics in Memorial and Thirkill Courts were converted into 41 bedsitting rooms, at a cost of £93,000. Both projects were again paid from College funds.

Late in 1979, discussions began in earnest about the need for, and the feasibility of, building a new undergraduate or 'tripos' library. The existing Forbes Library in Old Court had become somewhat cramped and inadequately provided and many felt that there was a need for more space, both for readers and for books. The matter was not uncontroversial, both in terms of the need for a new library and in terms of possible locations. It was generally agreed that if there was to be a new building, it would have to be placed somewhere within the curtilage of Memorial Court. There were advocates of a building in the north-west corner and others of something across the opening at the west side. What was eventually agreed, not quite unanimously, but – Clare being Clare – without any kind of acrimony, was that a scheme to build in the centre of the court, proposed by Philip (later Sir Philip) Dowson, Senior Partner in Arup Associates (and later President of the Royal Academy) – who had, as a matter of incidental interest, himself had rooms as an undergraduate in Memorial Court – should be accepted.

The College could not then easily have found the funds for a new building from within its own resources and it was agreed once again to appeal to Clare members. And again, members came up trumps. Professor Nick Hammond directed the Thirkill-Ashby Appeal, which succeeded in raising just short of £1,700,000, and included major benefactions from Paul Mellon, who gave $500,000, and the

LEFT: *Forbes-Mellon Library: entrance hall with view through to Reading Room.*

100

BELOW: *Forbes-Mellon Library: Reading Room.*

Inlaks Foundation, in memory of Indurkumar Shivdasani (1938), which gave $250,000. This more than covered the construction and furnishing of the new building; a small part of the sum remaining was used to assist graduate students in need and the balance of around £26,000 was transferred to the current Development Fund.

The final phase in the twentieth-century building programme was the completion of the Colony. Through the 1970s and 1980s, most of the College's lodging houses had become College hostels, managed not by landladies but directly by the College staff. In 1985, four houses on Castle Hill were refurbished and converted into a College hostel by the then Domestic Bursar, Darnton Holister, to provide 27 student rooms; and in 1990, Holister and Sidney Furness worked together on the design and construction of Castle House, a new hostel for which there was (only just) space, between Castlebrae and the Castle Street houses. This was built out of College funds at an overall cost of just over £1,500,000 and provided an additional 41 undergraduate rooms.

At the start of the century, the College had been able to accommodate perhaps thirty or forty students in Old Court, and a few more scattered in lodgings in the town. By the end of the century it is able (just about) to accommodate all of its 440 undergraduates and most of its 175 graduate students. It has also provided the greater part of the investment needed to fund the first phase of Clare Hall, as well as building – with the generous support of its members – the splendid new Forbes-Mellon Library and investing around £500,000 in student computing facilities. On top of that, it has just completed from within its own resources the extensive refurbishment of Memorial Court, at an overall cost over seven years of almost £4,000,000.

Investments

The strong possibility of continuing high inflation after the war, the repayment of loans from capital on the scale involved in the above programme, together with the need for heavy recurrent spending on maintaining the establishment, postulated an investment strategy that achieved a high income, and capital growth which at least maintained the real value of the College's investments. The formulation of that strategy after the war – and its success – make up one of the more interesting and gratifying chapters in the College's financial history.

Immediately after the war, the College's investments were held largely in commercial property, farms and government securities. The income from properties subject to regular rent reviews would have provided a hedge against inflation, but that from those let on long leases, at fixed rents, and that from government securities, were obviously vulnerable.

Brian Reddaway, then a University Lecturer in Economics and a Fellow of Clare, who was to become Professor of Political Economy in the University, and Brian Cooper, University Lecturer in Engineering, who became Bursar of Clare in 1949, were aware of the dangers. They formed the view that a switch into equities would make good sense, since equities were likely to produce at least a stable real income and probably an increasing one. They came to believe also that the statutory prohibition on investment in anything but property and government securities applied only to *corporate* capital and they persuaded the College to seek a change in its statutes. This was agreed and soon afterwards a new statute empowered the Finance Committee 'to purchase, sell or transfer property, real or personal, and securities (including stocks, funds and shares) of any description.' On 19 February 1953, a sub-committee comprising the Master, the Bursar, Dr Taylor (then the University Treasurer and a Fellow of Clare) and Mr Reddaway was set up and authorized to invest up to £100,000 in equities. This limit was increased several times during the 1960s and was quite soon afterwards removed.

Several of the principles on which the sub-committee acted in investing in equities in the early years were, to say the least, unconventional. Many might have considered them unadventurous and few, probably, would have given them much of a chance of consistently out-performing the FT All Share Index. A summary in one sentence would be *don't try to be too clever*; in detail they were:

- to remain fully invested
- to invest for the long term (the next century – or two!) and not in the hope of quick profits
- to invest for current and future income rather than for quick capital gains
- to presume against making future changes – which always involved costs
- to invest in a widely diversified portfolio, holding shares in companies in all major industry sectors
- to invest roughly equal sums in each holding: and so not to invest a disproportionate amount simply because a share was thought to be undervalued in the market

- to meet as a sub-committee only once a year and then to focus mainly on those purchases and sales, if any, to be made to keep the size of holdings roughly similar.

The Investment Sub-committee presented a paper setting out these principles to a meeting of the Finance Committee in October 1954, which endorsed them; and, though sometimes 'bent' in small ways, in the light of unusual or special circumstances, they have stood the test of the second half of the century.

The Sub-committee was, it is true, concerned from time to time about the relative proportions of the portfolio which should be held respectively in equities and in bonds; and in the twenty years between 1953 and 1973 the College did switch to a quite considerable extent into and out of bonds.

In most years, Brian Reddaway (the prime architect of the College's policy) has written one or more articles for the *Investors Chronicle*, under the pseudonym 'Academic Investor', in which he has reviewed the performance of the

LEFT: *Brian Reddaway.*

102

College's portfolio and pondered its significance. Reviewing the equities vs. bonds issue twenty or so years after the College took the plunge into equities, Reddaway came to the conclusion that 'all things considered, the College might just as well have stayed (entirely) in equities'; and he went on to show that the actual outcome at the end of twenty years was no different from that which would have resulted had the College simply sat tight on its original purchases of equities in 1953, held no annual reviews and made no other changes in the portfolio's composition. He concluded that 'the case for becoming more active in our management seems to be extremely weak' and his advice – in somewhat unacademic terms – was that '… if you know a better hole than equities, go to it!'

The College stuck to its policy through the crash in share prices and the high inflation of the 1970s and in most years out-performed the All Share Index to an extent which 'Academic Investor' confessed 'has always been a bit of a mystery to us': in an article in August 1995, he showed that over the forty years to June 1993, the capital appreciation for a notional unit trust held in the College's portfolio had been from £100 in 1953 to £5,068 in 1993, although all the income received had been paid out to the College (rather than re-invested.) For comparison, £100 'invested' in the All Share Index would have been worth £3,776. Moreover, the College's annual pre-tax income from that £100 would have been £239, while that from the All Share Index would have been £148. In no year up to 1993 had the College's income failed to exceed substantially that of the All Share Index.

'These overall results' concluded 'Academic Investor' in 1993 '… did nothing to suggest a change in basic strategy …'

And yet in 1997, the College *did* embark on a significant change. In the light of what seemed peculiar circumstances, the Investment Sub-committee decided at the annual review on 23 July to back its own judgement against that reflected in market prices – the first time it had done so since 1953. At the root of its decision was the view that share prices were too high and would very likely fall substantially – though just when this would happen could not be predicted. At 30 June 1997 – the date of the annual valuation – the All Share Index was up by some 18 per cent compared with a year earlier and the dividend yield was only three-and-a-half per cent. On top of this, it was felt that the decision in the latest Budget to discontinue payment to pension funds of the ACT tax credit would make

shares less attractive to this important body of investors relative to bonds or commercial properties, while the Chancellor of the Exchequer's announcement that there would be a phasing out of the tax credit to charities (like the College) after 1999 was a long-term reason for reducing the proportion of UK equities in the portfolio as against assets, which still had favourable tax treatment.

The College decided to sell about one-quarter by value of its UK equities and to invest the proceeds about equally between gilt-edged securities and commercial property.

At the annual review the following year the decision was taken that most of the College's equity portfolio should be invested *pro tem* in tracker funds – and in January 1999 the Sub-committee noted that the performance of the College Equity Index Fund had shown growth of 16.7 per cent (capital and income) against a fixed benchmark of 16.1 per cent. At the review meeting the following July, it was decided to sell the entire holding in the North American Equity Index Tracker Fund and to invest the proceeds in long-dated US Index-Linked Bonds.

The changes of 1997–99 represented a fairly radical shift in the College's strategy. Only time will tell whether or not the changes were worth making. In truth, the College has always eschewed short-term decision making and has seen itself as invested for the next century – or two! And the first of these has only just begun.

Students fees

After the war, social and political pressures to widen access increased. The Government's acceptance of the Anderson Committee's proposals (see page 93–4) was generally welcomed in academic circles, including Oxbridge colleges. But as with the grants paid to universities since early in the century, public funding of student fees was by no means an unmixed blessing for colleges, since it inevitably, if indirectly, involved the State – as controller of the purse strings – in their financial affairs.

Before Anderson's proposals came into effect, colleges had had a considerable degree of control over their own economies. They could to an extent vary the nature of their investments to produce more or less income and, within reasonable limits, they could control the income that came in from student fees and charges.

Post-Anderson, college and university fees were paid in respect of individual students not by the students themselves, or their parents, but through their Local Education Authorities. As far as colleges were concerned, there was little change during the 1960s from what had gone before – they simply claimed their estimated needs, expressed as fees, from LEAs rather than from students.

In the inflationary 1970s, the Treasury began to apply the brakes. A new system required colleges to budget their financial needs for a coming year. These were aggregated for all colleges and presented in a claim to the Department of Education as a single sum. This was negotiated between the Fees Sub-committee, a committee of college bursars, and the Department. The settlement agreed upon was then distributed among colleges by the Sub-committee. Divided by the number of students in residence in a college in the year concerned, this became the college fee for that college in that year, and LEAs were advised accordingly by the Department and the Colleges. Claims were based on reasonable estimates and these were generally accepted by the Department. As the decade neared an end, however, negotiations became tougher, and this was even more the case after the Conservatives, under Mrs Thatcher, came to power in 1979.

The Thatcher administration's primary aim was to bring down inflation and it believed that rigorous control of public spending would be critical. Moreover, notwithstanding talk of the virtues of deregulation, cuts in public spending went along with a growing tendency for government to exercise tight control from the centre. And these tendencies – strict control of public expenditure and greater central control – have been just as characteristic of the New Labour government that came to power in 1997. Indeed, a new determination to bring fees in Oxford and Cambridge more into line with those in non-collegiate universities, while continuing the squeeze on overall public spending, has resulted in a harsher regime for students and a greater threat to the independence of colleges than had been experienced under previous administrations. In the eight years since 1992–93, the college fee for students at Clare rose (or fell) in percentage terms by 1.55, –1.0, 2.4, 1.7, nil, 1.0, –0.7, –2.7.

On 17 March 1998, the Government announced that college fees paid in respect of individual students through their LEAs would cease. Thereafter, what had been college fees would be paid as a single component of the annual block grant to the University from the Higher Education Funding Council (HEFCE). HEFCE would 'provide elements' in their future grants to the University *'for the purpose of funding [colleges] at a level representing two-thirds of the current ... level, the adjustment to the lower level ... to take place linearly over a ten year period commencing in 1999–2000'*. The

reduction in college income (over the ten year period) will thus be one-third of the additional funding received by Cambridge as part of what had been the college fee. The loss to Clare – once the ten years have passed – will be about £350,000 a year in today's money. In the context of the Clare economy, this represents a very considerable sum. Moreover, it may well increase if – as seems distinctly possible – the graduate fee also comes under review.

The terms of the new dispensation have been defined in a Memorandum of Agreement between the University and the Colleges. Some colleges, Clare among them, will be required to make significantly larger payments into a central fund – the Colleges Fund – for distribution to poorer colleges which have an inadequate capital base. The form of accounts of colleges will be revised and made more transparent. College accounts will be subject to central audit by the University, which becomes responsible to HEFCE for ensuring that public funds paid to the colleges through the University are properly used. (Some of the details of audit arrangements remain to be agreed but the principle has been conceded.)

The College's response has been to try, wherever prudently possible, to increase revenues from sources other than fees. The shift in investment strategy towards a rather higher proportion of the portfolio in commercial property and bonds; strenuous efforts to build revenues from conferences held during vacations; increases in student accommodation charges (which have had heartening support from students) to bring them more into line with market levels – such measures have been combined with a programme introduced five years ago to reduce costs, again wherever prudently possible. Finally, in anticipation of what has happened, the current development programme was set up in 1995. This aims to raise £7,500,000 by the end of 2001. Thanks overwhelmingly – once again in the College's history – to the generosity of the late Paul Mellon – but also to several substantial and many smaller contributions from, members, the College is well on its way to achieving this target.

The College, at the end of the century, is not unconfident that the struggle to maintain its financial integrity might be won. Anxious, perhaps, but not unconfident. Of greater concern than the financial challenge, as the new century starts, is the wider threat to the independence of colleges under the new arrangements. As the Master pointed out in his introductory note to the 1998–99 *Clare Annual*, '...

103

104

this can be seen from the Terms of Agreement negotiated between the University and the Colleges which spell out the contractual obligations which the Colleges must fulfil in order to qualify for payment. We are now supplicants to the University for our 'share' of the income made available by HEFCE to the University to replace the college fee … (and) the absorption of the Colleges into a centralized and bureaucratic system of government financing poses a substantial threat in the longer term.'

This is a somewhat depressing note on which to end an account of 100 years of the College's financial history. But all, most certainly, is not gloom and doom. With the help of members, the College has become the flourishing and vital society that it is today. With their continuing help – and a fair wind – the struggle to maintain its financial viability and at least some room for independent manoeuvre will go on.

1 J. Dunbabin, 'Oxford and Cambridge College Finances 1871–1913' in *Economic History Review, 2nd series*, 28(1975).

2 G. Johnson, *University Politics*, Cambridge University Press, 1994.

3 'Singing the Blues,' *London Review of Books*, 15 April 1993.

4 Council minutes, 24 February 1899.

5 *ibid.*, 5 March 1909.

6 *ibid.*, 10 and 24 November 1905.

7 *ibid.*, 30 May 1901.

8 H. Godwin, *Cambridge and Clare* (Cambridge University Press, 1985), pp. 65–66.

9 C.N.L. Brooke, *A History of the University of Cambridge*, Volume IV 1870–1990 (Cambridge University Press, 1993), p. 511.

10 *ibid.*

11 R. Eden, *Clare College and the Founding of Clare Hall* (Clare Hall, Cambridge, 1998), p. 46.

12 *ibid.*, p. 54.

13 *ibid.*, p. 216.

14 Now renamed the Andrew Mellon Foundation.

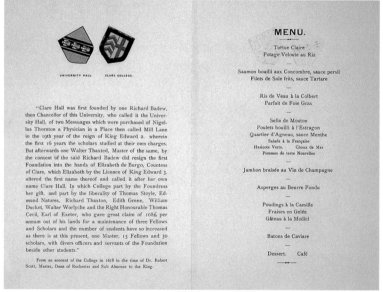

Menu for Commemoration Dinner, 1912.

BRIAN SMALE-ADAMS AND MICHELLE CALVERT

Clare has been very fortunate in its benefactors. Over the centuries since its foundation, they have contributed generously to the College's needs, supporting particular academic purposes, student welfare, building projects and a variety of other cultural and general purposes. Among the latter were the provision of advowsons, which enabled the College to put ageing Fellows "out to grass" – the pensions, perhaps, of their day; gifts of silver plate for the adornment of special occasions and of daily life; collections of books for College libraries; and the funding of particular projects, large and small, like the refurbishment of the Junior Combination Room or the purchase of a rowing eight.

The twentieth century has exemplified the generosity of a wide range of individual members. In the early decades of the century, major sums were donated by Denman Baynes to set up a studentship in the physical sciences; by William Senior to provide for the study of comparative law and legal history; by Harrison Watson, in the memory of his son Aubery for research in the medical sciences; and by D.J. Gordon Dickson for the College's general educational purposes. Elizabeth Dyer gave funds for a scholarship in memory of her son Francis, and Elizabeth Wardale provided for a scholarship in memory of her husband, father and grandfather – all former Fellows of Clare!

Pre-eminent among twentieth century benefactors, however, was Paul Mellon, who died in 1999. His several considerable acts of generosity are described in some detail in Duncan Robinson's chapter (pp. 107–109), but mention of some of them should be made briefly here too. Mellon set up an interchange between students at Clare and Yale University – the Mellon Fellowships – which continue to enrich the social and educational experience of students of both these institutions; he was a major contributor of funds for the construction of both Memorial and Thirkill Courts, the establishment of Clare Hall and the building of the new Forbes-Mellon Library. Finally, just before he died, he bequeathed the very considerable sum of $5,000,000, partly for the maintenance in perpetuity of Old Court, Clare Bridge and the College gardens, and partly for the College's general endowment.

The Thirkill-Ashby Appeal, which funded the construction of the Forbes-Mellon library, also attracted considerable benefactions from the Inlaks Foundation, in memory from Indukumar Shivdasani; Mrs E.N. Neild, in memory of her husband William Cecil Neild; and the Timken International Fund, in memory of Stephen Fredric Bennett. Notable contributions were received also in memory of Sir Geoffrey de Freitas, Professor Robert Salmon Hutton, Dr A.H. McDonald, J.F. Wilward and Colin Price. An anonymous Fellow paid the costs of the Appeal, which succeeded in raising from these donors, and a large number of other members, the funds required for the new building.

Other interesting and valuable gifts made during the twentieth century were received from:

- Edward Atkinson, Master, who gave 300 liturgical volumes and a fund for poor students.
- Cecil Sharp, who bequeathed his manuscripts of folk songs.
- Mansfield Forbes, who left his own books for the use of undergraduates, so forming the nucleus of the Forbes-Mellon Library.
- Alexander McFarlane-Grieve, who endowed a Shrove Tuesday dinner, which is given annually to this day.
- F.I. Wane, who left silver and rare books,
- Godfrey Wilson, Master, who gave pictures and furniture.
- Eric Lane who endowed a Visiting Fellowship in support of study and research relevant to the advancement of peace and social harmony.

106

- Royalton Kisch, who endowed a fund for students of Music.
- Alma Royalton Kisch, who gave funds to support study promoting inter-faith understanding.
- Mary Bliss, who gave the college a 14th-century bell, donated to an unknown religious foundation by Elizabeth de Burgh, Clare's foundress.
- an anonymous donor who provided funds for a Decanae Scholarship, to be held by a graduate student in Theology who also takes an active part in Chapel life, assisting the Dean with services and pastoral work.

During the final decade of the century, the future of state funding, which had been a major source of College funding since the Second World War, became increasingly uncertain, with the abolition of the college fee, and the distribution of public moneys distributed to colleges by the University. Not only does this new system infringe, in significant ways, the financial independence of colleges, but it is to be characterized by real cuts in state-funded revenues over each of the next ten years. However, in the tradition of past decades and centuries, Clare set its sights firmly on the future. It has determined to raise funds to maintain and enhance the excellence of its education, and the unique opportunities it offered – intellectual, cultural, social and sporting – as a small and thriving community. Members' response to the resulting development campaign has been generous and heart-felt, and by the close of the century £6 million had been raised. As well as gifts for the general endowment of the College, a number of special funds were established, some in honour of Fellows of the College: The Geoffrey Elton Fund now regularly supports a graduate student in History; The Brian Reddaway Fund provides support for the teaching and study of Economics; The Miles Heseldin Fund provides bursaries and hardship grants to students studying a range of science subjects; as previously mentioned, the Paul Mellon Clare College Trust provides for the upkeep of the College's oldest buildings and grounds.

The above lists only a few of the hundreds who have supported the College so generously during the course of the century, and only hints at the many forms and purposes of the support given. Though space forbids a fuller exposition, the College remains deeply grateful to each and all of its donors.

DUNCAN ROBINSON

The following appeared in a volume of essays entitled In Praise of Paul Mellon, which was written and presented to him by a group of his friends to mark his eightieth birthday on June 11, 1987. It was written by Duncan Robinson, then Director of the Yale Center for British Art and Adjunct Professor of the History of Art at Yale University.

'Cambridge I loved, and I loved its grey walls, its grassy quadrangles, St. Mary's bells, its busy, narrow streets full of men in black gowns. King's Chapel and Choir, and candlelight, the coal-fire smell, and walking across the Quadrangle in a dressing gown in the rain to take a bath.'

Paul Mellon

LEFT: *Paul Mellon with his father, Andrew Mellon, at Clare for his graduation, 1931.*

Paul Mellon's own recollection provides an irresistible starting point. More than thirty years later, when I went up to Clare College, not much had changed. The only baths in Old Court were still those at the foot of A staircase under the Chapel, although gas-fires had been fitted into most of the fireplaces to replace coal as the only source of heating in students' rooms. Many of the regulations which have since been relaxed were still in place; College gates were locked at night, and gowns had to be worn in the streets after dark. First-time offenders were fined six shillings and eight pence by the Proctor, whose two 'bull-dogs' were recruited from the ranks of College porters; supposedly one was a sprinter and the other a long-distance runner trained to overtake any undergraduate fool-hardy enough to run for it, and to ask with firm polite-ness, however breathlessly, 'Excuse me, sir, are you a member of this University?'

In 1929, Clare numbered some two hundred and sixty junior members. William Loudon Mollison was master and disliked so much the telling portrait which Henry Lamb painted of him for the College (see p.143) that he commissioned a substitute by an artist who worked from photographs. As far as the undergraduates were con-cerned, it was (Sir) Henry Thirkill, or 'Thirks,' then Senior Tutor and later Master, who ran the College in conjunction with Dean Telfer and Bursar Harrison. Unlike the pre-collegiate Yale from which Paul Mellon graduated in 1929, Cambridge University existed only as an association of fiercely and financially independent col-

108

legiate foundations. Admission then as now was to individual colleges. As the second oldest, Clare can lay claim to more than six centuries of intellectual and social activity, not all of it distinguished, but, as the sexcentennial College history which was published in two volumes, 1928–30, is at pains to underline, its transatlantic connections run deeply. It was sometime fellow of Clare, Nicholas Ferrar, who assisted Sir Edwin Sandys as governor of the Virginia Company in drafting the constitution under which the first representative assembly convened in America met on July 30, 1619. As relations between England and her American colonies deteriorated, the College's loyalties were evenly divided; the Hon. Charles Townshend, Chancellor of the Exchequer 1766–67, and Charles Carroll of Annapolis, appear to have been contemporaries at Clare in 1742. Cornwallis was admitted to the College in December, 1755.

It seems unlikely that Paul Mellon's choice of Clare was coloured by any of these associations, but he was presumably welcomed by the society which valued them and by one fellow countryman, Henry Pierce. Pierce read English while Paul Mellon sat for the History tripos, but both men fell unavoidably under the influence of the editor of the College history, lecturer and librarian, Mansfield Forbes. 'Manny' will survive the century as one of Clare's more colourful legends. When Roger Fry and his friends next

door in King's set out to champion Post-Impressionism in painting, Forbes organized a rival exhibition in which he painted all of the pictures himself. In Clare he was responsible for the Dilettante Society, an informal and convivial forum for both students and dons. To Paul Mellon falls the rare distinction of belonging both to this and to its inspiration, the Society of Dilettanti founded in London in 1732. While Henry Pierce gravitated towards the Cambridge stage (he began in a walk-on part at the New Theatre, beside Lydia Lopokova, later Lady Keynes, and went on to become in 1930 President of the Footlights), Paul Mellon turned to more literary pursuits. In 1930 he became the editor of the *Lady Clare Magazine*, specializing as a contributor in the sonnet form. In his own words he 'hunted with the Fitzwilliam regularly, occasionally with the Quorn, the Belvoir, and the Pytchley. I rowed regularly in non-hunting seasons in our college boat on the Cam, and I even learned to navigate a punt.' The modesty is characteristic of the secretary of the Boat Club for 1930–31, who rowed bow in the Clinker 4, 2nd Lent 8 and 2nd 9 in the May Races of 1930 and 3 in the 2nd 8 in the Mays of 1931.

On June 23, 1931, Paul Mellon was presented by his College for the degree of Bachelor of Arts of the University of Cambridge. At the same congregation, Andrew W. Mellon, who was to be named US Ambassador to the Court of St. James's a year later, received the honorary degree of LL.D. and, in July of the same year, was elected to an honorary Fellowship, the highest honour which the College could grant.

As a direct result of Paul Mellon's experiences as an undergraduate at both Universities, in 1932 the A.W. Mellon Educational and Charitable Trust established an exchange fellowship for recent graduates of Yale and Clare Colleges. In October, 1932, William Marvel, Yale class of 1932, moved into G1, Old Court, the set of rooms which Paul Mellon had occupied a little more than a year earlier, to become the first recipient of an award which has continued, apart from the inevitable interruption imposed by the Second World War. (Financial responsibility for the scheme was assumed by the Old Dominion Foundation in 1948 and rests currently with The Andrew W. Mellon Foundation.)

Twenty years ago, on May 1, 1967, Mellon Fellows from both countries gathered in New Haven to celebrate thirty-five years of transatlantic exchange. Many of them wrote of their experiences, the Americans unconsciously echoing Paul Mellon's words as they recalled the ambiance of

BELOW: *Paul Mellon, leading Mill Reef into the winner's enclosure after the Epson Derby, 1971.*

Clare, the unkind winter climate relieved at last by the riot of daffodils and croci along the Backs, and the Fellowship: Thirks, Telfer and Manny Forbes passing on the torch (and the traditions) to John Northam as Senior Tutor and Sir Eric (now Lord) Ashby as Master. As David Grimes (1948–50) wrote, 'No-one had my personal experience at Clare and no-one will. I loved it.' Yet Phil Smith, whom he remembered fondly as his gyp, served the College for fifty years and still looked after D and E staircases when I lived there in the mid-sixties. Not everyone can claim, like John Hershey (1936–37), that 'I wrote a novel while I was there,' even if it was 'later deposited, with a sense of relief, in a trash basket on the corner of 76th Street and Lexington Avenue in New York, labelled (the trash basket, not the novel): YOUR CITY – HELP KEEP IT CLEAN.'

Nor has everyone fallen under the familiar spell. Stanley Riveles (1963–65) left Cambridge convinced that it 'remains insulated from the mainstream of modern British life, that the gates should be taken down and the ditches filled.' He echoes the impatience of a decade which resulted, in both Universities, in those constructive changes such as co-residence to which we owe so much of our present vitality and strength. In 1967, James English (1949–51), then a banker, mused that 'the educational opportunity which I had has not been used either directly or in educating others.' He is now President of Trinity College, Hartford, and would presumably agree with John Gille (1956–58) that his Cambridge experiences 'have left me with a feeling of having inner resources which may be used and enjoyed for my whole life.'

As a former recipient, I plead guilty to stressing the value of the Mellon Fellowship which have for more than half of the century benefited both of Paul Mellon's universities. They initiated an impressive catalogue of benefactions which range widely, from capital projects to specific and always thoughtfully appropriate gifts. For example, the handsome *Catalogues of the Plate of Clare College Cambridge*, published in 1939, bears a discreet credit line to Paul Mellon, while an undisclosed sum, in 1959, helped to secure for the College one of the most important pieces of contemporary sculpture in Cambridge, the bronze *Falling Warrior* by Henry Moore. The College's endowment funds have benefited on more than one occasion, and in 1964, the Old Dominion Foundation made the first of two generous donations to Clare Hall, the new College which Clare established (and by doing so, revived its own former title) as a community for graduate students. A gift to the Fitzwilliam Museum helped to pay for the building of its rare book room and, among the works of art which Paul Mellon has donated, perhaps the most apposite is the *View of Newmarket Heath* painted by John Wooton, 'lovely Newmarket, its long straight velvet training gallops racecourse, to me the most beautiful one anywhere.'

In 1980, The Andrew W. Mellon Foundation endowed at Cambridge the Paul Mellon Chair in American History. Most recently, a personal gift of $500,000 from Paul Mellon did more than help to launch Clare's appeal for funds to build a new College Library. Designed by a distinguished Clare graduate, Sir Philip Dowson, its siting is controversial within the embrace of Sir Giles Gilbert Scott's Memorial Court (1924–35) and facing the University Library (1931–34) by the same architect. Opened in 1985, it is, with more than a little justice, named the Forbes-Mellon Library.

As all of these generous activities attest, Paul Mellon has retained a lively interest in his English University. In 1960, his name followed his father's onto the rolls of the honorary Fellowship of the College and in 1983 he returned to Cambridge to receive his honorary degree. The University Orator spoke at length, and with Pindaric eloquence, but one sentence in particular stands out: "Cantabrigiae si huius munificientiae documenta requiritis circumspicite."

Bronze bust by Tessa Pullan

PAUL MELLON

a last interview with nick hammond

ANTHONY SNODGRASS

Nick Hammond (1907–2001) was known to most people for his extraordinary career in wartime Greece as a Special Operations Executive. The secrecy, danger and excitement of these missions, both in mainland Greece and in Crete, are described in detail in his absorbing book Venture into Greece. *In this interview, he talks with Anthony Snodgrass about his life here in Cambridge and, in particular, his role as Senior Tutor at Clare (1947–54). He died while this book was in preparation, on 24 March 2001, aged 94.*

There have been three 'Nick Hammond periods' at Clare: (i) as a young Research Fellow and later Fellow, from 1930 to the outbreak of World War II; (ii) as 'the Tutor,' 1947–54; and (iii) after his retirement (and a further year in Wisconsin), as Honorary Fellow from 1974 until his recent death.

Since Nick had previously published two short pieces in this vein in the *Clare Association Annual*,[1] this interview was more selective than it would otherwise have been – referring back to comments in, especially, the latter piece; and also omitting the rightly famous war exploits in Greece and elsewhere.

Our interview took place on a beautiful August morning, sitting in his ground-floor apartment off Chaucer Road. The day before, I had attended the funeral of the previous holder of my own post as Laurence Professor of Classical Archaeology, a Clare man (1928–31) who had died soon after his 91st birthday. I once asked him who had been his main teacher(s) as a Clare undergraduate, and he replied 'Well, Nick Hammond of course.' But the fact is that the age-difference between the two men was little more than 18 months, one of several things that are unimaginable today. We took that year, 1930, and those differences, as our starting-point.

[AMS] Could we begin with an economic question: how well off you think you were in 1930, compared with somebody in your shoes today – a newly-elected, resident Research Fellow?
[NGLH] Well, of course, Clare in those days was a celibate community, and so you could live entirely, as I did, in College, and you had your free evening meal: you were OK, but not particularly well off, because you didn't earn very much apart from your £300 Fellowship, and you had to furnish your rooms at your own expense, and you paid for other meals from the kitchens; whereas now you would have furnished rooms and meals at College expense; and hold a University post concurrently, at least as an Official Fellow.

But how soon did you become an Official Fellow?
After six years. Harrison was the Bursar and he held me back, because I was paid less, you see.

He wanted to save the College money?
That's right.

Well, I spoke to Brian Reddaway today about economic comparisons in a Fellow's position. His estimate of the cost of living increase since 1930 implied that, in real terms, you were actually worse off financially than your counterparts today. He also stressed the issue of Cambridge housing, where the increase has been, in money terms, some hundreds of times over, and even in real terms, disproportionately high. So by escaping housing costs, resident Research Fellows today are also saved a lot more. Maybe they are better off than you were, though they probably wouldn't admit it! But they are also mostly five to ten years older than you were.
Yes. So it's reasonable that they should be paid a bit more.

The other thing that is so memorable about the 1930s, in your memoir of a few years ago, is the incredibly funny stories about the Fellowship. This is an old lament about the decline of eccentricity:

but why is it that we have ten times as many Fellows, but we couldn't tell nearly such good stories as you did?
I think it was due to the fact that you lived entirely in College, and it was a very close, small community, which developed oddities and eccentricities. Manny Forbes was a University Lecturer, but he never worried about University lecturing. He said 'I'm like a bird that lays an egg occasionally, and I fly away.' And I think that that was true; and there were also Fellows who didn't care about, or had given up, their University work. You see, Thirkill and Harrison didn't teach any more, or do research.

Well, that's another very big difference between then and now, that presumably when you go into College today, you are surrounded by people who are active researchers and scholars, as indeed you still are yourself. In a way, I suppose, that makes Clare in 2000 a more congenial community for you than Clare in 1930? Or didn't you feel that?
Well, one had a different aim, you see. In the 1930s, if you were a Fellow of a college, your life was devoted to the College; University lecturing didn't matter – I mean, you did it, but you didn't worry to do it well. All your effort went into College life, and it was very rewarding because you made friends, particularly in my case being about the same age, and it was a very satisfactory existence; and one was given teaching. You see, I had 25 Classicists to teach *everything* – I taught them Part II stuff as well; so you were absorbed in a close community, which was devoted to the College and which was mainly concerned with teaching. It was quite different from the modern set-up, which is of course far more outgoing, and concerned with University work and research. I mean, it was a strange period: with the small number of Fellows – only eight or ten – the teaching wasn't all done as a college. Law and History were taught by coaches – Barnes taught Law to anyone, and White taught History. You didn't have Fellows in those subjects. It was a very strange set-up really.

Well, it seems strange to us, now that the College aims to cover practically every subject. But can I switch subjects and ask about Clare as distinct from other Colleges? You've recalled a number of things that used to happen in Clare, like precedence in going in to Hall, in speaking at Governing Body and so on, which have disappeared. But are there still things which tell you that this is the same College as it was in 1930, and in some way different from any other college?

Well, what differentiated it in the 1930s was devotion to the undergraduates: the inward-looking nature of the College. You see, Thirkill gave up his Lectureship, in the 1920s I suppose, and devoted himself entirely to the undergraduates, and he did the admissions right up to when he was Master. And so, he had this closely bound, 'old Clare men' type of College, which was concerned not with academic distinction, but with producing decent chaps. 'Men with nice instincts' as Thirkill put it.

Yes, I remember that phrase. Some people would say – Geoffrey Elton was fond of saying – that Clare continued to put the interests of undergraduates way out in front of any other interest, even to the 1990s. Perhaps that is a resemblance that still distinguishes Clare. Was it a very different college from Caius [where NGLH had been an undergraduate], as seen from your angle?
Yes, it was. Caius was a much more intellectual college: the Fellowship was much bigger, and distinguished academically; and one was pressed academically to do well; whereas in Clare that wasn't so in the thirties.

Was Clare unusual then in having <u>such</u> a small Fellowship?
No, probably Magdalene had very few, and so on. There were other small colleges. The academically strong colleges had big Fellowships – King's and so on. That was really one of the distinctions.

Do you still sometimes look today at Cuneo's 'Conversation Piece' painting?
Oh yes, indeed: frightfully good. It absolutely got the relationship of these three men: Thirkill entirely dominant, and the other two very friendly with him but following his line – particularly Telfer, who was very like 'Thirks': he had great devotion to the undergraduates, and a sense of humour, but he was also still interested in his subject, and so became Lady Margaret Professor of Divinity; whereas Thirkill abandoned Physics altogether. So in a way Telfer was more versatile. But as a team, they ran the College and that relationship is very well brought out by the picture. Terence Cuneo painted it, and he came to stay in College and got to know them a bit. I remember it well. He was the first artist, I think, who depended on photography for his art: he made his name with advertisements for the railways, which were based on photography. He came down and photographed these three men in that position, and he only came back once afterwards to check that his painting fitted all right.

They're good likenesses, are they?
Very good; and it got the relationship very well.

Could we jump to your 'second period', when you come back as Tutor after the War? Thirkill is now Master, and there are big changes about to happen in the College – particularly the one you have singled out, the increase in the undergraduate numbers.
Yes, and the first real growth in research students: I think there were about sixty research students when I left Clare *[in 1954]*, whereas before the War there were one or two at the most. And the College went up from about 250 to about 400 or 450, including the graduates, which of course altered the whole thing. With 250, one knew each other: it was a much closer community.

But Thirkill wanted this to happen with the minimum change to the Fellowship; and achieved that, more or less?
Yes: he resisted even having Research Fellows. I persuaded him that the College must follow the general line and have Research Fellows – one in the Arts and one in the Sciences, and we started with Clare men only: Brian Pippard and Duncan Forbes were a good pair to start with!

You mean he wouldn't have had them at all, without persuasion?
No. Pippard had a research studentship at Pembroke at the time, and we made him a Fellow *[in 1947]*. But Thirkill wouldn't have had him back, I think, if he had not come as an official Fellow with a University post.

Was Harrison still Bursar then, so the financial factor was still influential?
Yes, he was desperately keen to spend as little as possible on the Fellowship, because he wanted to do the buildings: his memorial is the Memorial Court, and the whole idea of all the money going into producing College accommodation. And of course it was justifiable really.

Another thing you mentioned was the causes you supported, or in some cases initiated, often in the building line: such as the building of Thirkill Court, the conversion of the Memorial Court attics (which didn't happen straight away but happened eventually), and bringing freshers to live in College in their first year. These are all now part of life in Clare, and nobody can imagine it without them. But were there other things that Clare should have done and never did in those years? Did it 'miss the bus' in any respect?
I have a feeling that it was too restricted in the subjects that it was interested in, as compared with other Colleges. It had less distinguished research, on the whole. It did miss out on those sides. But it was a strange community: you see, games counted for so much, it was quite extraordinary. Team-spirit was all connected with College loyalty, with Thirkill admitting mainly sons of old Clare men – this idea of a Clare tradition.

And did Clare do very well at team games as a result of this policy?
Yes, we won Cuppers at rugger one year, I remember, and things of this sort. Now of course they don't play games at all, do they?

Well, very much a minority, as far as team games go.
Thirkill and Telfer would go and watch the rugger matches from the touchline; you can't imagine it now. I did too, of course; in fact I even played for the College when I first went, because I was so young.

And nobody objected?
Well, they wanted me to play in Cuppers too – I was a hooker, you see – but I was debarred as a Fellow.

Conversation Piece
Terence Cuneo, 1949

Henry Thirkill is standing, with William Telfer on his right and William Harrison, on his left.

In between your second and your third periods at Clare comes the Ashby Mastership [1959–75], almost all of it. Presumably this dramatically changed some of the things that you've been talking about?
Yes, well of course the admission of women made a big difference; he [Eric Ashby] was very nice, he sent me copies of all the minutes of the debate about it; he treated me as if I was still a Fellow, because I had been Senior Tutor. And of course the enlargement of the College, which was largely the continuation of an earlier process; and more research – again, that was going on, but he developed it further. But introducing women was the big difference, and by the time I came back to Cambridge, they were here; and I think a great improvement in many ways.

Do you think that any Fellow today can possibly have as close a rapport with the undergraduates as you had when you started?
I don't think so, because in my case it was a combination of age, a celibate college, living in College, and other Fellows living in College. It was a much tighter social unit; plus the fact that Thirkill made that his primary concern. He went on as Master, continuing to admit the sons of 'old Clare men' – whereas now admissions don't have that in mind at all.

Also, the idea of one person handling everything to do with admissions would be just a joke today. When you came back after the War, did you have a say in admissions, as the Tutor?
No, none at all, ever. I did all the administration as Tutor; they were my concern once they arrived. He didn't interfere at all.

He handed you a fait accompli, *and told you to get on with it?*
That's right, absolutely.

Whereas today at least Senior Tutors can feel that they are themselves partly responsible for which people are admitted; so that if something goes terribly wrong, they have a share of the responsibility. Did anything ever go terribly wrong in your day? Because it would surely have been difficult, if the Master was the sole person who had ultimately brought them there.

I don't remember anything. I think there was one suicide, but no one ever knew why – like most suicides, it was entirely illogical. But what were you thinking of?

Major academic failure, perhaps caused by a wrong choice at admission stage?
Ah well, academic performance didn't matter. The only people who were expected to get Firsts were Scholars. The others were quite content even to have a Special.

And Thirkill didn't regard that as a blot if they did?
No, no. It wasn't an aim. Again, it was this 'College spirit'. Every year there were a number of people that took a Special, having failed the Honours degree. But that wasn't thought to be a fault of the system or anything. 'Decent chaps'!

No lengthy discussion at Council! But is there anything that we haven't covered, which you think it's important to bring out, about the change over the years?
I think the chief thing to emphasize is that if you became a Fellow of a College, you devoted your life in the University to the College, not to the University. What you did in the way of research or of lecturing was of secondary importance. Your primary function, if you accepted a Fellowship, was to devote yourself to the College and do whatever it required – even to the extent of giving up your University Lectureship, if you were a Thirkill. That doesn't exist any more. He chose that course voluntarily; he was one of a very brilliant group, of Rutherford and company, at the Cavendish, but when he came back after the [First] War, he accepted a Tutorship and gave up lecturing fairly soon after that.

It's such a very different background: it's worth recording it.

1 A memoir of Henry Thirkill in 1971, pp. 8–15 and some reminiscences in 1994-95, pp. 8–12.

clare college in the mid-thirties

EDGAR BOWRING, MELLON FELLOW (1937–39)

Edgar Bowring is the oldest surviving Mellon Fellow. He was at Yale 1937–39, the fourth Mellon Fellow to make the exchange. His predecessors were Geoffrey de Freitas, Eric Cawston and Bobby Allan. Later Mellon Fellows have included Duncan Robinson (1965–67, see pp. 107–109 and 193–202) and Peter Ackroyd (1971–78, see pp. 82–84).

I was fortunate to find myself at Clare College in the autumn of 1934. I was the youngest of four brothers and there were only five years between the eldest, Tom, and myself; Tom's example was an inspiration for so many aspects of my subsequent life at Cambridge and afterwards. We were all born in Southern California, where my father was growing oranges. He was the youngest son of seven sons and three daughters of John Bowring, who, in turn, was the youngest of five sons of Benjamin Bowring, a clockmaker in Exeter who emigrated to Newfoundland during the Napoleonic Wars. Benjamin Bowring was the founder, in 1811, of the Bowring trading, shipping and insurance businesses, later known as Bowring Brothers in Newfoundland, Canada and the USA, and C.T. Bowring & Co. Ltd in the United Kingdom and elsewhere. Most of his elder brothers were in the family business, of which the two eldest, Sir Frederick and Sir Edgar, were Chairmen in their turn, but one, William, had already gone to California to grow oranges.

We were all registered as British citizens with the British Consul in Los Angeles and our parents decided that we should all be educated in England. We originally came over in 1920, leaving the two eldest at preparatory school in Liverpool, and finally returned for good in 1921, after which our parents bought a house and apple orchards in Goudhurst, Kent and sent us to a preparatory school near Hastings.

However, as Tom had only been educated in England for a short while, he was unable to pass the Common Entrance Examination for any of the Public Schools at which our cousins were and the Headmaster of our preparatory school recommended Eastbourne College. Thereafter we all went there and were, I believe, well educated. Tom had left before I arrived and had gone on to Emmanuel College, Cambridge to read Economics.

Since there was only one year between myself and my nearest brother, Fred, he and I were very close together at preparatory school and Eastbourne; at the former, we were both in the same cricket and football teams, although Fred was much better at games than I was. At Eastbourne he got his school colours in both the cricket eleven and the rugby fifteen, whereas I did not achieve either, although I think that I was only dropped from the latter as a result of an ankle problem.

Also at Eastbourne, the Headmaster, G.V. Carey, and one Housemaster, 'Beefy' Howell, who was in charge of rugby, were Cambridge rugby Blues and we never thought of any other University. Indeed, at that time, we had three cousins playing rugby for Cambridge: Peter Ralph Bowring from Rugby School who never got a Blue because two years running, having been selected for the Varsity Match, injury prevented him from playing, and W.H. (Barney) and W.J. (Jack) Leather from Sedbergh School. Barney & Jack played for several years and, in my first term at Clare, which was also Jack's College, he had stayed on for a fourth year in order to captain the Cambridge XV.

Before leaving Eastbourne, my brother Fred decided to follow Tom to Emmanuel College and subsequently got a First in Mechanical Sciences. He was also a leading member of the Emmanuel rugby XV. Since Fred and I had been so close and I had always been following him, I felt that it was time that I adopted a more independent existence. I asked Tom which college he would recommend, other than Emmanuel; I hardly knew the names of the other colleges. He took time to reply but when he did, after consulting with his friends at other colleges, he said that the unanimous view of himself and his friends was Clare College, and he gave good reasons for that, particularly its academic and sporting achievements and the character of its members.

Consequently, I immediately asked for an application form which I duly completed with the help of my housemaster at Eastbourne, who had been at Clare. In due course, because I did not have a School Certificate in Latin, and despite expecting a Higher Certificate in Mathematics and having School Certificates in most other principal subjects, I was asked to take the College Entrance Examination. I did that, although I was not too happy with my performance in the Latin paper and expected to be turned down. However, the next stage was an interview with the College Senior Tutor, Henry Thirkill (later Sir Henry, Master of the College and Vice-Chancellor of the University). He asked me many pertinent questions, but I enjoyed that, and I later learnt that he had quite a reputation for selecting a broad spread of candidates from different schools with wide interests, both academic and sporting, particularly cricket, rugby, hockey and athletics, and that Clare had an outstanding reputation for Blues in all of those sports as well as academic performance. When I was offered a place at Clare, I was surprised and delighted.

I left Eastbourne at Christmas 1933 and decided to follow another of Tom's ideas, a few months in France. He had been at a Château near Blois in the Loire Valley. Anyone who has seen Terence Rattigan's play 'French Without Tears' will know exactly what it was like. When I was there, there were six or eight other British boys studying French. It was run by an Englishman, Mr Gardner Beard, and his pleasant but rather aristocratic French wife who had inherited the Château from her parents. They had two young children and an English nanny who was a central character in the set-up. There was a long obituary of her in *The Times* a few years ago. According to the obituary, the current Duke of Wellington must have been at the Château in the same year as I was, but not at the same time. At my time, we did have one future duke, Lord Brackley, later Duke of Sutherland, and several other delightful people, although one was a nephew of Sir Oswald Mosley and was not too popular for that reason. During the Second World War, Nanny, who always asked the students to bring her tea from England, later earned a reputation in an escape chain enabling British soldiers

and airmen to get through France and Spain and thence on to England.

On arrival at Clare I was told that I had been allocated rooms at a street number in Thompson's Lane, a lane on the right shortly before Magdalene Bridge, and that the name of the landlady was Mrs Frost. When I got there I learnt that there was one other Clare freshman allocated rooms there. His name was Fraser Bird and we have been friends ever since, although with long gaps due to war and business. Fraser lived in Tunbridge Wells and we found that we had some mutual friends. We had separate bedrooms but shared one living room and agreed to share one decanter for our sherry, taking it in turns to fill it up. However, we soon found that someone else was sharing it with us, obviously Mrs Frost. I cannot do better than quote from what Fraser recently said in a letter to my son, Anthony, who also went to Clare.

'Our friendship began in Thompson's Lane in Michaelmas 1934; our Landlady was a Mrs Frost, who used to drink our sherry, much to your father's disgust and my fury. A few drops of "becacuanha" which I put in one of our bottles brought this sad little story to an end – at least so far as Edgar and I were concerned.'

Fraser was always more courageous and outspoken than I was; he was reading Law Part I and I was reading Economics Part I and we soon found our way round the College and the University, together with its lecture rooms and public houses. We also got to know many of the other Clare freshmen and those who had started a year ahead of us. Fraser was a good and keen cricketer and hockey player and played for the College at both. I only played rugby occasionally for the College. I remember that Fraser was keen to be elected to the Hawks Club, the sportsmen's club, which he achieved at an early stage. Ever since, he has been one of its most active members, particularly encouraging other members to attend the Club's annual dinner in London. Later I joined the Pitt Club, whose members were better known for their hunting, shooting and fishing interests.

I was keen on horses and politics. Again following Tom's initiative, I joined the University Cavalry Squadron and persuaded two other Clare freshmen, 'Bunny' Ramsay and Donald Carden, to join at the same time. They had not, previously, done any serious riding, but under tuition from a regular cavalry sergeant, we all soon learnt the hard way. We also occasionally went out with the University Draghounds.

116

My interest in politics and debate, since I had started a debating society at Eastbourne, was exercised at the Cambridge Union. I was keen on debating, although not very good, and had an ambition to become President of the Union, a position later achieved by some of my friends, such as John Simmonds, son of Gavin Simmonds QC, later Lord Chancellor under Winston Churchill, and Philip Noakes. I think that I was the first freshman of my year to be given a 'paper' speech, which meant that my name was printed on the announcement of the subject for the debate and the proposers and seconders for and against the motion. At the end of my first year, my name was proposed for the Committee, but I failed by a narrow margin. Thereafter my attendance at the Union debates was infrequent and, instead, I concentrated on the CU Conservative Association, of which I became Chairman. The President was Kenneth Picthorne, a Don at Corpus Christi, who later became the University MP, although the existence of University MPs was abolished by the Labour Government after World War II.

One of the merits of belonging to the Union and the CU Conservative Association was that one met so many people from other colleges. I do not remember any other Clare members of either, although there were some who joined the Union for its club facilities – i.e. meals, library and reading rooms. Particularly good friends of mine were John Simmonds and Evelyn Boscawen from Magdalene, Philip Noakes from Queens and Jessan Beer, a Norwegian and member of the Norwegian Davis Cup team, from Trinity. At Clare, apart from Fraser Bird, I got to know Bunny Ramsay (with whom I shared a set of Don's rooms in the New Court in our second year) and Donald Carden, already mentioned. Also there were James D.R. McConnell, who later became a housemaster at Eton and was an author under his middle names of Douglas Rutherford, H.B ('Bertie') Chrimes, later a prominent Liverpool citizen and businessman, Ronnie Canney, an excellent surgeon, Max Stamp, an important economist, and others in my year.

Of those a year ahead of us, I remember particularly R.A (Bobby) Allan, later Lord Allan of Kilmahew, with whom I started a CU Anglo-American Society and who preceded me as Mellon Fellow to Yale, Tom Howarth, whose first student I was when he returned to the College after getting a double First in History, since I was then reading History Part II. He later became Second Master at Winchester, one of General Montgomery's personal liaison officers during World War II, Headmaster of King Edward's School, Birmingham, High Master of St. Paul's School, and Fellow and Senior Tutor at Magdalene College, Cambridge. Of those a year after us: Gethyn Hewan, who got Blues at both cricket and hockey and followed me as the Mellon Fellow at Yale, Peter Studd, a cricket Blue and later Lord Mayor of London, and Joe Inglis, a rugby Blue, who also played for Scotland.

Also good friends of mine, both at Clare and later in the USA, were the Mellon Fellows who came from Yale to Clare during my time at Clare: Richard (Dick) Danielson and John Hersey. Dick, who had rowed for Yale, came from a Boston family, although his first marriage was to an English girl, Chris Andreae, whose father owned a yacht which competed with Lipton's Shamrock V for the honour of representing this country in the America's Cup. Dick's parents lived at Groton, near the private school of that name which Dick had attended, with houses also in Boston and on the Massachusetts coast. Dick's mother (née Deering) acted in many ways *in loco parentis* for me and was Master of the Groton Draghounds, which I followed on a number of occasions.

Dick's mother had inherited the famous Deering house in Miami, called Villa Vizcaya, which is now a tourist attraction. Bobby Allan and I visited it with Dick at Christmas 1937, and I visited it again in the late 1980's for Dick's 75th birthday at a lovely house which he had had built in the grounds of the Villa.

John Hersey was rather different, extremely intelligent and serious but not, so far as I can remember, particularly interested in sport, politics or girls. He only stayed at Clare for one year because he wanted to get on with his career. He lived in New York, where we met on a few occasions, and he had taken a job with a newly established, but very successful, weekly newspaper. He later became a famous author and ended up as Master of Pearson College, Yale, and an Honorary Fellow of Clare.

Sadly, of all the names I have mentioned, only Fraser Bird, Sir Peter Studd and Philip Noakes (of Queen's College) are, so far as I am aware, still alive.

HOMAGE TO DR ARNOLD

or

IN THE FOOTSTEPS OF A GREAT TRADITION

The College is evidently taking itself seriously, if one may judge from the text of the latest form issued to Bedmakers.

Clare College, Cambridge

This form to be returned to the Porter not later than 10.15am
If no Undergraduates are ill, the word "none" should be written below.
STAIRCASE ....
The following Undergraduates are confined to their rooms by illness:

....
Signature of Bedmaker.
Date ....

An end, sir, to this life of self-indulgence! Positively no slumbering after 10am! Cold baths and clean living for all! Back to the public school!

And why not, sir? Very fine institutions. May I suggest the introduction of the following rules in the College. We must get rid of dilletanteism and dormitory talk, and all that sort of thing.

BEDROOMS

All undergraduates must be out of bed by 7.30am, and beds turned back by 8. The Falcon-in-charge will see that this is done.

No undergraduate may enter another's bedroom except to go to the beer-cask.

No talking with bedmakers, except so far as necessary in the exercise of their functions. They have a great deal more to say than you have.

CALL-OVER

Call-over will be held in the Great Dining Hall at 8.50 (Sundays 9.30). Undergraduates must see that they are pricked-off before going to lectures.

CASTLE BRAE DURING THE SEXCENTENARY CELEBRATIONS IN 1926

GAMES

All undergraduates must play some kind of field game. A healthy body is the essential complement to a healthy mind. The man who shirks games will never come out at the top of the Tripos lists.

When "cuppers" are being played, all undergraduates must turn out and cheer. (In winter, greatcoats should be worn.)

THE FALCONS

The Falcons are appointed on their own athletic merits as responsible officers in the College, for the persecution of the Bursar. Other undergraduates should treat them with obedience and respect. But in any case of bullying or excessive heartiness, an undergraduate may appeal to his tutor.

GOWNS

Each gown should have its owner's name and college number clearly printed inside, to prevent loss.
Any undergraduate found wearing another man's gown, will be reported.

CHAPEL

Undergraduates must behave with reverence in the College Chapel, and not stare about them.
The choir is out of bounds.

ETHELREDA IN THE 1930S

DINING-HALL

There must be no disorderly conduct during grace. Translations of the College Grace may be obtained from the Dean, price 3d., if gentlemen will subscribe their praenomina in the Buttery. (Proceeds to the College Mission in Rotherhithe.)

HEALTH

Hot baths should not be taken in the morning.

Be regular in your habits. Cases of constipation should be reported to your tutor immediately. (A daily apple is beneficial.)

MISCELLANEOUS

When at a club or society dinner, do not write anything on your friend's menu which you will not think funny in the morning.

Especially when about to enter dance halls or other public rendezvous, ask yourself, would Lady Clare approve?

If you must drink, remember that still waters run deep; and so does the bath.

Undergraduates should behave in a manner consonant with gentlemanly standards at all times. "Once you have soiled your old school tie, it will never be the same again."

Lady Clare Magazine XXXI/1, Michaelmas Term 1936

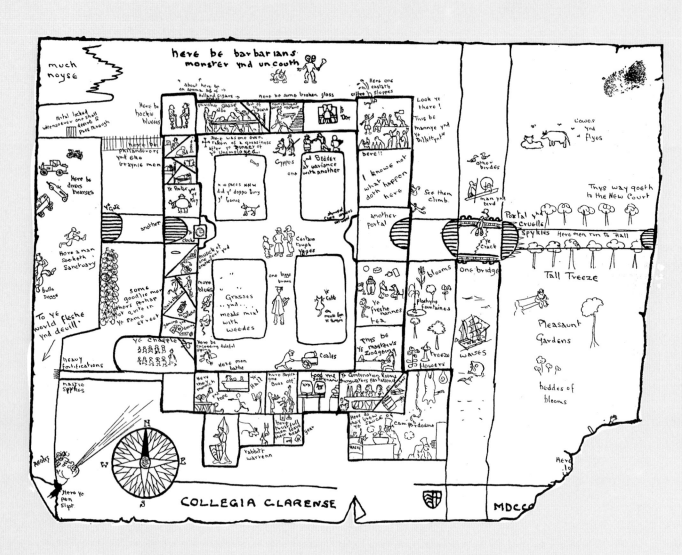

MAP, *COLLEGIA CLARENSE*, FROM *LADY CLARE MAGAZINE* XXI/2, LENT TERM, 1927

ANTHONY SNODGRASS

It is unusual for news of a death at the age of 96, though accurate, to be widely disbelieved. Yet that was the case with Noel Odell: he had seemed indestructible. Tall, upright, steady in his gait – you could still tell that this was a man who had most likely distinguished himself in some field of physical activity. His connection with Clare covered a long period, from his enrolment there as an (already seasoned) research student in Geology in 1931 and his later election as a Fellow Commoner, to his last dinner in College as an Honorary Fellow, a couple of days before his death in February 1987.

He was one of the outstanding all-round mountaineers of his generation, as he proved time and again, in a career that extended from Edwardian times to the late 1970s, and covered not only the Alps, Rockies and Himalayas, but a huge area of the Arctic, from Alaska to Spitsbergen. His leading part, in 1936, in the ascent of the 25,650-foot Nanda Devi, which for the next fourteen years remained the highest summit known to have been reached by man, would in normal circumstances be seen as the worthy culmination of his career. But in fact he was much more widely known for a fleeting episode which had occurred earlier, on the afternoon of 8th June 1924: a moment whose reverberations were to range from an audience for Odell at Buckingham Palace with a concerned King George V, to a mention in inter-war literature (in W.H. Auden and Christopher Isherwood's play *The Ascent of F6*).

In the third and last of the 1924 Expedition's attempts on the summit of Everest, Odell, alone and acting in close support of the climbing pair, G.H.L. Mallory and A.C. Irvine, was ascending in their tracks, a day behind them, to the camp from which they had that day set out for the top. Going strongly at about 26,000 feet, he saw the clouds part to reveal the whole summit ridge of Everest. Just below the sky-line, silhouetted against a snow-patch,

were two figures 'moving with considerable alacrity': he watched, fascinated, as first one and then the other launched themselves on a projecting rocky obstacle on the ridge itself. The leading figure then clearly emerged at its top, before the clouds closed in again. The time was 12.50pm and the obstacle was probably the 'Second Step', at 28,230 feet.

Since Mallory and Irvine never returned, Odell's sighting of them took on an extraordinary importance. The mountaineering world, indeed the world at large, was spellbound by his tale. Though some were later to question the reality of his observation, most of those who knew him well – as the Fellows of Clare did – believed that it must have happened as he said. The important thing about Odell's sighting was that it was not just a few seconds' glimpse, but several minutes of intent watching by a keen-sighted man, utterly free of fanciful notions, who was nowhere near the limit of his powers (as he was to prove by his unparalleled solo exertions in searching for his lost friends over the next two days); and that the details of it were compatible with the topography of the mountain. I have more than once tested his version by observing, on other mountains, silhouetted climbers at a comparable distance – some 1,400 yards, looking steeply and diagonally upwards – and there is no risk of more than momentarily mistaking 'rocks' or 'birds' for moving human figures, as sceptics later argued he had done.

The whole question enjoyed a great revival of interest in May 1999, with the discovery of Mallory's fallen body, at a height intermediate between those of the observer and the observed 75 years before. (Odell himself, incidentally, had deplored previous attempts to instigate a search for the lost climbers). On the assumption – anyway long since accepted as extremely probable – that the final accident happened on the way down, the site of this discovery is fully compatible with Odell's report of them,

122

much higher and some way further west. The fact that Mallory's snow-goggles were found packed away in his pocket suggests that the fall happened after sunset: if so, then there are at least seven hours to account for between the two events. If the climbers spent, say, half of this time continuing upwards and the other half descending, then a real possibility still exists that, with the aid of their oxygen apparatus, they completed the remaining 800 feet or so to the summit. This is of course the question which gives an apparently endless appeal to the story; and it perhaps justifies devoting so much space to five minutes in a life of ninety-six years.

His equable, obliging temperament (like his exceptionally slow pulse) had much to do with Odell's achievement as a climber. Mallory's choice of the inexperienced Irvine, rather than the supremely fit Odell, as his companion for the final attempt, has ever since been roundly condemned by mountaineers; Odell himself was not discountenanced by it at all, seizing the unexpected opportunity to practise his geology at unprecedented altitudes. Pressed to take part in the 1921, 1922 and 1933 expeditions to Everest, he eventually turned the invitation down each time in order to honour prior commitments; rejected for the 1936 expedition as 'too old', he was belatedly included again, at the age of 47, in 1938, and once more went high. Meanwhile, he had taken part in a whole series of explorations in Spitsbergen, Labrador, Greenland and Alaska, making an array of first ascents of peaks, and achieving equally notable things in the Canadian Rockies (where a peak was later to be named 'Mount Odell'). Perhaps his career is best summed up by the story of the Britannia Hut, 10,000 feet up in the Valais Alps: donated to the Swiss Alpine Club by its British counterpart in 1909, it was ready for opening on 17th August 1912, and later that afternoon received its first British visitors, a party including the 21-year-old Odell. Could anyone have imagined that, when the anniversary of the hut was celebrated 72 years later in 1984, the same Noel Odell would be the guest of honour in a party which crossed the Chessjen Glacier to attend?

Even if he had never set foot on a mountain, Noel Odell's would have been an interesting and varied life. His graduation as a geology student at Imperial College, London, was delayed until the age of 31, primarily by World War I, in which he was three times wounded as a Sapper captain (he was again to serve in the Sappers in World War II). Thereafter he worked as an industrial and later as a consultant geologist in Iran and Canada, before moving into the academic field. He held a teaching post at Harvard before coming to Clare to undertake his research, then others at McGill and the University of British Columbia, before taking the Chair at Otago from 1950 to 1956, and holding a final Professorship at the University of Peshawar until he turned 71. His marriage to Gwladys Jones, whom he had met when on leave in North Wales from the Western Front, lasted from 1917 to her death in 1977, and Odell lived to see their only son reach retiring age. His circle of friends, former pupils and admirers spanned the entire globe.

ANTI-WAR IN CAMBRIDGE

H. V. KEMP

I am not so much concerned in this note with the Anti-War Movement as such, though I was a delegate to the Paris Congress in September last, but rather with a specific item in the programme of the Anti-War Movement, namely the demonstration carried out in Cambridge on November 11th, and the actions which some members of the University thought fitting as a response to that demonstration.

It is true that November 11th in Cambridge is the occasion of a great deal of ragging in the town: it is true that elsewhere it is the occasion for display and pageant in many parts of Great Britain, as the photographs in the illustrated weeklies prove. The demonstration organised by the Student Anti-War Council was a protest against both these uses of that day, and against Imperialism as the fundamental cause of war. Many different points of view were represented, and it was a sincere avowal that the best response to the dead that we can make is to organise now against war and war preparation, so that 1914–18 shall not be repeated on a more terrible scale – and certainly with the improved technique at the disposal of the war-makers another war would mean annihilation on a scale far more devastating than the last.

It was intended that the demonstration should be sincere, peaceful, and orderly, and it would have been but for a display of unwanted rowdyism which is known to have been organised in one college at the invitation of the Conservative Association. This opposition took the form of crying down at a preliminary meeting someone who was attempting to assert his right as an English citizen to free speech; of pelting the demonstrators with fruit and eggs; and of attacking the main body of the demonstration itself. Furthermore, hooligans overturned the barrow of a fruitseller who refused to supply them with missiles, and made personal attacks on individual demonstrators which resulted in one serious case of concussion.

This may be a controversial subject; but these are facts, and I maintain they should be widely known. For it should be possible to make a peaceful and democratic expression of opinion in England upon any subject whatever, and it is this right which the rowdies attempted to deny. Surely a difference of opinion upon an important subject does not warrant an attempt at forcible suppression of one side by the other?

This statement has been seen and approved by the following members of the college before publication:

D.M. Balme	J.W. Jeffery
L.D.S. ten Doesschate	G. Knott
C. Thatcher	T.R. Shaw
A. Marriage	J.W. Harris

These types of articles banned after this edition.

EDITORIAL

Since the last number of LADY CLARE was published there has been much discussion and disagreement about the policy of the Magazine, and, as a result, the policy which has characterised the last few numbers has been given up. It has been decided that from this number at least all political articles should be excluded.

Although politics may enter considerably into the lives of some members of the College, we feel that political discussion is best left to verbal conflict, when red ties and black shirts may be viewed from afar and cultivated or avoided at will.

This number has been produced by an editorial committee. As he explains elsewhere, the Editor has been obliged to resign.

We would not claim that the magazine approaches the glories of some four years back, but at least it is not controversial. It will be enjoyed, we hope, as befits our cloistered seclusion, floating idly down stream from Grantchester or under the willows in Byron's Pool.

* * * * * *

We regret that since going to press the Editorial Secretary has seen fit to resign.

CORRESPONDENCE

To the Editor of LADY CLARE.

Dear Sir,
The Editorial Board has asked me to write explaining why I resigned from the Editorship of LADY CLARE at the last moment as I did.

The immediate reason was their refusal to allow an article of mine on "Soviet China" to be published in the magazine. This at first sight seems to be a personal, and perhaps petty, reason for resigning. I did not intend it to be so, and I do not think it is.

The article was banned because of its political intention: one member specifically objected to a statement about "the contradictions of world capitalism," and of course there is more than a fortuitous connection between the development of "dangerous thoughts" in the Japanese Manchurian army and in the minds of British under-graduates. The difference is, in Japan one is beheaded: in England, symptomatically, articles are banned. Never-theless, these contradictions exist. Fish is destroyed in England, coffee in Brazil, wheat in Canada, pigs and milk in USA, and there is a general restriction of production while millions are unemployed and millions starve. Are these not contradictions?

It is said that undergraduates are not "interested" in these problems: yet some are "interested" enough to sup-press free discussion of them. It is said a college magazine is not the "right" place to discuss them: but since when have social problems ceased to be a topic of conversation at universities, and who are "rightful" contributors to a college magazine if not the members of the college themselves?

Clearly on the basis of these views I could not contribute an article to the LADY CLARE one day, and on the next ban it in my capacity as Editor. So I preferred the straight role of a writer of banned articles to the famous personality of a Jekyll *alias* Hyde.

But I sympathise with the last-minute labour of responsibility which the Board has brought upon itself.
Yours etc.,

H.V. KEMP.

Lady Clare Magazine XXXI/3, Easter Term 1937

WAR IN AIR

Entr'acte

"Apothecary, an ounce of civet, to sweeten my imagination!" – Lear

Cambridge is a place for shouting. One shouts about politics; one shouts about God – preferably in the Market Place, or at breakfast time – one shouts, very loudly, about peace; or finally, and still more loudly, and sometimes alcoholically, about oneself. We make up for our lack of experience by the abundance and vigour of our opinions. We even take up zealously the cause of the busmen, or join, with well-fed enthusiasm, in hunger-marches. We have already seen God, and are anxious that others should see as we do. We join battle against the enemies of peace. Or perhaps we merely content ourselves with deciding that life, and/or woman, is vanity. In fact, in this cloistered clam, it is surprising how much we know.

However, we do look out, quite seriously sometimes, over the edge of this delectable, though expensive nest, and find it difficult to know where to join our clamour. "We are re-arming," say the Government, "for the peace of the world." And yet a vague suspicion tells us that we have heard that one before. Wasn't the last war the war to end war? But it seems so convincing. "I will serve my country to the best of my ability," says the new King. But who was it who said to the miners: "Something will be done?" Negroes are busy extracting wealth from holes in the ground in Africa, while governments are busy putting it back in their own private holes in the capitals of Europe and America. "The cure for unemployment," say the economists, "is *(a)* the Raising of Wages, *(b)* the Lowering of Wages." Children in the industrial districts of the North are hungry and dirty, while at Cambridge young men throw coffee-cups into the river.

"Trust in God!" say the Group. Yet one remembers that states do sometimes come to amicable arrangements, but churches never. And the wars of religion are usually the bloodiest. In what then shall we put our trust?

The blackbird outside the editorial window paused for the moment in the extraction of a worm, and looked at us gaily out of the corner of her eye. "The trouble with you, young man, is that you think too much!"

Well, anyhow, May Week is not far off!

Lady Clare News, XXVIII/3, Easter Term 1934

clare college in wartime

PHILIP RHODES

To go up to Clare in 1940, as I did, was somewhat sombre. October 1940 was only four months after the near miraculous Dunkirk evacuation as the German Panzer divisions overran northern Europe and it was around the time of the air Battle of Britain. There was great uncertainty about the probable outcome of the war.

Candidates for degrees were mainly those reading medicine or engineering. Undergraduate students in those subjects were in what were called 'reserved occupations'. This meant for the student that if he (the College was all male then) progressed steadily in his studies he would not be called up for military service in any of the forces. There were frequent air raids in many parts of the country. Several cities, including my own of Sheffield, had been subjected to blitzes of night time bombing by hundreds of German aeroplanes. These raids were essentially aimed at factories, railway marshalling yards and steelworks in attempts to damage production, especially of armaments, and their transport. There was the useful collateral side-effect for the enemy of undermining civilian morale too, for many were killed in these raids. Indeed several citizens after such raids called mutely for an ending of the war by surrender.

It was extremely worrying to hear the air raid warnings with the eldritch rise and fall of the sound of the sirens, with stomach churning in rhythm with them, to be followed by the sinister drone of aero engines and soon after that by the crump of bombs exploding on the ground not far away. Rationally of course most of us were not in much danger, though it was difficult to convince oneself of that, and there was uncertainty as to whether one would be under the next cluster of bombs. Occasionally lone enemy aeroplanes would fly low over a town and spray it with machine gun bullets, as happened at least once in Trinity Street, making pedestrians and cyclists scurry for cover. Not only were there raids on industrial targets but on some towns of historic and ancient interest such as Norwich and Coventry. These became known as Bædeker raids after the famous series of tourist guidebooks. There was anxiety that Cambridge and Oxford might well become targets for such terrorizing sorties.

Every college and public building had to take precautions against attack. There were designated areas, preferably underground, to protect against blast injuries, where all could muster. Walls of sandbags protected apparently vulnerable doors and windows. Many of us were trained in fire prevention duties, for often incendiary bombs were dropped and if that should be on the roof of the College they might wreak havoc, if fires were allowed to spread. There were buckets of sand in many places, so that bombs could be covered, and there were stirrup pumps of which one end went into a bucket of water to be pumped out by hand through a short length of hosepipe. I was seconded for night firewatch duties at various times to Addenbrooke's Hospital, then in Trumpington Street, and also the University Library, and later I joined a uniformed Home Guard bicycle platoon. We rode out into the country and engaged in futile exercises, sometimes late into the night. These extracurricular activities all took a lot of time, energy, effort and organization of one's time. They were duties which had to be fulfilled, and they were not conducive to academic work.

In retrospect these measures were a pathetic response, but at least it felt like some sort of defence, morale boosting perhaps, and a form of defiance, for there seemed little else we civilians could do against such odds. But those odds against being bombed soon lengthened after the Battle of Britain in 1940, when the number of enemy bombers getting through the squadrons of Spitfires in southern England diminished greatly. Nevertheless some enemy penetration of the defences still occurred, and it was then encouraging at night to see the searchlights looking for hostile aircraft and, when they were caught in the intersecting beams, to hear the crackling sound of anti-aircraft (ack–ack) batteries seeking the bombers, and we might see the shells exploding high in the air. Yet we soon seemed to get used to these threats from the air and even tended to ignore them, at least to some extent. We had seen the devastation wrought by many of these attacks and there were photographs of it in many places, yet large areas remained untouched even after the heaviest bombing. The chances of being hit were definite, yet often seemed very remote, though ever present.

This tension was constantly in our background, and it was added to by the fact that many of our contemporaries and relatives were serving in very dangerous theatres of war. We never knew where they were, but that did not prevent us worrying about their safety, and we nearly all knew someone dear to us who had been killed somewhere. But I must not give the impression that we lived in constant fear. We did not. Like everyone else we simply got on with what we had to do in our day to day academic tasks. It was rare for us to be very near to any bombs. Nevertheless there was always the spectre of war in its many guises forming a background to everything that we did. This made a difference to college and university life of the time.

There was some anxiety, even slight guilt, too as to whether we should have been in the forces alongside our contemporaries, and not reserved for later service. We were uncomfortably aware of the hardships endured in the forces, compared with the relative comfort of university life. The Regius Professor of Physick, Dr John Ryle, had made it plain in his inaugural lecture to undergraduate medical students that our service was to be in full and devoted application to our studies, so that we could be part of the future rebuilding of our country. The future had to be looked to as well as the present. This naturally gave us some unexpressed sense of duty and urgency in our work which perhaps earlier and later generations may not have felt with the same intensity. There was of course much enjoyment, but it always seemed to some extent to be tempered by the background against which we were living.

These ever present feelings probably detracted from the normal fullness of College life. This revolved round dinner in Hall and going to each other's rooms for coffee and gossip before returning to our rooms to bash the books. The medical student's week was very full with a lecture from 9 to 10, practicals from 10 to 12, a lecture from 12 to 1, an hour off for lunch then practicals or time in

the dissecting room from 2 till 4, followed by a lecture from 5 till 6, and all this for six days a week. There were Long Vacation terms too, lasting five weeks with many lectures and practicals, mainly in pharmacology. We medical students were therefore resident in Clare for at least 30 weeks of every year. With this overload most evenings had to be spent in writing up notes and reading, and this had to continue in the vacations at home. There was not much incentive to go out for there was a universal blackout after sundown so that the courts and streets were dark and uninviting, with few people about. If we went out we had to wear cap and gown. It was a fine game for town boys to ride by, snatch the cap off one's head and pedal off into the darkness laughing. The caps were never seen again.

For my first year I was in digs in the town in a house overlooking Jesus Green. There I had an insight into the way of life of pre-war undergraduates. I had my own first floor sitting room, with sofa and two easy chairs beside the metered gas fire, while in the bay window was a gate-legged table with two dining chairs. Upstairs on the second floor was my bedroom and across the corridor was my own bathroom. Mr and Mrs Bob Addison brought me tea in bed in the mornings, and served breakfast (cooked of course) to me at my table. If I wished for lunch on Saturdays and Sundays, that was provided too. This was the life of a gentleman, which I had not expected, though my predecessors had done. It was a style that soon disappeared under the influence of wartime privations, even though these were relatively minor. My second year I shared rooms in Memorial Court (L staircase) with a friend who was later killed as the navigator in a bomber flying over Germany. My third year I was on my own in rooms on L staircase. This too was luxurious with chair and table, basket chair to sprawl in, bookshelves and a coal fire. Coal scuttles were filled daily by one of the gyps, who also laid the fire ready for lighting. The bed makers were excellent. Of course there was the small kitchen and a bathroom between two sets of rooms. I was very comfortable.

Negotiating one's way from Memorial Court to the Old Court for dinner was a problem on moonless winter nights. Because I sometimes forgot to take a torch I had learned to count the number of paces on each leg of the journey from the steps of Memorial Court, across the road, through the trees to the gate and then up the avenue to the gates at the entrance to Clare Bridge, then to the arch into Old Court and across it to the steps to the Hall. Even so it was all too easy to crash into one or other of the gates

128

which were scarcely visible on some nights. We welcomed the moon and the longer evenings of summertime. There were few cafes and restaurants open, and food was monotonous and uninteresting because of rationing. However the kitchen staff of the College, and the gyps pressed into waiting at table, coped manfully with the problems, producing a variety of dishes out of meagre resources. Ration books were issued to everyone in the country. The buying of butter, meat and eggs and many other foodstuffs for households meant that coupons from the book had to be surrendered as well as money. The amounts allowed on each coupon were strictly controlled by law. Undergraduates had to hand in their ration books at the beginning of term and take them back again when they returned home. The College kitchens worked wonders on the scarce allowances of food they had at their disposal.

There was fun and enjoyment in the conversations in Hall and in the rooms, and in occasional excursions to the cinema, but there was little else. My pleasure outside work came largely from playing soccer for the University. I was a regular member of the side for three years, being secretary in my second year and captain in my final year. We were able to travel some distances to play service sides and to Oxford. This was mainly by train and bus and rarely by coach. None of us had cars at our disposal. We trained on Tuesday afternoons and played against other sides on Thursday and Saturday afternoons. Only occasionally could I play for the College XI, because my time was so full. To accommodate my football schedule to the lectures and practicals I had to undertake one hour of practical in physiology then scoot over to the biochemistry practical for an hour, and vice versa, or go to the dissecting room. To keep up with the lectures I had to get a friend to tell me what the subject had been and then read it up in the text books. There used to be a strict rule of signing into lectures and practicals and the register was overseen by a lab assistant. How I managed to do this when I was away so much of the time I do not now remember. But I think it was known that I was a University soccer player so that I was treated with some leniency. Certainly it was known to Mr (then) Henry Thirkill, the Master who was also my Tutor. It was he who allowed me a third undergraduate year when so many of my contemporaries worked for a two year degree. It was amazing that he could carry out so many duties with assiduity and perfection. I suspect that it was largely he who kept the College functioning as well as it did through the war years. Ably assisting him were no

doubt others, but the one who most directly and helpfully influenced medical students was Dr (then) E.N. Willmer, who was supervisor in physiology. He was quite outstanding in his teaching methods and in inspiring us to learn. Generations of Clare men, and now women, owe him an immense debt of gratitude. He induced a sense of the methods and delights of science, as well as demonstrating his extraordinary skills in the arts and garden design. Other supervisors seemed to come and go and few were very valuable, except for Dr R.I.N. Greaves, a pathologist, but he was at Caius, where we had to go to meet him.

In many ways we were the lost generation of Clare undergraduates because there was so little collegiate life. Moreover several undergraduates were up for only a year. That was intended to give them a taste of university and college life in the hope that they might be inclined to return to academia after war service. Most of them were expected to join one or other of the cadet corps of the University, the most popular being the air squadron. But this constant changing of people in the College and faculties, except for engineers and medics, did not make for stability in the undergraduate population. Many of the Fellows too were in the forces or helping the war effort in many ways and in many places. It was a disruptive time for everyone.

Because of these experiences I felt somewhat detached from the College after I left. There was always a sentimental attachment which remains now and has been felt through all subsequent years, but there were no strong continuing ties because of the distracted lives we led during the war. Nobody at Clare seemed to notice my progress in soccer, for I went on to captain the English Universities, the Corinthian-Casuals and the Combined Oxford and Cambridge teams, out of which sprang Pegasus, the renowned amateur football club which won the Amateur Cup after the war. Nor was there a ripple in the College as I became the first, and probably the only, Cambridge graduate to be appointed to a Chair in Obstetrics and Gynaecology in the University of London or indeed anywhere else. And later I became Dean of the Medical School of St. Thomas's in London and then held a similar office in the University of Adelaide, and Medical Postgraduate Dean in the Universities of Newcastle upon Tyne and Southampton. It was not noticed that I was for some years an examiner in obstetrics and gynaecology in the Cambridge Final MB, nor that I was Chairman of the Examiners in those subjects for three years. It was as if I had never been to Clare, for all the interest there. On the other hand why should the College be interested in the affairs of its graduates after they have left? I realize now that I should almost certainly have been more persistent in keeping in touch with the College. It should after all be a two-way process in which I was deficient. Perhaps it was assumed that doctors owe more allegiance to their hospitals than to Clare and Cambridge. Academic clinicians tend not to be much respected nor understood in more scholastic and scientific academia.

There do presently seem to be greater attempts to keep past Clare men and women in touch with their *alma mater*. Translated as 'benign mother' that is perhaps as it should be, for a parent should remain interested in all her children as they should be in her. These initiatives are welcome. I attended one reunion at Clare and there was no one else of my year present. It seemed as if all of us of the war years had slipped out of sight, never to be seen or heard of again. That is why I now welcome *Clare News* and the *Clare Association Annual*. They do tell us of the present but it is now perhaps too late for this lost generation to remember and be remembered. This should not now happen to those who came to Clare after the war and particularly from the 1960s onwards, because of the serious efforts being made to preserve and communicate with the nexus of Clare graduates, after they have gone down. No one can have been at Clare without recalling it with affection and gratitude. It is good that the College authorities now recognize that and show that they care for those who have been educated there, even after they have left to join the wider world.

the flying twins

JOHN DAVENPORT

ABOVE: *John (left) and Peter (right) Davenport in flying gear, June 1944.*

John and Peter Davenport, identical twins, were sent to Clare in October 1941 on an RAF Short Course, to study Engineering as a foundation for flying training. The University Air Squadron covered basic RAF training, while college activities included singing in the Chapel choir under a brilliant organ scholar, John Sidgwick and Rugby football in the Clare XV. Wartime University regulations required the wearing of cap and gown after dark. One offence (no cap) by the writer led to a fine of 6/8d levied by the Senior Proctor!

After training as pilots in Canada they joined 502 Squadron Coastal Command flying Halifaxes from St Davids before and after D Day on anti U-Boat patrols in the Bay of Biscay. Later, from Stornoway in the Hebrides, the Squadron changed to blockading night movements of German supply ships around Norway and Denmark, using radar in conjunction with flares or moonlight to make bombing attacks. John was awarded an immediate DFC for sinking two German ships at night, one with two, another with three, direct hits against fierce anti-aircraft fire.

On demob in 1946 the opportunity arose to return to Clare, reading Economics with Professor Brian Reddaway as supervisor. The adjustment to academic life, even to writing weekly essays was quite a test. The College seemed to recognize this and helped also to smooth the mix of ex-school and ex-service undergraduate intake. Rugby football and Eton Fives in sporting activity, with a resumption of choral singing in the Chapel or with the Canaries College Choral Society, beer at the Volunteer and contract bridge all helped. Tea with David Attenborough in his rooms on the same staircase in Memorial Court remains a pleasant memory.

John left in 1948 to join Tootal in Manchester. Peter started with Shell in London. Peter died in 1983. John retired in 1984 and now lives in Alton, Hampshire with dinghy sailing and contract bridge to fill his spare time.

A FRESHER'S 1941 DIARY

JOHN SPENCER

131

3RD OCTOBER 1941

No record of the experiences and impressions of a freshman during his first term at the University, could be complete unless it commenced the day before his arrival. It is during the War, and this fact has increased the necessity to gather together all my belongings before leaving home, realizing how difficult and unreliable it is to delay making the necessary purchases. Many things, my crockery and linen, were already in the house, and packing has proceeded steadily for one or two days. To-day, Friday, we had a day out, going to 'The Reluctant Dragon' and Kew and Richmond, and it was late by the time we reached home. I packed my trunk, and after dinner was surrounded by numerous pieces of baggage – a trunk, a hold-all, two large boxes and one small one, and a suitcase. The urgent requirement was to dispose of the small box, since the numerous packages in the carriage would make travelling impossible. I sat in each chair in my room successively, viewing the possibilities from all angles, arguing endlessly with the former generation. Eventually the problem was solved, but the ceaseless work of tying up lasted until the following morning.

The more notable objects which my luggage contained, besides my ordinary clothing etc. are here tabulated:

SUPPLIED FROM HOME:-

Linen: sheets, pillow-cases, toilet covers, towels (ordinary & bath), table cloths, napkins, dusters.
Cutlery (for 4)
Crockery: white, edged with black and gilt pattern; glass (for 4)
Wireless (Pilot: 'Little Maestro' – £5.19.6 – March 1940)
Clock (Boots, Richmond, 8/6 Jan. 1940)
My Bike; procured second hand 1938 and completely rebuilt except for frame and handle bars!

Bought:-		£	s	d		Budget (29.9.41)	£	s	d
	Tea pot, milk jug, sugar bason –				1.	University fees	45.	.=.	=
	Pewter – Robertson, Kilburn	2.	2	=	2.	Labs fees	12.	12.	=
	(Bread board Whiteley's		6	3	3.	College fees	37.	10.	=
	(" knife "		6	9	4.	Long Vac.	20.	=.	=
In	(Butter " "		2	9	5.	Dinners in Hall	21.	.=.	=
Uniform	(Serviette ring "		2	=	6.	Rooms (Memorial Court)	60.	.6.	=
Wood	(Mustard, salt, pepper pots on stand;				7.	Groceries	20.	=.	=
	Deacons Windsor,	15		=	8.	Kitchen	25.	=.	=
	(Toast rack		4	6	9.	Commons	8.	10.	=
	2 white dishes, jug. Pyrex butter shells (7d ea.)				10.	Laundress	6.	=.	=
	Small glass dish (11d)				11.	Books	10.	=.	=
	Glass bowl Harrods	2		=	12.	Travelling	10.	=.	=
					13.	Tailor	40.	=.	=
					14.	Clubs etc.	9.	=.	=
					15.	Coals	7.	=.	=
						TOTAL	£331.	18.	=

Other initial expenses already paid:-

Feb. 10.41	Registration fee	1	=	=
Feb. 17.41	Deposit	2	10	=
Apl. 12.41	Admission fee	2	=	=
Jly. 2.41	Caution money	30	=	=
do.	Matriculation fee	5	=	=

£40 .10 =

4TH OCTOBER

Surrounded by my elaborate paraphanalia, and to the usual onslaught of questions, I was hustled between two hefty boxes in a taxicab bound for Liverpool St Station. The journey was successful, though patience played an important part. On arrival at the station I was ushered with much delay and no bike, into a taxi and duly delivered at Memorial Court.

In my rooms I found notes from the Master, to visit him at 4.15pm, a tailor, advertising a cap and gown, and a Chapel notice. I scattered some of my baggage about the floor, and repaired to look for the tailor and a china shop, to buy some College-crested china as a present from M. I could not find one at all, so having obtained a cap, gown and surplice (which I later found unnecessary, as they are provided in chapel) I collected my bike from the station, and took it straight to a garage for a new front mudguard! On my way, however, I passed Matthews & Son of Trinity Street, who sold me my china, though a rather old collection in view of low stocks. This was delivered while I underwent the ordeal with the Master.

After being admitted by the maid, and having deposited my macintosh in the hall, I crept up the thickly carpeted staircase, and approached 'the 3rd door on the right', when a voice behind me checked my motion, and after brief introduction (we had met previously at the College entrance exam) I continued my expedition. On entering the room, four men were gazing at me, as silent as doormice, and then a slight relaxation ensued, the whole process repeated when the door opened again for another fresher.

The six of us were told the principle regulations, and then interviewed separately about our work.

6TH OCTOBER

Dinner at 7.30, and afterwards I drew rations (having chosen not to have breakfast in College) of tea, butter and margarine and sugar; we waited until 8.15 for the ARP warden to appear, and we then suffered a pi-jaw on the rare night watch once a fortnight.

8TH OCTOBER

Most of the days I spend looking for things that don't exist, e.g. pens and books in shops which don't stock them. A 2/2d pen was (bar a 17/6d one) the only one. (I had hurled mine accidentally twice on the floor with fatal results to the cap). The three books I obtained came from three different shops, none of which stocked either of the other two.

Breakfasts and lunches are going to prove difficult; the former may be obtained by the week in Hall if desired. Breakfast is possible as toast goes a long way, but lunch must be more filling, and although pork pie, a polony (to-day) and a tin of salmon (irreplaceable) are quite satisfactory, they have to be found, and when lectures start to-morrow and I'm working 9 – 1 each morning, the problem increases.

10TH OCTOBER

I procured a couple more polonies, and had one with a plate of soup for lunch. The afternoon was spent repairing a puncture and filling in forms at the STC HQ. I automatically enrolled in the Home Guard. One form has:

'Surname .... Christian Names ....

What is your name? ....' !!!

Before dinner we had a Boat Club meeting ... King Peter of Yugoslavia was there, referred to as 'Peter.' I charged in at first and started babbling away without knowing him.

After dinner, I confined myself to my rooms until 10 o'clock (and after) on 'fire watch'. I am a reserve.

11TH OCTOBER

I am getting in a muddle with STC. I have lectures two afternoons a week, and the STC want two, and the rowing wants three, all in six weekdays! I don't feel I can drop STC, and rowing will have to suffer.

13TH OCTOBER

I've been looking for some geometrical instruments, but I cannot find any.

14TH OCTOBER

I chased round looking for a tailor to get a blazer, a decision that was made absolute by the arrival of 12 clothing coupons from M.

I fixed up with the STC for Mondays and Fridays, which leaves only Wednesdays and Saturdays for rowing.

I bought some instruments, for 22/3d, the last lot in the only shop in Cambridge which had any …

15TH OCTOBER

I wrote to G to thank her for sending 8 clothing coupons for … a pair of trousers.

19TH OCTOBER

One item I have omitted. The d … d inkpot, without its top on, spilt all over the papers on the desk, and on my trousers. Fortunately the papers were old or unnecessary, and my trousers can be cleaned, but I am destined to wear my suit for a day or two.

27TH OCTOBER

Milk of 1 pint per day cut to ½ pint yesterday and to ¼ pint today. (Half pint restored 6th November).

30TH OCTOBER

The gyp's customary knock, or rather, knocks at my door, woke me from my slumbers, but after emitting a raucus "Alright", I promptly turned over and fell asleep again. Next, at 8.50, there was a clattering at my door, and again I emitted my harmless "Alright", but was suddenly interrupted by "ten-to-nine, sir" … I was sitting, panting and breakfastless, in the Mineralogy labs at 9.01am, before the lecturer had appeared.

31ST OCTOBER

I had a lousy night, being kept awake for most of it by toothache, and it persisted in a lesser degree throughout the day. I survived however, even through a Corps parade, and after dinner sat down in front of a roaring fire and did some Chemistry.

4TH NOVEMBER

… After dinner, I went up to P (B2) and listened to him on his piano, which he has hired at £2 a term. He is jolly good.

10TH NOVEMBER

The customary full day, with STC parade in the afternoon. It rained miserably – so we had lectures indoors. They were extremely pleasant, however, and whereas I have never learnt less in a given time before, I have probably never laughed more. Apart from usual jokes which Sergeant Newbury, with caustic interjections from CSM Simmonds, produced, the latter got into fine form on the exposition, and final ejection, of a certain 'Neighbour' (pun – of course) who had apparently signed on the Infantry by mistake!

Although we did no drill to-day, this might be a convenient place to mention Sergeant Fowle, the third member of the RE instructional staff. One occasionally hears efforts at imitation of Sergeants drilling squads with voluble, but quite unintelligible ejaculations, which one never believes to be entirely justifiable. No imitation of the volubleness, unintelligibleness, or 'Army-Manual-learnt-by-heartedness' could possibly exaggerate the manifestations emitted from this chip off the old block. During a recent drill of ¾ of an hour, during which it was his privilege to teach me the 'turnings at the halt', (repeating word for word the expressions adopted on the first occasion) I counted 29 'In this (or that) manner's, of which one was 'in the normal manner' – pronounced in a gutteral voice all of his own. Other regularly repeated expressions are 'I will now give you a complete demonstration'; 'I will show you exactly what I mean' – and, probably his finest piece of repertoire, with that nasal stress on the final vowel, 'When I say … , this is exactly what I want to see you do.'

For a merry gang, always picking fun at each other, we could have no better example – it does one good to see them so good tempered.

15TH NOVEMBER

I went down to the river and we launched a 2nd VIII. I always refer to 'a' 2nd VIII instead of 'the'. The reason for this is that the war has reduced the days on which we can row to three, and several of us can only row on two – owing to STC etc.. All of us cannot always row on the same days. Thus the crews change, though they are fairly constant for any given day …

Our cox's ignorance of the subject was quite inconceivable. Among the many occasions on which we nearly missed and only by shortening our oars, avoided, the bank, was one notable occurrence … Having successfully manoeuvred round a bend, the cox carried the bend round across the river, thus to clear the way for an oncoming boat. We were paddling firm at a decent rate of striking and the boat nearly rammed the bank, so that the cox had to swing us round the other way, i.e. the stern into the grassy verge. At 7, with practically no warning, I suddenly found my blade overlapping some three or four feet of land. At this moment, a willow caught it, and the full momentum of the boat was taken by my blade … and me. The oar bent round an astonishing curve but even so, the boat was still under powerful way, and I was compelled to lean back to encourage the handle to come over my head … the net result was that my head and shoulders were ducked over one side of the boat, while my feet dangled peacefully over the other – with stroke kindly securing them there! The pull of my feet had wrenched the rests of the stretcher off the cross bar to which they were screwed and the consequent looseness prevented my pulling on them. The sympathetic coach, of course, merely remarked that this was unnecessary in any case, as one should only press on the stretcher!

21 NOVEMBER

… We drew our Home Guard uniform.

26TH NOVEMBER

Physics in the morning and an appetizing lunch on polonies! In the afternoon down to the Boat Club, where the 2nd VIII embarked and after some difficulty managed to raise the stroke to a firm paddle. We rowed over the course. Stroke caught a crab, but we quickly recovered and went on brilliantly after that. Just before the railway bridge, we overhauled, without any difficulty, a Peterhouse* boat being used by an LSE VIII, which must have started a full minute ahead!! Our coach, seeing that we had to swing out to pass them, bellowed at them to tell them to move – as surely they could see we were rowing a course. The meek reply floated gently back – 'So are we!.'

After a rest, we set off again, but 2 had cramp, and R. took his place. Then when we were nearly back, an extra spurt of energy from 4 cracked, and bust in two, his oar at the button. So ended the outing.

---

*   My humblest apologies, Peterhouse. This should read LSE, who use Peterhouse boats.

KURT LIPSTEIN TALKS TO TERENCE MOORE

Throughout the twentieth century Cambridge has provided a haven for a number of scholars and scientists seeking a refuge from their own countries. Their reasons for coming vary. Sometimes the causes are political, sometimes racial, sometimes religious, and sometimes scholars simply did not wish to return to their home countries where basic democratic freedoms were lacking. Clare has played its part in welcoming and providing a base for some of those in need. Some alumni will recall, amongst others, Geoffrey Elton, Bob Hepple (our current Master), Paul Rubiczek and Colin Turpin.

The period leading up to the Second World War, and the years of the War itself, were inevitably a particularly fraught time for non-British residents. One Fellow's wartime experience is unusual, partly because his background is unusual. Kurt Lipstein QC, *honoris causa*, Professor of Comparative Law, Clare Fellow from 1956, born and brought up in Frankfurt-on-Main, had close links with England, his great grandfather having settled in Liverpool in the mid-nineteenth century. His father's brother lived in England and Kurt used to spend school holidays here, becoming fluent in English from an early age.

As he pursued his law studies in Berlin, Kurt always had at the back of his mind an intention to do the Bar exams in England. As it turned out, however, his opportunity to study Law in England came sooner than he expected, and in very different circumstances. He was working as a Clerk to the Courts in Frankfurt on that fateful day in April 1933 when a law was passed in Germany forbidding anyone of Jewish origin from holding office. Though he went to work as usual, he found himself barred from going to his office. 'I suppose you'd better have some leave of absence,' he was told regretfully by the President. Less kind were the brownshirts who marched him out of the building.

Kurt was aged 24 when, later that year he came to England, his family unable to send him money because the Nazi regime did not permit the transfer of funds. Fortunately Kurt's British uncle rode to the rescue and supported him through his graduate studies at Trinity. Kurt retains a special memory of the peace and tranquility of Trinity's Great Court, crystallized one warm July evening as he heard the clock on the northern tower strike six, twice, first the male and then the female chimes.

Kurt began his Ph.D in the field of Roman Law in the Michaelmas term 1934, spending, he recalls, two happy years at Trinity. Less happy were the vacations. Kurt went home to Germany, partly to see his family, partly to be less dependent on his uncle for money. Life in Germany, however, was growing ever more strained for those of Jewish origin, and, as the prospect of war loomed darker, crossing borders became more and more fraught. How does a young graduate student with no Ph.D, no Fellowship, persuade the immigration authorities at Dover that he, a German, should be allowed in? Kurt recalls on one occasion being granted permission to stay for just three months. All this changed, however, through the good offices of Professor H.C. Gutteridge QC and a promising young academic lawyer, Glanville Williams, later a well-known Professor of Law. With their backing Kurt was given first a year's permit for 1936–37, and later, in April 1937, a labour permit.

Anxious to reduce the financial burden on his uncle, Kurt began a time of excessive supervising, not only for Trinity undergraduates reading Law, but also for other Colleges including Clare. At this time his load was staggering – he supervised regularly 10am–1pm, 3pm–7pm and at times 8pm–10pm, notching up more than thirty hours each week. Thus he joined the group of private teachers acting at that time in Cambridge, which included young lawyers starting to practise in London, who would come down to Cambridge to do their supervising and stay overnight. These were known as 'carpetbaggers'. Some,

136

RIGHT: *Professor Kurt Lipstein and Dr Peter Knewstubb in Old Court, summer 2000.*

like R.E. (Ted) Megarry, became eminent lawyers and held high judicial office.

Sunday 3rd September, 1939, meant for Britain the outbreak of war with Germany, and for Kurt the need to register with the police. Then, in the spring of 1940, the Panzers divisions overran the Netherlands, making a mockery of the 'impregnable' Maginot line. The rumour in England was that the Germans living in the Netherlands had actively aided the invasion. Churchill wasn't prepared to take the risk of the same thing happening in England. 'Intern the lot' was his response to what to do about German nationals living in England.

Kurt's internment, initially at least, was a civilized affair. On hearing from his friend Clive Parry of Downing, later Professor C. Parry, that the police had come to arrest him but had told him to have lunch first, he joined the crowd of enemy aliens assembled in the Guildhall.

The next step in the internment process meant an abrupt departure from Cambridge. Kurt, along with other foreigners in Cambridge, was taken by bus to Bury St. Edmunds and dumped in a cowshed. That cowshed should have a plaque on it recording the distinguished figures who, however briefly, resided there. The names would include Max Perutz, OM; Michael Kerr, later Lord Justice of Appeal and Honorary Fellow of Clare; the man who later became Astronomer Royal for Scotland; H. Lehmann, who, after service as a Lieutenant Colonel, RAMC, became a Professor of Chemistry and a Fellow of Christ's College.

The British Officer in charge happened to be a friend of another internee, Richard Samuel, later Head of the Department of Germanic Studies in the University of Melbourne, so internment at this stage was quite amicable. The move to Liverpool a week later was far less so. Walking from the station through the streets of Liverpool was, Kurt recalls, a decidedly unpleasant experience as it meant passing through a gauntlet of hostile Liverpudlians,

not shy of expressing their views of foreigners. Conditions in the camp, too, were decidedly primitive.

However, the people interned, intelligent and energetic, soon set about making a community of themselves. They wanted things run properly and Kurt was actively involved in running the Camp Office. Subsequently drawing on their combined expertise they organized lectures, including one, Kurt recalls, by an expert on the sugar beetle. What made this period especially strange and uncanny to men used to digesting reports of world affairs, was not only the isolation of the camp, but also its insulation. For three months, until August 1940, they had absolutely no news of what was going on in the world outside the camp.

Unbeknown to them, pressure was building up in the country for their release. One advocate, the Bishop of Chichester, recognizing that the internees included extremely talented people, argued that it was ridiculous that men who would be useful outside were being kept inside. After four months in the camp Kurt was released in September 1940, required only to report to the police and obey a curfew from 10.30pm – 7am, a curfew that did not prevent him from fire-watching duty as an active member of the ARP. Re-settled in Cambridge, Kurt resumed not only teaching, included taking over as Secretary of the Faculty, but also the research into those fields in which he was to become eminent – Public International Law, Conflict of Laws, EC Law and, of course, the subject he professed, Comparative Law.

As the war entered its final stages Kurt's life changed very much for the better when he met and, soon after, married Gwyneth. In 1946 he became a University Lecturer in the Law Faculty and continued until 1948 as its Secretary. Some years later, supported by Lord Wedderburn, then a Law Fellow at Clare, Kurt joined the College in 1956. Thus began a long stint of service not only to the lawyers in Clare but also to the greater good of the College as a whole. It is a stint that, fortunately for us, still continues.

clare both sides of the war

J.G. RAWLINSON

I was at Clare on both sides of World War II, coming up from Oundle in 1939, and then returning in 1946 to complete the Natural Sciences Tripos.

In 1939 I had digs in 3 Fitzwilliam Street (Mrs Baxter). My one regret about a very enjoyable life at Cambridge was that I never had rooms in College, apart from a few days before coming up, sitting the Entrance Exam and Littlego.

That year, the first year of the War was hectic. Apart from work (Chemistry, Physics, Maths and geology – the latter a half-subject to make up three), and hockey, I joined the CUOTC gaining a Certificate B. This gave me immediate access on call up to OCTU and a commission in the Army. I also joined the CUMC (Mountaineering Club) with a couple of meets in Wales and the Lakes. The Summer of 1940 was marked by the CUOTC defending the many aerodromes around Cambridge. I was at Oakington, and on arrival we put up railway sleepers on the grass runway to prevent planes landing. Shortly after, we removed them and welcomed our first Blenheim bomber to the field.

In 1946 I returned to Cambridge, a place having been promised by 'Thirks' – Mr Henry Thirkill, Senior Tutor in 1939 and Master after the War. I was then married and lived in a flat in Park Parade off Jesus Green. Many old friends had returned, and I found a marvellous mix of 'old sweats' coming from up to six years in the Forces and 'youngsters' straight up from school. We mixed very well and happily. One memory is of prams outside lecture rooms – brought in by fathers on the way to lectures, and collected by wives on the way to shopping. Another memory is the custom being re-introduced of locking doors at 10 pm. On return to our flat, after an evening out, I opened the door for my wife who promptly entered and shut the door demanding a penny to admit me!

Work on the Tripos was hard after six years away – I found that one of the lecturers was using the identical notes he had used in 1939. There was much skating on the Fens in the hard winter of 1947, and big floods following the thaw. Later we had a canoe holiday on the Cam and Ouse West rivers.

My three years is a time remembered with real joy, it was a fabulous experience never to be forgotten. I went on to a job in the chemical industry as personal assistant to Richard Bennett (Oundle and Clare), MD, of Thorium Ltd in London.

139

BELOW: *1945 matriculation photograph, showing returning scholars in uniform.*

thirkill retires

THE CLARE ASSOCIATION ANNUAL, 1958

Old Clare men will think of this year as the end of an era; for it is marked by the retirement of Sir Henry Thirkill, Fellow from 1910, Tutor from 1920, President from 1930, and Master since 1939. Apart from his distinguished service in the First World War – and many will remember his stories of war and wireless in East Africa – he has lived the full Clare and Cambridge life. Giving up his work in experimental physics he devoted himself as Tutor to the destinies of the College, and then as Master, also to the affairs of the University, serving on the Council of the Senate, the General Board of the Faculties and the Financial Board and, during critical years for the University, as Vice-Chancellor. In public service he took a leading part, whether in ways that received due acknowledgement in his Knighthood, or in many kindnesses that only those close to him knew about. But it is Clare affairs that we have in mind. There are many old Clare men who will recall with gratitude and affection his interest in them on coming up, through their College days, and in their careers on going down – a continuing interest that reinforced his remarkable memory for faces and circumstances. It is good to know that, as Fellow of the College in his retirement from the Mastership, he is still in College – in the Old Court, in his old rooms on F staircase, where he can carry on the hospitality which has marked his long period of office. The devotion of old Clare men to him as to the College was seen in the support which they gave to the building of the new wing in the Memorial Buildings, and they will be happy to hear that this court has been appropriately named 'Thirkill Court'.

In the election of Sir Eric Ashby as Master, the College promises to go from strength to strength. He will bring to us not only the exceptional ability and wide experience that have set him among the leading Vic-chancellors of the country but high personal qualities and a vital interest in undergraduate life – in which Lady Ashby shares fully. They are remaining in Belfast until the Master finishes the major projects which he has initiated there. Meanwhile, Dr H. Godwin is acting as his deputy, and we enjoy the Master's regular visits. We look forward to welcoming him and Lady Ashby, and their two grown-up sons, when they come into residence in the Lodge next October.

*Sir Henry Thirkill
(Master 1939–58)*
W.G. de Glehn, 1947

Oil on canvas,
49" x 39.5"

RICHARD EDEN

Closing years of the old order: 1900–1920

In 1900 the Reverend Dr Edward Atkinson, at the age of 80, was in his 44th year as Master of Clare. The University reforms of 1856–82 were beginning to bear fruit and there were an increasing number of courses and examination options available to undergraduates.

Advanced students were making an appearance in the University to obtain degrees through research projects in science laboratories and in libraries. The reforms had also led to new requirements for college teaching, though the slowly changing Fellowship meant that private tutors from outside the College were often required for supervisions in the new subjects.

Atkinson had been admitted to Clare as a sizar[1] in 1838, the year in which Queen Victoria came to the throne. It was a college of modest distinction and size with a total of about 40 undergraduates. He read Classics and was in the first class in 1842, having taken the Mathematics Tripos earlier in the same year.[2] He became Senior Tutor in 1850 and Master in 1856, and initiated a remarkable period of growth in student numbers, to 70 in 1870 reaching 210 in 1910. This was achieved in a competitive environment in which Clare benefited from the provision of good sporting facilities and notable successes, particularly in rugby. Links were established with the new public schools, including Marlborough College, whose first Headmaster, Matthew Wilkinson, had earlier been a Fellow of Clare.

The academic quality of the Clare men who took honours degrees was good, but they formed only one third of the student body, and the remainder took ordinary degrees or left without a degree. For the honours group in the ten-year period to 1910, half of the Clare candidates in the Mathematics tripos were in the first class, and of those reading sciences about one third obtained Firsts.[3] In Classics and History, Firsts were more rare, with Clare averaging only one every two years.

LEFT: *The Passing of the Old Order. Sir Adolphus Ward, Master of Peterhouse, wearing a mourning rosette in his square for the funeral of Dr Edward Atkinson in 1915, greets Dr H.M. Butler, Master of Trinity, outside the Senate House.*

142

The Senior Tutor, William Mollison, had been 2nd wrangler and Smith's prizeman[4] in 1876 and became a Fellow in that year. He married in 1877 and worked for a period as a mathematics coach, also holding a lectureship at Jesus College. During 1880–94, he was Tutor in Clare, then Senior Tutor until 1913, when he was appointed *Locum Tenens* for the Master. From 1904–15, he was Secretary to the University's General Board of Studies, responsible for all arrangements for academic teaching by the University and the confidant of several Vice-Chancellors. He was Master of Clare 1915–29.

Elections to Fellowships in the nineteenth century were dominated by mathematicians, selected from those who came high on the list of Wranglers. However, the most distinguished scientists in Clare in 1900 were a geologist and a botanist[5]. Thomas McKenny Hughes, Professor of Geology since 1873, became a Fellow of Clare in 1882 and had a major role in developing the Department, including the building of the Sedgwick Museum on the Downing Site. Walter Gardiner, Bursar 1895–1913, obtained a First in the Natural Sciences Tripos in 1881, specializing in botany, and was elected to a Fellowship of the Royal Society for his research on the structure of plant cells. Harry Godwin observes that Gardiner was probably responsible for introducing into the Fellows' Garden at Clare many of the uncommon trees that still flourish there.

Walter Gardiner's predecessor as Bursar, Lucas Ewbank, Senior Fellow in 1900, had been a Wrangler in 1857. G.H.A. Wilson, another mathematician, was Bursar 1913–26. H.M. Macdonald, elected in 1891 after obtaining a Smiths Prize, left in 1904 to become Professor of Mathematics in Aberdeen. J.R. Wardale[6] took Classics and was elected to a Fellowship in 1882. He became Professor of Latin at University College, Cardiff in 1883, but returned to Clare in 1888 as Tutor, and was Senior Tutor during 1915–20.

The Reverend W.H. Fulford was first elected to a Fellowship in 1877. Harry Godwin[7] describes him in 1926 as 'an amiable cleric, who still retained the familiar name Fluffy, conferred on him (when he was Dean) by generations of pre-war undergraduates'. H.M. Chadwick, the University Professor of Anglo-Saxon, was 'a loveable bucolic-seeming man with a soft Yorkshire accent and beyond doubt the college's most distinguished scholar'. In 1922 Chadwick married Norah Kershaw, a student in his own area and also a scholar of great distinction. Together they produced a work of commanding authority, their three-volume book *The Growth of Literature*.

Despite his lack of worldliness, Chadwick had an important role in the development of English studies in Cambridge. Before 1917, English was examined as part of the Mediaeval and Modern Languages Tripos, and only after that year did it became possible to take two parts of the English Tripos and obtain a degree without studying another modern language. Chadwick's ventures into university politics were encouraged and substantially guided by Mansfield Forbes, universally known as 'Manny'.[8] He had taken the History Tripos and in 1912 was elected to a Fellowship in Clare at the age of 22, but a year later he was lecturing to third-year students of Mediaeval and Modern Languages on Anglo-Saxon charters and then on Anglo-Saxon poems.

Both Chadwick and the Professor of English, Sir Arthur Quiller-Couch ('Q'), supported the objectives for the new English Tripos. The aim was the study of modern literature with an emphasis on literary criticism, rather than traditional teaching on philology and the relation to early English. However, there was only one University Lectureship, which had been left vacant following the death of the holder in 1914, so the success of the new approach depended on finding freelance lecturers from scholars in wartime Cambridge in 1917 and from those who returned in 1919. Q was remote from this scholastic scene, but Manny was at its heart, so it was he who found the lecturers and, to a large extent, determined the content and ethos of the new Tripos. These included: B.W. Downs and T.L. Attenborough, who had taken the English section of the old Tripos; S.C. Roberts[9] from Classics and History; E.M.W. Tillyard from Classics and researching in archaeology. I.A. Richards had taken Moral Sciences but was contemplating becoming a mountain guide when Manny persuaded him to lecture for the English Tripos.[10]

During the First World War, emergency statutes for Clare were approved in 1915, and accommodation was provided in college for 50 army cadets. Five Fellows were given leave of absence: Wilson for work in the War Office, Harrison as an instructor in gunnery, and Thirkill as head of wireless with the army in Africa, where he was awarded a Military Cross. Roberts, the Tutor for medical students, and Philip Crick, the Dean, were also away. Crick returned after the war for only two years before becoming the Bishop of Rockhampton.

Some time before the war the Fellows had become concerned about the need for more accommodation for undergraduates, and there is a note in the College Order

143

W.L. Mollison
(Master 1915–29)
Henry Lamb, 1926

Oil on canvas
26 ⅝" x 21½"

144

Book for 29 May 1915, 'that assent be given in general principle that (i) a New Lodge be built for the Master in the Fellows Garden, and (ii) the old Lodge be converted into College rooms. The site refers to the Far Garden, where the Memorial Court now stands, the present Fellows Garden being called the River Garden, and in 1911 it had been decided that it would be too difficult and costly to build there. The idea of a new Masters Lodge was evi-

dently abandoned after the death in 1917 of Mrs Mollison, resulting from a fall on the service stairs of the Lodge. In June 1921 a buildings committee was formed consisting of the Master, Wilson, Thirkill and Roberts, and in November of that year Mr Gilbert Scott was asked to confer with the committee with a view to undertaking the new building.[13]

Building on the past: 1920–1945

The loss of income from student fees during the war and the two-fold inflation of costs caused a crisis in the finances of the University, and help was sought from the government. The Colleges had their own financial problems and were already helping the University through a 'colleges tax' imposed by an Act of Parliament in 1881, giving an annual transfer of about £30,000 to the university. The government provided a similar amount of emergency aid in 1919 and set up a Royal Commission. By 1926, the Universities of Oxford and Cambridge had new constitutions, and the statutes of both Universities and the Colleges had been revised. The independence of the Colleges would be preserved, and in Cambridge the University would receive an annual grant from the government from which lecturers would receive their primary salary, which might be supplemented by a college if the lecturer held a Fellowship.

At the first meeting of the Clare Governing Body in 1926, when the new statutes came into effect, Dr Mollison was Master and there were eleven Fellows. Fulford, Chadwick, Wilson, Thirkill and Harrison had been Fellows since before the war. More recent Fellows were: W.J. Landon – Secretary (chief administrator) of the Engineering Faculty, the Reverend W. Telfer – Dean and later Master of Selwyn, Raymond Priestley – Secretary of the newly formed Board of Graduate Studies, A.D. Nock, a young Classics Fellow who left three years later for a professorship at Harvard, and the Junior Fellow, Harry Godwin, a botanist and a pioneer in the modern development of quaternary research.

'Manny' Forbes was absent from the meeting. Brilliant, likeable, eccentric and wildly disorganized, he was no respector of people or conventions, least of all if they were businesslike and seemingly dull.[14] His lectures for the English Tripos were famously complicated, original and chaotic, and perhaps brilliant, though note-taking was almost impossible.[15] But his writings were slight except for his history of the College, *Clare College 1326–1926*, which is

ABOVE: *Professor Harry Godwin with students during a Botany School excursion.*[10]

From left to right:
Back Row – Dr David M. Churchill (Senior Asst. in Research), Mr Oliver Rackham (Ph.D student), Mr Jim H. Dickson (Ph.D student). Front Row – Student (Unidentified), Dr C. Donald Pigott (Lecturer in Ecology), Professor Harry Godwin.[11]

massive. His whimsical research for this book followed leads that had little to do with the history of Clare and for some years created chaos in the Fellows Library and extended into the Combination Room. Two years late for the 600th anniversary, he produced a two-volume work, heavy and handsome with some 750 pages and 240 plates. The College bore the cost, said to be £6,000, amounting to about one-quarter of the yearly income from endowments. When he died in 1935, his personal collection of books formed the nucleus of what is now known as the Forbes-Mellon Library.

Raymond Priestley had served as a geologist with Shackleton and then with Scott on major Antarctic expeditions. On Scott's last expedition, he led the northern party for an intended six-week reconnaissance equipped only for an Antarctic summer, but they could not be re-embarked due to abnormal ice and, with five others, Priestley survived the winter months in an ice cave bombarded by gales, before trekking to a second rendezvous, where they learnt of the disaster that had overtaken Scott's party. During the war he had a distinguished record in signals and was awarded the Military Cross. After the war, he took a Cambridge degree before becoming Assistant Registrary with responsibility for all graduate students. Later he became Vice-Chancellor at Melbourne University and then at Birmingham University. He was a friend of Paul Mellon's uncle, Percy McMullen, and it may have been this friendship that led to Mellon coming from Yale to Clare.[16] In 1970, on learning about Paul Mellon's gift to Clare to help with the founding of Clare Hall, Priestley said to Terence Armstrong (a Fellow of Clare Hall), 'I'll tell you something about that: I was in my room in the College (in Memorial Court overlooking the entrance from Queen's Road) when I saw Percy McMullen walking up the path. I went up to him and asked what he was doing in Cambridge. "I'm on my way to Trinity College[17] to make arrangements for my nephew to go there" was the reply. "Oh no you're not", I said, "Come up to my room."'

Henry Thirkill came to Clare as an undergraduate in 1905 and was elected to a Fellowship in 1910. He researched on the conduction of electricity in gases, and became a demonstrator in the Cavendish in 1912 under J.J. Thomson, the Cavendish Professor, who rarely remembered when to pay him. He once received his cheque during a chance encounter in King's Parade when J.J. used Thirkill's (not inconsiderable) back to support his

LEFT: *W.L. Mollison (left, Master 1915–29) and G.H. A. Wilson (right, Master 1929–39) in the Combination Room, beneath the painting of Lady Elizabeth de Clare (now in an oval frame in the Hall), 1926.*

BELOW: *Joseph John Howard (the College Clerk) examines the remains of an early master which were discovered in the Chapel, 1935.*

chequebook. In 1920, Thirkill succeeded Wardale as Tutor of Clare, and was Master from 1939 to 1958. He remained unmarried and was entirely devoted to the College; his many personal friendships with former students inspired an impressive flow of letters, up to fifty a day during vacations. The *Conversation Piece* (see p. 112) showing Thirkill with Telfer, the Dean, and Harrison, the Bursar, is a rare illustration of the influence and power

146

that was more commonly concealed by his modest style and genial personality. His wider influence extended into the University through his trusted friends and his long and skilful membership of key committees.

Holding the line: 1945–57

Thirkill was Vice-Chancellor during 1945–47, the most critical post-war period, when new appointments and strategic decisions were made that would affect the University far into the future. These included the appointment in 1945 of Harold Taylor (Clare's Mathematics Fellow in the 1930s) as University Treasurer on his return from war-service. Thirkill was earlier involved in the appointment of John Baker (Fellow of Clare, later Lord Baker) as Professor and Head of the Faculty of Engineering. Nick Hammond, who had succeeded Darby Nock as Director of Studies in Classics, became Senior Tutor on his return from distinguished war service with partisans in northern Greece, for which he was awarded a DSO. Charlie Moule was Dean 1943–51, when he became Lady Margaret Professor of Divinity; Brian Reddaway returned to teach Economics after war service as chief statistician in the Department of Trade; Brian Cooper directed studies in Engineering from 1944, also becoming Bursar when Harrison retired in 1949. After war service in the Army Medical Corps, Michael Stoker came from Sidney Sussex to become a Fellow of Clare and Tutor for medical students.

In 1951, I was elected to a Fellowship, and admitted at the same time as John Robinson, the new Dean, later to become Bishop of Woolwich and famous as the author of the best-selling book *Honest to God*. I was Director of Studies in Mathematics, replacing Robert Rankin who had gone to a professorship in Birmingham and later in Glasgow. Although I was required to supervise for only six hours a week, I was responsible for arranging the supervisions in Mathematics for about 12 men taking the Mathematics Tripos, and about four times as many taking Natural Sciences, so there was quite an organizational problem. My solution was to raid Trinity, a College so replete with Mathematics Fellows that they did not think to use their research students to help with supervisions, the best of whom had been near the top of the Tripos and were better at supervising than most lecturers. This also gave me a pool of contacts which could be traded for help from Shaun Wylie in Trinity Hall and Frank Powell in Caius when I was on leave of absence.

Thirkill was responsible for admissions to Clare from 1920, when he became Tutor, until 1956, only two years before he retired as Master. His admissions policy was the key to determining the character of the College, and its conservatism tempered by his good judgement made Clare a very pleasant community. There was nearly automatic acceptance of those reaching the standard for an entrance scholarship or exhibition, and priority was given to the sons of old Clare men. More generally, admissions were centred round a group of public (fee-paying) schools where he had established good relationships with the headmasters. Provided a headmaster sent him some clever students, others of more modest academic ability would be accepted. Fortunately, mathematicians came mostly from the first of these groups; all those gaining a scholarship or exhibition were accepted, and we also collected some from Trinity who had placed Clare as their second choice.

In the 1950s, Clare Fellows were encouraged through a miniscule grant of expenses to entertain students in their homes, and in the absence of the more interesting social life that has prevailed in Clare since 1972, they appeared to welcome such occasions. My wife and I were then living in a large flat in Belvoir Terrace, in Trumpington Road opposite the Botanic Gardens, and many visiting students became lifelong family friends. My early Clare students included Tim Smiley, whom I attempted to supervise in Applied Mathematics for Part II of the Tripos in 1951. Relieved of the burden of learning uninteresting things, he obtained a Distinction in Part III of the tripos, a PhD in Mathematical Logic and a College Fellowship. He became Professor of Philosophy in the University and was twice acting-Master of Clare. Of a slightly later vintage was Donald Lynden-Bell, who went on to research in Astronomy and gained a Research Fellowship, later becoming Professor of Astrophysics in the University. David Hartley turned from Mathematics in Clare to Computing, and became Director of the University's Computer Service, and a leading government adviser in this area. In 1959 Walter Bodmer was elected to a Fellowship and took over directing studies in Mathematics for the natural scientists. His PhD had been concerned with mathematical genetics, and this led him to a professorship in the Medical School at Stanford University. Returning to the UK, he was Director of the Imperial Cancer Research Laboratories, a post that had been held earlier by Michael Stoker, and was later the Principal of Hertford College in Oxford.

147

Eric Ashby
(Master 1958–75)
Brian Organ, 1975

Acrylic on canvas
60" x 60"

148

Times for change: 1957–72

In January 1958 we offered a place in Clare to a mathematics candidate from Newcastle who had nearly reached the standard for an open exhibition. In interview, I learnt of the educational obstacles that he had encountered, initially through failing the eleven-plus examination, and moving later to a comprehensive school with no experience of teaching for entrance to Cambridge. Eventually, because he had not studied Latin, he declined our offer of a place. When I told this story in June of that year at a Mathematics examiners' lunch in Newnham College, Ray Lyttleton suggested that we should start a movement to remove this obstacle to Cambridge entry. Success came a year later in June 1959, when the Regent House voted to abolish the University's entrance requirement of a qualification in a classical language.

I was less fortunate in seeking to introduce a theoretical physics tripos in the Mathematics Faculty during 1957–58 and had to settle for the second-best option of a Maths with Physics tripos based on a selection of lectures from two faculties. Five years later in 1964, working with Volker Heine of Clare and Neville Mott, the Cavendish Professor, we were able to set up a Theoretical Physics Tripos based in the Physics Department, which I joined in that year. Amongst my research students, who came via this new tripos, was Michael Green, who joined Clare as a Denman Baynes Student, was one of the discoverers of 'String Theory' and later became a Royal Society Professor and a Fellow of Clare Hall. Clare had a strong presence in the Cavendish including Brian Pippard, who succeeded Mott as Cavendish Professor in 1971, and Ken Riley, Lecturer in Physics and Tutor in Clare. In 1972, with remarkable support from many of our colleagues in the physics department, Ken and I set up an interdisciplinary research group on energy studies in the Cavendish, in which 35 graduate students obtained PhDs on subjects ranging from the use of eigenvalue methods for heat flow in buildings to the consumption of energy in villages in Northern Sumatra.

Thirkill's judgement on admissions of undergraduates had been equally good in the selection of new Fellows, but it had consequences that he may not have anticipated, which made Clare College a leader in the times of change. In 1957, when the time came to choose a successor to Thirkill, few of the post-war Fellows had been Clare undergraduates. Their diverse backgrounds made them reluctant to choose a traditional 'Clare man' as the new Master. This ruled out two distinguished Fellows, Harry Godwin and Harold Taylor, who had been so closely associated with Thirkill, and had been key architects of a General Board Report in 1955 that attempted to hold back the tide of change by seeking to limit the growth of faculties and departments – in effect to hold back the growth of new opportunities for research and funding. So a majority of the Fellows wanted to go outside Clare, and the result was the election in 1958 of Sir Eric Ashby, then Vice-Chancellor of Queen's University in Belfast.

When he took up residence in 1959, Ashby staunchly supported John Northam's policy as Tutor to admit students from a wider variety of schools and to set new academic criteria for admissions. It was difficult to explain to old Clare men that their sons would no longer receive priority, but it was equally hard to extend the range of schools to those that had no previous connection with Clare and often no connection with Cambridge. Northam brought in other Fellows to assist in visiting schools and encouraging new applicants.

The need to increase the numbers of Fellows had exercised the Governing Body for some years before the arrival of Ashby, but Thirkill had skilfully diverted their enthusiasm into the well-known cul-de-sac of referral and reports from committees.

The brakes came off with the arrival of Ashby and the number of Fellows increased from 32 in 1958 to nearly 50 in 1963. The number 50 proved to be a ceiling, and for some time it was breached only indirectly by the foundation of Clare Hall as described below. A separate development in 1964 came from the initiative of the Bursar, Brian Cooper, in purchasing St. Regis to provide accommodation for the College's increasing numbers of graduate students.

In 1963 there was a preliminary skirmish about the presence of women in Clare. In response to a request from students for permission to bring women guests to dinner on one night a week in full term, the Governing Body had a lengthy discussion first about whether such an allowance should be granted to Fellows. The vote was 13 to 12 in favour, and subsequently the students' request was also granted. A year later, it was decided that Fellows Designate of Clare Hall would have full lunching rights in the College and at a weekly Clare Hall dinner in the Masters Lodge. The first five included two women, and since we forgot to tell them that women guests were not allowed, there was a third woman at lunch from time to time, much to the puzzlement of those who thought we had elected only two.

ABOVE: *Clare Hall apartments designed by Ralph Erskine for visiting Fellows and their families.*

Talks about the admission of women to Clare began in February 1966, immediately after the legal formalities for founding Clare Hall were completed by the signing of a Trust Deed and its recognition by the University as an Approved Foundation. The initiative came from John Northam, Senior Tutor from 1957 to 1966. Ashby gives credit for its successful outcome to him and his two successors, Tim Smiley and Charles Feinstein.[18] A decision could be implemented only after a change of Statute that required support from two-thirds of the members of the Governing Body, and this caused some delay, but was achieved in May 1970. The following year the first two women Fellows were elected: Dr Lucy King and Mrs Alison Sinclair. In 1972 Clare admitted 30 women undergraduates and was one of the first three of the undergraduate colleges in Cambridge to become co-residential.

Founding Clare Hall

I have written elsewhere about how Clare College came to found Clare Hall,[19] but should mention here some of

150

those involved. On 11 January 1964, the Governing Body gave unanimous approval in principle to a proposal to set up a Clare centre to include: visiting Fellows, research Fellows, permanent Fellows and graduate students, and to be built on Clare land in Herschel Road, about five minutes walk from the Memorial Court. A programme for development, worked out by Eric Ashby, John Northam and myself, included the name Clare Hall that had been suggested by Harry Godwin (later Sir Harry). Brian Cooper and Brian Reddaway played a crucial role through their management of Clare's finances that made the development possible, and Paul Mellon was a major benefactor to the new foundation. Don Holister gave architectural advice, in particular leading to the appointment of Ralph Erskine as the architect for the new buildings that included twenty houses and apartments for Fellows and their families living on the college site in Herschel Road. One of the continuing arrangements between Clare College and Clare Hall allows any Fellow of Clare College on leave of absence to take up the rights of a Visiting Fellow in Clare Hall, and in most years one or two Fellows of the College take up this option.

On the formal foundation of the College in 1966, Brian Pippard (later Sir Brian) moved from Clare College to Clare Hall as its first President, and was succeeded in 1973 by Robert Honeycombe (later Sir Robert), Goldsmith's Professor of Metallurgy. Sir Michael Stoker, formerly medical tutor in Clare College, was the third President during 1980–87, when Clare Hall was granted its own Royal Charter. Anthony Low, Professor of Commonwealth History, was President during 1987–94, and was succeeded by Dame Gillian Beer, King Edward VII Professor of English Literature.

In the year 2000 Clare Hall occupies two sites in Herschel Road, its new West Court providing an additional twenty apartments for visiting Fellows and their families and more accommodation for graduate students. There are about 40 visiting Fellows, 20 research Fellows, 30 permanent Fellows and 120 graduate students. Former visiting Fellows include three Nobel prizewinners, Ivor Gaever for Physics in 1973, Joseph Brodsky for Literature in 1987, and Kim Dae-jung, President of Korea, who was awarded the Nobel Prize for Peace in 2000. A former Clare student, Nick Shackleton, Director of the Godwin Institute for Quaternary Research, now a Professorial Fellow of Clare Hall, was awarded the Crawford Prize for Earth Sciences (equivalent to a Nobel Prize) in 1994 and was knighted in 1998.

The rest of the Century: 1972–2000

In 1966 I became a Fellow of Clare Hall and ceased to be a Fellow of Clare, though we remained as guest members of the College until our new buildings in Herschel Road were completed in 1969. With my involvement in Clare Hall and my new research in 'energy studies', my perspective changed. I noticed the Masters of course. Robin Matthews may not recall how we met in 10 Downing Street, territory more familiar to him than me, when Margaret Thatcher had a 'bash' for some academics and their wives. He came to Clare as Master in 1975, a few years later also becoming Professor of Political Economy, having earlier held a professorship in Oxford and been the Chairman of the Social Science Research Council.

I first noticed Bob Hepple, the present Master, in 1963–64, when the Governing Body was informed that the College had offered a place to a young lawyer, who had fled from South Africa after a period of imprisonment arising from his opposition to apartheid and his close association with Nelson Mandela. During 1964–66 Bob was a graduate student in Clare, and in 1968 he became a Fellow on his appointment as a Lecturer in Law in the University. He left Cambridge in 1976 for a succession of professorial appointments and five years as a full-time Chairman of Industrial Tribunals, before returning to Clare as Master in 1993, two years later becoming also a Professor in the Faculty of Law.

Happily, many of the Fellows who were my colleagues in Clare during the 1950s and 1960s are still active in their academic work and in the college. Kurt Lipstein, a Fellow from 1956, became Professor of Comparative Law, and at age 90 remains active and distinguished in his profession and on his bicycle. There was a family connection too, when I learnt that Brian Reddaway, who had first come to Clare in 1938 and became Director of the Department of Applied Economics, was still lecturing and supervising in 1994–97 when his granddaughter Lucy Crampin and my grandson James Eden were amongst his students.

Others are no longer with us. Duncan Forbes, a nephew of Manny Forbes, became the first Clare Fellow in Modern History in 1947, and was the only Fellow in modern times who could cycle with impunity through the Old Court. During the war he had won the instant award of a Military Cross for holding a key position against repeated attacks on his unit of the Seaforth Highlanders near the Anzio beachhead. His military style was evident to the many students whom he marshalled in his role as Praelector, a post he held for 25 years. Geoffrey Elton, a legendary history teacher and research supervisor, joined the Fellowship in 1954. His books on the Tudor period were classics and his influence on the nature, method and purpose of history was immense. He became Regius Professor of Modern History in 1983 and was knighted in 1986.

The two developments in Clare in the twentieth century that have most changed the character of the College are the admission of women and the rise in the number of graduate students. Amongst the latter were James Watson and Andrew Wiles.

James Watson came to Clare as a research student in 1951, having already completed a PhD at Indiana University, and joined with Francis Crick in the Perutz-Kendrew unit working on the structure of protein molecules in the Cavendish Laboratory. Watson convinced Crick that the structure of DNA might be more fundamental than the structure of proteins. Using prior chemical knowledge and the X-ray diffraction results of Maurice Wilkins and Rosalind Franklin, Crick and Watson developed their double helix model of the structure of DNA, now accepted as one of the most important scientific discover-ies of all time. In 1962 (after the death of Rosalind Franklin), Wilkins, Crick and Watson shared the Nobel Prize for physiology and medicine.

Andrew Wiles[20] came to Clare as a research student in 1974 and was elected to a Research Fellowship in 1977. In Princeton in 1994 he completed one of the most important developments in mathematics in the twentieth century by establishing a proof of Fermat's last theorem, a task that had defeated many of the world's greatest mathematicians since Fermat wrote it down without proof over 350 years ago. The theorem states that the equation $an + bn = cn$ has no solution in non-zero integers n, a, b, and c, if n is greater than or equal to 3.

In 1963, Eric Ashby wrote:

Competition would drive the University towards even greater emphasis on academic quality and research, and the role of colleges would thereby be diminished. There would be greatly increased graduate schools, nests of specialists and a constant stream of visiting scholars. Their social life would revolve around the University departments and the Graduate Centre but not the Colleges, and members of the Faculties would be increasingly

151

LEFT: *Clare Hall West Court showing Gillian Beer House and, to the left, part of the Robert Honeycombe Building.*

152

reluctant to accept the responsibilities of College Fellowships, which would be in competition with their research. Colleges would be very different places – no closing of gates at night, no exclusion of women from senior or junior membership, gathering at lunch but not much communal dining at night, admission of students on academic merit, and the executive Fellowship of the college reduced to (say) a dozen people, paid full-time or part-time by the College . . . The response by colleges to the threat from the development of departments or research groups as the social units in Cambridge would be to seek a complementary role that matched their strengths. One of these is the traditional role of undergraduate supervision, which the College should seek to strengthen by an increase in the fellowship. In research the college could increase the numbers of graduate students and aim to provide facilities or Fellowships to scholars, particularly in humanities, where other support is scarce, this could include support for visiting scholars.[21]

He might have been looking into a crystal ball.

1   Sizar: an undergraduate in receipt of a room and meals or a grant towards living costs.

2   Until 1851, candidates for Honours in Classics (except for the sons of Peers) were required to have obtained Honours in Mathematics.

3   *Cambridge Historical Register 1910,* (Cambridge 1917).

4   Wrangler: First Class in Mathematics. Two Smith's Prizes for Mathematics were awarded each year.

5   C.N.L. Brooke, *A History of the University of Cambridge,* vol IV, *1870–1990,* (Cambridge University Press, 1993) p. 64.

6   See also: J.R. Wardale, *Clare College,* (Robinson, 1899).

7   H. Godwin, *Cambridge and Clare,* (Cambridge University Press, 1985).

8   H. Carey, *Mansfield Forbes and his Cambridge,* (Cambridge University Press, 1984), and Godwin, *op.cit.*

9   S.C. Roberts was already at the University Press; later he became Secretary of the Syndics, then Master of Pembroke.

10 See Carey, *op.cit.* See also E.M.W. Tillyard, *The Muse Unchained,* (London, 1958).

11 This action photograph was taken in March 1962 during a Botany School student excursion at Holme Fen. Professor Harry Godwin, equally at ease in the field as the lecture-room, can be seen here sharing his encyclopaedic knowledge to fire the imagination in all of us. He was the friendly, quintessential teacher, enthusiastically tossing a specimen that showed the contact between reed and Sphagnum peat as he reflected on the different conditions needed to form each. Professor John Corner called it 'forensic botany'.

12 The synergy of that period can be seen later, with Dr Oliver Rackham setting new standards for our understanding and appreciation of the English countryside; Dr Dickson's scholarly work on British moss plants; Professor Pigott's disciplined experimental science and humanism (in the best tradition of Clare College) are mutually supportive and necessary. Professor Godwin perhaps saw the potential in all of us before it was manifest, while uniting us as pupils and providing us with a role model at the very heart of education.

13 See the extract from the memoirs of Harry Godwin, pp. 53–63.

14 For example, see Carey, *op. cit.,* chapter 7.

13 See Knox Cunningham in *Clare Association Annual, 1975–76,* pp. 10–16.

15 In Paul Mellon's autobiography, Paul Mellon & John Baskett, *Reflections in a Silver Spoon,* (John Murray, 1992) p. 117, he says his uncle Percy was a friend of the Head Tutor at Clare College and had offered to arrange for him to go there.

16 Priestley's room in Memorial Court was not on the way to Trinity from any plausible direction (the building of the new University Library had not yet commenced), so I wonder whether Percy McMullen was joking, and was in fact on his way to talk with Priestley or Thirkill about admission to Clare. (RJE)

17 Eric Ashby in *Clare Association Annual 1986–87,* pp. 7–13.

18 Richard Eden, *Clare College and the Founding of Clare Hall,* (Clare Hall, Cambridge, 1998*).* Copies may be obtained from the Clare College Development Office.

20 The son of Maurice Wiles, formerly Dean of Clare.

21 Discussion paper by Eric Ashby, prepared for the Clare College Governing Body Meeting held on 11 January 1964, at which the decision was made that led to the founding of Clare Hall. See also Eden, *op. cit,* pp. 113, 114.

A speech by Lewis Elton at the Commemoration Ceremony for his late brother, Sir Geoffrey Elton, Regius Professor of History, FBA, 20 May 1995.

My task today is not to praise a great historian ... but to throw some light on his early years and on his relationship with his parents, both of whom played important roles in his genesis as a historian. I have been, however, sufficiently influenced by my historian brother to know that I must base my talk on primary sources.

Geoffrey Elton was born as Gottfried Ehrenberg in Tübingen on the 17th of August 1921, into a family of historians. He was, as the German phrase goes, 'erblich belastet' – hereditarily burdened. When he was one week old, his father presented him with his first book, a volume of German lullabies in heavy gothic print, as the 'Grundstück senior Bibliothek' (the foundation of his library) and throughout the first year of his life the progress of our future historian was recorded by his doting father in a sketch book.

Soon Geoffrey was writing historical plays, which were performed by him, his younger brother and their friends, and lovingly preserved by his mother. Here is an example, 'Das Attentat im Laufe der Zeiten' (Assassination through the ages), which had its first – and probably its last – performance on 27th May 1934, when Geoffrey was not quite 13. A friendly critic reviewed it well. It consisted of four tableaux, three tragedies and a comedy, in which Caesar, Gessler and Wallenstein went to their deaths, while Dollfuss, the Austrian Chancellor at the time, was saved by a button which deflated the assassin's bullet. A year later a second attempt at Dollfuss's life was successful and heralded the Nazi menace.

About the same time, Geoffrey's first book appeared, which he had not only written, but also illustrated, typed on his own typewriter with – unbelievably – left *and* right hand justification, and bound. This last skill was due to father having decreed that his sons should not be just bookish, but should learn a craft, and it naturally was that of book binding.

By then the clouds were gathering, although in Masaryk's Czechoslovakia we were sheltered from them until after the Munich agreement in 1938. At this point mother took it into her hands to be responsible for the family fortunes, and while father may have been a major influence on our historian's early years, it was his mother who saved his life and mine. Many years later she told the story in her book of reminiscences, but this is of course only a secondary source. The primary source are the letters of December 1938 and January 1939, a selection of which I presented to Esther Simpson, on the occasion of her University of London Honorary Doctorate in 1984. Esther was the Secretary of the Society for the Protection of Science and Learning and she became one of our guardian angels. On 11th January 1939 she wrote to us that the Home Office would: *'raise no objections to father, who had been awarded a grant by the Society, bringing his family with him'.*

In those dangerous days, one guardian angel was not enough. A second appeared in the shape of A.J. Costain, the Headmaster of Rydal, a boarding school in Wales. Here I must add, particularly within these walls, that I do not believe in angels – guardian or other. My formulation is that in the statistical distribution of refugee fortunes we were at least three standard deviations from the mean on the lucky side. It was Mr Costain and the governors of Rydal who gave Geoffrey and me free places and so made it possible for the family to leave. Mr Costain's letter arrived on the 19th of January and we left Prague on the 10th of February. The story, widely reported in the press recently, that mother bluffed her way past immigration by claiming that her sons spoke perfect English is not correct.

154

At this point I must interpose some recent news. Rydal has just decided to revive the tradition of free places for Czech boys and now also girls, and has instituted a scholarship, to be named the Ehrenberg-Elton Scholarship in memory of my family. I feel both humble and proud to have played my part in this and am assigning my late father's on-going royalties to the Fund. I hope that others, perhaps at this gathering, may also contribute to this venture, details of which are available from the Headmaster of Rydal who is here.

Back to 1939. We arrived in England on the 14th of February, St. Valentines Day. More that sixty years later Geoffrey wrote: *'within a few months it dawned upon me that I arrived in the country in which I ought to have been born.'*

I found the primary source for this statement among Geoffrey's papers after his death. It is an essay which he wrote at Rydal, and although it is undated, internal evidence places it in June 1939, when he had learned English from scratch for just four months. Let me read you the first paragraph of it, to give you a flavour of his English at the time:

The course of events is not directable by our feeble hands, which arrangement is sometimes most fortunate, sometimes less. I decidedly came to the latter conclusion when the second month of the new year saw me leaving home and everything I was fond of, and going away to a country the language of which was known to me less than vaguely, the manners and customs even absolutely strange.

Geoffrey just failed to get an Oxford scholarship ... so he had to take an external London degree, with University Correspondence College Cambridge, and here again both my parents played a very important part of his life. Geoffrey did not find the discipline of the correspondence course to his liking and the essays which he wrote for the long suffering Mr Hemming, his tutor, were much too provocative for the purpose of safely passing the perhaps somewhat pedestrian examination. Even then Geoffrey was Geoffrey, but his mother managed to tame him, so that he got his BA. Father contributed in another way. The London degree contained a special subject, for which the College was unable to tutor. So father took over and that is why the future Tudor historian's first published paper is concerned with the terminal date of Caesar's proconsulate. Uniquely as an external student, Geoffrey was awarded the Derby studentship and after two years in the army started historical research in London. His marriage to Sheila, another historian, completed his formative years.

As the years progressed and Geoffrey wrote book after book, both his parents to the best of my knowledge read and commented on most, if not all, of them in manuscript, as long as they lived. His mother's last extant letter, written in feeble hand, partly English and partly in German, dates from two years before her death. She died on Geoffrey's 52nd birthday, the 17th of August 1973.

I have told you something about how Geoffrey became a historian. Let me end with two little poems from a collection which his – and my – mother wrote bilingually, each poem in both English and German, sometimes the English first, sometimes the German. I am joined in this by my son Ben.

Questions

Where do we belong on earth?
Is it death, is it re-birth?
What is lost and what is found?
Where is, in a deluge, ground?
Who is weak if not the strong?
Are we right, the others wrong?
Do we ask what lies ahead?
Is there hope, not only dread?
Who's still with me, who is gone—
Questions many, answers none.

Frägen

Wo ist unser Heim auf Erden?
Ist es Sterben, ist es Werden?
Was Verlust und was ist Fund?
Wo ist in der Sintflut Grund?
Wo ist Kraft, wenn nicht im Schwachen?
Sind wir's, die es richtig machen?
Fragen wir danach, was droht?
Gibt es Hoffnung, nicht nur Not?
Wer lebt noch und wer ist tot?
Seid Ihr da? Bin ich alleine—
Viele Fragen, Antwort keine.

There is no going back

When moving on,
We should not think that we shall find
The things again that we have left behind,
For they have gone.

Unless we know
We are not going back to what we knew,
but ever moving on to something new,
We should not go.

Es gibt kein Zurück

Denkt nicht, wir gehn
Und können wiederkehren, wenn wir wollen,
Die Dinge, die wir hinterließen, sollen
Wir nie mehr sehn.

Ist Euer Blick
Im Suchen nach dem Alten so verblendet.
Daß Ihr nicht wißt, daß Iht im Neuen endet.
Geht nicht zurück.

CLARE IN THE 1950S

My only particular memory of Clare is going up from my north country grammar school to take the scholarship exam in early December 1954. When I arrived at the Porter's Lodge there was a message for me to see the Master (Sir Henry Thirkill). I duly went along to the Lodge at the appropriate time and was overawed to be met by the Butler in a tailed coat etc.. I was shown into the Lodge dining room where the Master sat in a pool of light by a long polished table. We had, I remember, an amicable conversation about all sorts of things (including Yorkshire cricket about which the Master seemed to know a great deal). The whole interview was conducted in a gentle, probing, yet entirely courteous manner. At the end, the Master got up and said 'Mr Hardy, if you come to this College you will do your National Service first. Good afternoon.' At that point I realized it was time to go. It was my first experience of Cambridge and getting on for 50 years later, it stays with me with absolute clarity. Henry Thirkill clearly knew whom he wanted in his College, and whom he did not. I am glad to say that ultimately I was awarded an Exhibition, but I guess the interview was a critical element in all this.

The Right Reverend Robert M. Hardy, MA
Lord Bishop of Lincoln

A UNIQUE EXAMINATION

I visited Clare from Loretto during the summer of 1941 to take the College Entrance Exam. I had been unable to attend on the regular date, so was on my own.

I was admitted to the Master's Lodge by a maid who directed me upstairs to meet the Master, Henry Thirkill. Smiling and affable, he welcomed me and then escorted me into a beautifully proportioned room overlooking the gardens and the backs. I was led to a Chippendale chair and table placed beside an open window. Here the sun shone and gentle breezes wafted in the scent of flowers in full bloom.

An examination paper in Maths was handed to me, after which I was left alone amidst these beautiful surroundings. After about an hour, the maid entered with a tray bearing a glass and a decanter of sherry! 'The Master thought you might like some refreshment, sir', she said.

Those were the days!

F.L.M. Pattison, Ph.D., Sc.D., MD.

1956 MAY BALL POSTER.

This May Ball Poster from 1956 was sent in by Christopher White, who writes:

It was great fun organizing the Ball that year as we were risking some fundamental changes. Up till then the May Ball had consisted of dancing in the Hall and supper down in the crypt, which at that time was dirty and dusty and – I believe – only used for that one occasion a year.

We decided to have dancing to a leading London band on a floor laid in a marquee in the court (which some of the Fellows were not too keen on at first), with supper in the Hall, a 'Night Club' in the crypt, and an open floor across the river in the garden for dancing to a Caribbean steel band. In those days it was all considered to be rather ambitious. Luckily it was a beautiful clear evening and was very well supported.

Unfortunately I cannot remember the details of what the costs were, but I believe we could buy champagne in quantity at below £1 per bottle and the offer of a free bottle was meant to be a good attraction to help ticket sales.

the college staff

TIMOTHY THOMPSON

'The Master desires that Bedmakers and other college servants take notice that the pouring of slops or soapy bath water into the gullies in the court, and the alteration of the Electric Light wiring, or of the flexible cords connected with the lamps, are absolutely prohibited. Any servant who offends against this prohibition will render himself liable to instant dismissal.'

Thus wrote Dr Atkinson on 13 March 1907. It might be seen as a forerunner of a Health and Safety policy now required by Government legislation, but the threat it contains could hardly be in any way appropriate under current employment law! Much has changed in the last century as conditions of employment of the original servants improved and the title 'servant'

BELOW: *Instruction from Dr Atkinson to bedmakers, 13 March, 1907, regarding slops.*

was dropped (only in the 1970s). However, the overriding theme throughout has been one of great loyalty and devotion to the service of the College by servants and staff who have never been particularly well paid, but who have always felt that the College as their employer had a caring nature.

This chapter is about these people and must start with the obvious apology that the vast majority of them cannot be mentioned and their omission must not be taken as a slight on the great contribution they have made to the life of the College throughout the twentieth century. As a general rule the author has had to limit mentioning individuals to those who served the College for more than 30 years – and there are many of those!

Family Connections

In many cases whole families have been involved and even several generations. As far as the Fellowship is concerned the Fellows' Butler has always been someone whose primary function is their care and attention. The turn of the century found Mr Henry Charles Phipps in this illustrious post; he joined the staff at the age of twenty in 1866 as a gyp and became Fellows' Butler in 1879, holding the office until his retirement in 1919 and having clocked up fifty-three years' service to the College. Phipps was known to many students, as well as Fellows, for his unfailing cheerfulness and courtesy and an extraordinary memory; he kept the Combination Room and the College silver in pristine condition and became the 'father' of the servants in his later years and a leading light in their social gatherings. He enjoyed the honour of waiting on the Prince of Wales in 1878 when Dr Atkinson was Vice Chancellor; the Prince drove down into Old Court in a carriage and pair and was the first person to smoke in Hall, which broke the ice for future generations. The turtle purchased for the soup on that occasion weighed 120lbs. Henry married

RIGHT: *Mr Henry Phipps and Mrs Phipps, c.1919.*

Elizabeth Frances Shirman in 1868 and, although she had no official College appointment, she proved a great helpmate in her husband's duties. Their photograph, taken on his 70th birthday, is reproduced from Volume II of *Clare College 1326–1926*.

We are fortunate today to have similar devoted family service from the current Fellows' Butler, Mr Peter Allinson, who was appointed Under Butler in 1976 and promoted to Fellows' Butler in 1982. However, in contrast to the Phipps, Mrs Allinson not only provides great support for her husband and family, but has held a key appointment as College Senior Housekeeper since 1986, having been a Hostelkeeper at the Colony since 1978. 'Billie', as she is affectionately known, runs the largest department in numbers of staff and is responsible for the bedmakers and janitors who look after the three College sites, both in term and during our busy conference seasons. The Allinsons' photograph appears alongside the Phipps', although perhaps it is a moot point as to who should be sitting. As with Henry Phipps, Peter Allinson has waited on royalty in the form of the Chancellor, Prince Philip and the Prince of Wales on occasions in Hall. He continues the important task of care of the College silver and is renowned for his devoted care of the wine cellar and his valuable advice on its contents. The Allinsons' connections with Clare are much more extensive because Billie's

160

BELOW: *Braeside 1958–59, with the reunion* (RIGHT) *in 1989.*

parents both worked for the College and lived at the Colony. Her father, Mr Arthur Bass, worked in the Combination Room for eight years and her mother was the Hostelkeeper of Braeside at the Colony for thirty-one years from 1958. The photographs show her students who matriculated that year and at their reunion with Mrs Bass in 1989, her 80th year. As Hostelkeeper in the 1950s, it was her responsibility to ensure that girls were out of her young men's rooms by 10pm and that the men were in by midnight; she provided their breakfast every morning and allowed them the use of her kitchen between 4 and 5pm only. The ground floor windows of Braeside were locked to keep students in, rather different from today when the purpose is to keep intruders out.

Another family's two generations span the years from 1933 to the present day with just a two-year gap between father and son. Mr George Hearn hitch-hiked to Cambridge from his family house in Norfolk in 1933 to start a labouring job at the University Library site, but because of his smart appearance he was noticed by the Bursar who immediately offered him a job, initially as bedmaker and a short time later as the T staircase gyp. His duties included heaving coal from the cellar at 6.30am to remake the fires in his gentlemen's rooms after they had left for lectures, cleaning the complete staircase with the bedmaker Florrie Cornell and cleaning shoes and dirty crockery from dinners taken in rooms the night before. At about 11.30am he went to Old Court to help serve lunch and have a meal himself before going home. He returned at 5pm to wash-up the gentlemen's afternoon tea and then over to Old Court again for service of dinner; he had to check that 'gated' students were in their rooms by sunset and was seldom home before 9pm, and much later for special functions. He also found time to work at the Pitt Club as Under Butler when not required at Clare. He ruled T staircase with an iron hand until his retirement in 1975 and was once incensed to discover a gentleman from another College using one of his baths; after a moving one-way conversation the student left in rather a hurry. But he also cared for his students like a father and one young man who did a lot of entertaining would never have got to early lectures without George's assistance. On his retirement the man concerned gave George lunch at his Chambers in London.

George's son, Richard, joined the College Portering Department just three years after his father's retirement and has given valiant service for the last twenty-two years, mostly in Old Court, where his attentive eye seldom misses an illegal cycle being wheeled through the Court. He was appointed Senior Porter for Old Court in 1990 and his wife, Shirley, who has worked as a Tourist Custodian here in recent years, is now helping the Head Porter in his important role as College Safety Officer.

Miss E.L. Greenwood rendered devoted service for 38 years as Housekeeper of the Master's Lodge until her death in 1952; her period of service included three Masters' terms and she treated all visitors to the Lodge with unfailing courtesy. Her brother Tom Greenwood was the Senior Porter in Memorial Court at that time and went on to complete nearly 40 years, finishing as Head Porter before retirement in 1961 – a kind and wise man.

Gyps and Bedders

G.A. Roberts served the College from 1924 to 1957, starting as a gyp on F staircase, before promotion to Fellows'

RIGHT: *Henry Thirkill and G.A. Roberts, College Servants' Match, c.1937.*

Butler after the Second World War; he proved a real martinet to the terror of some of the more junior Fellows, especially those who failed to book in for meals. The picture shows him playing bowls with the Master, Sir Henry Thirkill, at the annual Fellows-Staff sports day.

Ballad of My Bedder

A Bedder is a lovesome thing
So dainty and so debonair.
The mighty Milton could not sing
His gracious lady of the stair:
How then, O Princess, should I dare
Where angels fear, to be a treader?
Forsooth, I do not greatly care;
I'll sing the praises of my Bedder.

My Bedder wears a wedding ring;
My Bedder has a haughty air;
And of the heartfelt praise I bring
I fear she is but half aware.
Tea, sugar, love with her I share.
I have adored her and have fed her.
Please to strike up my favourite air.
I'll sing the praises of my Bedder.

162

What grace of action she will fling
Into the washing of a pair
Of cups or saucers, shattering
My china with a savoir faire
I have not met with otherwhere.
Surely some happy Fate hath led her
To make my comfort her affair.
I'll sing the praises of my Bedder.

Princess, within your lonely lair
Be thine to make thy nose the redder.
And mine this pleasant task to bear.
I'll sing the praises of my Bedder.

Jacques 1924

On his retirement in 1966, after 47 years at Clare, Phil Smith wrote the following for the Clare Annual:

It was on 9th February 1919 that I entered Clare College with a letter of introduction from Professor Chadwick to see the Bursar who was then G.H.A. Wilson. I had no reference, only that I was a Corporal with a good army record. The Bursar engaged me to start on that same day to be under-butler to Mr Phipps, a grey-whiskered man in his sixties. I waited in hall that night and my very first undergraduate was A.C. Chibnall. He had just come back from the war and I think he was Captain of the Boat Club. The Master was then Dr Mollison with whom I came into contact quite a lot. At that time I also remember Sir Henry Thirkill, who had just come back from the war, crossing the court dressed in the uniform of a Major.

In June 1926 the College celebrated its 600th birthday and Princess Mary came and had lunch in the Combination Room and the Butler asked me to wait on her. In September of the same year the Bursar, then Mr Harrison, asked me to take over 'D' staircase. It was then that I came to know the undergraduates more.

I was very interested in Rugby and during the Lent Term of 1927 I had the pleasure of having J.S. Synge on 'D' staircase (he was capped for Ireland). When he returned from vacation he brought me a big bunch of shamrock which I planted in my garden at home but the next year it turned out to be a lovely patch of white clover! Six years later I was to have the Scottish International A.W. Walker on 'D' staircase. After each match his father would give a dinner party for about twenty people in D6 – what a night!

Then in 1939 the war started, but I knew that I would not have to go because I was invalided out of the 1914–18 war. The College set up a Servants Fire Service and we did firewatch duty until 1940, after which the undergraduates took over. Sir Henry

Thirkill, then Master, and I did many hours duty in the crypt together.

Time passed and then Sir Eric Ashby became Master of Clare. He sent for me soon after his arrival and asked me if I would continue to help him with his parties and dinners. This I have done, even after my retirement, and I hope to be able to do so for as long as I can because it is always such a pleasure to help the Master and Lady Ashby.

And now I should like to take this opportunity of thanking all the men on 'D' staircase, and those who lodged at Histon Road, who very kindly contributed to the handsome cheque and lovely signature book that the Master presented to me and my wife at the farewell party the Master so generously gave me on my retirement on 27th September 1966.

I also want you all to know that I still race my pigeons!

Stan and Doris Barker were the last husband and wife partnership working on the staircases; he joined the College in 1935 as a kitchen porter carrying meals to undergraduates' rooms, even four-course dinners as far afield as the Colony. He left at the outbreak of war, served in the Royal Artillery and returned to the College in 1963 as a gyp. Meanwhile his wife, Doris, had started work as a bedmaker in 1954, firstly on A and B staircases but moving to Thirkill Court when it opened in September 1955. They both retired in 1975 and he was the last survivor of that antediluvian race, the gyps. We have been glad to welcome Stan and Doris at the annual gathering of College pensioners for many years.

Porters

The College has been well served by many members of the Portering Department throughout the Century. The Head Porter's appointment has been a key one in all Colleges for many years and Porters' stories are legion, for they are always in the 'front line' and have to deal with an extraordinary variety of 'customers'. 1955 saw the retirement of Dick Neaves, who for 36 years had served as a gyp, porter and Head Porter; his sterling character, helpfulness and ability to recognize and welcome returning alumni was much praised. Doug Taylor, former Army Major, died whilst on duty as Head Porter in 1976 and his death was mourned by all.

Joan Leaven (now Carter) served as a loyal, kindly Hostelkeeper at the Colony from 1964 to 1995; after the death of her first husband she married Gordon Carter, the Colony Porter, in 1990.

The College Clerk

Again, fulfilling the tradition of long service, we find that only three people have filled this key appointment throughout almost all of the century. Mr J.J. Howard was appointed as the first ever College Clerk in 1904, on a weekly wage of ten shillings, which was doubled after one year. He served for forty-nine years with great distinction and resided in Etheldreda at the Colony for much of this period. His distinctive, elegant figure could be seen making its way to the College Office on foot every day with gloves, cane and a rose of Sharon buttonhole. He once had occasion to reprimand a firm who sought payment before the despatch of goods by pointing out that the College had never failed to meet its obligations in six hundred years! His son-in-law to be, Mr Christopher Emery, joined the College in 1935 at the age of 19 years

and was called up for service with the Royal Air Force during the War. Howard stayed on after the retiring age for about a year to see in the new Bursar, Mr Brian Cooper, and then Chris Emery was appointed in 1953. Apart from his war service, Chris Emery gave the whole of his working life to the College, fulfilling a wide range of responsibilities with great ability; he kept meticulous accounts, looked after buildings and dealt with all staff matters – appointments, salaries, pensions, discipline and welfare. He invariably brought the opened post to the Bursar with suitable replies already drafted. He was well supported by Percy Smith who retired in 1966 after 40 years service as a clerk.

Outside work Chris Emery was well known in the City, being an active member of the Friendly Society, the Ancient Order of Foresters as Chairman and Chief

164

Ranger of the East Midlands region and an active member and treasurer of the City Hockey Club. Like his father-in-law before him, he delayed his retirement to smooth the takeover by another new Bursar, Mr Brian Smale-Adams, in 1979. Thereafter the Emerys continued to live in the Lodge at the Colony and he worked part-time on the Library Appeal for several years; he died in 1996 at the age of 80 and his funeral service was held in the College Chapel. His family, which includes his son who is Chief Clerk at Trinity, presented a fine bench in his memory which graces the Scholars' Garden.

Chis Emery's successor, Mr Peter Barron, completes the trio who have scrupulously guarded the College's finances over the century. Peter joined the College at the tender age of fifteen years and has already completed over forty years unbroken loyal service, although with plenty more to go! He succeeded Chris Emery in the newly designated post of Chief Clerk in 1979 and has provided stalwart support for Mr Smale-Adams and his successor, Brigadier Thompson. One of his many achievements in the last decade has been to mastermind the change to computerized accounting systems for, not only the accounts themselves, but also salaries and automated payments to contractors and suppliers.

Sports Staff

Rowing has been a keenly fought competitive sport between Colleges throughout the century and Clare has been fortunate to have been very well served by the three Boatmen whose loyal contributions have spanned almost the whole hundred years. Fred Masters was appointed in 1893 before the building of the Clare Boathouse in 1898–1900, which incidentally was designated a Listed Building in 1996. Masters worked for an amazing fifty-three years and handed over to Henry Benham after the Second World War. Of Masters it is recorded that 'he was a short, heavy man with cheeks a wintry red and proverbial white moustache … he combine[d] the attributes of a legend, an actuality and a dependable hypothesis,' always cheerful and in good spirits 'whether November winds swept down from Ely or Henley swelter[ed] beneath a breathless June evening.'

Harry Benham had been apprenticed to Masters from 1936, but was called up and served in the Royal Air Force throughout the war. Under his able coaching and impeccable care of the boats and other equipment, Clare rose to be Head of the River in 1949. He died in the tragic circumstances of suicide in 1963, leaving the Club in a desperate situation.

The College was extremely fortunate to obtain as his successor Peter Frost who was to serve so very well for thirty-five years. Coming at the very difficult time of his predecessor's death, shortly to be followed by a mutiny against their Captain by the first May Boat and then another tragic accidental death the following year, the Club was only saved from being closed down by the personal intervention of the Master, Lord Ashby. Oarsmen of that difficult time in 1964 got to know Peter as a strong, kind, quiet man who gave them wonderful support, despite the fact that his own job was under threat. The Club recovered due in large measure to Peter's work as an excellent craftsman and superb coach; his customary cheerful welcome at the Boathouse, especially for returning members, was regularly backed up by a welcome and a cup of tea from his wife Vera. His reputation as the best Boatman on the Cam led to several approaches by the University Blue Boat but he never waivered from his loyalty to Clare. Peter remained in harness despite the onset of cancer from which he died in August 1998, his 65th year., thereby sadly denied the pleasures of retirement which was due the following month. His funeral was attended by his family, many members of the College and colleagues; in November 1998 a large gathering of former 'Boaties' returned to Clare for his moving Memorial Service in the Chapel, and we have been pleased to welcome Vera to the annual pensioners' lunch since then.

The College sports ground at Bentley Road was laid out on land bought from Trinity College and first used in 1938. The pavilion was built just before the war when the ground was then ploughed up for growing vegetables to help the war effort. It was the formidable task of Ernie Hobbs, our first groundsman, to turn the 'cabbage patch' back into the splendid ground it soon became and is today. Ernie came from good sporting stock, being the nephew of Sir Jack Hobbs the great England cricketer; in his younger days Ernie was an accomplished player for Cambridgeshire. He served for thirty-six years and many generations of Clare sportsmen will remember him with great affection, not only for all he did to improve the facilities available, but for his shrewd and relevant advice about their sports. Some will similarly remember both Ernie and Mrs Hobbs as caring College 'landladies', since for several years Clare undergraduates had rooms in the Bentley Road pavilion. When Ernie retired in 1973 they

FRED MASTERS: AN APPRECIATION

1893-1931

A HEAD-WIND whistles down the Ditch. A shivering knot of eight men, whose stomachs seem long since to have fled through the soles of their feet, stand nervously on the bank and swing their arms or prance the tow-path in vain efforts to keep warm. The last day's racing of the Lents is about to begin. The past Clare captains and the old Trial Caps stand grouped about a short, heavy man in overcoat and cap with cheeks a wintry red and a proverbial white moustache. New faces are at the old thwarts. Familiar names have changed to strange. The clinker is new. The old tholes have given way to swivels. Freddy alone, of all the old traditions, seems to stand unchanged in years. There is, in fact, considerable question as to whether Freddy will ever alter very much. And the crews that with fresh hopes each year creep into their ship at the bank know this, and they too depend, as did once their fathers who now look admiringly on, upon this quality in Freddy to launch them on their last race with an accuracy and efficiency which has passed into history. For Freddy is for them the hope of the future moments, as he is a link, for older men, that binds them to the present. He is of the past, the present and the future. In this he is strangely timeless, for he stands as the foundation of past successes, the mainstay of the present, and the hope of rowing generations yet to come. He combines the attributes of a legend, an actuality and a dependable hypothesis, and it is impossible to imagine Clare rowing without him. Past years have seen captains who have failed and secretaries who have forgotten, but Fred has neither failed nor has he forgotten, and above all, in remembering, rarely has he been heard to complain. Whether November winds sweep down from Ely, or Henley swelters beneath a breathless June evening, he is always the same, always cheerful and in good spirits.

For nearly forty years he has been the faithful follower of Clare's triumphs and disasters, the loyal friend of all those who, like him, have cherished in their hearts a true affection for college rowing. It is impossible at this time not to feel a debt of deep gratitude toward the man who, through his patience, devotion and willingness at all times and in all seasons to work toward the founding of a great rowing tradtion, has meant as much to the Clare Boat Club as any single man in the past hundred years.

*Lady Clare Magazine XXV/*3, Easter Term 1931

166

moved to a College flat in Queen Edith's Way, where Mrs Hobbs still resides.

Today we are fortunate that Mr Roger Pearl, who was appointed Groundsman in 1979, keeps the grounds in the immaculate condition in which Ernie left them and is responsible for the reputation of the cricket ground as up to, or better than, the standard of Fenners.

The Head Gardener

Longevity of dedicated service has also been the hallmark of the College gardeners; although little is recorded about the gardens in the early part of the century, Walter Barlow, who was to become Head Gardener after the war, first joined the College as an under-gardener in 1929 having previously received his training in Welch's Nurseries on the Huntingdon Road. After service in the Second World War he succeeded G. Clark as Head Gardener in 1945, inheriting gardens which had inevitably suffered, not only from neglect, but also having been used extensively for growing vegetables like the Sports Ground. Under the direction of Professor Nevill Willmer, whose article is reproduced elsewhere, plans were drawn up in 1946 for rehabilitating the Fellows' Garden and carried out quickly by Walter Barlow and his staff. In a few years they transformed that garden and the rest of the College

grounds from a veritable wilderness into a setting which attracted visitors from afar, as it does still today.

In August 1951 Mr Brian Arbon joined the gardening staff at the tender age of 15 and, except for a two-year break of national service in the RAF, he has served the College with great dedication ever since. In 1961, Walter Barlow died suddenly and Brian was appointed Head Gardener, a post that he still holds today, after thirty-nine very successful years. His efforts were recognized by the award of the British Empire Medal in the Queen's' Birthday Honours in 1992 and the presentation was made by the Lord Lieutenant of Cambridgeshire on 30th September in the Master's Garden. He was also presented with the Royal Horticultural Society's Long Service Award by Professor Willmer the previous year. Brian Arbon will retire in 2001 and plans to leave, not surprisingly, before the next May Ball; in more recent years these Balls have caused him and his faithful team considerable anguish and extra work.

The Catering Department

Prior to 1924 the Kitchen Manager was not a College servant, but ran all aspects, kept any profit and bore any loss; after this time Colleges were made more responsible for their catering and employed staff accordingly. Some of these stalwarts of the kitchens include Arthur Bye, who was 2nd Chef from 1951 to 1981 and then worked part-time in the gardens, and Cyril 'Mickey' Rookard, who retired in January 1980 after no less than 50 years as Pastry Chef. Ernie Tookey was Head Chef from 1933–1981. Bernard Brittain managed the department from 1924–1974 with a break for war service in the Catering Corps; his particular achievement was to feed the College successfully from temporary kitchens in Old Court for nearly two years during the last major refurbishment. Edgar Brookman died in 1950 after 40 years service in the Buttery and as a 'Marker' in Hall, where he demonstrated unique powers of memorizing faces and names, so important in that role.

The work of the Department has expanded significantly with the advent of conferences, catering for outside functions and wedding 'breakfasts' which now average a dozen a year. Mr Riccardo Chieppa came to Clare as Butler in 1981 and took over from Henry Fleck as Catering Manager in 1988; he manages this busy department with skill and devotion, providing a high standard of catering for all.

BELOW: *Mr Brian Arbon with the Lord Lieutenant of Cambridgeshire, 1992.*

The College Nurse

The following poem by an anonymous student in 1937 shows how that nurse and her successors have been greatly valued:

Lines Composed on Hearing The Advent of
The College Nurse

Hail! Mistress of sad fortune's ills
With your thermometers and pills
We wait your
Diagnosis.

On stepping from our morning bath
A thousand foes beset our path
From warts to
Varicosis.

When night has lengthened into day
And still the snakes are green and play
Protect us from
Neurosis.

But, O white angel, this we pray
Who read the papers every day
Spare us
Halitosis.

Buildings Repair and Maintenance

The College did not employ maintenance staff in the early part of the century, but recruited its first decorator in very unusual circumstances. The Master, having found a gyp in bed with his housekeeper, insisted that they get married, which would have been laudable had the gyp been single; his enforced marriage was shortly followed by a jail sentence for bigamy! However, he put his time to good use by learning the trade of interior decorator, and was re-employed as a decorator by the College on his release.

Ron Frost joined the College in 1960 as our first carpenter and was followed a year later by David Parfey, who had learnt his trade as a plumber working with the lead on the roof of King's College Chapel. Thus began the fledgling Maintenance Team that was to expand considerably. Ron retired in 1987, but returned to help the Catering Department at Feasts and other large functions until the late 90s.

David Parfey rose to become Clerk of Works and led the team for many years before moving on to look after major projects and the Graduate Housing properties in his last seven years; in this latter role he supervised most of the major refurbishment of Memorial and Ashby Courts, before retiring in August 1998 after 38 years devoted service.

Alan Watson joined the Maintenance Staff in 1968, rising to become Deputy to David Parfey and later Maintenance Supervisor in charge of the team, which now numbers 11 craftsmen in all. He is now Clerk of Works and will retire in 2001, having completed 33 years of exceptional service.

Much more could be written about the great contribution made to the life of the College and the well-being of our Fellows and Students by the dedicated men and women who have worked here during the twentieth century as servants and staff. However, in drawing this chapter to a close, apologies should again be made to those whose names it has not been possible to mention.

clare sport through the twentieth century

KEN RILEY

I came up to Clare in the mid-fifties, and am still here, so I have some acquaintance with what has happened since then. However, I have had to rely on the writings of others for the first half of the twentieth century, and my principal sources for this have been chapter X of *Clare College 1326–1926*, edited by Mansfield Forbes and published in 1929 to celebrate the College's sexcentenary, and a selection of the club reports that appeared in the Lady Clare Magazine over that same period. The relevant chapter in the College history was largely compiled by Dr (later Professor and then Sir) Harry Godwin, then a recently appointed Fellow.

Sports as we now know them hardly existed in Cambridge before the start of the nineteenth century. Of the games currently recognized – loosely defined as those in which there is now at least one annual competition between Cambridge and Oxford – only a form of football was played, and that was confined to the precincts of particular colleges, but probably included Clare. The ban on extramural football arose out of a University match played in 1579 against a town team from the Chesterton area, which degenerated into a battle in which 'many University representatives had their heads broken by staves and others had to take refuge in the river'.

The early 1800s saw the start of some organized sports at both University and college level, and the first competitions held against Oxford were at cricket (1827) and rowing (1829). Varsity matches in the two football codes did not follow for another fifty years or so – rugby in 1827 and soccer (at that time Association football) in 1874. This period also heralded a time in which Clare produced far more Blues and internationals than its share of University numbers would indicate it should. For the last two decades of the nineteenth century and the first of the twentieth, Clare was probably the dominant college on the sporting front. By the same token, the first decade of the period

under review was, in general, the College's most successful on the sports field, though other purple patches were to follow in particular sports. Since a number of Clare's alumni from the last twenty years of the previous century achieved some of their most notable successes in the twentieth, I have taken license to include them in this review.

In the early days, individual clubs were formed as a result of groups of enthusiasts banding together to form teams or to share a common interest in more individual activities. These clubs ran themselves and financed their activities by individual subscriptions, occasionally augmented, it would appear, by donations from the Fellows.[1] However, the cost of some subscriptions, particularly to the Boat Club, were high, and, with typically Clare egalitarian spirit, it was decided in 1886 that a single uniform subscription should allow a man to take part in any form of sport at which the College was represented.

Thus the Amalgamated Clubs came into existence and took over the running of all the clubs, meeting major expenses such as looking after the ground and the purchase of boats. The basic funding of Clare's sport continued along these lines for more than three-quarters of a century, though when, following the Second World War, the Government introduced scholarships, and later grants, for university students, part of the cost was met by the fee element of the awards. Clare College Amalgamated Clubs remained under that name until the early 1970s when a change was made to reflect the fact that other, non-sporting interest groups, such as the Music Society, the Christian Union, the chess club and the darts team, had come under its wing. The CCAC became the Clare College Students' Association with a constitution drafted by a committee consisting of the present Master (then Mr B.A. Hepple), Matthew Parris (then President of the JCR and later an MP and columnist of *The Times*) and myself (then Senior Treasurer of the CCAC). Later still, when students started to acquire 'rights', as a result of both the general climate of opinion and parliamentary legislation, the name became its current one, the Union of Clare Students, a change that not everybody thought was for the better. However, this final change of name has not affected the way the student body runs the sports clubs and interest groups, though it has been accompanied by the introduction of voting rights for the Junior Members' representatives on the major College committees and representation on nearly all other committees and working groups.

The history of the various Clare sports grounds is also worth recording, not least because for fifty years or so we have had at Bentley Road what is generally acknowledged to be one of the best sports grounds in Cambridge. Many, especially batsmen, would argue that it is *the* best and, as a bowler who spent many fruitless hours trying to get some movement off the pitch to straighten the away-swinger, who am I to disagree? The quality of the ground is not confined to just the cricket square; the hockey pitch has been the venue for many high level matches, and the tennis courts have been in regular demand for county matches and championships over a long period.

The first Clare ground appears to have been established, presumably roughly in the area which is now occupied by Memorial Court, in 1865, but it soon became apparent that it was too small and in 1876 an arrangement was made with King's to have a joint ground in the same general location. This was the ground which saw the College sports into the 20th century and hosted its most successful period on the playing field. During the First World War it was commandeered to establish the 1st Eastern General Hospital, the first open-air hospital to be put into service. At the end of the war the hospital huts remained, and even when they did cease to be used as a hospital, local government used compulsory purchase orders to acquire the Kings-Clare ground for temporary housing. All this led to a move of the two colleges' joint arrangements to the site on Barton Road which is currently the King's-Selwyn sports ground. There the Clare sports field remained until, in 1937, the College purchased from Trinity the freehold of the present ground (including, as it did at that time, the land on which the Cambridge University Press is built). In the meantime, the original King's-Clare ground had been set aside for the new University Library, which was later to be designed by Sir Giles Gilbert Scott, the architect of Memorial Court.

The Bentley Road ground was, however, destined for an unsettled early existence. In 1942 it was ploughed up on instructions from the wartime local agricultural committee and given over until 1946 to producing wheat and potatoes. It was re-sown the following year and, as will be well known to nearly all readers, brought, over the next few years, to the immaculate state to which we have long grown accustomed, by the painstaking work and loving care lavished on it by Ernie Hobbs. During this difficult period, Clare's sportsmen had to rely on the generosity and cooperation of other colleges, and arrangements were made to borrow the grounds of Pembroke (1943–45), Fitzwilliam House (1946) and Corpus (1947).

The nephew of Sir Jack Hobbs and no mean cricketer himself, Ernie ruled the field and, in particular, the cricket square, until he retired in 1973. Ernie Hobbs' retirement more or less coincided with the time when, under financial pressure as the cost of maintenance and wages started to outstrip the income it received, the CCSA agreed with Peterhouse that they would share use of the Bentley Road ground, an arrangement that continues to this day. At that time we were already offering sports facilities to the newly founded Clare Hall (the name by which

LEFT: *The Treasurer of the Amalgamated Clubs.*

170

the College was known until 1857), which is a graduate College established largely through gifts from Clare College and the Old Dominion Foundation, a philanthropic body in which Paul Mellon was the leading figure.

With the closure as a college sports field of the Peterhouse ground (in Barrow Road), the Peterhouse groundsman, George Dowsing, took charge at Bentley Road. However, not long afterwards, George decided to move to a different type of job and the post fell vacant. Clare was fortunate indeed to attract immediately to Bentley Road a worthy successor to Ernie Hobbs, Roger Pearl, who came to us from the Pembroke ground. Roger had played some minor counties cricket for Cambridgeshire, and, like Ernie, knew exactly what was needed and how to achieve it. He later told me that he had not needed much persuading, as he had always regarded the Clare ground as the best and most attractive in Cambridge and the one he had set his heart on if ever the chance came.

It is now time to turn to individual sports and pastimes and individual Clare members who distinguished themselves (or did otherwise) whilst taking part. I include 'otherwise' because not only are the triumphs on the College, Varsity and international stages recorded, but so are the not-always-favourable critiques which were a regular feature of the *Lady Clare Magazine* in the early part of the cen-

tury. In terms which nowadays would be reserved for half-time talks behind closed doors, the following end of term reports were published for all to read.

Our forwards this term fell away and played like eight babies – they used their feet on neither the ball nor their opponents. The halves played like two old men of eighty, never getting up to the scrum till the ball had been out some considerable time. The three-quarters got nothing to do and did it badly …

[Rugby report 1904]

There then followed the team list, so that every culprit could be identified. The Association Football report of 1913 was even more direct, as the following extracts show.

H. Hall is not a very satisfactory goal-keeper. He is too fond of picking the ball up when hard pressed.
Hill, the right-half, is a robust but clumsy person.
Ellis, the outside-left, centres well, but has no control of the ball.
Lane, inside-right, is not a great success as a forward.
Oliver, outside-right, is a neat player, but has not enough go in him. He doesn't seem to like rough opponents.

I am not sure what H. Hall was expected to do, but the reporter rubbed salt into the wounds of the unfortunates by also including the following.

Murdoch is the best full-back Clare has had for four years. His kicking is magnificent.
Vestey, centre-forward, is easily the best man in the team when he feels energetic. His dribbling and passing are exceptionally good.

Having shown that not everything in the garden was rosy, I now turn to positive achievements, beginning, perhaps surprisingly, with lacrosse. Today no college has its own lacrosse team and all activities centre on the University club. But in the first few years of the twentieth century college interest was very high, especially in Clare. The inter-college cup was won in three successive seasons from 1902/3–1904/5, and in 1904 every member of the Clare X had played for one of the two Varsity teams. Such was the success of lacrosse in Clare that the Captain of rowing was provoked to protest about its effect on recruitment to the river. Just as quickly as it came, Clare's interest in lacrosse disappeared, and although we have had the occasional University player, including the captain, Alex Cheyne, in 1997–8, there has been nothing significant to report on the College front since 1907.

ABOVE: *Association Football Team 1903-04, Winners of the Inter-Collegiate Cup: J.K. Mathews, O.L. Trechmann, R.G. Lowndes, O.W. Mackrill, C.K. McKerrow, J.G. Aithchison, G.L. Mellin (Hon. Sec.), E.G.U. Robson (Capt.), C.C. Page, K.B Anderson, G.B. Potter.*

Another activity which, in a competitive sense, can be said to have finished before the First World War began, is winter sports. As with lacrosse, Clare still boasts the occasional Blue in the annual ski races with Oxford, and in most years the Clare Ski Club, founded in 1992, organizes vacation trips abroad. But these can hardly compare with the visit to Engelberg made by a group of Clare men during the Christmas Vacation of 1908, to compete against, amongst others, teams from other Cambridge colleges. Clare won the three-mile bobsleigh race and some individual events. O. Hughes, who also appears later as a cricketing hero, won the Veterans' Trophy for skiing, showed that he was a skilful ski jumper, and was only prevented from winning more prizes by the need to meet bothersome University regulations about residence in the Lent Term. Long before Clare went mixed, its winning bobsleigh team included a Miss A. Conran, whose real identity may be revealed to those who know, but not to me, by the parenthetical information 'The Clare Flapper'.

The end-of-the-century replacement for winter sports is the Clare Rats. Formed in 1985 as the re-foundation of an earlier climbing club, the Rats (who describe themselves as the Rock-climbing And Trekking club when seeking financial support) train all over the UK and have sent dozens of Clare junior members to the top of Mont Blanc (22 in 1991 alone). They have also climbed in the Himalayas, Africa and South America, and (as individuals) on some buildings in Cambridge where they should not be. The Rats at one time reached a membership comparable to that of the Boat Club and its 'fame' appears to have reached at least some schools, as it is sometimes given as a reason for applying to Clare.

We turn now to those sports which have survived, and sometimes thrived, throughout the century. As cricket was the first of these to be played against Oxford it may be appropriate to start with it. With the gradual change over during the period from largely amateur to wholly professional international cricket, it is not surprising that Clare's stars are drawn from the early years. In 1926 the great authority Mr P.F. (Plum) Warner was invited to give his opinion of Clare's cricketing alumni from the previous fifty years. He picked out A.P. Lucas, C.J. Burnup, A.F. Morcom, C.H. Gibson and K.S. Duleepsinhji, and I can do no better than make the same selection.

Lucas was described as a very sound bat with a beautiful style, but rather short of strokes. He was, apparently, attractive to watch even when scoring very slowly (or even not at all). He opened the England innings with W.G. Grace on many occasions in the 1880s, and such was his defence that it was reported that Australian opponents of the time wondered how he ever got out. Burnup is another whose inclusion here is only justified by Warner's 1926 assessments, but, in terms of achievement, he qualifies with ease. Although he never played in a test, in 1896 he made a century against the Australians and in his first-class career maintained an average of nearly 35; he was also a useful swing bowler and a very fine out-fielder. If more were needed, he captained Cambridge at soccer and represented England at the same sport.

171

BELOW: *K.S. Duleepsinhji, 1925–28.*

172

Moving on to those in Warner's selection who were resident during the twentieth century, we come to A.F. Morcom, who was considered by Plum to be a good, but not a great bowler. Curiously, Warner stated that he might be placed into this latter category if he were playing at Lord's – 'where the slope in the ground helped his natural break-back' – and presumably operating from the same end as that from which he bowled Cambridge to victory in the 1905 Varsity match. Fifteen years later C.H. Gibson was another Cambridge bowling hero in the match against Oxford, taking three wickets in each innings. However his greatest achievement came at Eastbourne a year later when he helped England to inflict the only defeat of their 1921 tour on the Australians. With the Australians needing only 196 to win in their second innings, Gibson took six for 64 and the tourists fell a few runs short of their target. Warner described Gibson as a fine bowler, with a beautiful action and a difficult flight that seemed to make the ball 'wobble'.

However Clare's cricketer of the century was undoubtedly K.S. Duleepsinhji (1925–28), whom Warner rated as 'the most promising young batsman in England', and 'quite definitely a better player at his age than Ranji (his illustrious uncle Ranjitsinhji, the Jam of Nawanagar, who had been a student at Trinity). In June 1927 Duleep broke the Fenner's record for a Cambridge batsman by making 254 not out, from the total of 366 for five recorded against Middlesex. His double century was reached after only three-and-a-half hours, with the total then standing on 285. After he had gone down, Duleep played for Sussex and the *Clare Association Annual* of 1929 records that the ex-Trundler and country's fastest scorer (excluding those who were merely hitters) had made 202 *v* Essex in under three hours, 115 *v* Kent in 105 minutes and a further 246 in the second innings of the same match. Sadly Duleepsinhji's career was dogged by illness and he did not play for England as often as his talents would have justified.

This may be the moment to digress on the subject of the Trundlers and Long Vacation activities. The Trundlers probably grew out of the pre-World War One practice whereby large numbers of undergraduates came into residence for the purpose of playing cricket and tennis matches on alternate days. There is no mention of academic work in the *Lady Clare Magazine* of 1910, despite the College being full! The most distinguishing feature of an ex-Trundler is not his ability with bat or ball, but the grotesque colouring of his cap and tie, which consists of broad stripes of yellow, pink and purple. This bizarre combination was said to have arisen from the need to form a combined team with Corpus Christi and King's, probably in the difficult times around 1919. Whatever the reason, the Trundlers continued to operate as a long vacation cricket team in Clare until the late 1960s, but alas with no one even vaguely approaching Duleepsinhji's class in sight.

After the Second World War fewer undergraduates came into Long Vacation residence, and, of those that did, most had at least a few lectures or laboratories to attend; this was the position reached by the mid-fifties. The highlight of each Long Vacation cricket season was a match between eleven junior members, of disparate abilities, and as many of the College Staff as turned up. By the mid-seventies a significant part of the University's teaching was done during the Long Vacation period (particularly in scientific subjects), and undergraduates would only come into residence if they had a compulsory course to follow. For this reason the Staff cricket match became one between the Staff and the Fellows, or between mixed teams of each. As the number of women on the College Staff increased significantly over the last forty years of the century, with bedders replacing gyps, a rounders match was played at the same time. Regrettably, not even this arrangement has survived, and now the demands made on the College Staff by the conference trade, and on academics by teaching and research assessment exercises, have resulted in the Staff Sports Day being (at least temporarily) abandoned altogether.

We now return to serious cricket, but at the college and University, rather than international, level. Although Clare had a number of blues in the first decade of the century, its college cricket seems to have been at best average. However, the arrival of O. Hughes, already mentioned for his prowess on the ski slopes, seems to have made all the difference. He rightly gained his blue, but, in addition, found time to score an undefeated 201 against Christ's and, in the following season, an undefeated century against Pembroke. His contributions were enough to give the College an unbeaten summer in College matches.

It is also recorded in the *Lady Clare Magazine* that De Freitas played a faultless innings against Pembroke and 'made history on the Trinity ground', without even hinting at how this was done. The following year the same Mr J.M.de Freitas 'really lived in London but every now and then kindly stayed a day or so in Cambridge and appeared on the cricket field. His batting revealed no falling off from last year …'.

As the century unfolded the number of college and University cricketers who made the transition onto the county scene declined, in Clare as in most other colleges. Nevertheless, a few did, amongst them Alan Hurd who joined Essex after leaving Clare in 1959 and John Minney, who although he never got a blue, was a successful batsman for Northamptonshire. National recognition was also accorded to the first of Clare's women cricketers. In 1991 Kate Dunham gained the last of her blues, captained the University side, led the Clare Ladies to victory in the six-a-side Cuppers, and was made a member of the Young England Squad.

Nor was there a lack of excitement in these later years, as demonstrated by the 1986–87 Cuppers. Although Gavin Canham played regularly for the Varsity side, the Clare team contained no blues, but by sound team performances had reached the quarter-finals. In their allotted overs Clare scored 165 for six, and, with one ball of the match remaining, Magdalene stood on 165 for eight. Their ninth wicket fell from that one ball, as the attempted winning hit was caught, and Clare prevailed by virtue of losing fewer wickets. And so to the semi-final, where the opponents were Emmanuel. Batting first, Clare made the modest total of 113, but Emmanuel were held in check by determined bowling and fielding and when the last ball of the match was to be bowled their score was 109 for nine. Again a wicket fell on the last ball and Clare had squeezed through once more. It was perhaps a blessing that the final against St John's was rained off and the trophy shared!

One aspect of Clare cricket which remained essentially unaltered over a long period was the connection between Clare and the Southern Counties, Sussex in particular. The pattern was that sides such as the Sussex Martlets would come to Cambridge during the Clare cricket week and the Clare XI and stand-ins (sometimes under the name of the Clare Trundlers) would tour the Sussex area after the Easter Term was over. Reports of three such tours undertaken in 1933, 1951 and the late 1960s are remarkably similar. In later years the tours took in other areas, that in 1978–79 ranged from Southampton to Birmingham, whilst the 1987–88 tour was to Holland, finishing with a match against Amsterdam. Sadly, as the interest in cricket, both in school and college, has waned, so these traditions have fallen by the wayside, and most students today spend their summer vacation either working to supplement their student loans or taking their last carefree chance to see the world.

Soccer is a sport that seems to have flourished at Clare only early and quite late in the century, with a distinctly barren period in the middle. In the late 1970s the team included soccer blues Graham Morris and Nick MacNay; the latter is probably the only Clare player to have been on the books of a Premier (then 1st Division) League club, Leeds United. He was also the University captain when winning the last of his three blues. Most of Clare's inter-college honours on the soccer field have been gained by the Clare Ladies, who won Cuppers in '91 and '92 and the League title in '93, and have had a sprinkling of blues since then.

The other football code figures more prominently in the College records with highlights in the 1930s and 50s. There had been a steady stream of rugby blues and internationals at Clare since the turn of the century, and the Cambridge teams against Oxford in 1926 and 1927 contained respectively three and four Clare men. In the early 1930s several internationals were in residence at the same time, including Tallent, Dick, Johnston and Jones, not a firm of solicitors, but the holders between them of a good number of English, Scottish and Welsh caps. Phil Smith, the college gyp who looked after D staircase, later wrote that in 1932 he had nearly a complete staircase of internationals. Clare also provided successive University captains in 1934 (R.B. Jones) and 1935 (W.J. Leather), whilst the 1935–36 College side was under the captaincy of Cliff Jones. Cuppers was won in 1934 and the final reached again in 1939, though it took eight years for the result to be reported – lost to St Catharine's after two replays!

In the 1950s the College was almost as well represented at the Varsity, if not the international, level, and particularly so amongst the forwards. In 1955–56 both of the University props, Jim Turner and Nick Tarsh, were Clare men, and Dick Boggan held what is today called the No. 8 position. Even when the former two went down, your reporter found it hard to secure a place in the front row of the College scrum, as Joe Vaux then came up. The College pack of 1957 was considered sufficiently strong that it was invited to Grange Road to give the Blues pack some practice; afterwards we did not feel that we had disgraced ourselves. Like the cricket teams, the rugger teams of that time went on tour during vacations, to areas such as Cognac, Barcelona, Milan and La Rochelle. One of the games in Milan was televised, but hardly drew the crowds as both AC and Inter were playing at home that day!

174

RIGHT: *G. Lowe (1902–06), University Tennis VI, English International.*

ABOVE: *Hockey Team 1904–05, Winners of the Cambridge University Hockey League. T.A. Grose, H.W. Scott, C. Palmer, H.M.A. Ward, J.J. Quill, E.H.Y. Williams, R.K. Henderson (Hon. Sec.) L.D. Gelling (Capt.) D.P. Robinson, F.B. Adams, R.S. Preeston.*

In more recent years, Clare's rugby blues have been few and far between, but Nick Herrod, nationally known for having played six times at Twickenham before he finished up on the winning side, to some extent makes up for that. He followed three losing undergraduate years at Oxford with two more postgraduate ones at Cambridge, but finally left Clare with a winning blue, a Clare wife and a Research Fellowship at Girton. (This is perhaps the only positive mention of academic study likely to appear in this review.) In college Rugby, the Clare Ladies had rather more success than their male counterparts, winning the league in '91–92, and both Cuppers and one of two equal leagues in '93–94.

Something should be said here of the Clare Unemployed, a club which most people associate with rugby, as it was the name under which the Clare third XV played throughout the fifties. However it's origins are much older and more diverse than that. In 1901 the Unemployed Cricket and Hockey Club was formed and took as its motto 'They toil not, neither do they spin',[2] and, as its colours, the familiar olive green and pink. The latter decision was expedited by the elected Captain (R. Hargreaves) and Secretary (E.S.H. Johnson), offering the selection

committee three designs, of which only the one chosen was not totally impossible. Perhaps one of the rejects was later taken up by the Trundlers! The other notable election was to the office of 'Brake Driver' to which J.H. Howell was appointed.

In its first year the Unemployed played seven cricket matches and five hockey matches against local teams – as well as holding a Smoking Concert in the Lion Hotel and composing its own song, sung to the tune of *The Vicar of Bray*.[3] At the time of its 1920 AGM the Unemployed had more than 100 members and – first things first – it was 'unamiously (*sic*) decided to have a dinner at the "Lion" early next term, and then to organize a number of rugger, football and hockey matches against local sides, some against other colleges, but mostly against schools and town clubs. Currently only two of Clare's dons sport Unemployed ties, both ex-Senior Tutors; one of those is well over ninety, though he shows no signs of calling "no-side".'

Hockey is the one Unemployed sport not yet covered, and also one in which Clare can be said to have taken a lead. Before the University Club was formed in 1890, hockey had been taken up in Clare and Trinity and casual matches between the two were arranged. A league was instituted in 1903 and Clare was the first winner; its next real successes were some thirty years in coming. In 1932 T.A.D. Hewan captained the University and six years later G.E. Hewan followed suit. During the thirties the final of the Cuppers was reached on a number of occasions, several Claremen gained their blues and R. Fison, an ex-member of the Hockey Club, captained England. The fifties and early sixties were similarly sprinkled with successes including Cuppers wins in 1951 and 1961, and an unbeaten league championship in 1958–59.

The last quarter of the century brought further recognition for Clare's hockey players, with the women contributing their full share. Amongst the earliest of these were Pam Thornton, who captained the University side in her final blues year, Ruth Honey and Margaret Hannah, who each gained two blues, and Candy Taylor who was the leading goal scorer for the Varsity side in two successive seasons. Candy also won a half-blue for sprinting. The Clare Ladies won the hockey Cuppers in '91–92 and Sharon Mulroy gained her blue. To keep the male flag flying Mike Meredith, like Nick Herrod (rugby), a postgraduate import from the other place, added Cambridge blues to his Oxford ones and captained his adopted University.

The remaining major group of sports to review is that involving racquet and ball, namely squash and the two forms of tennis, lawn and table. (It should be three, but I can find no information on Clare men involved in Real Tennis.) In the early days Clare produced only one tennis player of note, and that was F.G. Lowe who played for the University and later for England. Blues have appeared scattered across the years, and D.N. Jones captained the University in 1934, but real College success did not come until the late fifties when the league was won in '58–59 and both the league and cup the following year. The league was won again in 1965. Since then only Jill Cottrell, who played at Junior Wimbledon before coming into residence and captained the University side when up, has made any real impact on college tennis; she also won a blue for squash, to which we now turn.

Squash became popular in the University in the late 1920s and can truly be said to be a twentienth-century sport. The *Lady Clare* magazine of 1930 contains an impassioned plea to the 'Powers-that-be' for a Clare squash court, emphasizing that it would never be regretted, how cheap it would be to run, and how it would give a chance for even the hardest of workers to obtain *some* sort of recreation – enough to last for two or three days in less than an hour's play. Clare court or not, success came quite quickly and several Claremen won their blues. Amongst the achievements reported in 1935 were victory over a strong team of Classical Dons and an Unemployed Squash match arranged with Girton in which the form(s) of the visitors struck the Clare spectators favourably.

The Clare Squash Club was again riding high in the mid-fifties when half of the University VI were members of the College, though it is rumoured that none of them, or indeed any other junior member, had ever managed to beat the then Senior Tutor, Alex McDonald, another Classical Don. Perhaps it was due to judicious restraint on their part, but, more likely, to the fact that Alex had been runner-up in the Australian Open and played exhibition matches with the world champion.

After another lull, Clare squash again reached the heights in the fifteen years or so starting in the mid-1970s, with most of the success down to the women in the College. One or more blues were gained by Jane Randall, Shealagh McCracken and, as already mentioned, Jill Cottrell, and the Women's League was won in '78–79. Carrying the flag for the men, Chris Harland captained the University in the following year and won the British Universities' Championship. A few switchback years followed; a disastrous plummet to the lower divisions of the league, a climb through four divisions in one season, and then a mass exodus of the best players, conspired to leave the 1984–85 men's team in the first division, but outclassed. It didn't beat any other college on the courts but survived by employing the cunning plan of conceding fewer walkovers than the other weaker teams. Later in the decade, Kathie McGurk came into residence. Already a Belgian international, she was declared to be too good for women's inter-college matches and had to play for the men's team. At University level, she led the women's side and played regularly for the men's Second VI.

Finally, in this group of sports, we come to table tennis. Not much is recorded, though it is of interest to note that the College club was formed in 1937 and immediately set about trying to demonstrate just how disgusted it was at having been placed in the second division of the College League. The College's star performer at the table was almost certainly Lu Shi Qin, who came to Clare from China in 1980, *via* a one-year A-level course at Warrington College for Higher Education, and a test paper in Maths and Physics set and marked by your reviewer. He carried the College side into the first division, playing every match and remaining unbeaten throughout his three years in residence. A decade later Clare won the inter-college league with an unblemished record.

Athletics is a sport in which Clare has had a steady stream of blues throughout the century, though I can find no evidence of any particularly successful College teams. Amongst those from the early years, W.R. Seagrove won the AAA mile in 1924 and ran in the Antwerp and Paris Olympics; he also ran in four cross-country matches against Oxford. A few years later J.W.J. Rinkel, competing in all the sprints, won the AAA quarter-mile at Stamford Bridge. In the following decade Geoffrey de Freitas, President of the Union and later an MP, gained several blues for both track and cross-country, and E. Hudson Bennett was, if the *Lady Clare* report is to be believed, only prevented from winning College matches on his own by the rule restricting any one man to only three events! No doubt he specialized a little more when first Secretary, and then President, of the University Athletics Club.

Clare's other athletic high spots came late in the century, the first in 1975 with Anthony Gershuny, who won both the 100 and the 200 metres and was a member of the winning sprint relay team in the match against Oxford. He was also second in the long jump. The other bumper year was 1996–97, when Clare's women won the cross-country league and no less than six Clare students competed in the Varsity athletics match. Esther Casson contributed in no small measure to both College and University success during her four years in residence.

Though not concerned here with what has happened on the water (though I do recall a year in which Clare won the sailing Cuppers at Grafham Water), it would be wrong to omit our successes *in* the water. Swimming has played a small but significant part in Clare sports throughout the century, and at one time there were College swimming races. H.D. Darbishire got the century off to a good start with easy wins in the 50 yards races against Oxford in 1901 and 1902. Fred Clatworthy, a graduate student from New

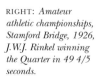

RIGHT: *Amateur athletic championships, Stamford Bridge, 1926, J.W.J. Rinkel winning the Quarter in 49 4/5 seconds.*

Zealand, ended it in 1994 by representing Cambridge in the 200m, the 400m and the 1500m freestyle, winning the middle distance of this gruelling triple. In between, there have been many others including Barry James from the late eighties and Patricia Greenhalgh and Jane Brown from a decade earlier. All three had success at the national level of university competition, and the latter two were in the first batch of five Cambridge women to receive full swimming blues. In 1959 Richard Dyball reached a similar standard and represented Britain at breast stroke in the World University Games, as well as helping the College to win the Medley Relay. To touch on related sports, the same Fred (not his real name) Clatworthy was the triathlete world champion in the 25–29 age group in 1999 and Lisa McGuire represented Great Britain from the diving board in the same year.

The one major sport not yet covered is golf and here, although Clare has had its fair share of blues, and some like Henry Longhurst have gone on to achieve national fame, the College's lasting contributions to the sport were made by its members, not so much as players, but as those working to foster the game. The aptly named Johnnie Law, after coming close to winning the Amateur Championship at St Andrews in 1901, became chairman of the Rules of Golf Committee, and, as such, helped to frame the modern game. He was also a founder member of the Oxford & Cambridge Golf Society, and donated his 1901 putter as a trophy for which its members still compete annually. In a parallel development Harry Colt was said to have invented the science, or art, of golf course design in about 1907, and altogether designed or remodelled some 250 courses all over the world, starting with Rye and Sunningdale. Another Clare name to have a lasting place in golf's history is that of Halford Hewitt; his name is that associated with the annual competition played at Deal and Sandwich between teams of alumni from the Public Schools.

There is not much scope for a college golf team and success has to be measured by University representation. In the 1930s both I.K. Macrosty and Hugh Neilson captained the University side and both D.A. Drayson and J.S. Rowell held the post of Secretary. Some twenty years later, in 1958, Clare provided three of the team to play Oxford, W.P. Cooper, G.T. Mills and B.H.G. Chapman. When Brian Chapman graduated that year, he had won no less than fifty singles matches for the University.

Needless to say, there are many other sports and games

LEFT: *W.R. Seagrove (1919–22), President of the University Athletic Club, 1921, Olympic runner Antwerp, 1920, Paris, 1925.*

178

that have been played at college and University level but which have not yet been alluded to. It would be tedious to list them all and I hope that no reader will feel offended if their particular sport gets no more than a passing mention, or even no mention at all. Sophie Llewellyn Smith pulled two such sports together; she shot for the University, at both small and large bore, and represented it in 1993 in the newly competitive activity of ballroom dancing. A year later Sarah Cutmore and Syed Ahmed led the Cambridge dance team to victory in the Varsity match. On the netball court Clare's most successful player has been Ann Pullen, who captained the University in her first year as a research student and then played for two more years. Sarah Porter had the distinction of being awarded an honorary when she missed the Varsity match with appendicitis. She had been awarded a more conventional one a year earlier in the 1985–86 season, as was Linda Stuart four years later. Ann Pullen's counterpart on the judo mat was Ken Hori, a black belt who in 1990 led a University side, containing three other Clare members, to their fourth consecutive British Universities Championship and to their 15th consecutive win over Oxford!

In the less physically active sphere of mind games, not much is reported until the later parts of the century, when Clare had one or two distinguished performers. In the early eighties, Allan Beardsworth twice played as top board against Oxford and achieved the distinction of winning the University chess championship twice in successive years. At the green baize table, Clare's Bridge teams and members have had some successes. In 1984–85 Steve Dannell and Chris Tofts were members of the winning Cambridgeshire county U-25 team in the Home Counties Championship, and in the following year teamed up with Richard Lawrence and Alan Marshall (borrowed from Clare Hall) to win the Bridge Cuppers. Some ten years later Graham Hazel came into residence and was soon representing England at U-21 (and later U-25) level and was part of the U-25 Team which won the European Championship. He was also a member of the winning pair in the national junior (U-25) championships of 1998.

Finally, half-blues awarded to Lackie Forbes and Edward Hynes (both boxing), James Morrow (archery), and Paul Klenerman (fencing and swimming) – he also fenced for Great Britain at two Student World Games and at the Los Angeles Olympics whilst still a student – allow us to at least nod in the direction of a few more sports.

Where does all this leave us? The perennial answer always appears to be '…they don't seem to be as committed to, or as good at, sport as they were in *my* day. Too much is now determined by success in academic examinations, and admissions policies do not pay enough attention to qualities of leadership which…'. The truth is that for the last forty years or so Clare has been able to demand the former without compromising the latter. All sports have their ups and downs, and those who complain almost invariably happen to stand on one of the loftier peaks. But they should heed the words written by a former Master, Sir Eric Ashby, when addressing past members of the College through the pages of the *Clare Association Annual*:

'But let me defend the undergraduates now up at Clare: their good old days will measure up to yours.'

He wrote those words in 1962, but they could have appeared at almost any time in the century we are now celebrating.

1 I note with interest, as Senior Tutor of Clare for some twenty years, that, according to the report of the Universities Commission of 1874, the Tutor [of Clare] (as he was then called) received one eighth of all College fees. If this laudable practice had been continued into the late 20th century, some further donations might have been made.

2 Matthew VI, 28.

3 The first and last verses and the *chorus* were:

When summer was a-coming in,
And groundsmen made a wicket,
Some men of Clare did meet and swear
To form a club for cricket.

And this is law, I will maintain,
Until my dying day, Sir,
That whatsoever Dons may reign
This Club has come to stay, Sir!

Good fellowship to thus promote,
The members all endeavour
So give the toast both guest and host,
'The Unemployed for ever'.

Chorus as before

ADRIAN TRAVIS

Ah, you come from Cambridge! I am so sorry to hear that you did not manage to beat Oxford this year!'. It can come as a slight humiliation at academic conferences in Asia to discover that Cambridge is almost more famous for the Boat Race than for any of its intellectual achievements. The college boat clubs play a crucial role in supplying the talent which goes each year into the University crews, and W.P. Pulman (1907) even claimed that 'Clare ... Boat Club is not an end in itself, but only a means to an end, and that end is the success of the CUBC'.[1] Although Clare was not the first college to enter a crew in the Bumps, it is thought to have been the first college to start a boat club, in 1831.[2] Rowing at Cambridge began as part of a picnic excursion when students would hire boats which had to carry all the kettles, pans and cutlery that went into picnics of the time, and therefore weighed almost half a ton. It could only be a matter of time before an element of competition entered these excursions, and five colleges got together in 1827 to start what became the University Bumping races. Clare first entered a boat in 1831, but it must have been a cheerfully relaxed affair by comparision with today's tense sportsmanship, and the appearance of Clare crews was sporadic until the 1840s. Nevertheless the Colleges quickly learnt that they could gain an advantage by building their own lighter boats, and although these were three-foot wide luggers with hefty rudders, keels, no rowlocks and certainly no sliding seats, they must have been a relief after what went before. The oars also were little better than planks of wood, and Clare is one of the few colleges still to have one of these early oars.[3]

However some things don't change. Rule 15 of Clare Boat Club, revised on 28th October 1865[4] lays down the following fines:

'(1) For not being at the Boat-House at the time appointed by the Captain, any sum not exceeding 2s 6d...

(2) For any person (except the Captain and Steerer) giving orders or speaking in the Boat on Racing Days, or on any other day, after silence has been called, any sum not exceeding 2s. 6d.'

Such a familiar problem, and such an excellent solution.

Judging by its position in the Bumps, Clare's commitment to rowing in the nineteenth century was indifferent, with exceptions. There must have been an exciting last day's race in 1870 when Clare 2nd VIII were rowing for their oars and got their bump, only to hear the crew in front claim to have made their own bump half a second earlier. Very sensibly the 2nd VIII ignored this nonsense and awarded themselves full honours, and their picture now hangs in the Boat House. By 1887 Clare had risen to fifth on the river, but slumped back as the century drew to its close. It cannot have helped that a Clare rower, E.S. Campbell, died in 1888 in the first of the new Lent Bumping races. He was rowing 4 in the Clare boat which had just bumped and pulled in to the bank at First Post Corner when a Trinity Hall boat, trying to escape its pursuer, crashed into Clare and its bows went through Campbell's heart. VIII's now carry a rubber ball over their bows, partly in an attempt to reduce injury if this ever happens again.

In its early years Clare Boat Club was paid for by members' subscription, and it is clear that there was a precarious and slightly strained relationship with the yard where the Clare boats were kept. But in 1886 a combined fund was set up to pay for all sports in Clare, and this seems to have made the position of the Boat Club more secure. Then in 1898 Clare built itself the Boat House and in 1899 appointed its first boatman, Freddie Masters.[5] By this time out-riggers had been introduced[6] and boats were being built which were thinner and longer and looked more like those we use today. But it was only the first division which was allowed to use these boats, and then only in the Mays.

180

Furthermore there were still only two crews rowing in the Bumps, so the Boat House was considered to be remarkable for its spaciousness. As one member wrote, 'One of its marvellous features is a spacious and extensive shed stretching away from the river illimitably, far, far and away into the fen-country'.[7]

Freddie's loyalty must have been tested in those early years because in 1901 Clare dropped into the second division and stayed there until just before the start of the First World War when all rowing ceased. Influenza was clearly a problem at the time and is reported on occasions to have put rowers out of action all term. Other colleges must have shared the problem. Perhaps Freddie and the new Boat House were responsible for a detectable note of optimism in reports from that period. In 1907 the Clare first

VIII took two and a half hours to row down to Ely to watch the Varsity trials, and presumably took at least this time to row back. They comment that 'It is a great pity that the custom has died out, and it is to be hoped that this will be a precedent for future years: it is in such small matters as this that the true spirit of the College is seen'. The following year the same remarkable crowd decided to go to Henley, a slightly more complicated exercise than today. Two members of the College kitchen staff and another to manage them were brought along to prepare meals, and it took Freddie three days to move the boat to Henley.[8] There were successes as well as enthusiasm: E.D.P. Pinks won the Colquhoun Sculls in 1909, thus becoming the College's first 'Champion of the Cam', and there were regular entrants for the Varsity trials.

As far as the Bumps were concerned things continued to go badly when rowing began again in 1919, not least because there were only three or four from the pre-war era left to teach the old skills.[9] Of these W.P. Pulman is said to have been particularly inspiring and Clare decided to send a crew to the 1919 Henley regatta, where they narrowly missed winning the Remeham Cup for Clinker Eights when they were beaten by half a length in the final by Caius.[10] Nevertheless the Boat Club clearly enjoyed this success, and in 1922 after winning the Junior Cup at Marlow, entered the Thames Cup at Henley and again just missed winning, this time by two-feet to Worcester College, Oxford. It was in 1923 that Clare finally climbed back into the first division of the Lents, although still in the second in the Mays. Much of the success of these three years is attributed to Stiffy Pain who came up in 1920, galvanized the Club into action, and continued to coach the first VIII for more than forty years.[11]

A period of steady improvement now ensued, and in many ways the years up to the 40s were halcyon times for the Club. It was a strange time to be rowing because there was little consensus about what was the correct stroke.[12] Some coaches encouraged their crews to lean almost horizontal as they pulled out the finish[13] (less extraordinary when you consider that sliding seats were still not fully accepted) and some taught that the oar should be in the water for the greatest part of the stroke possible.[14]

In 1924 the newly arrived Geoffrey Ambler went straight into the University crew, then was President of CUBC in 1925 and 1926. Clare was now regularly putting three boats into the Lents and Mays and was gradually climbing in each, so it was in good condition for the ball put on to celebrate the Boat Club's centenary in 1931. That year also brought the arrival of Charles Sergel, who was also in the University crew for three years, and CUBC president in his last.[15] Clare's arrival back in the first division of the Mays in 1932 was rather overdue, so to rub it in Sergel coached them to win the University light fours that year. R.B.F. Wylie, who went on himself to get a rowing blue the following year, reported that Sergel, who was the son of a missionary, was reluctant to swear and clearly caused some amusement when by way of a substitute he would 'beat his thigh furiously with his fist'.[16] In the following Lents the first VIII burst from 18th position to 4th and the other four VIIIs made similar gains, winning 36 places between them. Chasing for a double over bump in order to win their oars, the third VIII must have spoilt

Magdelene's repose when they suddenly appeared three lengths behind at the Railway Bridge, but unfortunately they had a quarter of a length still to close by the finish.

By 1934 the Clare First VIII was second in the Lents, and by 1937 it had risen to sixth in the Mays, but they still hadn't got to the head of the river. Maybe this suddenly didn't matter because in 1937 the Boat Club's regular attendance at Henley finally paid off and, after having to re-row a dead heat in the semi-final, Clare won the Henley Regatta Ladies Plate. A week later the crew were guests of E.T.U.F. Rowing Club at the international regatta at Essen in Germany, where R.F. Stratton reports that all eight participants in one heat, including Clare, departed on 'Are you ready?', and the umpire thought better than to try calling them back. Stratton also reports with understandable satisfaction that he nicked their swastika.

It was as the Second World War broke out that Clare came Head of the Lents, then Head of the Mays in 1941 which lasted until 1944. This must have been a great reward to Freddie Masters, who had been the Clare boatman for 47 years and had stayed beyond the retirement age in order to carry the Boat Club through the war years. Freddie, by now something of an institution, retired in 1946 and was replaced by Harry Benham. At about the same time and after various pinks, yellows and whites since its foundation, Clare Boat Club had adopted the in-your-face yellow that its oars are painted with today.

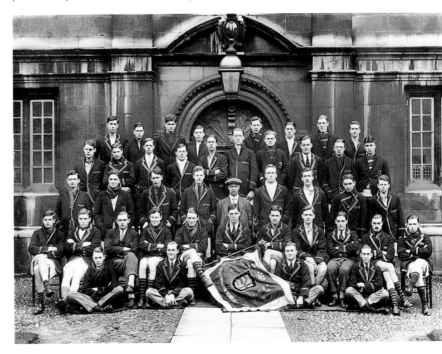

BELOW: *Clare Boat, 1923.*

181

182

In 1949 the College repeated its success by coming Head of the River for the first time, in peace, in the history of the College.[17] By tradition this meant that an VIII had to be burnt, and perhaps it was in view of our last accident with the College buildings that the Club was encouraged to do this somewhere other than in the middle of Old Court. There were so many other successes that year and in those that followed that it is easy to get muddled: Clare won the light fours twice, the Forster Fairbairn Pairs and the University Pairs, and the Visitors' Challenge cup at Henley. Perhaps it is otiose to note that David Jennens went on to become a legend by stroking the Blue Boat three years running, the winning British VIII at the European Championships in 1951, and the 1952 Olumpic VIII in Helsinki. He used to tell an entertaining story of how in Helsinki he struck up quite a friendship with one of the Russian crew despite having to communicate whenever no-one was looking through a wire fence in an unknown language.

By now the numbers of students both within the University and within Clare was considerably greater than before the war, and the Boat Club was regularly fielding several VIIIs in the Lents and Mays each year. The amalgamated sports fund simply wasn't big enough to sustain this level of activity, so various alumni banded together on the 9th of February 1955 to form the Clare Boat Club Fund. The aim of this fund was to provide the boats, oars, commissions and transport costs needed to allow members of College to row, and although some students are unaware of the extent of the generosity from which they benefit, most realize when they talk to rowers from other universities. The Fund has become increasingly important over the years, not just for financial reasons, but also in helping the captains of the Boat Club with advice and coaching.

Clare won the light fours again in 1953 and 1954, and sent another oarsman, J.A.L. Russell, to the Olympics in 1956. The College remained in the top eight places of the Mays and Lents until 1957, but then its performance began to falter. This wasn't necessarily a failing; many fewer freshers were coming up who had previously rowed (two in 1967, one in 1968)[18] and the Club was simply having to learn how to train novices from scratch.

In 1963 Harry Benham died, and Peter Frost, who had done a five-year apprenticeship as a boatbuilder at Banham's boatyard, joined the Club. With Peter's encouragement it clawed its way back and, in the Lents, the first VIII got blades in 1966, 1967, and just missed them in

RIGHT: *G.H. Ambler (1923–26), President of the University Boat Club, 1925–26.*

1968, reaching third place. In 1970 Clare went Head of the River for one night, then clinched the Head of the River again properly in 1973.

1972 brought ladies to the College and into the Boat House, where they were of course treated with great enthusiasm. This may have faltered when the women proceeded to go straight to the head of the new Mays Ladies Division and to stay in the top five for the next ten years. Perhaps this steeled the resolve of the men because membership of the Club blossomed, and in 1981 Clare had three women's IV's and eight men's VIIIs including a graduate VIII and a Fellows' VIII rowing in the bumps. There seems to have been particular delight when, on the last night of the Mays that year, the gents' boat bumped the Fellows' boat to the cheers of the onlooking rugby boat. In its first ten years as a 'mixed' club, the Clare Boat Club produced three CUWBC presidents, nine women's Blues and got a number of ladies into Blondie. Nicola Boyes and Penny Sweet rowed in the British VIII at the

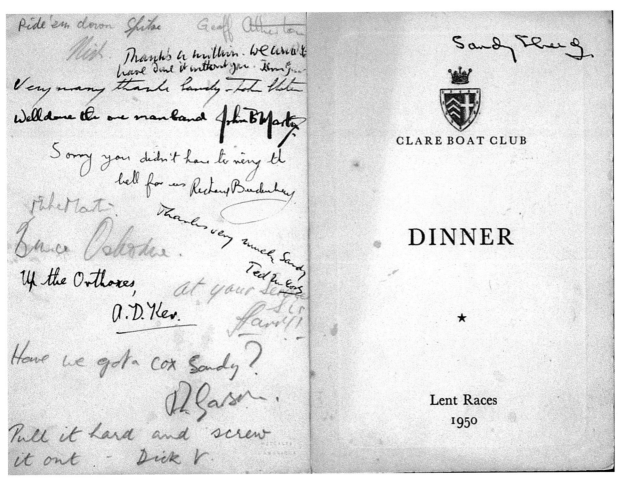

LEFT AND BELOW: Boat Club Dinner Menu, 1950, Lent Races.

Moscow Olympics, and Celia Duff, who rowed at national level, has recently returned as a Fellow of Clare and Trustee of the CBC Trust Fund.

With the highest average percentage of rowers in the University, and the increasing enthusiasm for rowing, the Boat House (which originally accommodated only two VIIIs) was getting crowded. Every rack had a boat on it and two were kept permanently on the floor. Furthermore Peter was doing not just the maintenance and small jobs which Freddie and Harry had done, but also all the major repair work which, until the firm closed, had been done by Banhams. Peter was quite capable of this of course, but he had no space. So the College built a workshop on the upstream side of the Boat House, and for a time this ameliorated the problem.

In 1990 the positions of the first and second IVs were amalgamated as the Ladies' Mays moved from IVs to VIIIs, and this brought them several places down the ranking. Since then they have progressed steadily upwards and are

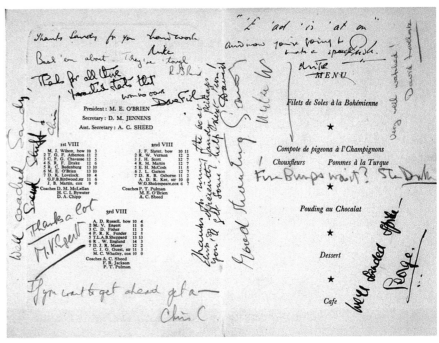

184

RIGHT: *Clare Boat bumping Jesus on Grassy Corner, Lent 1973, to go Head of the River. The Jesus' cox's arm is raised to acknowledge the bump, the river empty ahead.*

looking increasingly strong. At the beginning of the 90s the men's First VIII made a quick visit to the second division of the Mays, and appeared strangely keen to repeat it. But it was in the Lents in 1996 that the men's First VIII found themselves as sandwich boat chasing St Catherine's in the first division, and being chased by a strong Selwyn in the second. There followed a demonstration of true Clare grit: each day Selwyn got agonizingly close to Clare, overlapping by a considerable margin on at least one occasion, and each day Clare held them off to the end of the course. Exhausted, Clare then had to use what remained of their energies to chase the whole way down the course again after St Catherine's, before repeating the experience the following day. It is remarkable that Selwyn never got them, and Selwyn Boat Club were chivalrous enough to have the whole of Clare First VIII to their dinner after it was all over.

1 *Lady Clare Magazine* XXV/3, 1931.
2 *Lady Clare Magazine* XXIV/2, 1930, 'Clare Boat Club 150 years', p. 5.
3 J. Durack, G. Gilbert and J. Marks, *The Bumps. An account of Cambridge University Bumping Races 1827–1999* (Clare College, 2000), p. 52.
4 *Clare Boat Club 125.*
5 *Clare Boat Club 125*, p. 2.
6 Durack, Gilbert and Marks, *op. cit.*, p. 54.
7 *Lady Clare Magazine*, Long Vacation, 1898.
8 *Lady Clare Magazine* VIII/1, March 1908.
9 *Lady Clare Magazine*, 1919 and 1931, no. 3.
10 *Lady Clare Magazine* XXV/3, p. 97.
11 See note 2 above.
12 *Lady Clare Magazine* XXV/3, p. 98.
13 *Clare Boat Club 125.*
14 Durack, Gilbert and Marks, *op. cit.*, p. 56.
15 *Lady Clare Magazine*, 1933.
16 *Clare Boat Club 125.*
17 *Clare Association Annual*, 1949.
18 *Clare Boat Club 125*, p. 14.

LEFT: *Clare Boat on the river, summer 2000.*

RIGHT: *Clare Boat, 2000 in front of the boathouse and* (BELOW) *a Clare ladies' boat.*

NORMAN DAWSON

LEFT: *The Cricket Club on tour in Worthing in 1954 with Ernie Hobbs the groundsman on the left.*

Cricket at Bentley Road was under the fiefdom of Ernie Hobbs: groundsman par excellence, some-time minor counties cricketer for Cambridgeshire and nephew of the great Sir Jack Hobbs of England and Surrey. He told tales of his uncle's disenchantment with MCC ('*Surrey* was *his* county') and on one occasion ordered a Clare player to remove his MCC sweater. 'Not in *my* pavilion, please.'

Bentley Road was the finest batting wicket in Cambridge, including Fenners, and Ernie nursed the square like a baby. Players were required to inspect the soles of their cricket boots when they returned to the pavilion. Any hapless individual who had lost a stud (they were nailed or screwed into the leather soles in those days) was required to go out and retrieve it before it could damage the pristine blades of Ernie's wicket cutter. As

188

dusk fell, a forlorn figure could occasionally be seen still engaged on this thankless task.

The Pavilion was ruled with equal sway by Mrs Hobbs, Connie, who provided the ample cricketing teas and took a motherly interest in the private lives of the team members. I was gratified that when I wrote to her many years after we had left, she still remembered us and particularly mentioned John Light, Yorkshireman and opening bat.

Old Alleynian's were well represented amongst Clare cricketers: brothers Nigel and Neil Bennett and Peter Howland (Captain in 1968). Ernie generally compared them (unfavourably!) with Nick Cosh, who had preceded them from Dulwich through the University (though not Clare) and played in the Varsity match in each of his three years. None of my contemporaries made it into the Blue side but Jim Paul (Captain in 1967) had games for the University. Rab Murray (Captain in 1969) and Mark Mildred were a formidable opening attack for the Crusaders.

I recall a game on a hot day in May in which our leg spinner, Keith Lloyd, was bowling with an approach between the umpire and the stumps. In the nature of such bowling, he over pitched and was driven straight back down the wicket. Keith swayed to the side to avoid the ball which went on to strike the unfortunate umpire full on the temple. He fell to the ground unconscious and was ministered to by one of several nurses who were attracted to Cricket at Bentley Road around that time. Eventually we saw the casualty into the ambulance and off to Addenbrookes Hospital (then on Trumpington Street). Only as the ambulance disappeared from view and the cool evening breeze began to blow across Bentley Road did we realize that we had also dispatched various sweaters and other items of cricket gear wrapped round the waist of the said Umpire. I guess he was gratified to be visited by most of the team that evening. He made a full recovery.

In June we had cricket weeks when we played games against the Quidnuncs and entertained touring sides including The Free Forresters and The Sussex Martlets.

After the end of the Easter terms we toured to Sussex. Our first game, *en route*, was always against the Staff College at Camberley, followed by games against Horsham, Ditchling, and a Sunday game against Rottingdean. We lodged at a pub in Worthing, and late into the night Ernie recounted tales of Cricket matches long past and, out of earshot of Connie, tales of conquests of a more intimate variety.

The Rottingdean ground is in a natural amphitheatre in the downs. On Sunday afternoons cars would park round the boundary. We were always well entertained at the clubs we visited but at Rottingdean the club secretary would particularly encourage us to recount the story of the tour so far: cricket and social. As we took the field for the next session, his familiar voice would resound over the public address system with a pen picture of each Clare player's achievements.

In the long vacation term Clare fielded a summer side: The 'Trundlers.' Its particular achievement was to award a tie: broad stripes of pink, yellow and purple which makes the 'bacon and egg' of MCC look restrained.

The highlight of the Trundlers' season was the match against the College Staff captained by the Steward. The College side fielded the usual eleven but the staff played with as many as turned up … twenty or so. This was not an illusion consequent upon the ample refreshments.

BELOW: *The same team, minus two, sitting on Ichabod, a 1932 London taxi bought by R. Morris for £12. The Morris 8 on the left belonged to Ernie Hobbs. Ichabod was used for several years by the Boat Club for tours and visits to regattas at Bedford, St. Ives, St. Neots etc.*

RIGHT: *Ice hockey on the Cam, 1963. From left to right: Julian Platt, Sam Wilson, Tony Gaitskell, Tony Roberts and Chris Greening – all of whom subsequently became members of the 23 Club, which provided the initial funding for this book.*

Photographs of the big freeze were taken by another member of the Club, Ben Wrey.

John Berryman (1914–72) was of a generation of American poets whose work innovated form and meter. Berryman coupled emotional, sexual and mental self-analysis with the new rhythms and forms inspired by jazz and beat. Typical of his poetic generation, Berryman's creative life was lived out in a context of heavy drinking, multiple marriages, serial affairs and nervous collapse; what the critic Ian Hamilton has described as 'the confusion between psychic disrepair and tortured vanity.' Or, in Berryman's more direct phrasing, 'Madness and booze, madness and booze/Which'll can tell who preceded whose?'

When he came to Clare in 1936–38, he was still in the mode of the scholar poet, and when he returned to America he published *Poems* (1942) and *The Disposessed* (1948). His excavation of the work and life of the seventeenth-century New England poet Anne Bradstreet, *Homage to Anne Bradstreet* (1956), demonstrated his originality of mind and voice, but *The Dreamsongs* (1964) are considered by critics to be his finest, most individual collection. Written over ten years, they began as 77 poems with an imaginary protagonist, Henry, and to those he added another section in 1968, *His Toy, His Dream, His Rest.* His *Collected Poems* were published in 1990, with *The Dream Songs* kept intact as a separate section.

The poems reproduced here are from *Love and Fame*, which followed *The Dream Songs* in 1970. John Haffenden has described *Love and Fame* as 'teeming with idiomatic and moral risks and raising fascinating problems of form.' These three poems recall his trip out to Cambridge in 1936. The last line of *Transit* is poignant: Berryman killed himself in 1972 by jumping off a bridge in Minneapolis, into the frozen Mississippi, waving as he did so to passers-by.

Much of Berryman's work is permeated by a sense of loss, for which his own suicide was probably the ultimate resolution. (His father, too, had committed suicide when he was a child.) When he died his last book, *Delusions etc.*, was in press and has some marvellously spare, bleak moments of resignation:

Age, and the deaths, and the ghosts.
Her having gone away in spirit from me.
Hosts of regrets come and find me empty.
I don't feel this will change.
I don't want any thing
or person, familiar or strange.
I don't think I will sing
any more just now;
or ever. I must start
to sit with a blind brow
above an empty heart.

Away

Ah! So very slowly
the jammed dock slides away backward,
I'm on my way to Bumpus' & the Cam,
haunts of old masters where I may improve.

Now we're swinging round, tugs hoot,
I don't think I was ever better pleased
with the outspread opening world & even myself
O when The Nation took my epitaph.

In fifteen minutes I have made a friend
a caricuturiste for Vendredi
who has been covering the elections
& a young tall Haitian doctor joins us now

It beats the Staten Island ferry hollow
I used to take to Clinton Dangerfield
to type out from dictation her pulp Westerns
I'm impressed by the bulk of the ship

192

Yeats, Yeats, I'm coming! It's me. Faber & Faber,
you'll have to publish me some day with éclat
I haven't quite got the hang of the stuff yet
but I swamp with possibility

My God, we're in open water
I feel like Jacob with his father's blessing
set forth to con the world too, only I plan
to do it with simple work & with my ear

London

I hardy slept across the North Atlantic.
We talked. His panoramas,
plus my anticipations, made me new.
He drew large cartoons of me

reclining in my bunk, needing a shave.
(Dean Hawkes had said to me at the end,
about the British differences & my behaviour in Cambridge,
'And, listen, for God's sake, Berryman, sometimes shave.')

Mr Wharton did give me his sad volume
of the medieval genius thief in Canadian.
I told his wife I didn't know how to play bridge,
which (against my principles) was a lie.

Donga debarked at Southampton, tenoring 'Christmas!'
I made up a brief rapprochement with the pouting Haitian
(when girls pout, I used to be available)
and then we docked, south of London.

I took with my luggage a cab to the 'Cumberland Hotel, sir,'
near Marble Arch, the only hotel I'd heard of
& near Bumpus' in Oxford Street:
we arrived & I looked at the entrance

reminding me of the Hotel Pennsylvania
no place for me, not yet met Bhain, not yet met Saul, O my
    brothers,
& said in American 'Let's move on,
I want a small cheap hotel near here, let's go.'

In half an hour, alive after crossing Oxford Street,
that bloody lefthand traffic,
I was downstairs in Bumpus', O paradiso
where I grabbed the Oxford collection of Keats's letters
& the Sloss & Wallis edition of Blake's Prophetic Books.

I went to feel the Elgin marbles, I fed at Simpson's.
Ignoring whores, I walked to a naked night-club
off Piccadilly, leaving early,
& took a 9:06 train up to Cambridge.

Transit

O a little lonely in Cambridge that first Fall
of fogs & buying books & London on Thursday for plays
& visiting Rylands in his posh rooms at King's
one late afternoon a week.

He was kind to me stranded, & even to an evening party
he invited me, where Keynes & Auden
sat on the floor in the hubbub trading stories
out of the Oxbridge wealth of folklore.

I joined in desperation the Clare ping-pong team
& was assigned to a Sikh in a bright yellow sweater
with a beard so gorgeous I could hardly serve;
his turban too won for him.

I went to the Cosmo, which showed Continental films
& for weeks only Marx brothers films,
& a short about Oxford was greeted one evening
with loud cunning highly articulate disdain.

Then I got into talk with Gordon Fraser
& he took me home with him out to Mill Lane
to meet his wife Katherine, a witty girl
with strange eyes, from Chicago.

The news from Spain got worse. The President of my Form
at South Kent turned up at Clare, one of the last let out of
    Madrid.
He designed the Chapel the School later built
& killed himself, I never heard why
or just how, it was something to do with a bridge.

clare's buildings: continuity and change in the twentieth century

193

DUNCAN ROBINSON

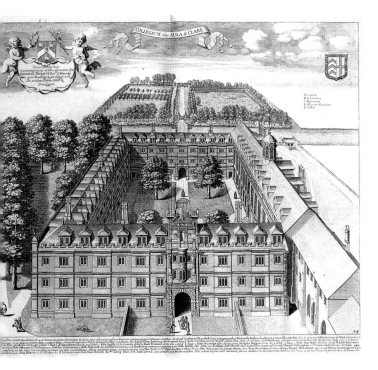

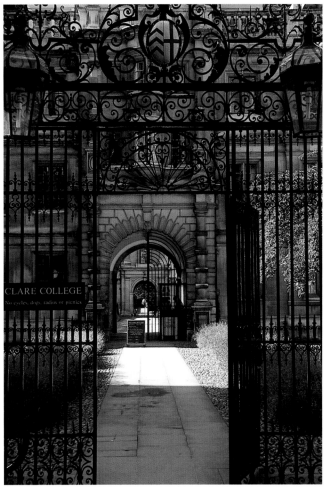

FAR LEFT: *View of the College in 1690, J.F. Loggan, engraving.*

LEFT: *The main gate from the west, 2000.*

The Old Court of Clare is not simply a jewel, it is unique among the Cambridge Colleges founded before 1800 in standing alone, isolated in its architectural integrity from later accretions. When our seventeenth-century predecessors decided not to extend the small medieval courtyard, which was roughly half the size of the present one, but to demolish it by stages and replace it with the buildings we recognize without difficulty from Loggan's prints of *c.*1690, they could not have foreseen the obstacles with which civil war and pestilence would threaten their grand design. Yet by the end of that century it was virtually finished, with the exception of the northern part of the west range containing the Master's Lodge, completed in 1714, and the rebuilding of the chapel in the eighteenth century, to designs which combined the sophis-

ticated neo-Palladianism of James Essex with the enlightened amateurism of Sir James Burrough, Master of Gonville and Caius. Looking at our neighbours along the river, it is hard to explain why Clare resisted the temptation like King's, to throw out a Victorian wing towards the Cam or, like John's to build across it into the meadows. Apart from an early nineteenth-century face-lift, which enlarged

OPPOSITE: *View of the main gate from the east, 2000.*

LEFT: *View of Old Court, with the Hall still covered in ivy, in the early years of the twentieth century.*

the windows and exaggerated the classicism of the garden front to conform to Regency taste, Old Court remained intact, 'the palace in the jungle', as it was described by visitors approaching from the south. Looking back today on its twentieth-century architecture, distinguished as much of it is, perhaps the greatest achievement of the last hundred years has been one of restraint, to respect Old Court and to resist the temptation to introduce, as so many of our neighbours have, architectural elements of their own times to jeopardize what one eighteenth-century undergraduate (from another college) described as 'neat beyond description, and though it might not at first sight strike your fancy as much as Trinity, yet the more you consider, the more you admire it.'[1]

Recalling his undergraduate days, Sir Harry Godwin wrote that 'when College life was revived after the First World War, Clare was a small College restricted by its endowments to about a dozen Fellows, with an undergraduate population of roundabout 125 and with a single court which, although beautiful beyond all others in Cambridge, offered but scanty accommodation.'[2] Expansion was inevitable, and to that handful of Fellows and their

Master, it may well have been the constraints imposed by building on marshland which weighed more than the architectural value of Old Court, in the decision to cross the Rubicam and to begin that development of West Cambridge which was to be continued throughout the twentieth century by University and Colleges alike.

Together with its neighbours, King's and Trinity, Clare had benefitted in the nineteenth century from the enclosure of what was known as the West Field. It was converted by its respective owners into gardens and playing fields until Clare chose to build its second court there as a discrete entity. It was conceived from the start as a memorial to the Clare men who had lost their lives in the First World War, and it was completed over a ten year period, largely thanks to the resourceful management of the College's assets by Bursar Harrison. Having ignored the nineteenth century and its efforts to medievalise the centre of Cambridge, there was an element of ironic genius in Clare's choice of Sir Giles Gilbert Scott to design the new buildings. The heir to one of the great Victorian architectural practices associated with the Gothic Revival he rose to early prominence when, at the age of twenty-two, he won the

196

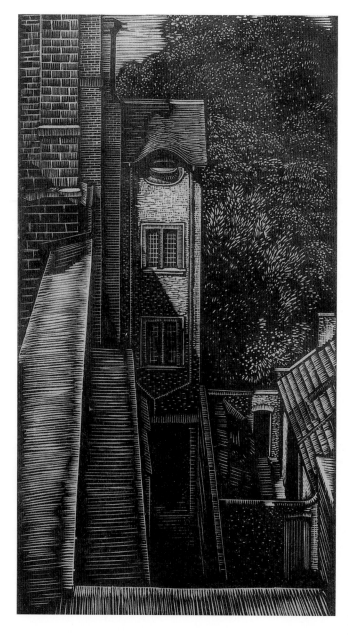

OPPOSITE: *Door to Chapel passage and stairway.*

RIGHT: *Grumbold's Tower and kitchen passage from Chapel leads, north range.*

Linocuts by J.F. Greenwood, 1925.

competition to design Liverpool Cathedral. Throughout his career Scott remained loyal to the tradition he inherited from his grandfather, while at the same time, like his contemporary Edwin Lutyens, he developed for his secular commissions a personal and simplified variant of Georgian classicism. Caught in the twentieth century's battle of the styles, he insisted on creative compromise. 'I hold no brief for the extreme diehard traditionalist or the extreme Modernist,' he wrote. 'Let us avoid being extreme even if it does pay in these vulgar days to be sensational ... let us aim at quality rather than novelty.'[3]

The first phase of Scott's Memorial Court was opened by the University's Chancellor, Lord Balfour, on Armistice Day 1924. It comprised the principal facade, the east range with its monumental memorial arch in which the entrance gates, framed by a massive stone surround, are inserted between two giant columns which support the entablature. On the other side of the arch a similar pair of free-standing columns supports a modified pediment, pierced in the centre to accommodate a large bell. The arch, under which the names of the Clare men who died in both World Wars are now inscribed, adds the appropriate touch of ceremony and solemnity to a complex which is perhaps described best in the words of the late Sir Niklaus Pevsner as 'handsome neo-Georgian with occasional simplified Adam details.'

The thick band of reconstituted stone which runs in a continuous string course above the first floor windows reinforces the importance of the horizontal organization of the court. In a deliberate departure from the towers, turrets and winding stairs of earlier collegiate architecture, resulting in vertical stacks of accommodation with little or no communication sideways, Scott designed staircases with wide, fan-shaped landings on each floor, around which at least four sets of rooms are arranged, together with shared facilities, lavatories, bath and gyp rooms on the same level.

Following closely upon the heels of Clare's decision to build to the west of the river, the University Library Syndicate decided in 1920 to recommend the removal of the Library from its impossibly overcrowded location in the Old Schools to a site which offered potential for future expansion. At first their choice fell upon Corpus Christi's Sports ground, which bordered on to Sidgwick Avenue where the Raised Faculty Building now stands. But in 1922 King's and Clare agreed to consider the sale of the Library's present site, due west of Memorial Court. From then onwards events moved swiftly and in Scott's direction. His responsibility for Memorial Court made him a natural choice as the architect of the new University Library and, although there was talk of a competition, in 1923–4, a matter of months before the opening of the east range of Memorial Court, he produced his first ideas for a building which would eventually face its northern and southern ranges, still to be built.

Initially, Scott proposed for the Library the same combination of grey brick with stone detail and dark red tiles that he had used in Clare. He explained to the Syndics

198

that 'the anxiety to avoid any self-assertiveness has led to the omission of any prominent feature such as a tower or dome.'[4] In profile his proposed library respected the horizontality of Memorial Court, while its entrance with four giant columns supporting an entablature suggested both a reflection and a development of the arch with column screen there. Three years later, however, the University Librarian had the delicate task of explaining to the architect that a potential benefactor was unimpressed by his designs. 'One may say generally', he wrote, 'that the facade was thought not to be sufficiently imposing ... Not that there is a want of dignity, but it is self-effacing, austere, and with no trace of richness.'[5] Less than two months later and long before it was common knowledge that the critical patron was John D. Rockerfeller, Jr, Scott had returned to Cambridge with a new design featuring a central tower rising above a pedimented entrance.

When plans were unveiled fifty years later to build across the middle of Memorial Court, public opinion divided sharply over the propriety of interrupting the ceremonial route which Scott had created through Clare to the University Library. The proponents of the plan, including the majority of Fellows of Clare, pointed out that Scott did not conceive the entire complex *ab initio*. Opponents argued, with equal justice, that plans for both buildings were finalized, presumably to the satisfaction of both the College and the University, long before the completion of the Memorial Buildings in 1935. As it happened, of course, the construction of the Library overtook that of the College; it was opened by King George V in October 1934.

BELOW: *Memorial Court, 2000.*

The architectural press has been on the whole grudging in its praise of Scott's work at Clare. His clients, on the other hand, went back for more after the Second World War and in 1955, following a successful appeal for funds to old Clare men, Thirkill Court was completed as an extension to the south range. With its greater number of 'singles' (bed-sitting rooms) at the expense of sets, and the introduction of corridors to the left and right of the entryways, it may seem less generous in its allocation of space, but with the introduction of post-war comforts, including electric heating, it more than compensated, especially for overseas students who were traditionally allocated rooms there to acclimatize slowly, between October and December, to the rigours of winter in the Fens. Among the guests of honour who attended the opening ceremonies, 'Sir Giles Gilbert Scott was especially welcome, and,' the *Annual's* Correspondent added, 'we may record our appreciation of the important contribution which he has made to the well-being of the College, as well as to the architecture of Cambridge. Both in beauty and in comfort his Memorial Buildings have provided, and – we trust – will continue to provide, one generation of Clare men after another with a fine setting in which to live their College and University lives.'[6]

In 1926, as work continued on Memorial Court, the College turned its attention to another site which had formed part of its estates since the late Middle Ages. In 1392 Clare acquired land and buildings under the shadow of Castle Mound. To that parcel, Master Wilfleet added Castle End Farm in 1466 and before the end of that century John Tapton, Master of St Catherine's, had donated yet another plot bordering on Chesterton Lane. For centuries, Clare managed its holdings in the parish of St Giles as tenancies. In 1889, twenty-two acres of the site were leased to the Reverend Samuel Savage Lewis and his wife Agnes, and it was Mrs Lewis and her twin sister Margaret Gibson who proceeded to build Castlebrae there. Distinguished scholars, they were both leading figures in the academic emancipation of women who used their personal wealth to make an architectural statement about their own aspirations; at the time Castlebrae was described as a house equal to any occupied by the heads of Cambridge Colleges. It was following the death of Agnes Lewis in 1926 that Castlebrae reverted to Clare and was converted into lodgings. With the construction of two more houses, Braeside and Etheldreda, both designed by H.L. Tomlinson, 'the Colony' came into existence. Its further development is one of the College's major achievements of the second half of the twentieth century.

In 1957 David Roberts was commissioned to design a hostel for 40 undergraduates, two caretakers' flats, two breakfast rooms and a kitchen. The result was hailed by Nicholas Taylor, the author of Cambridge New Architecture in 1964 as 'one of Cambridge's best post-war buildings. Its principal qualities are freedom and simplicity. There is freedom in layout and landscaping; freedom from the collegiate shibboleths of enclosed courts; and freedom from the gloom of academic introversion (colours are light and bright, with a Scandinavian tone in the staircases and breakfast rooms).'[7] What Roberts had anticipated was the next wave of emancipation. When students in the 1960s rejected the paternalism of college authority with locked gates, pernoctating tutors and prowling porters, Castle End and Wilflete resembled the blocks of flats which were replacing sub-standard terrace housing in every major city, cleansed by blitz and bulldozers to accommodate the young professional, upwardly mobile urban population of the swinging sixties. By 1990, writing in the *Annual*, Master Matthews could describe the Colony as 'in a very real sense the College's Third Court. In fact more students now live there than either in Old Court or in Memorial Court, Ashby Court and Thirkill Court. Many students spend two of their three years there.'

The transformation did not take place overnight. As a former Rooms Tutor, I recall with embarrassment the conditions under which students and resident housekeepers lived in the 1970s in our Castle Street properties and in St Giles and St Andrews. Slowly the College took old properties in hand, and with a combination of renovation and new construction, converted them into the 'third court' of which we are now justifiably proud. The four terraced houses, 14-20 Castle Street, epitomized the problems; demolition was one option but one which appeared to be insensitive at a time when there was a perceptible shift towards conservation of the existing built environment. The solution, which was to translate the four houses into four sets of six rooms, each with common facilities, has redeemed completely accommodation which used to be allocated to those unfortunate students who drew the worst lots in the annual ballot for rooms. The final component to the Colony was added just over ten years ago with the construction of Castle House, a purpose built addition designed to provide rooms for thirty-six undergraduates and six research students. Planned by the Cambridge

Design Partnership, it was masterminded by Darnton Hollister, Domestic Bursar 1962–78, whose gentle hand has guided so many of the College's architectural projects (and, as Director of Studies, its students of architecture) since he was elected to the Fellowship in 1962.

Around 1980 the College turned its attention to what had become a pressing problem. It was all very well to recall that until the 1930s Clare had not had an undergraduate library. Nor was it much comfort to point out to students with limited access that we were better placed than any other College in terms of our proximity to the University Library. With tripos results second to none, we could not ignore the painful fact that our College library was one of the poorest in Cambridge. After a series of feasibility studies carried out in the vain hope that the Forbes Library could be expanded somehow, even perhaps underground into the flood plain below Old Court, the Fellowship finally agreed that a new library had to be built on the other side of the river. The debates provided a kind of microcosm of those which had divided the University sixty years earlier and at issue, once again, was the relationship of a new building to Scott's Memorial Court.

In appointing an architect for what was bound to be a controversial scheme, the College was fortunate to be able to call upon the services of an old member, Sir Philip Dowson (1947), a Senior Partner of Arup Associates who in 1981 received the Royal Institute of British Architect's Gold Medal. He lost no time in rejecting the suggestion that the new library might be tucked discreetly between the north range of Memorial Court and Burrell's Walk, and boldly advocated the building of a pavilion on the central axis between the Memorial Gate and the entrance to the University Library. A year later the Master wrote plaintively in the *Annual* of the delays in obtaining planning permission, a thin cover for the controversy which was raging in the national press at the time. In supporting the scheme, the Royal Fine Arts Commission (of which Dowson was a member) acknowledged 'that there will always be two views about the siting of a building which blocks Giles Gilbert Scott's vista and ceremonial route through Memorial Court to the tower of the University Library.' The report went on however, in a judgment which was to be crucial in resolving the issue, 'to support wholeheartedly an exceptionally sensitive solution produced in difficult circumstances.'[8]

No-one can deny the subtlety and ingenuity of Dowson's design. His pavilion bisects Memorial Court

200

into two smaller courtyards, both of which serve to highlight the implicit domesticity of Scott's architecture. By a stroke of genius, he placed the entrance to the College Library on the side of the building facing the University Library, leaving a far from blank wall of solid brick to face the approach from the Memorial Arch. It displays the kind of confidence and assertiveness from which Scott too often shrank; Dowson would have embellished it with a fountain but the College preferred, in my view wisely, to site Henry Moore's Fallen Warrior (1956–7) in front of it as yet another subtle reminder of the elegiac theme of the archway. Students of Dowson's work will recognize his signature in the concrete columns of the entrance facade which are reminiscent of those he used twenty years earlier in Leckhampton House (1963–4). There they provide a structural framework, a kind of exoskeleton for the units of accommodation within; in the Clare Library they are integrated into a rather self-conscious display of references and quotations, from Brunelleschi's Pazzi Chapel in

Florence (1429) to Clare's own antechapel (consecrated 1769). It is perhaps worth recalling that Mansfield Forbes cited Geoffrey Webb's 'Architecture of Humanism' extensively in his two-volume history of *Clare College 1326–1926*;[9] one among many reasons why his name should continue to be associated with the Library, together with that of the late Paul Mellon, the College's principal benefactor of the twentieth century.

No account of the College's buildings and grounds would be complete without reference to the restoration of the masonry of Old Court and the creation of what is indisputably the finest riverside garden in Cambridge. At the beginning of the twentieth century the path running from Old Court to the Backs, once it crossed Grumbold's bridge, became a causeway raised on retaining walls of brick above the water meadows on either side. Changes began with the building of Memorial Court, which deprived the Fellows of their garden across Queen's Road. First of all the soil excavated from the site was used to

BELOW: *Forbes-Mellon Library, front view.*

widen the path to raise the lawn and to create the embankment which slopes down towards it. The present layout of the river garden derives from the plans drawn up by one of the Fellows, Nevill Willmer, now emeritus Professor of Histology, with more than a passing interest in garden design. As its centrepiece, he designed the sunken garden, a formal, rectangular enclosure around a lily pond, in which the level of the water corresponds to that of the river nearby. Its inspiration came, as he explained, from the ruins at Pompeii which he had visited twenty years earlier, in 1926. Around that central feature, lawns and borders curve in graceful informality, backed by shrubbery, framed in turn by mature trees. Willmer explained the challenge he faced: 'some Fellows enjoyed sunshine and bright colours, others preferred green and bosky shade. The Dean like to walk between the yew trees and the wall while preparing his sermons. One of the tutors enjoyed sleeping out near the summer house in high summer …'[10] The result is a triumph of landscape gardening, paying equal homage to the serpentine paths and concealed bounds of William Kent's eighteenth-century gardens, and to the combination of formal design and thickly planted flower borders which Gertrude Jekyll introduced into English gardens in the early twentieth century.

After almost three hundred years of exposure to the elements and the effects of pollution from the coal fires which burned throughout Cambridge, the Ketton and Weldon stones with which Old Court is faced had not only lost their distinctive honey colour but had begun to degrade to the point of danger. Under the Bursarship of Brian Cooper, a systematic campaign of renovation was undertaken to repair and replace where necessary, using like stone and the traditional skills of masons who worked their way slowly round the four sides of the Court. For several generations of undergraduates who occupied rooms in the attics, the presence (and after-hours convenience) of scaffolding from paths to parapets is an abiding memory; the final result is another of the century's unobtrusive but far-reaching achievements.

Of some of the renovations which took place behind those facades, on the other hand, the less said the better. Fortunately, by the end of the century the tide had turned against fluorescent lighting and wood in-grain wallpaper. The small dining hall underwent a particularly unfortunate modernization during the sixties, when the lower walls were given shiny black panels devoid of mouldings and the ceiling was timber boarded to reflect the rage for

Scandinavia in contemporary design. While it worked well as a flavour at Castle End and to perfection as the guiding principle of Clare Hall, it rapidly became a painful anachronism in the context of Old Court. Thankfully it was reversed twenty years ago, although the area surrounding it, beyond the screens, has yet to be rescued from the equally insensitive horizontal panelling which surrounds the ocean-liner stairwell with its glass panels and teak handrails leading downwards to the Buttery. At basement level, on the other hand, the present JCR and cafeteria represent a major gain of space and amenity. Twenty-five years after that successful excavation, the time has come for minor adjustments, along with a complete refurbishment of one of the most heavily and effectively used areas in Old Court. Finally the improvements to Memorial Court, which began with the ingenious attic conversions of the seventies, are nearing completion. When those rooms were built, gas fires and running water were luxuries; today's expectations include central heating and en-suite bathrooms.

Whatever the future holds for the College, the last century is bound to be regarded as its most active, architecturally, since the seventeenth. At its outset Old Court and the College were synonymous, even for those undergraduates who spent one or more years in licensed lodgings. Today Memorial Court and the Colony provide the bulk of our accommodation for undergraduates on sites which lie at some distance from each other and from our historic centre. In this essay I have tried to suggest that in different ways, each of these twentieth-century developments was innovative, both architecturally and socially. Both reflect changes in the structure of our academic community which has become less rigid and less formal than it was a hundred years ago. And although Old Court continues to function as the academic, administrative and social centre, the building of the Forbes Mellon Library in Memorial Court may in time prove to have been a further significant step in the social and architectural history of the College. The all too apparent lack of space in Old Court, and of flexibility in its use, adds weight to the argument in favour of reducing pressure there by adding amenities to the other two sites. Whether that happens or not will depend to some extent on our continuing evolution as a College which is responsive to the intellectual and social welfare of its members; on balance, our twentieth-century architecture suggests we are on the right track.

1 M.D. Forbes (ed.), *Clare College 1326–1926*, 2 vols., (Cambridge University Press for the College, 1928), I, p. 118.

2 H. Godwin, *Cambridge and Clare*, (Cambridge University Press 1985), pp. 19–20.

3 Quoted in G. Stamp, 'Sir Giles Gilbert Scott', R. Dixon (ed.), *Sir Gilbert Scott and the Scott Dynasty*, South Bank Architectural Papers, (London 1980).

4 Quoted in 'Notes from the Master', *Clare Association Annual*, 1981–2.

5 Quoted in C.N.L. Brooke, 'The University Library and its Buildings', Peter Fox (ed.), *Cambridge University Library: The Great Collections*, (Cambridge University Press 1998), p. 224.

6 Anon., *Clare Association Annual*, 1955.

7 N. Taylor, *Cambridge New Architecture, A guide to the post-war buildings*, published by the Editors at (Trinity Hall, Cambridge, 1964), p. 82.

8 Quoted in 'Notes from the Master', *Clare Association Annual*, 1981–2.

9 G. Web, 'Association of Humanism' in *Country Life*, 10 July, 1926.

10 N. Willmer, 'The Fellows' Garden', *Clare Association Annual*, *1988–9*, reproduced in this volume, pp. 235–41.

RIGHT: *Forbes-Mellon Library, light falling into the Octagon.*

PETER KNEWSTUBB AND PETER ALLINSON

Through the later half of the twentieth century, it has been possible for Clare students to see at least once in their time at Clare a display of the College silver. This has placed on view for one afternoon, an impressive array of pieces with dates of origin going back to 1525. Except for wartime interruptions it is likely that students in the earlier half of the century had similar opportunities to admire these treasures, which are well described in the book *Clare College 1326–1926*, Volume II,[1] and in other reference books on the silver held by Cambridge colleges.

The purpose of this chapter is to comment more specifically on changes to the Collection during the twentieth-century, a survey which will supplement the information in the older references. The Collection has received many interesting and valued additions through the generosity of its Fellows and former students, and sometimes through the generosity of their families after a death. The College's aim is to make use of its silver, often on a daily basis, rather than to lock it away for most of the year.

Table silver

It is very helpful to our aim of making use of the silver that prospective donors sometimes ask what would be useful. Clare has received several lovely pieces in this way which are in daily use on the table. Most recently, Dr G.H. Wright (Fellow) in 1997 gave a most elegant pepper mill of unique design and engraving, which includes both the College arms and those of Dr Wright's family (1)*. Equally delightful are a pair of sugar casters[2] given by Dr M.G. Bown (Fellow) in 1993 (2). Similarly in daily use are the two pepper mills[3] given by Professor A.C. Chibnall (Fellow) in 1964 (3). Professor Chibnall's pieces are individually designed, though both commemorate Richard de Badew, one of the original founders of the College when it

was called University Hall, before Lady Elizabeth rescued it from bankruptcy in 1326. Earlier in the century donors have had regard to other culinary needs in giving pairs of salt cellars of a rare 'reel' pattern (4), (G.N. Pitt in 1906, and W. Allis-Smith in 1934), and others covered mustard pots of more conventional pattern (W.H. Wing in 1901, G.V. Carey in 1929 and F.I. Wane in 1969).

The table is sometimes graced also by a very elegant water jug given by Professor H.M. Chadwick (Fellow) in 1950 (5), but we have only one such, and there are often many Fellows dining. Professor Chadwick was Professor of Anglo-Saxon and Norse Studies for many years, and the jug has features suggestive of Viking culture. A quite original design of tableware is the crème-brulée server given by Professor S.W. Jackman in 1971 (6), which combines both a ladle for serving with a hammer for the initial cracking of the top layer of caramel. There are some who aver that the recipe for crème-brulée was originally evolved in Clare College. Four Fellows gave toast racks of different patterns around 1960 (one is illustrated at (6)), but alas we seem only rarely to find toast on the menu now – perhaps that fashion will return. Dr A.R. Peacocke, Dean in the years 1973–84, made a novel and helpful gift in 1984, when he had the College grace engraved on a silver plaque then mounted on a reading board, replacing a printed version which was becoming worn and less easy to read.

A description of table silver is clearly incomplete without reference to candlesticks, of which Clare has a remarkable collection illustrating the styles from 1686 to recent times. On this account candlesticks and candelabra given in the twentieth-century (though often made at earlier times) are not always in use, yet have their own charm and are noted when they appear. They would most frequently be those from Professor N. Willmer (Fellow), given in 1993, made in 1906, and the gilt candlesticks of 1791 and matching dishes (made in 1852) from the estate

Numbers in brackets refer to catalogue entries at the end of this article

204

of R.G. Wall, given in 1986. The gathering of Fellows and their guests after dinner, besides offering a second occasion for the use of candlesticks, often sees use of a very fine coffee service (7) with an interesting history. Professor R.S. Hutton was the first Goldsmiths Professor of Metallurgy, 1931–42, and Prime Warden in 1942 of the Worshipful Company of Goldsmiths. At his retirement in 1949 the Goldsmiths presented him with the coffee pot, which he then gave to the College. Clare then commissioned a hot milk jug and sugar bowl in the same style in 1950. By 1964 the number of Fellows (and the calls for coffee) had increased, and Professor Hutton gave the College a second coffee pot of the same pattern. Then in 1971, after his death, his widow gave a second sugar bowl (with spoon) engraved as in his memory. Thus the whole set is associated with Professor Hutton. There was also in the Combination Room a cigarette box of very elegant modern design, given in 1964 by Sir Eric Ashby (as he then was) to mark his first five years as Master; few Fellows now smoke, but it is unfortunate that it was stolen from there in April 1988.

Chapel plate

The Chapel uses some of the oldest items which the College has, but there are notable twentieth-century items. The altar cross now in use for services, replacing a brass cross, is a silver-gilt design with a walnut back, made in 1955 and in part given by the undergraduates of that time (8). A chalice and paten were commissioned in 1953 (the year of the Coronation of Queen Elizabeth II) to reduce the frequency of use of the gold plate (*c.* 1618), and likewise the impressive alms dish given by Mr T.C. Brown (Fellow) in 1993, welcome as a splendid piece, also reduces the wear and tear, even with careful use, of the alms dish of 1671.

Other notable items

Among many other donations are two ornamental bowls given by the College on special occasions and generously returned by the family after death of the recipient. One is the rose-bowl given to Mrs Atkinson in 1906 by all members of the College in celebration of 50 years as Master of Clare of her husband, the Reverend Edward Atkinson. The other item noted is a bowl and cut cover, (also described as a rose-bowl, (9) presented to Professor H. Godwin in 1972. The presentation was largely occasioned by his tenure as Acting Master during the absence on leave of Sir Eric Ashby, at a time which coincided with the debates over admission of women to Clare. The unique design calls to mind Professor Godwin's work on the primitive botanical species *Dryas octapetala*.

Two pieces of fine modern design have an interesting history; a pair of silver-gilt mugs were engraved (one for each of them) and given to Mr and Mrs Galer in 1960, on their retirement from long College service (10). The mugs were eventually bought back by the College from the estate of Mr and Mrs Galer in 1967. Another item is much older, but also has an interesting history dating back to the admission of Henry Delves as a fellow-commoner in 1718. The fellow-commoners had some special privileges and were usually of the nobility, and Henry was the only son of a baronet. In 1722 he gave the College a fine cup and cover, suitably inscribed and in Britannia standard silver. Britannia was a higher grade than sterling, and was required by law to be used by silversmiths from 1697 to 1720, because the fraudulent clipping of the edges of sterling silver coinage had become so prevalent. Henry Delves' cup could legally have been made in sterling silver, but he apparently chose the higher standard. This was no doubt appreciated by Clare, yet by the mid-nineteenth century tastes had changed, or Clare had more cups than it needed, and in 1859 or thereabouts several pieces of silver were sent to Peters, the Cambridge silversmith, for the making to order of a set of candelabra, which the College still has and exhibits. The candelabra were engraved as the gift of the several alumni whose original gifts had been surrendered, presumably with the instruction that they be melted down to make the new items. The melting of the original gifts evidently did not happen, as at least three of the pieces have been seen since that time. We must presume that Peters had too much respect for the older craftsmanship to destroy it, and just used new sterling silver. It seems unlikely that the College would have suggested that the engraved pieces be sold on, even if the donors were then dead, but such sales must have happened. So it was that the cup and cover given by Henry Delves (11) came on the market at Sothebys in 1963, and was repurchased by the College, and we are glad to have it back in our keeping.

Those who have attended a Reunion Dinner at Clare may have seen exhibited on one of the tables the extraordinary 'pineapple' cup given by the Reverend E.E. Dorling in 1938 (12); it is said to be a replica of one dated *c.* 1500, but the whereabouts of the original, if it still exists, is unknown. Another generous gift was from the estate of

A.C.D. ('Stiffy') Pain, who had a lot to do with the Clare Boat Club in his day, and also as a hobby collected ancient silver. We were pleased to receive in 1974, and remember him by, a very valuable and interesting collection of spoons, in varying styles from the reign of each monarch from 1525 (Henry VIII) to 1705 (Anne). The single apostle spoon from 1525 is the oldest item in Clare's collection.

Two items with a somewhat humorous history must finish this list. We have an interesting drinking vessel, the Trinity Hall tun, bearing the arms of Clare and of our neighbouring College, to commemorate the time when their kitchens were out of order, and we fed them from our kitchens through a hole in the wall. Then we have two cricket balls from the 1930s, with silver shields attached to note the very effective bowling of Henry Thirkill in the Long Vacation matches of Trundlers v Old Trundlers (*i.e.* alumni). The figures noted were 7 for 32 (on 23 July 1932) and six for 56 (on 29 July 1933). The Trundlers were a combined King's and Clare Long Vacation cricket team.

Descriptions and illustrations of the numbered pieces (references may be found at the end):

1) Pepper Mill
    London 1996, Designer and maker Lucien Taylor
    Silver in lighthouse shape, the body of hammered finish with gilt sawtooth decoration round the base. The cap hexagonal with ball finial with further gilt sawtooth decoration (overall 8" high). The cap inscribed on one face with College arms, on the opposite face with Wright family arms, and on the other four faces a rose. Round the basal rim *1996 Dono dedit Gordon Herbert Wright Soc. Clarensis 1958.*

2) Sugar Casters (pair)
    London 1993, Designer and maker Christopher Bowen (of Ely)
    Both silver in lighthouse shape with round base and octagonal body, the perforated cap dome-shaped (6" high). Inscribed only with the College arms.

205

3) Pepper Mills (two) *ref. 3, items 34 and 35*
    London 1964, Designer Reginald H. Hill, Maker
    C.J. Vander Ltd
    Both pieces silver in lighthouse shape, one with reeded cap and reeded conical finial (8¼" high), the other with ball finial (8½" high). Both engraved laterally with the seal of University Hall, Cambridge, and in script *Ne Ricardi de Badew obliviscamur Auleque Universitatis,* and beneath the base *Ex dono A. C. Chibnall Socii.*

4) Salts (sets of four and of two) *ref. 2, p. 53*

Set of four reel-shaped, hammered, marked for London 1906–7 and engraved George Newton Pitt, M.D. 1906 a pair similar, but with a plain moulding encircling the stem, not hammered, marked for Sheffield 1922–23, Makers T. Bradbury & Sons, and engraved *Willoughby Allis-Smith, A.M. 1934.*

5) Water Jug *ref. 3, item 52*

Sheffield 1950, Designer James Warwick, Maker A. G. Fisher Silver jug chased with deep fluted decorations, those round the bottom representing the ocean and surmounted by an engraved Viking ship (overall 11" high). Beneath the spout engraved the College arms and *Socii in memoriam Hector Munro Chadwick: 1893–1947.*

6) Ladle *ref. 3, item 58*

London 1971, Designer and maker William Powell (in Cambridge) Plain with rat-tail ficoid bowl, and handle bicuspid at the base and reflexed at the top (12" long).

7) Coffee Service (six pieces) *ref. 3, items 18, 19, 20, 21, 41*
London 1950, Designer Reginald H. Hill, Maker Wakely &
Wheeler Ltd (earlier items).

First

Coffee pot, plain with ribbed decoration on borders and with ebonized wooden handle and finial of lid. Inscribed on the upper part of the body *The gift of the Worshipful Company of Goldsmiths to Robert Salmon Hutton, Prime Warden 1942 and first Goldsmiths Professor of Metallurgy University of Cambridge 1931–42. 1949.* Also engraved on one face the Goldsmiths' Company's coat of arms and on the other the College arms with *Aula de Clare Cantab.* (12½" high).

Also

A duplicate of the above but inscribed on one face only with the College arms and *Aula de Clare Cantab.*

Also

Hot milk jug, *en suite* with the above and inscribed on one face only with the College arms and *Aula de Clare Cantab* (11" high).

Also

Sugar bowl, *en suite* with the above and similarly inscribed.

Also

London 1971, Designer and maker David A. Thomas
Sugar bowl and tea-spoon, plain with two lateral handles springing from the plane of the upper lip, biconical in shape. Inscribed on the outside of the bowl the College arms, and on the outside of the basal rim *A gift to Clare College in memory of R. S. Hutton.* The spoon uninscribed.

208

8) Altar Cross *ref 3, item 1*

London 1955, Designer and maker Reginald H Hill
Silver-gilt with a walnut back to the cross (height 24"). The foot *en suite* with the altar candlesticks given by edward betenson in 1686. the inscription is the college arms and *Aula de Clare Cantab* MCMLV.

9) Rose Bowl and Cover

London 1960, Designer and maker Mortimer E. Gould
Silver, a wide shallow bowl with hammered finish on a circular foot, the bowl 4" high and the rim 10" diameter. A close fitting lid with cut decoration depicting the primitive bog plant *Dryas octapetala*, the knob cast in the College arms, giving an overall height of 6". The inscription round the rim is *Presented to H. Godwin by The Master and Fellows of Clare College in recognition of his services as Locvm Tenens for The Master 1958–1959.*

10) Mugs *ref 3, item 31*

London 1960, Designer and maker, A. G. Benney
Two mugs or tankards, plain cylindrical with hammered surface and substantial plain handles; silver gilt inside and engraved with College arms, and on the base, respectively, *Presented to Arthur Edward Galer who served the College from 1924–1960* and *Presented to Minnie Dorothy Galer who served the College from 1927–1960.* (5¾" high)

11) Tazza or Fruit Dish *ref. 3, item 42*

Birmingham 1937, Designer and maker, C.J. Shiner
Silver, with plain conical bowl and conical foot joined by a knop closely engraved with College arms, 1938 and three close lines of lettering *ex dono Caroli Gordon Grant winter a.m. Collegii de Clare alumni.*
(diameter is 12", 7" high)

Bowl or Bonbon Dish *ref. 3, item 8*
Birmingham 1938, same Designer and maker
Silver, without foot and plain except for College arms embossed in the centre, surrounded by large Roman lettering in three lines (same as the above)
(diameter 9",)
'The bowl was completed for the College when the designer of the tazza commissioned initially from the benefaction was less expensive to make than he had expected.'

12) Cup and Cover *ref. 2, p. 42 and ref. 3, p. 24*

London 1911–12, Makers Chapell & Mantell

Silver-gilt, a modified copy of a cup of German style of about 1500 (original source uncertain). Three figures serve as feet supporting an ornamented round base, on which is a cup in pineapple-style finish with a rim formed boldly in sixfold scallops, the cup 9" high. The cover is heavily ornamented with a fence-like form round the edge and with a swordsman as finial (14" high overall). A rather sinister inscription on the cover is *nisi Dominus*, with a drawing resembling a gallows.

13) Cup and Cover *ref. 3 item 22* (not illustrated)

London 1722, Maker William Lukin

Britannia standard two-handled plain cup with strongly domed cover and plain finial. The two handles joined to the cup with foliar thumb pieces and the body divided into two areas by a narrow reeded band, above which the body is engraved with College arms and *Collegium sive Aula de Clare,* and the arms of the donor with *Henricus Delves Filius unicus Thomae Delves Baronetti hujusce Collegii Socio-Commensalis DD* 1722. (11¼" high).

1. M.D. Forbes (ed.), *Clare College 1326–1926,* (Cambridge University Press for the College, 1928) II, Ch. VI, pp. 272–82.

2. E. Alfred Jones, *Catalogue of the Plate of Clare College Cambridge* (Cambridge University Press, 1939).

3. H. Godwin and R.J.L. Kingsford, *The Plate of Clare College Cambridge Supplementary Catalogue 1939–1971* (privately printed by the College, 1972).

209

JCR FOOD SURVEY, 1971

These are the conclusions drawn from the statistical findings of the survey, and our proposals are based on these conclusions:

FIRST COURSES

Of the soups provided that were covered by the survey, the least popular were French Onion (1.90), Leek (1.97) and Clear Vegetable (2.00). We propose that these be served less frequently.

It is clear that Fruit Juice (Orange) (2.97) and fresh Grapefruit (3.09) are both very popular, and not merely as a change from soup (*c.f.* result for Cod Fillet). We therefore propose that either Fruit Juice, or Grapefruit, or both, be provided as permanent alternatives to soup or any other hot first course under the new catering arrangements.

MAIN COURSES

The most unpopular meals were Braised Steak (1.55), Haricot Chop (1.72), Lancashire Hot Pot (1.73), and Pork Chop (1.95). We would therefore propose that these first three should not be repeated, and that the fourth (Pork Chop) be served less frequently. Chicken dishes, however, proved to be quite popular, as was Roast Pork.

VEGETABLES

Most cause for complaint seems to rest in this section. Vegetables generally scored markedly low. We suggest that a considerable part of the reason for this lies in the presentation and cooking of the vegetables. But, apart from this, it is quite clear that Leeks (1.09) are extremely unpopular and should not be continued. We also suggest that Cabbage (1.40 – 1.55) be less frequently provided, unless the presentation can be improved. We further suggest that the greater popularity of Sweet Corn and of Peas is the result of superior presentation.

POTATOES

Mashed Potato varied between 1.43 and 1.83. This is clearly the least popular form of potatoes, but it is also by far the most frequently provided, wherein may lie part of the explanation. We therefore strongly reccommend (sic) that Roast Potatoes (2.24) and Fondante Potato (2.10) and, under the new system, Chips be much more frequently served, and repetition of Mashed Potato for as many as 5 consecutive days be avoided.

SWEET

Sweets were marked consistently high. In particular, Apple Crumble and Ice Cream (3.10) and Blackberry and Apple Tart and Ice Cream (3.01) were highly popular and appreciated. At the other extreme however, Adolpae Creams (1.04) were particularly unpopular, and we propose that these should not be repeated. Bakewell Tart and Sliced Peaches also scored low.

Average Ratings of Dishes served during the Survey:
(Survey held over 13 days)

FIRST COURSES
Grapefruit 3.09
Oxtail Soup 2.41
Mushroom Soup 2.33
Scotch Broth 2.24, 2.33
Romany Soup 2.22
Cod Fillet and Egg Sauce 2.14
Mixed Vegetable Soup 2.12
Clear Vegetable Soup 2.00*
Onion Soup 1.90*
Leek Soup 1.97*

MAIN COURSES
Chicken Casserole 2.58
Roast Pork and Apple Sauce 2.51
Roast Lamb 2.38
Roast Beef 2.30
Curried Chicken 2.32
Steak and Kidney Pie 2.10
Pork Cutlet 2.07
Pork Chop 1.95*
Lancashire Hot Pot 1.73**
Haricot Chops 1.72**
Braised Steak 1.55**

VEGETABLES
Sweet Corn 2.15, 2.10
Peas 2.10
Sprouts 1.91
Diced Carrots and Peas 1.08
Carrots 1.05, 1.00
Cabbage 1.55, 1.40*
Leeks 1.15, 1.09**

POTATOES
Roast Potatoes 2.24
Rice 1.94
Mashed Potato (served 9 times) 1.43 – 1.83*

SWEETS
Apple Crumble & Ice Cream 3.10
Blackberry & Apple Tart & Ice Cream 3.01
Apple Crumble & Custard 2.81
Sherry Trifle 2.73
Apricot Crumble & Custard 2.00, 2.01
Pears Chaudfroid 2.58
Family Mince Pie & Custard 2.50
Francaise Pudding & Custard 2.42
Blackcurrant Flan 2.29
Bakewell Tart & Custard
Sliced Peaches & Cream 2.12
Adolpae Creams 1.04**

Where more than one rating is shown, that dish was served more than once during the survey.
* means that we recommend that the dish be served less frequently
** means that we recommend that the dish be dropped from the menu completely.
Ratings – 0 means inedible, 1 means poor, 2 means average or mediocre, 3 means good, and 4 means very good or enjoyable.

women at clare:
notes from the master

ERIC ASHBY, *THE CLARE ASSOCIATION ANNUAL*, 1970

In February 1879 the Statutory Commission appointed by Parliament to draw up reforms for Cambridge, having considered the statutes of Peterhouse and Clare and certain other Colleges, decided to demand of all Colleges that the tenure of a Fellowship should not be conditional upon either the taking of Holy Orders or on celibacy. No longer would it be obligatory for one third of the Fellows of Clare to become ordained; no longer would Fellowships have to terminate with marriage. A tragic break with five centuries of tradition, a shabby violation of the intentions of the pious benefactors, an irreparable secularization of college life; the loyalty of dons shared between the combination room and the marriage couch; the responsibility of being *in loco parentis* left in the hands of men who might preach and practice infidelity without restraint.

Well, something like it, but far less revolutionary, has happened again. In 1970 the Governing Body of Clare (which comprises all Fellows) met twice to consider the repeal of statute 21 (4) which read 'No woman shall be admitted a member of the College either on the Foundation or otherwise.' A change in statute requires a majority of two-thirds present and voting. On both occasions the majority in favour of repeal comfortably exceeded this ratio.

This change, like the change made less than a century ago, must be judged in the perspective of history, not in the perspective of the year 1970. So I cannot offer you a judgement of the decision, though I can put it into the context of contemporary thought in the world of universities. But first you may be interested in the way the decision was made. The College is *de jure* a corporation of Master, Fellows, and Scholars. The word 'scholars' in this formula does not mean what it means today: it means those students enrolled in the College who are not Fellows. In fact (and it is a fact that we are tempted to brush under the carpet these days) the 'scholars' have never played a part in the formal government of the College. My personal view about this (if I can digress a moment) is that our society is like a guild of masters and apprentices. The apprentices have rights, different from the rights of the masters – that is another story – and one of their rights is to be consulted before the Governing Body makes major decisions concerning the life of the guild. So, although the initiative for considering the admission of women to Clare came from Fellows, junior members were brought into the discussions and a joint committee of senior and junior members produced valuable material, some of which was used for the report which the College offered to send to you and which many of you have read. The decision, however, rested with the Fellows alone.

This has, I'm afraid, created a little resentment among a few Old Clare men, who wished they had been consulted before the decision was taken. On behalf of the College I would like to express my regret for this apparent discourtesy; but it is apparent, not real, for there were three reasons why we felt unable to consult you. One reason is diplomatic: that the matter had to be kept confidential because the press was liable to report gossip (and did, and got it all wrong) and rumours at that stage might have prejudiced the discussions and embarrassed other colleges. Another reason is legalistic: the *de jure* corporation of Master, Fellows, and Scholars, does not include ex-Fellows or 'scholars' who have left. And the third reason is simply practicability: to circulate, to some 6,000 Clare men, all the data required for coming to a decision was beyond our bureaucratic capacity.

Nevertheless, we do have some notion of the reaction of Old Clare men, for 137 of you were interested enough to write to ask for copies of the report on which the decision was based, and 54 of you were kind enough to give your views on the decision, some of you with refreshing pungency. I believe that some sort of acknowledgement was sent to everybody at the time, and I hope that they will regard this article as a further recognition of their kindness in writing. Of course those who replied do not constitute what the pollsters call a random sample (indeed it is commonly supposed that people are more likely to write to complain than to commend!). In any case, after the last general election, opinion polls are at a discount. All the same, the responses from the 54 Old Clare men are instructive if they are not taken too seriously, especially if they are analysed according to the vintage of those who replied. Here is a breakdown:

Entered Clare	In favour	Opposed	Total	Asked for Report
1901–10	1	0	1	2
1911–20	2	6	8	11
1921–30	8	6	14	32
1931–40	7	1	8	25
1941–50	10	3	13	28
1951–60	4	2	6	26
1961–70	3	1	4	13
Total	35	19	54	137

For what these figures are worth they indicate: (i) That 65 per cent of those who replied are in favour of admitting women to Clare – almost the two-thirds majority required by the Governing Body for a change of statute; (ii) The only span of years which contain a majority opposed to admitting women was 1911–20 – even my generation (most of whom are of an age to claim old age pension) were 8 to 6 in favour of the decision; (iii) It looks as though the First World War was the dividing line. But there is no sign that approval is a monopoly of youth; indeed, the only octogenarian to offer an opinion – and he a clergyman at that – wrote: "congratulations on this step forward." Nor, for that matter, is disapproval a monopoly of age: a very young Old Clare man, scarcely five years out of College, wrote: "I count myself very lucky to have been at Clare in an all-male society, which will now be completely destroyed …."

The interest of these figures is their close resemblance to a similar set of figures gathered from nearly 2,000 alumni by Princeton University, which recently decided to admit women not only to its classes but to its dormitories. The Princeton equivalent of the *Clare Association Annual* devoted a special issue to the question, peppered with statistical tables (including the replies to a question to elicit from undergraduates the number of week-ends they would spend away from Princeton with, and without, co-education!). The view of the Old Princetonians were as follows (this time they are expressed as percentages):

Graduated from Princeton	In favour	Opposed	No response
Pre 1915	40	56	4
1916–24	48	43	9
1925–30	53	40	7
1931–40	62	31	7
1941–50	65	31	4
1951–60	79	17	4
1961–	82	16	2
Total (%)	69	26	5

It is interesting to see this similarity of opinion between the alumni of Princeton and the alumni of Clare.

So much for the balance of opinion among Old Clare men, which – from these scraps of evidence – are not very different on this issue from the balance among Fellows of Clare. What are the circumstances which have moulded this opinion? Is it not part of a steady (some women would say sluggish) current of history? The course of women's education in Cambridge has been marked by a succession of what now appear to have been overdue concessions. Eighteen years after the first women passed Little-Go, women were admitted to examinations in the Tripos; that was in 1881. Sixteen years later, in 1897, a Grace for admitting women to degrees was rejected by the University; and another Grace for the same purpose was rejected in 1920. Women were not admitted to full membership of the University until 1948, 85 years after the first women were permitted to sit for Little-Go, 70 years after women were admitted to degrees in the University of London, and 20 years after women had won the vote. It was not exactly a reckless prediction to suppose that the differentiation in treatment between men and women in Cambridge would continue to diminish, and that co-residence – already a feature of a dozen British universities, not to mention Yale and Princeton – would spread to Cambridge. Already the University has changed its statutes to make co-residence possible; there are three mixed graduate foundations, one of them created by Clare itself; and already two other Colleges – King's and Churchill – have announced their intention to admit women. I'm not concerned to argue here whether these trends are desirable or deplorable.

214

The fact is that they are not passing fashions imposed upon us by the young; they are part of a long-term evolutionary change in the place of women in society. There will, in my view, continue to be a sustained pressure on single-sex institutions, not only in the educational world, to admit women. This pressure will generate counter-pressures against the admission of women on equal terms with men which may (as in the Anglican Church) succeed or may (as in the Royal Society and Lloyd's) fail.

So our problem at Clare was to make a positive decision about this issue, rather than to wait until we may be dragged by the current of change into a belated acquiescence. In a memorandum which I circulated to the Governing Body in March 1969 I put it this way: 'The decision which the Governing Body has to make, disregarding all pressures from outside, is whether, on grounds of education in its widest sense, the decision should now be made or deferred into the future.'

The detailed evidence upon which the Governing Body took its decision is in the report which is available to any Old Clare man for the asking. So all I add here are my personal impressions about the evidence.

The arguments against co-residence were strong. It would be a break with tradition, certain to change the character of the College. It would put the Master and Tutors to a great deal of trouble, for it would mean arranging new admissions procedures, suitable accommodation, and including women in the Fellowship. It might distract the young of both sexes and make academic quality not better, but worse. It might diminish the pool of athletic ability in the College. Why, then, embark on this disruptive operation now?

This was certainly the spirit in which some of us entered upon the discussions. Far from searching for arguments in favour of co-residence, some Fellows hoped to find compulsive arguments against it. First, we enquired how it works elsewhere. We consulted people who knew about co-residential halls in six other universities. The replies were almost unanimously favourable, indeed enthusiastic. The co-residential hall of residence is 'a better social community'; 'an unqualified success'; a community 'easier to run, pleasanter to live in … with fewer disciplinary problems'; there are 'higher standards of behaviour, friendships develop and dissolve naturally … without waste of time'; in brief, men and women work and relax together without the artificiality of contrived meetings merely for enjoyment. And – the most convincing evidence – new co-residential halls are being built and single-sex halls are being converted for co-residence.

Cambridge colleges, quite rightly, emphasize that education is not limited to the classroom; indeed, the most valuable education for many students is the civilizing experience of living in a collegiate society. The evidence we got indicated that the quality of this sort of education would probably be enriched, not impoverished, by co-residence. Another factor which we could not ignore is the rapid spread of co-education in schools, including some of the most distinguished public schools. Would it (we asked ourselves) be educationally bad, or good, to bring boys into an all-male society for three years after they had grown up in a co-educational school for the previous six or seven years?

We then turned to the problem of equity. The overall percentage of women undergraduates in British universities is 27; in Cambridge the percentage is 12. Discrimination on grounds of sex is surely no less reprehensible than discrimination on grounds of colour. There is a good case, therefore, for increasing the opportunities for women to come to Cambridge. The three existing women's colleges are being expanded, and Clare has contributed generously to the cost. If a fairy godmother could be found, it might be possible to endow a new women's College. But in view of the evidence in favour of co-residence from other universities, some of us began to doubt whether, in the long run, the foundation of new colleges confined to women would be the best educational solutions. The alternative contribution toward equity would be for some men's colleges to admit some women.

Thirdly, there is the question of academic standards. I see no great value in making a fetish of attempts to be top of the league in tripos results, any more than to be head of the river: the one distorts the purpose of study; the other distorts the enjoyment of sport. But Cambridge is providing a high quality education at public expense, and it is an obligation on colleges to select undergraduates who can make the best use of this opportunity. In some subjects the intellectual quality of women undergraduates in Cambridge is, on the average, distinctly higher than that of men at Clare. By admitting some women to Clare in these subjects the intellectual quality of those who gain places in the College would undoubtedly be improved.

Add together these potential advantages of co-residence – the demonstrable civilizing influence, the stimulus to music and drama, the prospects of improved intellectual quality, the contribution to redress the imbalance of opportunity between men and women in Cambridge, and other reasons which have influenced those who had to decide – and weigh them against the arguments for preserving the *status quo*: you will see (I think) how some of the Fellows of Clare came to reconcile themselves to the proposal that the College should admit women, and how others were enthusiastic about the proposal, notwithstanding all the work it will involve.

The decision carries various safeguards. For instance, the annual intake will be increased from 110 to 120, so that we shall admit about 90 men each year. On this basis, Clare will still remain one of the middling-size colleges in its population of men undergraduates.

It was after discussions on these lines, lasting over years, not months, that the Governing Body came to its decision. I think the view of some of the Fellows could be summarized as follows: that when you are taking a calculated risk, the better place to be is in the vanguard, not in the rear. Or (who knows?) in 90 years' time, or much sooner, it may appear to our successors to have been a change as natural, and as beneficial, as the abolition of celibacy for Fellows, made 90 years ago, now appears to us.

215

women at clare:
becoming senior tutor

POLLY O'HANLON

Many old members of Clare will have preserved, amongst the haphazard collection of images and memories of student life, some particularly vivid image associated with their first arrival in Cambridge. Mine was not of Clare itself, of the Memorial Buildings which, though I do not remember it now, must have impressed me with their bulk and their brightly lit windows in the semi-darkness of that autumn evening. The images for me are not of buildings or people, but of the journey beforehand: of the extraordinary flatness of the East Anglian landscape glimpsed from the windows of a speeding train, of a sense of incredulity at the expanse of its sky. My journey had begun in Plymouth that morning, where granite suburbs framed the horizon and the world always seemed shut in by hills. The contrast somehow seemed fitting, marking a movement from a familiar, closed world to one of infinite openness and possibility. Some of the possibilities seemed immediate and obvious: the chance to develop the history I had so enjoyed at school, to find new friends and explore new activities, to develop the personal independence that marks a successful transition from school to university life. There was a sense of challenge too: this was the first year in which any of the former men's colleges had taken women. It was not at all clear how women would fit into the older institutions in the College: its living spaces of staircases and common rooms, its sporting clubs, its largely male Fellowship and tutorial network. Clare had taken a bold step in admitting women: but in what style and on what terms remained to be seen. These were the immediate possibilities, and to this contemplative student on the train, what lay beyond them seemed too remote to be worth considering. Coming to the College as an undergraduate seemed astonishing enough: the Fellows and tutors there were clearly recruited from a different species, and it certainly never occurred to me that I might return to join them.

Many women have spoken of their experience during Clare's early years as a mixed College. There were some common themes: the sense of curiosity mixed with discomfort at our small numbers, the surprise at the superficial uneventfulness of women's assimilation into the College, the speed with which many women established a strong presence in College sports and social life. The sense of special difficulty faded very rapidly: by my final year, women in the College seemed to grapple with problems, work through challenges and enjoy successes that were common to all undergraduates. This sense of normality and stability came in large part from the atmosphere of quiet welcome created by the Fellows, and in particular by those who had worked so hard to bring about women's admission into the college: Eric Ashby as Master, the Senior Tutor Charles Feinstein, and John Northam. For me as an historian, it also came from our Director of Studies, Charles Parkin. Charles was special: a long-standing resident Fellow who brought qualities of quiet understanding, patience and humour to his teaching, and whose supervisions often merged into an extended rumination on the nature of history and its limitless possibilities, as learning, as discipline, as philosophy, as a form both of private solace and of shared understanding. It was from Charles, too, that students in the College often learned something about Clare as a community. As an historian, Charles naturally had a great fund of stories to tell, some inherited from older Fellows, some relating to his own early years as a young lecturer, and some to more recent encounters in the years when the College was contemplating the admission of women. But Charles conveyed something more about Clare than its local oral traditions. The College as a community was not a sentimental construct, an intellectual comfort blanket; nor was it simply the natural human attachment to Clare's peculiar beauty in its setting by the river. Community here meant rather a vigorous and often critical companionship between people who lived as well as worked together, for whom the dynamics of intellectual exchange, friendship and criticism provided an environment at once stimulating and nurturing. With a tutor like this, who could help wanting to be an historian too?

But an academic training as an historian involves departures also, and my own training led me to some years spent researching in London and then in India, where there were communities of different kinds to be explored, and new networks of friends and colleagues to be developed. When I returned to Clare as a Research and then a Teaching Fellow in the early 1980s, it was in the very different political atmosphere of Mrs Thatcher's period in government. Cambridge was not exempt from the sense of attack on the values and institutions of academic education. This seemed to be reflected in a new sense of anxiety and defensiveness in the College, which felt, in subtle, ways rather different from the pioneering and outward looking spirit of the early 1970s. There was anxiety about the future of the Cambridge collegiate structure, with its intensive teaching and tutorial system, which suddenly seemed very vulnerable in a context of declining resources for higher education. There were worries, too, that the University might be about to see a new wave of student protest reminiscent of the troubles of the 1960s, as undergraduates took up issues such as nuclear disarmament and South African apartheid with a new vigour. There were also changes within Clare, as the Fellowship expanded to take account of the growth of new courses and new specialisms, and as academic and new administrative pressures on teaching Fellows increased through the decade. When I became Director of Studies and a Tutor in the early 1990s, it was noticeable that pressures on students too had increased: there seemed much higher levels of student anxiety across a whole range of issues, from the burdens of work, to employment prospects and sexual health.

What was remarkable, though, was the robustness and imagination with which the College responded to these pressures. From the middle of the decade and under the quietly effective guidance of Terry Moore, steps were taken to modernize and strengthen the tutorial system, to pass on to support staff some of the administrative burdens that had accreted to teaching Fellows, and to expand the College's information systems so as to make them accessible to a wider range of teaching and administrative staff. Collegiality amongst the Fellowship emerged in new and strengthened ways. It was true, as some Fellows noted with regret, that fewer Fellows dined together in the evenings. Yet the Senior Common Room remained a busy centre of activity,

with Fellows finding new and imaginative ways to combine a sociable lunch with the discussion of teaching matters and the conduct of other college business. It was also encouraging to see the mature and reflective way in which students at the College responded to these new pressures. While some no doubt settled for a narrow contentment with their own relative security in the College, many others continued to look outward and to engage with wider issues in higher education: with the effects on less-well-off students of the declining value of the student grant, with the relatively limited constituency of schools from which Cambridge colleges still drew their applicants, and with the poor representation of women in the academic staff of British universities. This outward looking sense of many students at the College made it seem natural that they should gradually assume a role as responsible partners in an intellectual community, rather than its junior apprentices. This role received clear recognition when the College gave full voting rights to student representatives on all major College committees.

All of these changes provided a very heartening environment for a busy Director of Studies and Tutor. At about the same time, I also took on responsibility for the allocation of College rooms. This may sound a straightforward administrative task, but in fact few questions aroused stronger feeling amongst Fellows and students alike than the quality and size of their rooms. The role of Rooms Tutor in Clare is effectively one of hotelier to a lively and sometimes cantankerous group of guests, always slightly too large for the hotel. There are delicate negotiations with senior members over rights to particularly desirable rooms, students to see whose earnest desire to share has waned on closer acquaintance, and occasional brisk reminders to be issued that redecorating rooms or taking in paying guests might not be included in the rights of College membership. This range of responsibilities meant a great deal of variety and sometimes incongruity in most working days: a supervision on the Aztec empire might be followed by a session of pastoral advice to a student with family problems, and then by discussion with the Housekeeper as to whether goldfish constituted pets under the terms of the College's tenancy agreements. It was therefore with some relief that I was able to relinquish some of these tasks, and to take on in 1997 the role of Admissions Tutor in the Arts.

This was a more focused responsibility. I had the good fortune to be introduced to its complexities by Ken Riley as Senior Tutor, and to be working alongside William Foster, also a new Admissions Tutor in the Sciences. Ken combined

RIGHT: *All of the Senior Tutors in the Thirkill Room, September 2000: Tim Smiley, Polly O'Hanlon, Charles Feinstein, Ken Riley, Simon Franklin, Nick Hammond, John Northam.*

an encyclopedic knowledge of schools in all parts of the country with enviable database skills. I possessed neither of these in the remotest degree, so my learning curve in the first year was alarmingly steep. But these were interesting and contentious times for admissions, and so there was much incentive to learn quickly. After a decade or more of government pressure on all British universities to expand their numbers, the spotlight now began to turn to Oxford and Cambridge in particular, and to the relatively small numbers of state school candidates applying to Oxford and Cambridge Colleges. This was a serious matter for us, and not simply because the new Labour government quickly made plain its interest in the issue. It suggested that there might be a significant body of talented students in schools and colleges across the country that never considered applying to Cambridge. If the College were to maintain its very high academic reputation, it seemed important to widen the pool from which we drew our students, and to find ways of encouraging applications from schools who might never have considered sending us candidates. This was not at all an easy task. The image of stuffy and elitist Oxbridge colleges is very difficult to shift in public perception, and there is a dispiriting repetitiveness with which old images are recycled and reinforced in newspaper headlines. In common with other colleges searching more widely for talent, we quickly drew fire from both sides: from independent schools who suspected us of social engineering, and from state schools aggrieved at the cautiousness of our approach.

This was a very fertile ground for misunderstanding, and we did all we could to explain our procedures to schools, parents, applicants and old members alike. There was no question of our operating quotas of any kind, or of responding to external political pressures. It was, more narrowly, a matter of our own interest as a college committed to academic excellence and intellectual diversity, and continuing to look for those qualities across the widest possible field. Transparency itself was an issue, both in explaining our evolving admissions policy to members and old members of the College, and in the way that it was presented to schools and colleges outside. It was clear that considerable mystery often surrounding the way in which Cambridge colleges actually selected candidates for admissions, and the interview process itself was poorly understood in many schools without experience of Oxbridge. We therefore welcomed, in the autumn of 1999, an approach from the Vice-Chancellor's office to open up our procedures in Clare to a respected education correspondent from one of the national newspapers. After discussion in the Governing Body, and with the leading support of the Master and Senior Tutor, the College agreed to allow completely free access to all parts of the admissions process, including live interviews themselves, with the consent of candidates. No college in Oxford or Cambridge had done this before, and it was heartening and impressive to see the degree of consensus in Clare that the principle of transparency made the work and the risks worthwhile. The resulting newspaper articles reported very favourably on Clare's procedures, and contributed valuably to a wider public debate about access to Oxbridge. Shortly afterwards, the Chancellor of the Exchequer led a renewed attack on the exclusivity of Oxford and Cambridge colleges, and it was very helpful ourselves to be able to point to our own prior initiatives in this area. Over the last two years, we have seen a substantial increase in the pool of new schools applying to us, and we hope in due course that this will be reflected in the strength and diversity of our student body. These changes would not have been possible without the imagination of the Master, Bob Hepple, and of Simon Franklin, the Senior Tutor, who supported our work in admissions at every stage.

But College life consists of much wider issues too, and it was somewhat unexpectedly that I found myself moving from admissions to take on the role of Senior Tutor in the autumn of 2000. With Simon's move to a Readership in the university, the post became vacant, and it was with much trepidation that I accepted this new position. I would be Clare's first woman Senior Tutor, and my predecessors in Simon Franklin and Ken Riley had set very high standards in the imagination and humane efficiency brought to the task. Any new College officer is deeply dependent on the willingness of Fellows and students alike to give their skills to the work of the College, and to the Master for creating an atmosphere of support in which initiatives can flourish. Clare's robust tradition of collegiality, and its combination of stability for students and imaginative response to change provide a reassuring environment for a Senior Tutor new to the job.

The trains in East Anglia move more slowly these days, and it seems a very long time since my own first journey brought me to the College. But that early sense of openness and possibility have never been disappointed. These seem to me the most valuable qualities that a college can hold out to the new students that are its lifeblood, and my hope is that our own generation in the College will be as effective as our predecessors in sustaining them.

220

Punting into Clare by BARBARA BECK

YOU would think that a girl bright enough to be one of only 38 admitted for the first time this year to Clare College, Cambridge (formerly, men only), would have been encouraged by her teachers. But you would be wrong. When Vivienne May told her careers mistress at her grammar school in Gloucester that she wanted to be a doctor, she was advised to take up nursing. Vivienne ignored the advice and is now reading medicine at Clare —the first girl from her former school to get into Oxbridge.

Four of the girl pioneers at Clare told me similar stories. It was their teachers, not their parents, who tried to dissuade them. Nursing, a career in the forces, secretarial college, were all alternatives put to them. Fortunately, like Vivienne, they backed their own faith in their abilities. And, as Keren Hull of Bangor, North Wales, put it: "We realise how lucky we are. I appreciate it more and more every day."

Keren is also reading medicine after obtaining A levels in maths, physics, chemistry, and biology. She had wanted to be a nurse but her father, a potter, said: "Why not be a doctor?" Her older brother is reading philosophy at York and, according to Keren, her 16-year-old sister is the really intelligent one of the family. "How nice for your parents that they have three brilliant children," I suggested. "Oh no, they're the ones who are brilliant," she said.

Claire Cockram saw a television programme about Millfield, the progressive boarding school; when she was 15 and determined to go there. Knowing her parents wouldn't be able to afford the fees, she applied behind their backs for a scholarship and got it. "The advantage of Millfield was that so many were trying for Oxbridge; I wasn't marked out as special," she said. She read natural sciences for the first term at Clare and then switched to religious studies and gives the college full marks for their help and understanding. "They helped me to come to terms with myself," she told me.

And Rachel Symes, reading archaeology and anthropology, corroborated the other girls' stories of help from parents. "My mother knew about Clare admitting girls before my school did," she said.

Had there been any hostility from men at the college? Not at all, they assured me. On their first day, feeling just as nervous as the first day at grammar school, a group of third year men descended and "organised us." The organising seems to have consisted of punting on the Cam and taking them to parties. "They told us no one had done it for them and we must promise to do it for first years, next year." They all promised. Vivienne said: "It was the men and women in other colleges who were inclined to say: 'Oh, one of them,' as if we were a different species." Girton girls particularly, she added.

The girls think that the teaching staff probably went out of their way to disguise any opposition but are now entirely on their side. It was the domestic staff who were most vociferous in their opposition before the girls arrived. But now they are, if anything, "too kind."

The girls think their presence has given the college a boost; given it a greater community spirit. But they did admit that there was a certain amount of tension not just in Clare but in Cambridge generally, because of the unnatural ratio of men to women. "Social life is quite a strain," said Vivienne.

reflections from the seventies

CELIA DUFF

Have you ever known a full length mirror cause controversy? The Millennium landmarks have had their say this year. All are large, expensive and imposing; most of us have a view, often ill informed. All were designed to be noticed and commented upon and there should be no surprise at the level and noise of debate.

But a full length mirror?

Perhaps it was small beer. Well, yes it was in the scheme of things, but it was important at the time and posed a question that will have contributed to a standard we see today.

This controversy began in the autumn of 1972. Clare had admitted its first women as undergraduates to the College. Some of the background only becomes clear years later and even now much is a mystery to me. I tell of this time from my memory of then. I have heard that Directors of Studies were bound to an overall quota of at least one-third women. In the event, I have also heard, the admissions procedures took the course they should, with equality of opportunity applied without positive discrimination and the numbers shook out about right.

Not that we knew anything about this at the time. I was one of these women, admitted to Clare to read Medicine. I had heard of this new departure from my school, one of those boys' independent schools with girls in the sixth form. While commonplace now, in the seventies it was still unusual and many institutions were feeling their own way with similar implementation. I heard from my teachers that there had been a deputation from Clare to visit the school to learn about the successes and problems of such integration. It may seem comical now when we take social integration as the norm, but there were many painful lessons learned and prejudices to be overcome. I believe that matters discussed included the need for girlie accommodation, separate tutors for the girls to

address our moral welfare and the need for private space. There were worries too about behaviour (ours and of the men).

The upshot of all this was a designation of four staircases in Memorial Court for the women, rooms redecorated for the purpose, a female who would be available to us in addition to our subject tutor for girl problems and briefings for Fellows and Porters on what misdemeanours to expect.

And what of those full length mirrors? Advice received by the college included the need for the girls to have full-length mirrors in their rooms. All were duly kitted out. Above all the attention given to making our arrival comfortable, this was the single preparation most derided by our male colleagues. Why, they said, should we wish to see ourselves full length any more than they?

You might, at this point in the tale, be scoffing gently at these preparations. Remember, if you will, the times and also remember that this was to be a showcase, a project that could not fail. So we arrived, about 40 of us in all shapes and sizes, representing the spectrum of subjects offered including Chinese. We came from a range of backgrounds, most with no experience of living alongside boys other than in immediate families. Scary stuff!

Within hours the inspections began. Excuses to visit the girls in their rooms were wide and varied. There were clubs to join, coffee to be offered, sugar to be borrowed. Most of the visitors were from the two years above us. I think the boys in our year begrudged the attention we received. All in all it was harmless, but overwhelming to some. The attention lasted a mere week or two and then we became a part of the furniture, just as it should be. Most of us settled down pretty quickly, some were unhappy at the sudden and dramatic change in their lives. We had one girl with anorexia, little known and less understood than now, and several more who wanted to

222

RIGHT: *Celia Duff (1972–75, left) with Catherine "Catti" Moss (Newnham, 1972–75) and Andrew Starr (1971–74) outside Clare boathouse, 1974. Celia and Catti rowed coxless pairs.*

BELOW: *Cambridge University rows at the National Championships in Nottingham, July 20th 1975. The crew was a Newnham/Clare hybrid. From the bow: Sally Visick, Newnham, Nicola Boyes, Clare (first Clare Olympic oarswoman), Catti Moss Newnham, Celia Duff, Clare (first person, male or female, to get full blue for rowing from Oxford and Cambridge), Cox: Pam Harling, Newnham.*

leave with the unaccustomed pressure of feeling as if in a fishbowl of attention.

Considering our various academic pedigrees before taking up our places at Clare, the first-year results were poor. We felt it keenly then, almost as if it was a smack in the face of those who had faith enough to offer us the opportunity. Now, of course, I know that this is not an uncommon phenomenon. But it was enough to make most of us work rather more systematically with a resultant dramatic improvement in exam grades in our second year. So much so that, despite the fact that Clare had not been allowed to give entrance awards (a sop to the women's colleges who were concerned that all the bright women would be tempted away), several of us walked away from that second year with Foundation scholarships.

We moved into all aspects of Clare life. The choir took on new strength, the boat club adopted us quickly and even invited the women to share their showers. (You should know at this point that when the offer was taken up the men fled in shame.) The Music Society flourished and drama too.

But there remained pockets of resistance for some time. A traditional argument against the admission of women to formerly male only institutions was peddled. 'They will weaken our sports teams, they will reduce opportunity for men.' True, but why not? In weakening the pool from which to choose the 1st men's VIII was born the first and only Clare Olympic oarswoman and the first person, male or female, to receive a full rowing blue from both Cambridge and Oxford. And both of these from that first intake. Women from that first year have gone on to hold positions of national importance and make up the current complement of College Fellows. Sadly some expressed their resistance physically. I remember waking one night to find a strange man in my room, cursing rather drunkenly about the detriment to the College that I represented. The following morning we found our gyp room had been trashed. Underwear disappeared from the drying room with regularity. But the novelty and resistance soon died down.

Now, I believe, all rooms have full-length mirrors and each is decorated to a College standard. There is no discrimination. Staircases are mixed and men and women share doubles. The women have their own showers in the boathouse and compete for choral awards. And why not? It is nearly thirty years since I became one of the first intake of women into Clare. The College still feels the same but it is of course far more relaxed and less self-conscious. Those with doubts, I hope, have cast them aside.

Next time you look at yourself in a full-length mirror, consider whether the reflection is one of a traditionalist or of one accepting that some change is developmental. And then consider whether Clare was right to install the full-length mirrors at all. And then, when you have reflected, consider whether you would encourage your son or daughter to apply to Clare. I did.

Celia Duff (1972–75) is Consultant in Public Health Medicine, Eastern Region, and Director of Studies in Clinical Medicine at Clare College.

choosing clare for the wrong reasons 223

ALICE RAWSTHORN

There were lots of sensible reasons to have picked Clare as your Cambridge College of choice back in the late 1970s, but I chose it for all the wrong ones. Having always gone to mixed schools, applying to an antedeluvian single sex college would have seemed absurd. Wherever I ended up, it had to be mixed and, when I filled in my application form in autumn 1976, that gave you five or six colleges to choose from. I plumped for Clare because it was a) bang in the middle of town, b) had beautiful architecture with lovely gardens and c) a pretty name.

Nor did it occur to me to stay on at school to sit the entrance exam after 'A' levels. My school, a newly-formed comprehensive in rural Essex which had never sent anyone to Oxbridge before and, as far as I know, hasn't since, couldn't have coached me. Besides, all I wanted was to escape from rural Essex to lead an independent adult life, and saw no point in postponing it for another year.

So, I wrote Law at Clare at the top of my UCCA application choices and took the Cambridge entrance exam among a bunch of CSE retakees. I'd chosen the General Studies papers, because most of the marks came from a three-hour essay on a conceptual theme which, I reckoned, would put me at less of a disadvantage against the specially tutored post-A levellers. All I remember of what I wrote on "What if this heaven was the world's last night?" was mis-spelling Armageddon.

Undeterred, Clare called me in for an interview. As I lived an hour's drive from Cambridge, it seemed pointless to stay overnight which meant that, when I arrived at the Buttery for lunch, all the other interviewees were chatting in a friendly huddle, which I was too shy to join. (Later, they told me that I'd looked too intimidating to approach, and they'd spent lunch being terrorized by a boy who'd airily claimed that *Coriolanus* was the only Shakespearean play worth reading. Later still, we discovered that he

ABOVE: *The cast of a 1980 play in Trinity College Theatre, which was written and directed by Oscar Moore.*

LEFT TO RIGHT: *Alice Rawsthorn (Clare 1977–80); Sue Saunders (with bag) (Clare 1979–82); (behind) unknown; Oscar Moore (Pembroke 1979–82); unknown; (in front) Caroline Hardy (with glass) (Clare 1979–82); unknown.*

224

hadn't read it.) I don't remember a word of my interview, nor could I immediately afterwards. All I do recall is meeting my mother in Belinda's, the Trinity Street coffeeshop, and warning her to prepare for disappointment. A few days later I gave the same speech to my headmaster when he called me in to discuss the interview, only to be told that I'd been accepted by Clare and awarded an exhibition. I'd never heard of an exhibition before.

My expectations of Cambridge were ridiculously high. The big pitfall for top-of-the-class state school kids like me, or so we were constantly told, was that we were so unaccustomed to academic competition that Cambridge was a rude awakening. That sounded great to me. Having spent my teens as a frustrated culture-junkie longing to meet anyone who'd know one Verlaine from another (that meant proto-punk Tom from poet Paul in the late 1970s), I looked forward to three years among dazzling intellects. When I confided this to a friend's elder brother who'd just left Trinity, he warned me not to expect too much. Another cautionary note came when a friend of my mother's arranged for me to visit her son, a rowing blue who was graduating from Clare the summer before I went up. After giving me a guided tour of the College, he eyed my skinny frame and suggested I become a cox. 'If you don't row,' he said solemnly, 'you won't have any friends.' Silently, I wondered which would be worse. Rowing, or friendlessness?

The friends thing didn't daunt me, even though I wouldn't know a soul when I arrived at Cambridge. My shyness at the Clare interviews was not characteristic. My family had moved up and down the country throughout my childhood and teens. Having started afresh at so many schools, I was used to making new friends from scratch. But in other ways, I was ill-equipped for university life. I couldn't cook and had never even tried to operate a washing machine. 'Doing homework' had always excused me from helping with household chores. But off I went.

What did I find when I got there? First off, that skipping a year off had been a silly mistake. I might have perfected my French in Paris like Cherith Simpson, or had an affair with a poet in Greece, like Maria Margaronis, but I hadn't. The second realization was that I should have ignored my teachers' clichés about how 'generalists should study Law.' Only those who want to practise law should study it. I didn't and wasted two years plodding through the Law Society's obligatory qualification subjects, 'just in case you change your mind,' before being

liberated to read History of Art. Even then, the most 'recent' subject we could study was early nineteenth-century neo-classical architecture. Although, I must admit that, workaholic though I'd been before and have been ever since, my three years at Cambridge were the only time in my life when work wasn't a priority.

Shocker number three was that hardly anyone at Cambridge was into punk, or any other form of the pop culture, which I considered as indispensable as nineteenth-century literature or eighteenth-century paintings. I went up to Clare in September 1977, six months after The Clash had released their debut album and a month before *Never Mind The Bollocks – Here's The Sex Pistols* shot straight to number one. Me and my sixth-form friends had already cropped our boyfriends' hair and shaved flares into drainpipes. All the cool kids in my year at Cambridge had been cursed by bad timing, having left England for India in the dog days of hippydom, and missed punk completely. None of the rest seemed to have noticed what had happened.

Then there was the gender thing. Only one in ten of the undergraduates in my year were women. That mightn't have seemed strange to anyone who'd gone to a single sex school, but it was really weird for me, especially when some of the nine-out-of-ten males were tweed-clad, 18-going-on-80-year-olds from Magdalene, who kept beagles in outlying villages for a spot of wildlife slaughter before breakfast. 'Comprehensive boys are so much more comprehendable,' purred a Holland Park Comprehensive hip chick to a jejune public schoolboy in an otherwise forgettable Stephen Poliakoff play of the era.

Things got better through the three years, as mixed colleges like Clare shot to the top of the academic league table and more single sex colleges went mixed. But that didn't stop the local magistrates, who threw out a rape case in my first term on the grounds that any woman who went to a (particularly seedy) pub near Cambridge Station wearing jeans had been 'asking for it.' No wonder feminism swamped our intellectual agenda. Though our enthusiasm for consciousness-raising groups and pro-choice marches was dampened by the awkward feeling (which lingered into the mid-1980s) that by committing anti-feminist crimes like wearing lipstick or failing to come out, we never would be right-on enough.

One thing I didn't realize was how pampered we were. Not only were students given viable grants in the late

1970s (as they should be today), but rich colleges, like Clare, often topped them up. Book grants. Travel grants. Subsidies for this or that. Low rents for College rooms and even for out-of-college houses. Gina Campbell and I rented a two-up-two-down house in our second year for a few pounds a week. We took it all for granted.

I had little sense of belonging to Clare; maybe in the first few terms while we struggled to define ourselves, but definitely not afterwards when I'd found a circle of friends, some of whom came from the College and others who didn't. I loved Old Court's elegant architecture and the ancient roses in the gardens, but certainly didn't feel crushed by the weight of Clare's centuries of history. That may have been because it was a male history that I couldn't relate to, and, as the College had gone mixed a few years before my arrival, we really were reinventing its culture. In many ways Clare seemed to belong to its staff, rather than the students, not least because most of them were there for far longer than three years. When the Cam burst its banks one term and the gardens were flooded, I remember seeing the elderly gardeners wandering around the sodden flower beds in tears and realizing how many years of work and love they'd put into tending them.

It's only twenty years since I left Clare but most of my memories of it are hazy, possibly because my college friends have been my friends ever since and our relationships have evolved rather than being frozen in nostalgia. When I meet up with Sarah Moylan or Amanda Craig, we talk about what we're doing now rather than what we did then. But for all its sexism, the tweedy twits and our fashionable groans about how we longed to escape to London, my three years at Clare and Cambridge were a happy time. And, here are some of the reasons why....

The Arts Cinema. I can't imagine getting a better film education than spending afternoons, evenings and late nights soaking up 50p double bills of Buñuel, Fellini, Visconti, Cassavetes, Godard and Antonioni. Gin fizzes in Jan Buckley's room downstairs in Castlebrae. Kettles Yard. Victoria Fleming in her fluffy white rabbit coat. Reading *Domus* and the other imported art and architectural magazines in the faculty library. Sue Saunders and Caroline Hardy breakfasting on Special Brew six-packs. The great jazz albums on Andy's record stall in the market. Scoffing Chelsea buns from Fitzbillies with A.J. Close. Unearthing a Balenciaga ballgown from the Costume History Shop and scouring Saturday morning jumble sales for boxy 1960s suits and mohair relics. Thanks.

Alice Rawsthorn, now Director of the Design Museum, read Law then History of Art at Clare 1977–80. Before joining the Design Museum in spring 2001, she was an award-winning journalist and author. Alice wrote for the Financial Times *for 16 years as a foreign correspondent in Paris and as the FT's architectural and design critic. A trustee of the Whitechapel Art Gallery in London, she was a judge of the 1999 Turner Prize. Alice's first book,* Yves Saint Laurent: A Biography, *was published by HarperCollins in 1996 and her second, on the work of designer Marc Newson, by Booth Clibborn Editions in 1999. She is now writing a biography of the 1960s pop artist, Pauline Boty, to be published by 4th Estate/HarperCollins in 2002.*

women at clare:
life was a party

TERESA LEVONIAN COLE

'Don't go to Clare' said my teacher, in capital letters. 'They are Left Wing and they Won't Like You'. Coming from an all-girl boarding school, the prospect of a mixed college, coupled with the challenge set by this injunction, proved irresistible. 'Says here you are insubordinate' said Professor Feinstein at the interview. 'If Girton offered you a scholarship, would you go?' 'I'd sooner lop off my little toe' I replied (or words to that effect). So instead, I pruned my surname to a single inoffensive syllable, and went to Clare.

A stately dowager alongside the flamboyance of King's, Clare's façade – as approached via Senate House Passage – gives little away. Its charms are enclosed within the perfect symmetry of the warm yellow stone, and distantly glimpsed from Queens Road. I was immediately seduced: Clare was part of the great Confederacy of Punt-owning Colleges, boasting a privileged position on the Backs, and the prettiest bridge in Cambridge. Daily would I cross this bridge, which looked ripe for collapse beneath the weight of its ornamental globes, and walk along the avenue of seasonal snowdrops, crocuses or daffodils to my first-year rooms in Memorial Court. In those days, prior to the interposition of the College library, its spacious architecture formed a latter-day echo to Old Court's symmetry beyond the Cam, with the UL tower forming the nub of its axis. The location was perfect: a mere three hops from bed on J staircase to breakfast in the UL: cheese scones and gossip in the smokey tea-room being our local variation on absinthe and existentialism in the Deux Magots.

The Buttery, rather than formal hall, was a regular meeting place, its atmosphere that of Wimpy Bar crossed with early Habitat. This alternated with the Whim, a student haunt of dubious credentials, and the halls of Trinity and Magdalene (good chefs), till other eateries began to spring up. Cambridge was a gastronomic desert. Despite the ban on cars, someone could always be trusted to suggest an

RIGHT: Teresa studying on a boat to Granchester.

excursion to Ely, Foxton, Aldeburgh or Whittlesford, in search of food. The Tickell Arms was a favourite, owing to the barely-sane proprietor who would insult his customers, refuse to serve them, or simply treat them to Brunnhilde's Immolation scene played at deafening levels. A keen Wagnerian, he was always good for a laugh, God rest his soul.

In summer, the car would be replaced by the punt, and Clare came into its own. Armed with a wind-up gramophone, bottles of wine and a copy of *The Four Quartets*, we would shunt our way to Grantchester, riding perilously low on the water as we collected friends along the way. When we felt creative, we would feed the ducks bread soaked in vodka, which yielded new perspectives on synchronized swimming. And as we watched the ducks, the Japanese tourists watched us, through their lenses, no doubt marvelling at the rites of Albion.

Summer was, of course, the high point of the party season. It was also the time you made intimate acquaintance with the bike sheds – the illicit route into Clare after curfew, to which the benevolent porters turned a blind eye (handlebars and bruised ribs being punishment enough). Magdalene's infamous Wiley, *Vile Bodies*, James Stourton's lethal champagne cocktails in Thompson's Lane, endless carousing on lawns (the Beaufort, Pimms parties, cricket parties – any excuse) and the annual treasure-hunt stylishly organized by Christs' Anthony Oakshott, spring to mind. The latter event (I think it was during the year of *The Hunting of the Snark*) managed to elicit a full house of complaints from the Botanical Gardens, National Trust, traffic police and UL, without our even trying. And the whole jamboree culminated in a succession of May Balls, each college vying to outdo the next in inventiveness. I dimly remember my Cambridge career came to a close with three May Balls on consecutive nights – a practice not to be recommended, unless you wish to join the ranks of the Walking Dead.

When study became absolutely unavoidable, I would repair to the roof of Old Court. The camber of the lead tiles was such that you could lie semi-prone, sunbathe, support a book and oversee the activities on the Cam all at once. But the great horror of the summer term was not exams; it was the rooms ballot, by which most of us would be exiled from the cossetting of bedders in the world of Gown into the realities of Town – or, worse, The Colony. With no appeal. In other words, I moved out of College at the end of my first year, and into Number One, Petersfield, a large and perpetually open-house, shared with Tony Oakshott and Andrew Somper (Downing).

This coincided with my Part II studies in History of Art. Despite Duncan Robinson being a Fellow of Clare, I was (I think) the only Clare-ite from my year reading the subject. The Arts History Faculty was peopled, in the main, by members of Trinity and Magdalene, with a smattering of representation from Christ's and Trinity Hall. My supervision partner was Nicholas Coleridge (Trinity), whose sparkling talent for improvisation came in handy when having to discuss the essays neither of us had written. And so my centre of gravity shifted, and I spent less time in Clare – although returning to the College always felt like a warm welcome to a safe haven.

Clare had a strong bent for music and drama. Kit Harvey, along with Simon Butteriss one of the more colourful thespians in the College, directed an *al fresco Romeo and Juliet* around the fairy-tale pond in Clare Gardens. It remains memorable for the Romeo of Iain Softley, on loan from Queen's, who went AWOL just before curtain-up, much to the distress of the director. (All ended well: Romeo was located at the 11th hour, enjoying a

LEFT: *May Ball Poster, 1976.*

siesta). Ivor Bolton, now a successful conductor, was the Organ Scholar. I spent many hours in his rooms in Old Court, which were furnished with a grand piano, unwittingly serenading the unfortunate Chaplain upstairs with renditions of Brahms Ballades. And John Rutter, the composer and then-Director of the excellent Clare choir, has reappeared in my professional life as a music publisher.

I never did meet any Lefties at Clare. Perhaps, like the seriously brilliant mathematicians whom I also never met, they were too busy working. Work, alas, does not feature in my memories; although I do remember Tess Knighton – now Admissions Tutor at Clare, for her pains – carrying me bodily to my one-and-only first-year lecture on the handlebars of her bicycle. My memories, rather, in which eternal springtime and crocuses have replaced the bitter cold and driving rain of the fens, are of a sybaritic existence among friends numbering aesthetes and assorted eccentrics. 'It's like something out of Brideshead' said a visiting friend; and it was. Ivory towers, time warps and other clichés come to mind. But for me, the mood of Clare in the late 70s is forever captured in the form of John Newton, English Fellow, soulfully reciting *Lapis Lazuli* by moonlight beneath the weeping fig-tree. Or again by Yeats, as posted on the door of a noisy upstairs neighbour: *Tread softly, because you tread on my dreams.*

Teresa Levonian Cole (1976–79) is Music Editor at Oxford University Press

schoolmaster fellow at clare

PETER KING

I am the latest (1984) in an increasingly long line of schoolmasters and schoolmistresses to benefit from the wonderful opportunity to spend a term in Clare College 'for a period of intellectual refreshment freed from the normal pressures of one's job.' As Director of English Studies at the George Ward School, Melksham, in Wiltshire, an 11–18 comprehensive of 1750 pupils and an English staff of 17, I think I can claim to be particularly aware of those pressures. My special interest is eighteenth-century English literature, not the most popular period in schools, but absorbing in terms of the pronounced changes in taste, reflected especially in the visual arts, the main angle that I am now pursuing.

BELOW: *Parapet, top of Old Court, 1971–72.*

Settling in to such a warm, friendly and welcoming college as Clare was easy; disciplining oneself to academic studies with such unaccustomed freedom initially proved difficult. I shall return with greater sympathy for some of my lazier sixth formers! I am still marvelling at a week in which I attended an Easter carol service at Trinity College, a performance of Haydn's 'The Creation' in St. John's, Choral communion in Clare and the appeal concert at the Senate House, an excellent lecture which proved how limited my powers of concentration have become, and probably for the first time in my life, talked at length to two old Etonians.

I am a compulsive reader of College notice-boards, especially the menus, write a range of educational articles for anyone who will publish them, now umpire for Bath Hockey Club but occasionally play for their veterans, enjoy theatre-going, public speaking and meeting people. I admit to extreme difficulty in controlling a punt, soaking myself and any occupants, combined with a general sense of disorientation – though I have now found my bearings in Clare, including the 'delightful' dustbin-lined route to the television room. If you see me wandering around in the subterranean gloom of the buttery, however, desperately searching for an exit, please point me in the right direction.

One final reflection: I shall advise sixth formers to stop worrying about 'A' levels and concentrate on coping with eccentric washing machines or learning how to iron shirts: I now regard these as vital survival skills.

Postscript

I'd only been in residence a few days when I approached Old Court from the Queen's Rd entrance. I vaguely noticed somebody stretched along the ledge immediately outside one of the rooms above the entry arch. I was then lucky not to be showered with tea as the individual languidly emptied his cup!

I thought no more of it but then received this charming letter. I wrote back thanking the writer for the apology and, ironically, suggested that the incident had left me wondering if this was some sort of strange initiation ceremony for newcomers to Clare …

Dear Mr King,

I write in apology for last Saturday's regrettable incident outside Old Court. It is not my habit to precipitate hot tea, or anything else for that matter, onto the innocent heads of passers-by; I think my friend's action surprised me almost as much as it must have done you. I cannot account for his extraordinary action, and fear it may have confirmed your worst preconceptions as to the behaviour of undergraduates. Once again, my apologies; I trust that the rest of your stay in Clare will be rather more peaceful.

Yours sincerely,
Leon Bennun

THE GREEN COMMITTEE

THE CLARE ASSOCIATION ANNUAL

The Green Committee was set up by the Governing Body in 1989 to promote awareness and discussion of environmental issues and to foster sound policies within the College. It has four senior members, a representative of the Staff, two members from the MCR and three from the JCR. It is thus broadly representative of College life. Initially it was established for one year, at the end of which it produced a short report.

The Committee promoted a recycling scheme for glass, paper and aluminium, integrated with the collection schemes operated by the City Council. The use of recycled paper and low-energy light bulbs throughout the College has been encouraged. There was an informal audit which showed the extent to which environmentally sound practices are followed in the gardens and the housekeeping departments, including the design of the new hostel. Discussions were also held with other colleges. It was gratifying that Clare won an award made by the City Council for good environmental practices.

This has been a small-scale but encouraging beginning. The recycling was hindered by a national paper glut, and collection cannot easily be extended from Memorial Court to Old Court, but the College appears now to be thinking and talking about Green issues, and modifying its practices accordingly. Much more can be done, however, particularly in the conservation of energy, and the Governing Body has accordingly renewed the life of the Committee so that the good work can continue.

THE CAMBRIDGE GREEK PLAY IN DELPHI, 1981

by NANCY JANE RUCKER

My first year as a Classics and Modern Language undergraduate at Clare coincided with the triennial performance of the Cambridge Greek Play: since 1882, the Greek Play Committee has revived plays in the original Greek, the performances reflecting the cultural and dramatic preoccupations of each generation's encounter with the ancient plays. Having attended a performance whilst at school, I was fired with the desire to be part of this inspiring tradition, just at a time when Classics was undergoing a metamorphosis from text-based study to an increased awareness that ancient plays can only be properly experienced in live performance. It was therefore something of an ambition realized, as well as an instructive initiation for two Clare classicists (Imogen Broughton, 1978, and myself, Nancy-Jane Rucker, 1979), who became members of the Chorus of Euripides' *Electra* in 1980 on the boards of the Cambridge Arts Theatre, while a Clare musician, Philip Weller (1977) was part of the team which provided percussive accompaniment. This was a time of the reawakening of authenticity in performance and we learnt to chant our Greek in what seemed at the time a cross between modern Greek pronunciation and a Welsh lilt, certainly a long way from the Greek of our primers at school. We struggled with the complexities and rhythmic excitement of Greek choral odes, and even managed, in our flowing *peploi*, to remember the intricacies of our dance movements.

To be part of such a performance was in itself an experience to enrich and colour our subsequent appetite for Greek drama: but this was further enhanced a year later when the Cambridge Greek Play was invited to take part in an international conference on the production of Greek drama at Delphi in Greece. This proved to be something of an Odyssey in more ways than one: the cast had to be reassembled and parts relearnt, some of the travel – in particular to Ithaca – proved to be a challenge for those unused to Greek lifestyle and the charms of retsina. Our performance at the conference (on a modern proscenium stage) was one of a number of offerings from different countries, illustrating a variety of production techniques and approaches to translation, precipitating lively debate (I remember a memorable intervention from George Steiner) on the philosophy of translation. Our Cambridge version was the only one staged in the original Greek.

Our visit was transformed by the extraordianry diplomacy of the President of the Greek Play Committee, Professor Pat Easterling, an inspiring force for many years in the teaching of Greek drama in Cambridge. Whether by charm, persuasion, or even bribery, she managed to get permission for our production to be put on in the ancient theatre at Delphi itself, dedicated to Apollo, patron god of music and drama. By all accounts this was a unique achievement, since the archaeological authorities are wary of any activity which might erode this treasure amongst Greek sites. For anyone who has not seen Delphi, it is the most dramatic of sanctuaries: set on an escarpment overlooking a valley of olive groves, looking down towards the sea, it is dominated by the burnt orange cliffs of Apollo, called by the Greeks the 'Shining Ones' because of the glistening quality of the rocks, which tower above the site.

We started the production early in the morning, before the site was opened to tourists, and the misty quality of the light enhanced the sense in all of us that we had been touched by the oracular atmosphere of Delphi, home of the Sybil and the god of music and poetry himself. Acting in a Greek theatre is unlike any other dramatic experience. For the first and only time, we as the chorus were chanting and dancing in a real 'orchestra' – the round dance floor of the Greek theatre. The acoustic of the semi-circular cavea, even in the partly ruined state of the Delphi theatre, amplifies the voice and gives it a separate identity far removed from mere mortal intoning of the words. The production took its course, in an atmosphere of heightened tension: we were playing out our story in front of the patron of drama himself. The climax arrived, where Electra calls on Apollo for requital of her wrongs, aiming her voice high up over the stone seats towards the great cliff beyond the *cavea* – and the god replied, with an eerie echo of her words which sent a shiver of surprise through us puny mortals acting out our parts. Not even the professional classicists in our party had been aware of this freak of the Delphi theatre: that the cliff would act as a sounding board for the voices of the actors, and in Delphic and enigmatic fashion, add an unforeseen irony to the drama.

THE GREEK PLAY BEING PERFORMED AT DELPHI

232

LEFT: *1996 May Ball poster, provided by Norman Dawson (see pp. 187–88), who attended the Ball with his wife on the twenty-fifth anniversary of his (accepted!) proposal of marriage.*

NEVILL WILLMER

The Fellows' Garden at Clare is one of Cambridge's well kept (but well known) secrets. It is a brilliant balance, abundance punctuated by austerity, like pauses for breath. Shape, scent and colour are all designed to stunning effect: from the Dean's Walk to the sunken garden, Clare Fellows' Garden has astonished its visitors for half a century. Professor Nevill Willmer began its design in 1946 (when it was called the River Garden). There follows an article written by Professor Willmer in 1988/89 for the Clare Annual, *giving his own account of it, and an article by Michelle Calvert on the current Head Gardener – who has almost made his own half century – Brian Arbon.*

The land which now forms the Fellows' (or River) Garden was acquired from King's College in 1638 in exchange for a plot of ground near King's Chapel. It was known as Butt Close and lay on the frequently flooded water meadows. At this time the rebuilding of Clare's old Tudor Court, directed by Barnabas Oley, was about to begin on its new site nearer the river. The river bridge (designed by Thomas Grumbold) and a causeway across the marshy ground were built almost immediately, the latter resting on a mattress formed by the heads of forty willow trees and supported by brick walls. This gave members of the College direct access to what is now Queens' Road and the open country beyond. There was also a direct route for building materials into the new court.

At first, little seems to have been done with the newly acquired paddock. In the Loggan print (*c.*1690) (see p. 197) it is shown surrounded by trees, and the causeway is depicted with a single row of small trees on its south edge, and a double row on its north side, of which the outer row may have been in the paddock itself, i.e. at the lower level. By 1780 the paddock seems to have been bisected by a hedge running north and south; there was also a path along the river bank that ran between what look like pleached limes. The bisection persisted until the 1920s

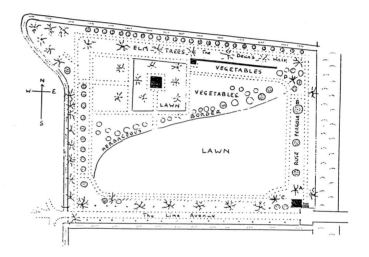

FIG.1: *The garden in 1945*

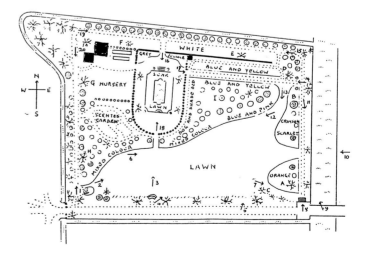

FIG.2: *The garden in 1954*

234

RIGHT: *Mixed border,*
Fellows' Garden.

and the western half was used as an orchard for the latter part of that time. In Victorian times the eastern half was divided more or less diagonally by a hedge running south-west to north-east. In front of the hedge was a lawn surrounded by a path; behind it the area was, at some stage, converted into a vegetable garden and provided with a wall along its north side for growing trained fruit trees. Beyond the wall was a row of elms and, along the Garret Hostel Lane boundary, a row of yew trees which were probably part of the same scheme, perhaps to act as a wind-break when the original elms became too large. The Judas Tree (letter A on the plans) and the Swamp Cypress (B) on the river bank were probably part of this first horticultural development, as were the isolated conifers between them. By the beginning of this century the paddock had come to resemble a typical country-house garden of the period with pleasance, orchard and walled vegetable garden.

While Memorial Court was being built (1922–35) great changes were made in the River Garden. The soil excavated from the foundations was dumped partly along the wall of the causeway (thus obscuring the brickwork and extending the embankment), and partly used to raise the level of the western end of the lawn which had by that time been extended so that the diagonal hedge and path ran almost all the way to the south-west entrance. In the 1920s also, a summer-house was erected in the orchard where it dominated the centre of the garden. It was surrounded by formal lawns and paths.

In the 1930s the garden received little attention. Its trees and shrubs became overgrown and the College deserved its title of 'the palace in the jungle'. Matters were not improved by six wartime years with a staff reduced to one ageing gardener, and by the death of the elms behind the wall from Dutch Elm Disease. Not surprisingly, when the Governing Body met at the end of 1945, rehabilitation of the garden appeared on the agenda. Several of the Fellows knew of my interest in gardens and their design, and that I had assisted Harold Taylor, the College Steward, to plan his own garden. I was soon asked for my opinion on what should be done. Would I put my ideas on paper?

To be asked to produce ideas for such an area in so prestigious a place as the Cambridge Backs does not occur very often and my answer was, of course, 'yes'. Knowing the tendency of colleges always to call in the expert (i.e. the professional), I was determined to accept the challenge and see if, on this occasion, the amateur could win the day. No doubt this was partly conceit but it probably

incorporated, if possible. The dead and dying elms would, of course, have to go.

Two other personal factors loomed large with me at this time: I was a very keen 'Sunday painter' of landscapes, and my research work at the end of the war had been concerned with some peculiarities of human colour vision. Both factors influenced my thoughts on design, pictorial composition, focal points, illusions of space, vistas and colour patterns. Thus I conceived the idea of creating a number of landscape pictures to be seen from certain important vantage points, e.g. the Master's Lodge and the windows of the west front of the College, the bridge, the middle of the causeway and a point near the exit to Queens' Road. Each of these views should have a special feature to act as its focal point. (The viewpoints are shown on figure 2; each one is numbered and the accompanying arrow indicates the direction of the vista). I therefore began to draw tentative sketches from various angles and spent much time in the garden trying to visualise the effects. Thus I saw in my mind's eye the old wall clothed with blue *Ceanothus* and *Solanum* mixed with yellow roses (Canary Bird, *R. cantabrigiensis*, and Golden Showers), and forming a back-cloth to a very wide herbaceous border also of blue and yellow flowers, e.g. tall delphiniums, anchusas, monkshood, achilleas and hieraciums at the back with smaller plants in front. After toying with some other grandiose ideas I saw too that if a path led away from the river and along the front of such a border, a splendid vista would be made if a matching border were created on its other side. This vista (viewpoint 14), seen from the river bank, could then end in a gateway in the yew hedge which I was thinking of using to surround an inner sanctum for Fellows.

To make this sanctum I proposed to relegate the summer-house (of dubious beauty) to a nursery section, there to be used as the gardeners' shed, and substitute a garden enclosed on three sides by a yew hedge with an extension of the wall on the fourth, and containing a sunk lawn with a central lily-pool. The axis of the garden would run north and south (viewpoints 3, 16), at right angles to that of the blue and yellow border. These two main features, in fact, set the key for the design for the rest of the garden. Fig.1 shows the garden as it was in 1945, and fig.2 shows the plan very much as it was submitted to the Governing Body, but as it had actually matured by 1954. (It should be remembered that, in the nature of things, there have been changes of detail since then. Anyone visiting the garden today may expect to find some differences from the plan.)

235

LEFT: *Guests admire the sunken garden and pond of the recently redesigned Fellows' Garden, 1955.*

also had a genetic basis, for gardeners of various sorts appear in both sides of my family tree.

What sort of garden did the Fellows expect? *Quot homines, tot sententiae.* The Dean (W. Telfer) liked to walk between the yew trees and the wall (the Dean's Walk) while preparing his sermons. One of the tutors enjoyed sleeping out near the summer-house in high summer. Both Fellows and undergraduates played bowls on the lawn, and they also had parties of various sizes. The dramatic society produced May Week plays in the garden. Botanical Fellows would like interesting or rare plants. Flowers were needed for the Chapel and the Master's Lodge. Some Fellows enjoyed sunshine and bright colours, others preferred green and bosky shade. Unlike most gardens in Cambridge, the Fellows' Garden offers few horticultural problems. It is well protected from winds, and the river ensures a high water-table so the loamy soil does not readily dry out in July and August as in so many Cambridge gardens on gravelly soils, nor does it bake hard like those on the clay. Severe frosts, periodic flooding and soil alkalinity are almost the only limiting factors.

With such a free hand it seemed to me that I should perhaps use Hidcote as my model and divide the garden into as many different sections as possible, giving each a special character with respect to such things as season, colour, scents, privacy and use. Certain existing features, e.g. the Swamp Cypress, the Judas Tree, the Medlar (C) and the old brick wall should certainly be preserved and

236

To my great surprise the plan was accepted without any of the usual wrangles about aesthetics, or calls for an expert. I was given more or less *carte blanche* to go ahead. Meanwhile a new head gardener, Walter Barlow, had been installed. Soon the elms had been felled, builders were repairing and extending the wall and transplanting the summer-house to its new corner, and Barlow with his two assistants was clearing away rubbish, preparing the new beds and marking out the plot for the Fellows' enclosure. It was during this general clearance that a valuable buck-eye chestnut was discovered among the dross, and many other plants and bushes were put on one side for possible future use. The yew hedge was planted in the autumn of 1946 and it had a rough time. The winter was exceptionally hard and the snow came when the ground was already frozen. It lay for several weeks and then melted so quickly

BELOW: *A view from the garden towards the Masters Lodge, featuring the vibrant reds and golds of early autumn.*

that there were floods everywhere. On emerging from the snow the yew hedge immediately disappeared under water. Yet every tree survived. In making the Fellows' enclosure the yew hedge was given the form of an apse with a gateway in its middle so that a main axis was established from a wrought-iron gate in the centre of the wall at the north end, through the gateway in the hedge and to a flight of steps leading down from the avenue (viewpoints 3, 16). The actual position of this axis was dependent on those steps since they had to be placed between two of the monumental trees remaining on the avenue. This therefore determined the position of the gate in the wall and, in order to keep this central, the length of the wall (and thus the width of the enclosure).

I had first been impressed by a sunk garden with a central lily-pool that I saw in Pompeii in 1926, and I had successfully used that motif in designing a garden for my father in Cheshire. In the Clare garden the lily-pool became a determining factor in several ways since its water level was set by that of the river. The average level of the water determined the approximate level of the sunk lawn, and the depth of that lawn also dictated its size in order to maintain pleasing proportions. Thus, although the plan clearly showed the main layout and primary shapes of this part of the garden, its detailed construction depended on an extensive use of pegs and string and a certain amount of trial and error, together with step-by-step modification. Because of the difference between a plan on paper and the scene when it is viewed on the ground this method of work applied throughout the whole development of the garden.

Anyone entering the Fellows' enclosure from the avenue first descends the steps that project on to the main lawn, then passes through the yew hedge and can descend again to the sunk lawn by the steps that project on to the lower level. Then, passing round the pool, one ascends again, but by steps that are recessed into the bank. This arrangement tends to create the illusion of going progressively down hill more than is actually the case. Similarly, by arranging specimen conifers of suitable size, e.g. *Juniper hibernica*, at the four corners of the sunken lawn, though actually on rounded projections of the upper lawn (see fig.2), with two larger ones at the end nearest the avenue and two smaller ones at the other end, the length of the sunk lawn is made to appear greater. This same illusion of distance from the entrance is also fostered by planting grey-leaved plants with 'pastel-shaded' flowers in the beds next to the wall. In designing the Fellows' enclosure its use

best. Later the mixed border along the main lawn takes over until it yields pride of place to the dazzle of the red border which is then unaccompanied by a golden resurgence of the blue and yellow border. Blue flowers are curiously restricted to the summer months; yellow flowers have a much longer season.

In planting these borders the new head gardener, Barlow, who had been trained in a local nursery, was a tower of strength. He knew his plants, their sizes, their habits, their seasons and their cultural requirements. The detailed planting was left almost entirely to him, and only for the exact positions of larger specimens and for the final shape of the beds did he call for help. The planting of the blue and yellow border was a particularly interesting task because blues vary from blue-green to violet, and yellows from yellow-green to orange. Between they thus include many pairs of complementary colours whose juxtaposition provides surprising visual effects. This was of particular interest when members of a conference on colour vision, housed in Clare in 1947, wandered about in the garden. So too was the surprising difference between the behaviour of the blue border and the red border as the evening light faded and the blue flowers became whiter and the red flowers blacker.

Perhaps the most important viewpoint for the garden as a whole is from the west front of the College and the Master's Lodge (viewpoint 10). For this reason it was proposed that the main lawn should remain much as it had been but the diagonally-running herbaceous border should be widened and given a gently sinuous front along which the eye could travel to a focal point at the far end (viewpoint 12). The border was modified accordingly, and the focal point provided by an upright conifer fronted by a small separate flower-bed whose contents can be varied with the season.

The remains of the rose pergola along the river bank were removed and the bed divided into two, each part being considerably widened and so shaped as to direct the

as an open-air theatre was borne in mind. Either end can be used as a stage, but the northern one has certain advantages with its three entrances and the seating of the audience at the end where they enter.

The higher level of the lawn had, of course, to be supported by a stone wall, and the pool edged with stone. In this damp situation York stone was preferred to the more horticulturally amenable oolitic limestone, which tends to disintegrate in frost. The rock walls provide excellent niches for rock-loving plants, and since these mostly flower in May they provide welcome colour before the main herbaceous beds are ready. Such seasonal succession in different parts of the garden was felt to be important. In early spring bulbs give colour on the avenue, and some of the shrubs in the scent garden make their contribution. Then the cherries, willows and anemones on the river bank dominate the scene. The rock plants follow, and by the height of summer the blue and yellow border is at its

238

gaze of observers in the desired direction. While most of the diagonal border has remained mixed in colour, at the end nearer to the College it was at first given a mixture of pinks (phloxes) and blues (Michaelmas daisies) in order to blend with the crimsons in the northernmost portion of the now-divided riverside border. Both portions of this concentrate on red flowers, but varying in hue from orange-red nearest the avenue through vermilion by the central pathway to crimson at the north end. Autumnal flamboyance has remained the key-note of these two beds. The *Thuya occidentalis* and the fastigiated Irish Yew remaining in that bed would act throughout the year like gateposts on either side of the main vista from the College. The deciduous *Taxodium distichum* (Swamp Cypress) and the *Cercis siliquastrum* (Judas Tree) also remained at either end of the red border. Because this border is also prominently seen from the avenue (viewpoint 5) it seemed a good idea to increase its apparent length from that aspect, hence the shaping of its front edge and the use of brighter and orange reds in the foreground and the more crimson, i.e. bluer, shades at the far end.

The original plan envisaged the mixed border and the crimson part of the red border as separated by only a narrow grass path, but when the garden was in the making the sapling buck-eye chestnut (D) was discovered near the point of emergence of that path. Its marvellous autumn colours suggested its use as a focal point at the end of the vista of the red beds as seem from the avenue (viewpoint 5), and the narrow grass path was widened and shaped accordingly. Similarly, when the bushes between the avenue and the Judas Tree were being tidied up it was noticed that a most attractive view of the bridge and the

steps up to it could be obtained from the lawn if some bushes were cleared away (viewpoint 7). Such a clearance was made and a grass pathway provided. Many commentators have called attention to the rather oriental character of the bridge and this suggested the planting of two weeping Japanese cherries, *Prunus subhirtella pendula*, growing on their own roots, and keeping a weeping willow on the river bank. By underplanting all these with *Anemone blanda caerulea* and *A. appenina* the river bank itself acquires a sort of eastern charm in the spring.

The path between the wall and yew trees next to the Garret Hostel ditch, the Dean's Walk, remained, but in place of the defunct elm trees a 'white border' was created against the wall. As part of this a *Davidia involucrata*, the pocket-handkerchief tree (E), and a *Halesia Carolina*, the snowdrop-tree (F), were inserted to break the uniformity of height at two points (viewpoint 15). The development of this bed was dependent on the disappearance of the elm stumps and roots by natural processes since it was impracticable to use heavy implements or explosives to

RIGHT: *Professor Nevill Willmer (1902–2001).*

BELOW: *The White Walk.*

239

remove them. As it happened, an unforeseen effect caused a modification of this plan: all the white flowers in the border turned their faces to the sun, so that much of the sparkle of white was lost to those walking along the path. When the elm roots had rotted away the path and border were interchanged. This improved matters but the white border has always proved rather 'spotty' in contrast to the coloured borders: white means white, with little of the variation of hue that is tolerated by other colours. Fortunately many of the white flowers are strongly scented, and this makes up for other lack of interest. There is certainly an air of quiet peace about this walk.

At the west end of the white walk the path turns sharply south to run along the garden's western boundary in a 'tunnel of gloom' under the overhanging yew and other trees. This walk was also designed to be deceptive, appearing much longer when viewed from the south end (viewpoint 1) than from the north. This was achieved by progressively varying the width and height of the tunnel and the width of the path. Two branches lead off from this path, the first to the nursery area and the second to an enclosed dell furnished with scented plants, shrubs and trees. These include *Tilia petiolaris*, the weeping silver lime (G), which has a strong scent of clover in August; and the balsam poplar (H) which casts a resinous aroma far and wide when its buds open in the spring. The scented bushes include *Viburnum bodnantense*, *Chimonanthus fragrans* (the wintersweet), *Philadelphus* Belle Etoile, sweet briars, *Skimmia japonica*, rose albertine and honeysuckle; and smaller herbs such as thymes, southernwood and lavender. Unfortunately the dell turned out to be a frost-pocket and the smaller herbs (and even such hardy biennials as wallflowers) are often killed or damaged in the winter and early spring.

Corresponding to the scent garden but on the other side of the Fellows' enclosure is a small area, much shaded by shrubs that had formed the original diagonal hedge, where the soil is correspondingly cool, peaty and rather damp. These are excellent conditions for Japanese and Himalayan primulae and for the blue poppy (*Meconopsis*) and foxgloves. Subsequently it also seemed the ideal site for the gift to the College of a *Metasequoia glyptostroboides*, the Dawn Red-wood (1), a tree that now forms a more attractive central feature of the garden than its predecessor in that role, the summer-house.

The Jekyll-Lutyens principle of using architectural features and a generous use of trees and shrubs ensures that a garden has interest at all seasons and for many years. Forty years on, it is gratifying to note that two recent books on Cambridge gardens both place the Clare garden in the first rank. Walter Barlow died all too soon in 1960, but fortunately he had imparted much of his knowledge and wisdom to one of his assistants, Brian Arbon, who succeeded him as head gardener at the early age of twenty-six. Since then the College has owed the beauty of its gardens almost entirely to him and his staff.

(Nevill Willmer died during the preparation of this book, 7 March 2001, at the age of 97.)

a half-century of clare gardens

MICHELLE CALVERT

In 1951, a young pupil from Sawston Village College responded to a two-column *Cambridge Daily News* advertisement for a 'Garden Boy'. Accompanied by his father (following a hastily aborted interview for another post with a gruff and intimidating country gentleman), Brian Arbon arrived nervously at Clare for an interview with the College Clerk. When offered the post, he accepted on the spot, taking on the six-day per week job for the princely sum of two pounds and five shillings per week – his father's polite suggestion of negotiating on the point of pay being equally politely declined by the prudent Mr Emery.

The Fellows' Garden, recently and beautifully redesigned by Professor Nevill Willmer, was quickly taking shape when Brian arrived. Together, the then Head Gardner (Walter Barlow, "a marvellous bloke"), two Under Gardeners and the new Garden Boy set to work on completing the transformation. In addition to this major undertaking, the regular seasonal gardening had to be done and, in those days before rotary mowers, Brian remembers one of his first jobs being to cut all the grass on the riverbank with a pair of garden shears!

At this stage, his work was not confined to horticultural activities. Full-time staff were not then automatically given lunch so, always ready for a hot meal by midday, Brian would run over to the kitchens to help serve the students, in exchange for a meal himself. And, in common with many staff members, Brian would help out at a range of May Week events to earn a little extra money. He recalls one May Ball, in particular, when he was on duty with one of the older Gyps. Not long into the evening, the young gardener noticed that all the collection and washing of glasses appeared to be the work of his hands alone. He carried on regardless until, in the early hours, he heard a rustling as he walked past a large bush in the Fellows' Garden. On further inspection, it turned out to be the wily Gyp emerging from a comfortable evening's nap –

who, nodding sagely to the new recruit, observed: 'When you're as old as me, you'll learn!' The theme of May Balls as the nadir of the gardening year was set to continue.

Responsibility for the College Gardens fell fully on Brian's shoulders in 1961, following the death of Walter Barlow. Though some worried that, at the age of 26, he was rather young to take on the Head Gardener's job, Professor Willmer was firm in his decision that Brian should be given the chance. His faith was fully justified, as the succeeding decades have shown.

Describing himself as a "working Head Gardener", Brian points out that there is no job in the gardens that he is not willing to do himself. His enjoyment of the work has evidently been shared by his colleagues, who have been remarkably few in number. Long service has been the norm, with many Clare gardeners serving twenty, thirty or even forty years. Brian is determined to make it to fifty.

Over the years, the seasonal gardening cycle has become a timetable "written in his head". 'To do' lists are unnecessary: the change of seasons and weather provide sufficient reminder of the tasks in hand. However – and fortunately for Clare – Brian has also committed much to paper. For the last forty years he has meticulously recorded each year's plantings, building a detailed picture of both subtle and substantial changes to the gardens with his annual inventories.

One of the most substantial changes during Brian's working life happened by accident rather than design. In 1978 the swiftly rising Cam submerged the Fellows' Garden in under twenty minutes. In some places, the water rose as much as four feet above the garden, and – to the horror of the Head Gardener – students were seen punting over his sunken flowerbeds. Sadly, the flooding destroyed many old and rare plants and Brian confesses to having shed a few tears for their loss. Nevertheless, regular hosing down of the gardens to remove river silt, com-

LEFT: *Brian Arbon in the Fellows' Garden.*

242

ABOVE: *The garden submerged, in 1978.*

bined with careful tending of the surviving plants and an active barter trade with other college gardeners, eventually restored the Fellows' Garden to its former glory. Or almost – Brian still insists that the delphiniums are not what they used to be.

The reputation of the College Gardens, as perhaps the finest in Cambridge, was well-established in the 1970s. Its profile was raised further when, in 1977, the BBC's *Songs of Praise* Christmas special was filmed at Clare. As the *Annual* of that year reports: 'in addition to carols sung by the choir in Chapel and in Hall [the programme] featured interviews with Fellows, students, and staff, and, incidentally, some beautiful colour photography of the buildings and gardens'[1]. Brian's memory of this occasion is rather more specific. The programme's producers were unconcerned by his self-confessedly vague notions of God; they were delighted by the views of the garden and anxious to film him at work. He duly started to dig a new riverside flowerbed and the scene developed beautifully, with a robin arriving to perch photogenically on his shovel. The film-makers were delighted and *Songs of Praise*'s first broadcast from a

Cambridge College was a great success. However, the following spring, it was at precisely this spot that the river burst its bank, and Brian has wondered ever since whether someone was making a point!

Garden 'traffic' has increased substantially over the years, with both a greater number of College activities and a dramatic leap in the number of visitors. College events have varied considerably, from elegant drinks receptions and lively summer plays to – the *bête noir* of College gardeners – the annual May Ball. Brian has seen forty-eight May Balls during his time at Clare and they have become steadily more ambitious, their reach extending ever further into his carefully tended patch. Though he likes to see the students enjoy themselves, he can nevertheless be seen for days afterwards, head shaking mournfully as he and his staff set about their task of garden restoration. And, as preparations for the next May Ball begin, Brian can hardly keep a smile from his face: he will retire before the big day!

Tours of the gardens have always been very popular with both individual members of the public and a range of community groups, but demand has grown in recent years. As well as being open to growing numbers of summer visitors, the College gardens have been specially featured in a range of events – from local charity fundraisers to the National Gardens Scheme Open Days. Such is the reputuation of the Gardens that Brian Arbon was awarded both the Royal Horticultural Society's Long Service Award (presented to him, appropriately, by Professor Nevill Willmer) and, in the Queen's Birthday Honours, the British Empire Medal for services to horticulture. The Lord Lieutenant of Cambridgeshire presented this medal to Brian, on Her Majesty's behalf, on 30 September 1992 in a ceremony in the Master's garden.

As Brian looks towards his retirement next year, fifty years after his arrival, his affection for the College gardens remains undiminished. When looking back on pictures from his early years at Clare, he is astonished to see how much everything has grown. The gardens' development, perhaps unremarkable from year to year, has been dramatic in retrospect. It is a testament, both to Professor Willmer's original design and to its devoted and skilful tending by Brian Arbon and his fellow gardeners over half a century.

September 2000

1 *The Clare Association Annual*, 1977–78, p. 20.

From the earliest days music was accorded a prominent place in the life of Cambridge University, playing a central role in chapel liturgies; several colleges
made a chapel choir part of their original foundation.
Over the centuries Cambridge alumni, especially composers, exercised a substantial influence within the
national musical scene. In Clare, however, music appears
to have had little prominence until the beginning of the
twentieth century, when the activities of two former students, Sabine Baring-Gould and Cecil Sharp, and the co-
incidental succession of musically active undergraduates,
gave Clare music a sufficiently high profile to earn it an
enthusiastic mention in the 1926 history of Clare College.
Volume one concludes: 'those [Clare musicians] who
show such direct, clean enthusiasm have become quite
single-minded in the zeal of their discovery that art can
bring the inestimable recognition of a life created within
life. If it is on its musical tradition that the College may
most congratulate itself in reviewing its recent generations, it is in the degree of this kind of enthusiasm that the
essence of that tradition lies, for it makes of its possessors
real 'new world' types. Such men as Cecil Sharp, Denis
Browne and John Shepherdson[1] do not occur with per-
functory, calculable regularity; but awareness that a tradition has, somehow, gathered into being, and of the outstanding values in the nature of that tradition, may help to
ensure unbroken continuity.' And so it has proved.

After the University's introduction of a music tripos in
1947, the consequent rise in the number of undergraduate musicians and the advent of a regular (and continuing) stream of ex-National Youth Orchestra players in the
'fifties, the impetus behind active university music grew
steadily. In time, this situation was reflected at Clare
where, in addition, a succession of music-loving Masters
and Chapel Deans, the introduction of a mixed choir and
eventually the appointment of a fully salaried Director of

Music in 1979 brought music to the forefront of College
life – so much so that by 2000 Clare could stand proudly
alongside King's and other musically-renowned colleges,
boasting its own academic successes, a thriving musical
society, an internationally recognised choir, and a growing
list of distinguished musical alumni.

Onward Christian Soldiers

A history of Clare music through the twentieth century
must surely begin with a mention of Sabine Baring-Gould
and Cecil Sharp, though their names nowadays may evoke
scant recognition and their national importance in the history of British music be now known to only a few. Baring-
Gould, a cleric and hymn writer, was the author of the well-
known 'Onward, Christian Soldiers' and 'Through the
night of doubt and sorrow'. Of more significance perhaps
was his hobby, folk music; he was amongst the first to collect traditional English tunes. Cecil Sharp, twenty-five years
younger than Baring-Gould, nonetheless became the older
man's collaborator in a seminal publication, *English Folk
Songs for Schools,* published in 1905. Thereafter Sharp, who

244

took a degree in Mathematics at Clare, became an ardent collector of folk tunes himself. His interests in folk music became increasingly wide (his study of Appalachian tunes, resulting in a collection amounting to some thousand airs and variants and attendant notes, is a major source of social history). His list of publications was prodigious, many of them intended for schools. He was granted a Civil List pension and in 1923 the University awarded him the degree of Master of Music *honoris causa*. After his death in 1924, Cecil Sharp House, the home of the English Folk Dance and Song Society, was built in his memory. His manuscripts of folk tunes were bequeathed to Clare.

Raymond and Agnes

Baring-Gould and Sharp were, at Clare at least, musical amateurs. There was no music don – indeed, there was no music tripos. Until the end of the second war, Clare music was, apart from those few musicians who read for a Mus Bac., an amateur affair. This changed when the first music Fellow was elected to Clare in 1961. The arrival of Nicholas Temperley created a co-incidental link with Sabine Baring-Gould. Temperley possessed a rare zeal to restore some credibility to nineteenth century English music, especially Victorian hymnody, the subject in due course of a major publication on the subject. A by-product of his interest in this period of English music was the revival in 1966, at the Arts Theatre, of Edward Loder's opera *Raymond and Agnes*. The production was almost exclusively a Clare event: conducted by the organ scholar, David Grant, solo roles were taken by members of the chapel choir, whilst the chorus, orchestra and backstage crew included many Clare men. The production attracted considerable notice in the national press.

Despite *Raymond and Agnes*, Temperley's role in Clare was principally academic. Inevitably, however, he took some vestigial responsibility for the choir, and also was involved in the purchase and installation of the new chapel organ.

The Chapel Choir loses its trebles

Until 1960, the Chapel choir had drawn boys from the town to provide the treble voices, enticed to sing as much by the promise of earning a few pence as by any musical ambition. Rex Langford, a chorister in the late 'forties, remembers that for him and his cousin the promise of 13 shillings a term, the Saturday soccer and cricket matches and the twice-yearly choir camp (run by Professor Moule and a few of the undergraduates) was inducement enough. It seemed

not to matter that he did not read music and had no vocal experience prior to becoming a chorister!

There are few published accounts of chapel music in the days of the men and boys choir. There were certainly highlights. In the 1929 edition of *Lady Clare* we read: 'The Choir, assisted by three outside soloists, gave an ambitious performance of Bach's Cantata *My Spirit was in Heaviness* in the Lent Term. P.B. Rogers, W.H. Wilson and the rest of the Choir are to be congratulated on a noble effort.' In the Lent term 1930 the choir sang Bach's *St John Passion* and 'at times reached quite a high level.' However, the liturgical repertoire was small by today's standards. In the Michaelmas Term of 1930 the choir managed two anthems and two settings of the Communion Service. Presumably its efforts were devoted to that term's carol service, which included traditional carols and two chorales from the *Christmas Oratorio*, accompanied by a small orchestra.

By the end of the 2nd World War, choirmasters (employees of the College who were apparently neither Fellows nor undergraduates) had been replaced by organ scholars. There being never more than one such scholar at a time, the new one had to master from scratch the job of recruiting and training the Chapel choir (including the town boys), on arrival as a freshman. He was also responsible for the College choral society (The Canaries). Such a baptism of fire suited some, such as Martin How (who went on to a distinguished career in the Royal School of Church Music). Others fared less well, with inevitable consequences for musical standards.

Whatever the state of Chapel music between 1930 and 1960, during the enlightened sixties the situation came to be seen as uncomfortable: it took boys away from their local parishes, and without the benefit of a choir school they received insufficient musical training or discipline. By then the musical standard was certainly far from creditable: it is reported that the boys could sometimes scarcely *read*, let alone read music. For a number of years Trinity College (once famous for its men and boys choir) had successfully managed without a treble line and the decision was finally taken to do the same at Clare. Numerous ATB arrangements in the choir library (including an important publication of anthems for mens' voices, co-edited by Nicholas Temperley) bear witness to the years without a top line.

By the early seventies, however, with the welcoming of women into the men's colleges, it was with some relief that the chapel choir could once again field a complete ensemble. Just at this time, Temperley was succeeded, in 1971, by the Purcell scholar, Peter Dennison, an able choir trainer who was to have a profound influence on the direction of College music thereafter. It was Dennison who established the first mixed choir at Clare, employing female volunteers from both Clare and other colleges. With the acquiescence of the College, he took over the direction of the Choir himself, relegating the organ scholar to the organ loft. His fanatical perfectionism didn't always endear him to his singers (or to the Fellows) but in a short time he made the choir a force with which to be reckoned. However, the temptation of a professorship in his native Australia resulted in a brief stay at Clare. His place was taken in 1975 by a recent Clare graduate, John Rutter, who was appointed as the College's first Director of Music, albeit non-stipendiary.

Carols from Clare

Rutter's career as a composer and carol arranger has brought him international recognition and placed him at the forefront of late twentieth-century British composers, despite the self-confessed 'popularism' of his compositional idiom. Like Arthur Sullivan before him, whose credentials as a composer many have been too ready to question, Rutter's skill as a tune-smith and as an orchestrator is superb. It is surely safe to suggest that in another century Rutter's name will be known when some of his contemporaries, more celebrated now, are long forgotten. That his compositions are almost exclusively vocal is perhaps the result of a fortuitous collaboration with David Willcocks, whilst still an undergraduate, in the compilation and editing of *Carols for Choirs II*. In any case, he developed an early association with the College choir as a bass volunteer, and in 1966 he produced a first recording of carols, *In dulci jubilo*, with the choir-based Clare College Singers. The 1967 *Association Annual* concluded its report of the event with some prescience: 'If the recording company likes it and the publisher likes it, it's a sure bet that the public will; they ought to'. Thirty years later 'Rutter' and 'carol' are more or less synonymous, though his output extends far beyond this genre to include a number of major choral works, including the *Gloria, Requiem* and *Magnificat*.

Keeping an active connection with Clare Choir after graduation, it is scarcely surprising that John Rutter was a natural choice as successor to Peter Dennison. He devoted to it prodigious amounts of energy and quickly proved the potential of a good mixed-voice choir. In four years he established a consistently high standard of service singing, to the point where he secured some notable broadcasts, including two memorable Advent meditations

with Charlie Moule, recorded in Ely Cathedral, and two special Christmas editions of *Songs of Praise*. There were also exciting concerts and tours, including one to Venice, and in 1978 Rutter produced another carols recording, *Carols from Clare*, which remains in the catalogue to this day. For the six hundred and fiftieth anniversary of the College he invited Herbert Howells to compose the motet, *The Fear of the Lord*. This began a series of commissions for the Chapel Choir which has continued ever since, most notably in 1998 with *The Silent Land* by Giles Swayne, commissioned by Phyllis Lee in memory of her husband Hardy (Clare 1929–1932), a stalwart of the College music society in his time.

Three 'firsts'

In all his work at Clare Rutter was strongly supported by the Master, Eric Ashby, the Dean, Arthur Peacocke, and ultimately by the Governing Body. They recognised the sig-

RIGHT: *The Chapel choir at work (1944) and* (ABOVE) *at play (1950).*

nificance of a formally-constituted mixed choir by the establishment of choral exhibitions for women, the first in Oxbridge. The pressure of Rutter's work as a lecturer at the Open University and as a composer finally made a move from Clare in 1979 inevitable. However, he retained a strong link with the College by setting up the Cambridge Singers, drawing largely on ex-members of Clare choir. Projects with the Singers soon led to the creation of the Collegium record label and a steady flow of recordings over twenty years. In 1999 came the appearence on the label of Clare Chapel choir; it's initial recording, *Illumina*, was subsequently nominated for a prestigious Gramophone Award.

With the resignation of John Rutter, the Governing Body faced a dilemma: recognising the value of Dennison's and Rutter's endeavours to give the choir a national profile, how could it ensure that a new Fellow in Music might have sufficient interest in it to continue his predecessors' work? In the end, it decided to create a new College lectureship which specifically involved the direction of the choir as well as the direction of studies. One doubts whether ten years on, with the increasingly difficult economic climate for Oxbridge colleges, a position that was in part non-academic would have been countenanced. But in 1979 Clare was prepared to lead the way and appointed Tim Brown as Director of Music. Since then many Cambridge colleges have followed suit by themselves appointing Directors of Music to promote practical music-making. In this appointment, as in so many other areas, Clare led the way.

In the last quarter of a century the College choir secured a niche for itself both within the Oxbridge choral scene and on a larger stage. The increase in the number of choral exhibitions over the years was a significant help. Numerous overseas tours and recordings earned it a formidable reputation and an increasing 'fan club'. It has been able to play a significant role in the work of the College's Development Campaign. In 1999 it received an invitation to take part in a BBC Promenade Concert, the first mixed voice Oxbridge choir to do so: on 26 August 2000, as part of the celebrations to mark the 250th anniversary

of Bach's death, Clare College Choir provided the chorus for the *St John Passion,* in a performance directed by Ivor Bolton, a former organ scholar (1975–78) at Clare.

Behind the glitter has lain a determination to maintain a consistent standard of music at services of worship. 'Extra' opportunities for the choir are therefore seen against the routine of thrice-weekly worship and the special chapel events such as late-night vigils and sung service of Compline. As we move into a new century the Chapel choir remains just that: a *chapel* choir which from time to time does other things. Secular music in the College remains a separate entity, and is the responsibility of an undergraduate committee.

The College Music Society

From the *Lady Clare Magazine* and *Association Annual,* reports of regular College concerts abound throughout the century. Generally they appear to have been lively affairs, especially in pre-war days, when they were presided over by a chairman (a College Fellow), who kept some order and to whom a vote of thanks would be presented at the conclusion of the evening. Sometimes matters almost got the better of him, as in 1909 when 'a gratuitous obbligato from the back of the room' threatened to disrupt proceedings, or when in the Smoking Concert held on 9 March 1910 a number of sportsmen, disappointed at the scratching of the annual athletics fixture with Oriel, 'drowned their sorrows in a consolatory dinner, with the result that a section of the audience conceived themselves to be participating in an acrimonious debate rather than a comparatively peaceful concert'. Somewhat pompously, the writer adds: 'Why it should be the general opinion that an audience can best show its appreciation by talking loudly instead of listening to the efforts of the Music Society, it is difficult to guess. It is merely a matter of treating the thing seriously: and if the audience want to talk the whole way through the programme, it would be better to go and do it in the court, than to baffle the efforts of the performers so completely as was the case on this occasion. The one item that was greeted with the attention it deserved was Hughes and Whitehead's wonderful conjuring'. Sad perhaps to say, conjuring has not been seen at any concerts within living memory. Fashions have changed. 'Smoking concerts' are no more: evenings involving a more or less random (and sometimes, one suspects, interminable) collection of miscellaneous items have given way to more structured programmes.

For many years the Music Society has presented a freshers concert at the start of each year, and on each occasion the range of talent is impressive, sometimes remarkable. One hundred years ago, when the annual intake of freshers was a mere sixty or so, there was only the smallest pool of amateur musicians to support the College's musical activities. Today there are at least 130 freshers who come from every possible background, including specialist music schools. Many have attended Saturday morning classes at the music conservatoires; some are choral exhibitioners. What comes across when reading the accounts of early concerts is the raw enthusiasm which pervaded the College's musical activities, when such luminaries as the singer and opera producer Clive Carey (1883–1968), composer of the College Song *Carmen Clarense*, the pianist and composer William Denis Browne (1888–1915) and Frank Haines (organ scholar 1907–1910) stimulated much of the music-making, including the formation of a College chorus. With a fairly desperate absence of vocal or instrumental balance there was nevertheless much fun to be had, such as that recalled in the account of an orchestral outing to Melbourn in January 1904. On this occasion the band consisted of half a dozen strings, an ocarina, clarinets, piccolo, cornet and euphonium, bassoon, two triangles, castanets, an assortment of drums, cymbal, and piano. A College magazine article entitled 'The Wanderings of the Clare Orchestra' describes the event as 'an immense sensation … the applause so affected our pianist that he proceeded to push the piano, together with a standard lamp, *off* the platform … The return journey to Cambridge was an eventful one; it was cold and the night was full of fog. We were soon convinced that the horses were in difficulties, and at last we were forced to alight and search for the road which, owing to the dense fog, we had lost. Having found it, however, we deemed it safer to appoint "out-runners", thus enabling the driver to keep the horses on the road. In this way the remaining eight miles were accomplished. Ultimately we arrived at our destination about three in the morning after both an eventful ride and pleasant outing.' The concert raised £10 for charity.

Accounts in *Lady Clare* make it clear that the fortunes of the Music Society were inclined to ebb and flow. In the late twenties and early thirties, the era of Paul Mellon, the College obviously had a number of energetic and entrepreneurial musicians who, like Clare men in the years before the First War, not only generated much musical enthusiasm in College but made a significant contribution to University music. There were regular concerts, and programmes included operettas as well as performances from visiting artists of the stature of the oboist Léon Goossens and singers Carrie Tubb and Topliss Green. In 1936 sufficient players were mustered for the College orchestra to be able to tackle *The Lark Ascending* by Vaughan Williams. But successive editions of *Lady Clare* make it clear that there was little consistency from year to year. In 1947 we read: 'Philistinism in Clare is rife; gentlemen are not supporting the music society'! In 1952 Peter Smart wrote of the 'decay of College Music: In the field of music Clare is without doubt one of the very least successful of all the Cambridge colleges.' 'R.P.C.', writing in the same issue about the Canaries' performance of *The Pirates of Penzance* was even more outspoken:

The real fault about The Pirates of Penzance *was that it should have been performed at all. It is nothing short of disgraceful that a College which has four musical Scholars or Exhibitioners in residence, backed by an Amalgamated Clubs expenditure of over £100 a year on music, should be content to devote its entire musical energies to a not impeccable performance of a work which may be heard and seen on the stage almost annually in any large town in England. There is a tendency in Clare to ignore a duty to the public incumbent upon a College with musical resources at its disposal which are denied to the rest of the community. We have the opportunity to introduce to the public new works, the great works of neglected composers, the neglected works of great composers. All of this we fail to do. A revolutionary departure is a concert of works by a living composer during the Lent term, but here the same criticism applies, for Vaughan Williams' music has been so successfully plugged by the BBC of late that he is now as well known to the public as, say Haydn. This failure is primarily due to an absence of any interest in music in the bulk of members of the College, and a lack of musical taste in the remainder. It is time that those responsible for music in Clare stopped providing sops for people whose musical development stopped short at their preparatory schools. The really musical members of the College spend their time listening and performing elsewhere in Cambridge. At the present moment the return shown for the expenditure on music indicates that the College and the Amalgamated Clubs are wasting their money.*

By the mid-fifties, with the influx of undergraduate music students after 1947, an increasing number of National Youth Orchestra players and students set on a professional musical career, often as conductors, the number of col-

248

lege musicians increased and the quality of College music steadily improved. Even though Roger Norrington, later to become an eminent conductor, stated in 1956 in *Lady Clare* 'Clare is not a musical college', that year Bach's *St Matthew Passion* was performed with some success (in Great St Mary's). By the sixties ambitious orchestral programmes were regularly mounted. Nowadays, it is not unusual for a fifty-piece orchestra to take the stage (often that of the University Music School as the College Hall is frequently too small to accommodate all the players); almost all of the players will be from Clare. Each year there is at least one concerto performance, frequently of near-professional standard. It is no surprise when such musicians subsequently end up as solo instrumentalists, members of chamber music ensembles, or as orchestral section leaders. 'We heard them here first' is a proud boast.

The Canaries

Vocal ensembles have been a continuous feature of Clare music in one form or another. Described in the early days as 'quartettes', enthusiasm was sometimes rather more in evidence than skill, in songs such as *Quibble's Cocoa* or Sullivans' *The Long Day Closes*. In 1928 a new society was formed, calling itself The Canaries. 'Any vocalists in the College who can sing a Bach Mass at sight and have a compass of not less than three octaves are invited to join the long waiting list for canarieship.'[2] In 1930 the club offered Elizabethan madrigals to its audiences. Though enjoyed by the majority of the members of the Club it was apparently not so successful from the popular point of view. The Col-

lege as a whole 'obviously prefers *Belinda's Dog* to Morley or Weelkes'.[3] In 1930, a second vocal ensemble, The Black Cats, was founded to sing negro spirituals and cowboy songs, following the vogue of those times. Like The Canaries, The Black Cats were a popular attraction at Smoking and Musical Society Concerts.

Later in its life, The Canaries became more of a choral society than a vocal ensemble, enjoying something of a revival in the years immediately after the war, under the leadership of the then organ scholar, Martin How. Sir David Attenborough is amongst those who remember The Canaries with affection: 'When I joined I was unaware that the ability to sing a Bach Mass at sight was the required qualification. Had I been so I would never have dared apply. Nonetheless, I did manage to stumble my way through Stanford's *Phaudrig Crohoore* – and greatly enjoyed the experience.'

By the seventies, the advent of 'pop' music had produced quite different kinds of close harmony and the Cats and Canaries had long since fallen from grace. Since then, *ad hoc* groups have sprung up every year, primarily to gain free entry to May Balls. From time to time a group will take its singing more seriously. In the early nineties a group of choral exhibitioners calling themselves 'SPAM' generated huge audiences for their sell-out concerts and the choir has recently spawned a group calling itself The Claritones. However Clare has yet to create its own 'King's Singers'. The nearest it has come is with 'Harvey and the Wallbangers', a group which was created by Harvey Brough in the late seventies, and which for a time enjoyed some commercial success.

College Support

When The Canaries gave their first public performance, they were greeted with tumultuous applause and 'canine noises from the Don's gallery'. Fellows' support for music has not always been so vocal, but at times in the century has been significant; mention has already been made of the decision to create a full-time Directorship of Music, and to enlarge the number of choral awards. The purchase of the von Beckerath organ in 1971 is a further example. It was a courageous step: Clare was the first Oxbridge college to depart from a conventional electro-pneumatic organ in favour of a tracker instrument in the Baroque style. The enthusiasm of individuals also played its part in no small measure. The interest of a host of Fellows and successive Masters has done much over the years to provide the kind

RIGHT: *Roger Norrington rehearsing the Appeals Concert, 1998.*

of environment in which college music can best flourish. Mollison, then Thirkill, both as Tutors and subsequently as Masters, were active and popular chairmen of the Music Society. The legendary Lodge concerts of Eric Ashby in which he was both host and participant have been re-created with great success by the present Master.

Alumni

A recent obituary for the composer Brian Boydell reminds us that many of the most successful Clare musicians read subjects other than Music; in Boydell's case, Natural Sciences. And so it has been since the time of Cecil Sharp. Sir Roger Norrington read English whilst Andrew Manze, the virtuoso baroque violinist, read Classics. Kit Hesketh-Harvey, celebrity of the cabaret scene, also read English. Some *have* read Music, including Richard Stilgoe, lyricist and cabaret singer, Ivor Bolton, Daniel Pailthorpe (flautist, co-Principal BBC Symphony Orchestra), violinists Margaret Faultless (Leader, Amsterdam Baroque Orchestra) and Marcus Barcham Stevens (Principal First Violin, City of Birmingham Symphony Orchestra), and two members of The Schubert Ensemble, Simon Blendis and Jane Salmon. The soprano Ruth Holton, and three cathedral organists, David Dunnett (Norwich) and Stephen Farr (Guildford) and Jonathan Gregory (Leicester), alumni of the chapel choir, also read Music. The balance of 'full-time' musicians and 'amateurs' is one of the factors that gives Clare music its particular character. This was shown to glorious effect in 1999 at the launch of the Development Campaign, when over a hundred Clare instrumentalists and singers, including a galaxy of *alumni* soloists gathered under the direction of Tim Brown and Sir Roger Norrington to perform a programme which included commissioned works, Bach's *5th Brandenburg Concerto*, and the Bach *Magnificat*.

Not all Clare musicians, of course, go on to performing careers. Each generation has produced its quota of academic musicians, such as the Professors of Music Brian Boydell (Trinity College, Dublin) Stephen Banfield (Elgar Professor of Music, Birmingham), Robert Orledge (Liverpool) and Michael Talbot (Liverpool). Others have had distinguished careers in the BBC or in the arts generally, such as Martin How, Bernard Keeffe, Stephen Plaistow or the composers Patrick Gowers and John Rutter, recently elected an Honorary Fellow. Over the years, the balance of academic and performing musicians has been one of the strengths of Clare music.

The Future

The same frustrations and grumbles that we read about in early College music reports will, I suspect, continue to surface from time to time. It will become no easier to find convenient rehearsal times, to secure the services of all the performers as and when they are required, or to persuade students to put aside their essay (or pint) or Fellows their marking or research (or dining) in order to create an audience. Yet despite the obstacles, each year throws up its Browne, Boydell, Norrington, Rutter, Holton, Manze – or its Cecil Sharp. This year another mathematician-musician arrived: Stewart French soon made us aware that we have in our midst a guitarist of rare talent. 'We heard him here first' … I wonder.

249

LEFT: *May Week concert, 1999.*

1 Cecil Sharp (1859–1924), English folk music collector and editor; W. Denis Browne (1888–1915), composer and critic; John Shepherdson (former organ scholar, later assistant to Dr Watson Mann at King's).

2 *Lady Clare Magazine*, Michaelmas Term, 1928.

3 *Lady Clare Magazine*, 1930.

a view of the river in the year 2000

UNA CLIFFORD

It's just everyday routine; cursing the sound of the radio alarm, forcing myself out of bed at what I am sure is an ungodly hour, then realizing somewhat guiltily that my bedder has been at work since 6am. As I struggle with the curtains, clambering up onto my window seats to open the shutters and let some daylight in, I don't suppose it really strikes me that the view that I nonchalantly choose to ignore is that of punts floating down the Cam, the fabulously beautiful Clare gardens and early-bird tourists, video camera in one hand, 'England's Top Ten Tourist Spots' in the other, eager to have their photo taken on Clare bridge, soaking up every last anecdotal detail that their guides have to offer. From the other side of my room the world-famous Chapel at King's is clearly visible – even on the mistiest of mornings.

Some people may think this all a bit surreal in the technologically advanced society in which we live. I know that if my friends back home were to read this, they may find it slightly alien to the world of student halls and crumbling town houses that they are used to. To me it's just my room, F staircase.

There is no-one to introduce reality into Cambridge life like a bedder. I can't count how many mornings I have stood in my room in a dressing gown, cup of tea in hand, chatting to my bedder, known fondly to me as the 'Dawn Chorus', about whichever soap has made the headlines at the moment. She is the person who brought me throat lozenges and Lemsip when I had the flu last winter and who tiptoed through my room when I was finishing off the essay so as not to disturb me. They become part-time mothers, nurses and friends.

We are blessed with a fabulous team of porters here in Clare as well. Always a smile, a joke about the mittens my mum sent me in the post to keep my little fingers from freezing during the bitter winter months, and providers of light-bulbs and useful advice when things go wrong. The member of staff who stood out for me during Freshers' Week last year was Norman, the Memorial Court porter. I admit I shed a silent tear when he left us at the start of Michelmas 1999. It's people like the bedders, porters and the College nurse who have made life here in Clare such a pleasure for me.

My first memory of Clare, after the blur of arriving as an eager fresher and saying goodbye to my parents, is Matriculation Dinner. The Master stood up and told us all to 'get a life'. I was shocked on two accounts; firstly, that someone important like the Master would know what 'get

LEFT: *A still winter's morning at Clare Bridge.*

a life' meant and, secondly, that he would have the gall to use it at so formal an occasion as this. I think I now know what he was getting at. Clare has offered me so much and when I first sat down at my computer I wasn't sure if I could fill out this chapter; now I can't decide what to cut.

I had few expectations about Clare before I came up. It had always been my dream to go to Cambridge, so I suppose that I didn't want to have too many hopes only to have them proved false. The only time I had been to Clare before Freshers' Week was for interview, and even

then it felt right, despite my stomach being so full of butterflies that I could barely breathe. When I am out at schools talking to students about applying to Cambridge I feel so proud and end up selling Clare. Perhaps that is the reason for our extraordinarily high number of applicants. At open days we can't keep ourselves from boasting about the achievements of our students, keeping in mind the reality of a Cambridge degree. We all complain about Buttery food and feel claustrophobic at times, but most of us can't help loving Clare all the same. That is its unique

252

selling point for me. Clare seems to be timeless. Even in the new millennium.

One of the most interesting parts of being a Clare student is marrying a 21st-century lifestyle with an impressive 17th-century, listed building and an institution dating back to the reign of Edward II. I wonder whether Lady Clare ever imagined that by choosing Clare College as her pearl of learning she would be laying the foundations for a centre of learning that, in the future, was to become home to the internet, email and, indeed, female students. Pretty impressive when I think of it like that. I tend not to. I just get up, press the play button on my CD player, turn on the computer for a quick scour of my emails in the hope of a reply from my Latin American literature supervisor, hit the switch of my millennium kettle and don a dressing-gown to set out on the long trek to the showers.

Day to day living for a Clare student is, I suppose, not a lot different from that of thousands of other students across the country, unless you are forced to stop and think about it. Clare has many advantages for today's youth; it's close to Sainsbury's, handily positioned for access to the University Library and all Arts departments, not to mention home to the best Entertainments in Cambridge. Quite an impressive résumé really. My favourite memory of Clare in the time that I've been here is sitting on the bridge one sunny Friday afternoon, shopping bags at my feet, trying hard to avoid the essay, watching the world.

Clare students pride themselves on displaying talent in many areas and have a desire to share this with the public. Our choir enthralled countless American crowds during their successful tour last summer, the Clare Actors mesmerized audiences during a fabulous production of Shakespeare's *Anthony and Cleopatra* in the gardens during May Week 1999, and the Clare Art Exhibition in the Cellars made the front page of both *The Cambridge Student* and *Varsity* in the Michaelmas term. The *pièce de résistance* of the exhibition was, without a shadow of a doubt, the collection of items that had been confiscated by the Housekeeping department, including a blow-up sofa, a full-size cardboard cut-out of some international sex symbol and even a fire-extinguisher. No wonder we Clare students are proud.

The highlights of 1999–2000 as a student of Clare College are different for everyone, but there are some things I don't think anyone could forget. The 1999 May Ball was a resounding success and thoroughly enjoyed by all. Even the President, Susanna Howard, assures me that, despite innumerable moments of panic leading up to the big day, she had a great time. Clare can never be seen through quite the same eyes after the magic of a ball. Sometimes I still walk across the bridge and expect to look to Trinity, seeing an impressive firework display through a sea of sparkling beads, and the soothing smell of that massage parlour still lingers in the air of Small Hall.

I have to say that, on the whole, student-staff relationships are very open here in Clare, but they have not been without some fraught moments, May Ball itself providing an emotionally fired debate within College last year. I think that every student would agree that the decision taken rather rashly by a sub-committee of Fellows to reduce the size of the university-renowned Ball, posing a serious threat to its survival, planted the seed that caused a dark cloud to hang ominously over Clare in the weeks preceding the millennial celebrations. No student was celebrating in Clare. As usual, however, a compromise was found that suited everyone concerned. Preparations are presently underway for what is sure to be yet another highlight in the Clare calendar.

The gardens, the main venue for May Ball, remain at the heart of Clare and every student remembers sitting on the riverbank, book in hand, valiantly trying, or pretending, to study for Tripos exams but actually more interested in the spectacle on the river. There is value in this of course. Some of the most interesting things I know about Clare originated from the guides who punt tourists up and down the river, quoting age-old myths about the Colleges and the many tricks that the students of the past got up to.

Many of my favourite memories of Clare are, naturally, personal ones, shared with closest friends. Among these I would have to include holding back homesick tears during a late-night performance of the spectacular Fauré *Requiem* by the Clare Choir, and sitting on the not-so-clean floor of the JCR one Sunday evening whilst three of my best friends stood in the much sought-after spotlight during Clare Jazz.

My biggest personal achievement since arriving at Clare almost two years ago was being elected President of the Union of Clare Students in Lent term of my first year. I find it hard to talk of what Clare means to a student at the turn of the millennium without thinking of what has happened in the ranks of the UCS over the past year. The job has brought me both highs and lows and has seen me doing everything from presenting papers to College Council, to carrying boxes of Freshers Handbooks down the Avenue,

LEFT: *A spring day on the river, 2000.*

practising the introduction to the UCS I had been preparing for our newcomers. There is even a photograph somewhere of me cutting up five bags of oranges and lemons to help make mulled wine for 200 people before the UCS fancy-dress party – dressed as a Christmas fairy at the time.

The events that the UCS has run throughout the course of the year have been the source of most of my highlights as President. The front lawn of Memorial Court after exams last summer was the perfect venue for our garden party. Never has bulk shopping been so fun as steering a trolley around Sainsbury's with three of my good friends deciding whether to buy 30 baguettes or to splash out and go for 35. Freshers' Week looks a bit different when you are organizing it – different but just as exhausting.

Naturally, as President of the UCS I have had the opportunity to see an area of College life not always available to the average Clare student. Getting to know a bit about how College works has been quite an experience and one that I have thoroughly enjoyed. Although at times the rest of the Executive would sigh in a defeatist manner when I would report back from meetings, telling of the formation of yet another sub-committee, secretly, I was quite pleased. Somehow I manage to glean some kind of perverse enjoyment from the delights of the Clare sub-committee, however exasperating they proved to be on occasions.

Often I have found myself leaving College Council and some concerned Fellow has stopped me to enquire about the health of my academic career, reminding me that 'student politics is all very well but study has to come first'. In this respect, Clare is, I suppose, no different from every other Cambridge college. It has not always been easy coping with Tripos work and running the UCS at the same time, but, like most other students here, I thrive on a challenge. On occasions I think most people become slightly disillusioned with work and indeed resort to that well-known phrase 'They must have been mad to give me a place here!' Clare students are, I feel, fortunate in that there is an excellent support system in place in College to deal with the trials and tribulations of academic work. I am not just talking about the tutorial system, but also friends and members of staff whom students meet and talk to on a day to day basis.

Bearing in mind that a college loses and gains one third of its students every year, you could say that it would be relatively easy for the atmosphere to change within a short period of time, and yet in every alternative prospectus that I have been able to get my hands on, dating back to 1980, the description of Clare has remained the same. 'An open and friendly college, students of all year groups mixing together.' Many students wish that the bar and

254

JCR were more welcoming places to spend time with friends but it doesn't seem to have hindered the growth of true friendship.

Clare has provided me with some of the best friends I could ever have, and I'm not sure where I'd be at times without those people who sit across the table at Buttery, tirelessly listening to my complaints during the peak of my week-five blues and putting up with the endless stream of excited monologues about the latest linguistic discovery. It's my friends here in Clare that make everything worthwhile, even when I seem to have set up camp in the library, partly due to an essay crisis, partly because of the unbearable cold in my room. I have lost count of the number of cups of coffee that my best friend has made me, either over a girlie giggle or a good old weep. When I look at my Matriculation photo I am proud to say that I can name every undergraduate in it, suits, ties and all. Clare has many faults but one thing that can't be ignored is the fact that, despite students living on three sites, a real sense of community is central to life here in college.

If I had to choose one thing that makes Clare a convivial environment for both students and staff, I think I would say that it is the willingness of everyone to fight for what they believe in and yet a determination to find compromise. We all have complaints at times, be it with the noise of drum and bass echoing up from the Cellars on a Saturday night or the Housekeeping rules. The fact

BELOW: *Summer 2000, time to relax on Clare Bridge.*

remains, however, that almost 700 years after the first admission of scholars to Clare College, students and fellows continue to live and work together congenially. This is quite an achievement and one that I feel everyone would wish to see continued long into the future.

So how does life in Clare relate to the reality of my world? It doesn't feel in any way strange now to phone home and tell of the pennying in Formal Hall last night, or the terrible supervision that I had yesterday due to the fact that the only article I hadn't read was the one that my supervisor had actually written. When I had my very cool sixteen year-old sister over to visit last year, even she was accepting of how things worked in our little bubble. She was, of course, amazed that I could possibly consider where I lived to be a 'real student room', and thought that the gardens were more fitting for a fairy-tale than a pre-exam cramming centre. It's strange having family and friends to visit, since it makes you see Clare through the eyes of a tourist. And perhaps I can see what all the fuss is about.

Getting emails from friends at other universities is another measure of how real or surreal life here actually is. It seems to me that the only difference lies in the fact that they count the number of essays they do per term or semester and I count the number per week. I am not complaining though, since few if any of them can say that they have the pleasure of pulling the curtains every morning to mist on the Cam or the kind of gardens we used to dream about as children. Clare fits easily into my reality. I still complain about the same things as my friends back home – poverty, the cold and men. Like almost every university student I have found friends for life and can say that, thankfully, there is more to my university career than books and essays.

I wasn't too sure how to end, so my Dad suggested to me that I look to the future since this is a book that has concentrated on the past 100 years of the Clare community. He asked me if I returned to Clare with my kids twenty years from now and had to choose just one place to show them, where would it be. I didn't even have to think about it – Clare Bridge. How many generations of Clare students have sat on the bank listening to the story of why the third arch isn't architecturally perfect, or leaned on its sides during a May Ball, gazing over at the fireworks in Trinity? How many of us have even wasted time that perhaps should have been spent writing an essay just sitting, shopping bags at our feet, watching the rest of the world go by?

Lady Clare, the years have flown
Since you laid the primal stone.
Did you picture in your mind
All the genius you would find?
Did you make romance, and say,
'In this lecture hall one day
Sat the Keeper of the Seal;
There's the imprint of his heel.
He with look so sinister,
Once was our Prime Minister.
In that seat, now mark it well,
Sat our greatest admiral.
Over there they dined in hall.
Fame hangs painted on the wall.'
Romancing is a power divine
To use and love when you recline.

From that grey and mossy wall
You may see a shadow fall,
Sinking softly to the ground
With an airy, muffled sound.
Then a window banged and barred
Echoes round the old courtyard;
While the undergraduate
Trembles at the porter's gate.
If a 'Bulldog' hoves in sight
He must run with all his might,
Chased and hunted through the town
And for morals good sent down.
Lady Clare, these men of fame,
Passing in your dreams, became
Living lights upon the wall,
Painted fame in dining hall.

F. A. N.

Lady Clare Magazine Vol XVIIII/1, Michaelmas Term, 1924.

a snapshot in time

SIMON FRANKLIN

Scene One: a courtyard. Huge lumps of ancient masonry lie smashed on the ground. Up above, remnants of a stone balustrade perch precariously, like gigantic loose teeth. Where are we? A long-abandoned palazzo in Tuscany or the backwaters of Venice, perhaps? The picturesque ruins of a Northumbrian castle? Wrong. This is Clare Old Court on Sunday 3 October 1999; Clare as presented to the new batch of freshers who had all arrived the previous day. An enterprising third-year at the top of D staircase had decided to sling a hammock in his room. His clever wheeze was to secure one end by a rope passed through his window and fastened to the balustrade overlooking King's back lawn, and to secure the other end by a rope passed through the opposite window and fastened to the balustrade overlooking the court. Like the Millennium Bridge: an elegant design; shame about the engineering. Fortunately, and fortuitously, nobody was hurt by the falling stonework, though the building bears the tell-tale scar: a suspiciously uncorroded section of balustrade at the south-east corner.

Scene Two: a courtyard. A half-finished tower of bare scaffolding stands incongruously in the middle, without obvious purpose. Passers-by pause in bemusement. The tower cuts off their path. Some of them pick their way gingerly around its base, or even stoop to walk through the gaps underneath it. No signs warn of any danger; no hard hats. Somebody sticks a few posts into the ground and semi-effectually tapes off the immediate area. Where are we? Some dusty third-world building-site where health and safety regulations come a poor second to quick-fix under-the-counter contracts? No. This is Clare Old Court on Friday 16 June 2000, the last day of Full Term, the first day of frantic transformations for Monday's May Ball. By Monday evening the bare scaffolding, suitably draped, has become a fountain of magical lights, with a multi-coloured phoenix rising from beneath it. By Tuesday afternoon it has gone. Uniformed cleaners with gloved hands scour the lawns for fragments of discarded wine-glasses, the last remnants of the revelry.

Somewhere in between these two scenes, an academic year went by.

Every academic year is both typical and unique. Thus, on one level, there is nothing to report. The normal, day-to-day life of the College has been lived much as it always is, with the same highs and lows and pleasures and tensions and stimulations and anxieties that make up our annual cycle; generically familiar (like the tableaux of Old Court) to those who have seen the cycle through all its phases; unique in the specifics (again, like the tableaux of Old Court), and of course unique as personal experience for those who live through the cycle for the first time. Maybe it's true that you can't swim in the same river twice. But then again, maybe it *is* the same river, and 'river' is not defined by the particular water which happens to be in it at any given time. Clare is Clare is Clare. My brief, however, is to hold the flow, to present the year as a 'snapshot'. Try taking a snapshot with a year-long exposure, and you'll end up with a very fuzzy picture. A year at Clare is not 'still life', not some Damien Hirst half-cow suspended motionless in a hushed gallery. Besides, most of the important things which make a year unique are things which the Senior Tutor doesn't see, or shouldn't see, and certainly shouldn't reveal. Senior Tutors can list Achievements, Activities, Issues, Projects, Plans, but systematic reports give a false sense of completeness. For the moment, therefore, I continue with a series of unsystematic recollections and impressions, strewn randomly in the chronological gap between the smashed balustrade and the disappearing tower.

This was the year in which I discovered that a 'server' is not somebody employed by the Catering Manager, that 'hubs' have nothing to do with wheels, and that 'networking' is not just another word for toadying up to useful people; in which the Porters Lodges came to resemble Mission

Control at NASA, with banks of monitors tracking every recess of the College through CCTV, and with up-to-the-minute databases with names like FORUM and CASC (don't ask . . .) spewing out instant answers to every inquiry, and not a scrap of paper in sight (though the bowler hats still come out for graduation); in which library books stopped walking out by themselves, because they now know that computers have them tagged; and in which College doors began miraculously to open at the mere sight of a specially programmed card.

This was the year of Two Cultures, as Clare finished top of the Tripos league in English, and bottom in the Natural Sciences; but, just to show we're still in touch, all our Part II Computer Scientists achieved Firsts; and both our Part II Philosophers achieved starred Firsts.

This was the year in which we elected more new Fellows than in any year in living memory (in History, Economics, Music, Clinical Medicine, Clinical Veterinary Medicine, Law, Materials Science, Astronomy, and in Molecular Sciences Informatics (what else?), plus a brace of Experimental Psychologists, not to mention our usual quota of two Research Fellows), yet we still have fewer teaching Fellows than we did in the early 1990s. I must ask a mathematician to explain how that trick works; except that we are still looking for a Fellow in Applied Mathematics.

This was the year when the students almost went to war over inflatable furniture; when the Fellows almost went to war over the siting of a bell (peace was reached with the aid of a step-ladder and a papier-mâché mock-up) and over the lettering of the proposed commemorative inscription for Paul Mellon (resolved by ballot); when the Liaison Committee set up a Working Party on Duvets (the last straw?); and when students and Fellows almost went to war over the saga of the red gloss paint (on the ceiling of the JCR). Meanwhile, elsewhere in the University, students did go to war over rents; in Clare the students voted overwhelmingly (89%) to accept a five-year series of rent increases.

As to external battles, the College continues to make its modest contribution to the political life of the nation. This was the year in which a Fellow became Leader of Cambridge City Council, and assured us that in consequence he would have much more time for the College (in opposition you do your own homework, in power the staff do it for you). At the weightier end of the political spectrum, this was the year in which the University gave a student permission to degrade because her academic work was likely to be disrupted by court appearances connected with alleged attempts to infiltrate nuclear bases: an honourable Clare tradition, initiated by the newly-enthroned (in 2000) Archbishop of Wales when he was Dean of the College.

This was the year in which we completed the refurbishment of Memorial Court, and then discovered that we still don't have sufficient rooms either for all students or for all Fellows; in which all first-years finally got central heating, but there was no winter (and then no summer). And this was the year in which the College finally achieved its aim of having every student room wired for telephones – at the very moment when the demand for fixed-line telephones collapsed because of the sudden proliferation of mobiles. No matter how fast we run, we can't catch up.

Happiest, silliest faces of the year: Clare Relics who came back and rowed (well, sort of).

The year's dampest squib: the first Governing Body meeting in the Latimer Room, newly prettified as a 'high-class meetings-room'. By far the most audible participant was the lawnmower on King's back lawn. However, the room redeemed itself at its first art exhibition, organized by a student at the end of the Easter Term. The decision to upgrade was controversial (where else can the Rugby Club spill – sorry, I mean swill – its beer?), but the Latimer Room does occupy one of the finest locations in Cambridge and deserves a degree of elegance.

Prize for evocative writing: the Tutorial Bursar's summary list of students' applications for travel grants. A small specimen:

SPS/Law; Tibet; culture and pilgrimage trek.
NatSci; Greenland; sea-kayaking and mountaineering.
Vet; Amsterdam; small animal congress.
Phil.; St Petersburg; IVS – restoring Tsarist Russia [?!]
NatSci; Provence; dry stone-walling [sic!]
SPS; Europe; prayer-tour of European cities
SPS; London; conference on Marxism
Egr.; Cuba; politics and photography.

And so on, and so on. An Incantation in Two Spreadsheets, a litany of enterprise and discovery, each line a concise and crushing reminder of things I will never do.

Trivia question of the year: which event at the May Ball caused most damage to the fabric of the College? Answer: the poetry-reading (the wanton vandalism of listeners draping themselves aesthetically across the trailing creepers in the sunken garden; next year I must suggest a more tranquil alternative, such as an abuse-and-beer-gut competition between English and German football fans).

258

This was also the year in which Clare was exposed not just to casual tourist snapshots but to the powerful glare of public spotlights; a year of the phenomenal growth of a kind of 'virtual' College, a College which bears some resemblance to that which we recognize as our own, but which acquired a quasi-independent existence in the pages of newspapers (features, editorials and letters, broadsheet and tabloid), in party political polemics, and even in that most controversial of media – correspondence with alumni. We ourselves were partly responsible. In December, at the request of the Vice-Chancellor's office, we became the first College ever to allow complete and unrestricted access to every phase of the admissions process, from preliminary briefings for Directors of Studies, through real interviews with real candidates, to the final discussions and decisions as to who would or would not be offered places. 'Want to get into Cambridge? Go to a state school', declared the mildly mischievous front-page headline which introduced Judith Judd's careful series of three long articles in *The Independent.*

And off flew the story, twisting and mutating in the re-telling, selectively misinterpreted in the reading. Apparently a place called Clare College (just like us) indulged (as we do not) in 'positive discrimination', 'reverse discrimination' 'political correctness', 'social engineering'. Our very own fifteen minutes of flak. All because we confessed – no, not 'confessed', simply 'stated' – that, when trying to judge academic potential, we give some credit to candidates who have achieved excellent results from low-achieving schools. There is nothing unusual or particularly new in this. A version of the same thing is flagged in the University Admissions Prospectus, as standard practice for all Colleges. It would be blatantly unreasonable to do anything else. Still, better that such issues are discussed and disputed in the light of facts than – as has always been the case in the past – on the basis of vague assumptions, rumours and recycled anecdotes. On the whole we felt mildly proud to be leading the way towards candour; though some of us also recall that 'glasnost' (openness) cleared the way for the collapse of the Soviet Union.

So when the next storm broke, we kept quiet. In mid-May the Chancellor of the Exchequer declared that Oxford (and by implication Cambridge) admissions were 'an absolute scandal'. Why? Because an excellent candidate from a comprehensive school was rejected by Magdalene and went to Harvard instead. Clearly, admissions tutors only pay attention to the accent and the school tie. The 'Laura Spence Affair' generated quite astonishingly prominent and intense coverage in the media, as for a good two

or three weeks (or a dreadful two or three weeks) the admissions issue filled the political stage at national level. This is not the place to re-rehearse the arguments in detail, but the episode did bring a number of points sharply into focus: the abiding power of the stereotype; our own inadvertent wisdom in establishing a position in advance; the likelihood that we – that is, Colleges in general – will continue to lose aspects of our traditional autonomy, so long as we remain in any degree dependent on public funding (Harvard, held up as an example of 'good practice', is of course financially independent).

I digress. A snapshot of the future would be altogether too ambitious. Back to this year: for the record, as they say, University statistics show that this year the success rate for applicants to Clare was virtually identical for all types of school.

And let us keep the debates in perspective. On 27 May, at the height of the political row, Clare hosted an open day for prospective applicants. Such occasions start with a general presentation in the Hall, including a question-and-answer session. Obviously the news stories would be in the front of everybody's minds, and we agonized about how best to respond to the inevitable pointed or worried questions. Never assume. Our visitors were too polite even to mention the issue. They were much more interested in courses and facilities and activities – that is, broadly, in their future education – than in the Chancellor or Fleet Street editorials. Admirable bunch of people, the young.

Hyper-introspection is a disease from which Clare does not normally suffer, but this was a year in which we did spend a bit of time contemplating ourselves. The Master abandoned us for the Michaelmas and Lent Terms, disappearing over the horizon into Memorial Court to indulge in frivolities like writing books. As he waved goodbye, he handed us a box labelled 'hot potatoes', with instructions that the box should be empty on his return. His accompanying letter presented most of the issues as consequences of external or internal 'threats'. This is true, at least in the sense that all change is a threat to the way we are, and for most of us the definitive (Platonic, timeless) College is the College in the year when we – whoever we are – first arrived. Finances apart, for me the most significant and deepest change is the gradual withdrawal of trust, on all sides. No longer is it assumed that institutions have the right, or the capacity, to order their own affairs in a broadly reasonable way, with few questions asked and few procedures or criteria specified.

Consumers and paymasters alike demand transparency, accountability, harmonization (or standardization, or centralization), monitoring, reporting, codification. More and more of our time is spent jumping up and down to somebody else's tune: sometimes indeed to promote or try to ensure good practice, sometimes for self-protection in an increasingly litigious world, and sometimes – sometimes it feels as if we jump up and down merely because we have to be seen to be jumping up and down.

Hence, while students planned their sea-kayaking expeditions or their trips to restore Tsarist Russia, the College's various Committees pondered, *inter alia* (in no particular order of preference or value): the University's Mission Statement; a draft of a proposed Cambridge University Students' Charter; a Committee of Vice-Chancellors and Principals Proposal for Higher Education Progress Files; the new Data Protection Act; College Policy in relation to the proposed Institute of Teaching and Learning; the University's Institutional Teaching and Learning Strategy; College Policy on Student-Run Web-Sites; Codes of Practice for the Provision of Computer Services; Guidelines on Procedures for Student Complaints, and a Review of our Review of Student Support. We also endorsed a Code of Practice for the Support of Students with Disabilities, and Inter-Collegiate Procedures for Dealing with Cases of Meningitis, as well as producing new Rules governing the Use of Public Rooms, Guidelines for Duty Tutors, and our very own written Guidelines for Dealing with Cases of Extreme Drunkenness. And (the ultimate test of the true navel-gazer) we convened two Special Governing Body meetings to consider the Governing Body.

I said at the beginning that there is, on one level, nothing to report. Nor should there be. Contexts change, methods change, presentation changes. Whether change breeds anxiety or excitement, it always breeds sub-committees. But the point is to protect and renew what is central to the College as a place of education, learning, community and discovery. Just as Old Court needs constant attention if it is to remain Old Court, so the College as an institution demands ever more intensive maintenance. In both cases that which is most easily described is the annual maintenance activity, the issues and discussions and achievements and disasters of a given year (which reminds me, this happens to be the year in which we initiated work towards the production of a Strategic Plan for Old Court). In both cases maintenance is essential, but it is not the essence. If done properly, it should leave intact the repetitively unique experience of being here. So: a picture of Clare in 1999–2000 is ... well, it's just a picture of Clare. 1999–2000 was of course the most important year in the College's history for those who were here; but more importantly, 1999–2000 was, I hope and believe, a year of no importance.

Come now, that really won't do. Surely there must be *something* crucial, *something* substantial and definitive? Ah, yes, now that you mention it. If you want profundity, then I suppose you want the True and Curious Tale of the Dean's Dirty Crockery? Sorry, but no. Even in the age of transparency, decorum demands that some issues are best left opaque.

259

BELOW: *From the inside ... looking out.*

masters and fellows

SERVING IN THE TWENTIETH CENTURY

MASTERS OF CLARE

Edward Atkinson	1856–1915
William Loudon Mollison	1915–1929
Godfrey Harold Alfred Wilson	1929–1939
Henry (later Sir Henry) Thirkill	1939–1958
Sir Eric (later Lord) Ashby	1958–1975
Robert Charles Oliver Matthews (election 1974)	1975–1993
Bob Alexander Hepple* (election 1992)	1993–

FELLOWS SERVING AT 1ST JANUARY 1901

W.S. Collett former Dean	1858
L.Ewbank Bursar	1865
J.P. Taylor former Dean	1866
W.L. Mollison	1876
H.W. Fulford Dean	1877
J.R. Wardale	1882
T.McK. Hughes	1883
W. Gardiner Bursar	1885
H.M. Macdonal	1890
J.R. Harris	1892
H.M. Chadwick	1893
W.E. Philip	1896
G.H.A. Wilson	1897
F.W.B. Frankland	1899
C.E. Garrad	1900

FELLOWS IN ORDER OF THEIR ELECTION

H.O. Jones	1902
A. Young Bursar	1904
F.G. M Beck	1905
P.C.T. Crick Dean	1906
W.J. Harrison	1907
T.R. Ellison	1908
H. Thirkill	1910
Ff. Roberts	1911
M.D. Forbes	1912
W.J. Harrison (2) Bursar	1913
H.D. Henderson	1919
G.V. Carey	
J.W. Landon	
W.Telfer Dean	1921
W.E.H. Berwick	
R.E. Priestley	1922
A.D. Nock	1923
H. Godwin	1925
E.T.C. Spooner	1929
N.G.L. Hammond	1930
O.T. Jones	
P.H. Dean	1932
H.M. Taylor	1933
J.D. Boyd	1935
R.S. Hutton	1936
E.N. Willmer*	
D.M. Balme	1937
R.M. Barrer	
W.B. Reddaway*	1938
G. Metcalfe	
J.H. Parry	
R.A. Rankin	1939
E.C. Bullard	1943
A.C. Chibnall	
J.F. Baker	
C.F.D. Moule Dean*	1944
B. Cooper Bursar*	
A.B. Pippard	1947
D. Forbes	
J.P.R. Riches	
M.G.P. Stoker	1948
P.H. Spencer	
R.J.L. Kingsford	1949
J.D. Smith	
A.J. Harding	1950
A.M. Macbeath	
J.R. Northam*	
J.A. T Robinson Dean	1951
R.J. Eden	
J.S.L. Gilmour	
A.H. McDonald	1952
K.W. Wedderburn	
T.H. Ellison	
D. Walker	
J.W. Glen	1953
R.G. West*	1954
D. Forbes	
G.R. Elton	
C.W. Parkin	1955
T.J. Smiley*	
W F Vinen	
R.M. Ogilvie	
K. Lipstein*	1956
C.B. Reese	
Sir E.C. Bullard	1957
R.J. Eden	
Sir Eric Ashby Master	1958
G.H. Wright*	
W.F. Bodmer	
I.S. Laurie	1959
G.C. Duncan	
M.F. Wiles Dean	
W.W. Black	1960
A. Korner	
R.L. Fortescue	
V. Heine*	
D. Lynden-Bell	
D. Russell-Davis	1961
P.A. Roubiczek	
M.G. Bown*	
C.C. Turpin*	
J.M. Newton	
K.F. Riley*	
B. Hartley	
R.S. Schofield	1962
F.D. Holister*	
R.L. Tapp*	
N.M. Temperley	
J.P. Chilton*	
D.R. Jenkins	
C.H. Feinstein	1963
J.H. Dickson	
P.G. Lowe	1964
D. Branson	

P.F. Knewstubb*
P.J.S. Williams
D. Williams — 1965
C.N.J. Mann
N.O. Weiss*
M.J. Mitchinson* — 1966
J.R.C. Lecomber
R.M. Blackburn*
A.R. Sheldrake — 1967
D.E. Moggridge
C.W. Thompson
D.L. Weaire
R.T. Hunt
M. Santer Dean
B.A. Hepple — 1968
W. Horbury
P.R. Stanfield — 1969
M.M. Bowie
P.G. Dixon
P. Patnaik
R.S. Schofield (2)* — 1970
C.E. Maloney*
A.K. Stevens
J.M. Newton (2)*
M.J. Ruel*
D.R. Dance
P.J. Dennison — 1971
A. Shaw
M.A.L. King
A.S. Sinclair*
D. Lynden-Bell (2)* — 1972
T. Scott
R.D. Gooder*
G. Bartram
A.R. Peacocke Dean — 1973
S.J. Patterson
T.J.B. Simons
S.H. Paine
A.B. Holmes*
I.C. West
P.A. McNaughton — 1974
D.W. Bullett
D.D. Robinson
R.C.O. Matthews*
K.M. Marriott — 1975
M.H. Hoeflich
R.T. Hunt (2)* — 1976
W.A. Foster*
N.C.T. Coote
E.M. Freeman*
T. Moore*
L.J. Hill
A.M. Snodgrass* — 1977
J.M. Rutter
D.J. Tolhurst
A.J. Wiles
P. Lake
S.R. Reid
M.W. Johnson — 1978
D.W. Bullett (2)
B.A.W. Smale-Adams Bursar
J. Woodhouse* — 1979

A.A.A.K.K. Appiah
D.E. Moggridge (2)
S.M. Kanbur
T.C. Brown*
L.M. Gillman
E.J. Anderson
H. Daneshyar
J.D. Lear
P.F. Leadlay*
G.D. Price — 1980
S.C. Franklin*
G.F. Parker*
R.F. Willis
P.S.M. Judd Acting Dean
S.B. Dunnett — 1981
R.A. Houston
R.W. Scribner
M.R. Weale
P. Cartledge*
A.L. Johnson*
P.J. Ford*
T.R. Astin — 1982
R.O'Hanlon*
A. Lucas*
A.B. Philpott — 1983
H.E. Elsom — 1984
W.T. Shaw
R.D. Williams Dean
T.J. Kehoe
T.R. Baldwin
D. Williams — 1985
D.A. Day
A.M. Miller
D.R. Howarth*
M.L.J. Ashford
P.J.P. Goldberg — 1986
T.P. Marsland
N. Sagovsky Dean
J.R. Northam (2)#
D.F. Hartley*
M. Cappelletti (Vis.Prof)
A.G. Thomason*
R.E. Palmer — 1987
D.J. Scott*
D.A. Street
V.F. Faull Chaplain
N.H. Woodcock*
L.C. Paulson*
R.L. Taylor — 1988
S.E. Alcock
A.R.L. Travis*
A.P. Blake
G. Brown*
G. Woan — 1989
J.M. Masters
R.H. Aylmore (withdrew)
T.K. Thompson Bursar*
S.C. Rowell — 1990
J.M. Goodman*
M.E.N. Majerus*
M. Lapidge*
J.E.E. Charman Chaplain

N.A. Seaton
G.J. Mason — 1991
P.D. Griffiths
P.A.W. Edwards*
R.D. Lund
M.J. Grant*
B.E. Croxson
R.T. Phillips* — 1992
J.M.B. Wallace
M.M. Lahr
J.L.W. Schaper — 1993
J.P. Clayden (resigned)
M. Webster — 1994
H.E. Thompson*
C.N. Jagger — 1995
H-J. Voth
J.C.B. Wells Chaplain, Dean*
N.H. Andrews*
D.D. Robinson (2)*
C.J. Clarke*
A.M. Swinton — 1996
T-M. Yong
C. Baesens
T.W. Knighton*
D.R. Squires
N.C. Greenham*
E.A. Foyster
A.D.E. Reed* — 1997
S. Derrer
R.M. Harris*
W.A. Harris*
G.E. Hardingham* — 1998
B.J. Thomson*
J. Helgeson
P. Fara*
M.M. Lahr* (2)
A. Gambles
M. Sprik*
D. Hedley*
A. Philpott* — 1999
A. Bejancu*
S.D. Snobelen*
T. Follini*
J.S. Chadha*
C. Harrop
W.A. Pullan*
C.H. Duff
P.D. Bristowe*
J. Scott* — 2000
H.F. Jahn*
T.M. Lewens*
M.J. Steiner*
N.B. Holdstock*
M. Frolova-Walker*
R.C. Glen*
L.K. Tyler*
N. Clayton*
G. Ogilvie*
S.M.S. Pearsall*

262

* denotes a Fellow still in office at the end of the 20th Century (the sequence of * thus gives the order of seniority of Fellows at this time).

(2) denotes a second election after absence.

\# seniority granted under Statute (9(7) of 1967).

CHAPLAINS OF CLARE

A list up to the time at which the office included election to a Fellowship; not initially so in order to further an intermediary status between Fellows and undergraduates.

A. Leeke	1935–39
(H.C. Blackburne appointed but diverted to war service)	1939–40
A.T. Howden	1945–47
S.W. Betts	1947–49
J.D. Wakeling	1950–52
F.S. Skelton	1952–59
C.J.V. Drummond	1959–62
J.O.C. Alleyne	1962–66
J.R.P. Barker	1966–70
M.G.V. Roberts	1970–75
D.G. Tennant	1975–76
P.S.M. Judd – elected Fellow (Acting Dean) 1980	1976–81
A. Pettersen	1981–85
V.F. Faull – elected Fellow 1987	1985–90

HONORARY FELLOWS IN ORDER OF THEIR ELECTION

The first provision for election of Honorary Fellows was in the Statutes of 1882, hence the following is a complete list of Honorary Fellows of Clare.

E.C. Buck KCSI — 1898
Indian Civil service

J.R. Harris FBA — 1909
Prof of Greek, Early Christian History

O. Seaman Bt.
Editor of *Punch* 1906-32

H.M. Macdonald OBE — 1914
Prof of Mathematics (Aberdeen)

W. Gardiner FRS — 1915
re-instituted the C.U.Botanical Museum

S.B. Gould (Rev) — 1918
author and hymn-writer

C.S. Terry Hon FRCMusic — 1929
Prof of History (Aberdeen)

A.W. Mellon Hon LLD — 1931
Secretary to the American Treasury

H.M. Chadwick FBA — 1941
Prof of Anglo-Saxon 1912-1941

E.B. Bailey MC FRS — 1944
Prof of Geology (Glasgow),
Director of the Geological Survey of G.B.

W. Telfer MC, Dean 1921–46 — 1947
Master of Selwyn 1947–1968

Sir Hubert D. Henderson
Chairman of Royal Commission
on Population

M.A. Cassidy GCVO CB — 1949
Physician to the King 1932–1939-

E.A. Gowers GCB GBE
Senior civil servant, reviser of
Modern English Usage

S.L. Sassoon MC CBE DLitt — 1953
Poet

Sir Raymond Priestley MC — 1956
geologist, also known for polar exploration

Sir Geoffrey Crowther — 1958
Editor of *The Economist* 1938-56

P. Mellon Hon KBE Hon RA Hon FBA — 1960
Art collector, philanthropist

H.M. Taylor CBE — 1961
Vice-Chancellor, Keele Univ.

Sir Patrick Dean KCMG — 1965
HM Ambassador in Washington

Sir Geoffrey de Freitas KCMG — 1967
MP, Privy Councillor

Sir Arnold Hall FRS FEng,
Chairman, Hawker Siddley Group plc

J.R. Hersey
writer and war correspondent

Prof J.D. Watson*
Nobel Laureate 1962 (joint discoverer
of the structure of DNA)

The Rt Hon Lord Guest — 1971
KC Lord of Appeal in Ordinary 1961–71

Prof Sir Brian Pippard FRS* — 1973
President of Clare Hall 1966–73

Prof N.G.L. Hammond DSO CBE FBA*1974
Classicist, Prof of Greek (Bristol)

Sir John Gray MB ScD FRS* — 1976
Prof of Physiology (London)

Sir Michael Stoker CBE FRCP FRS*
Pathologist, President of Clare Hall 1980–87

Kingman Brewster — 1977
Prof of Law (Harvard),
President of Yale Univ 1963–77

Sir David Attenborough CVO CBE FRS* — 1980
Broadcaster and Naturalist

The Rt Hon Lord Ackner PC* — 1983
Lord of Appeal in Ordinary 1986–92

Sir Richard Bayliss KCVO MD FRCP*
Physician to the Queen 1970–81

Prof N.E. Odell PhD
Mountaineer, Emeritus Prof
of Geology (Otago)

The Rt Hon Lord Justice Kerr PC — 1985
Lord Justice of Appeal

Sir Edmund Leach
Emeritus Prof of Social Anthropology

Rt Revd Mark Santer* — 1987
Bishop of Birmingham

Sir Walter Bodmer FRS* — 1989
Principal of Hertford College, Oxford

Prof N. Ramsey*
Nobel Laureate 1989,
Prof of Physics (Harvard)

Sir Roger Norrington CBE* — 1990
Conductor and musical director

Sir Nicholas Barrington KCMG CVO* — 1992
High Commissioner to Pakistan 1989–94

Sir Frederick Catherwood*
MP MEP 1984–94
Vice-President European Parliament 1989–91

Prof H. Daniels FRS
Prof of Mathematical Statistics (Birmingham)

Sir Philip Dowson CBE PRA RIBA*
President of the Royal Academy 1993–99

Sir John Boyd KCMG* — 1994
Ambassador to Japan 1992–96
Master of Churchill College

Prof C.H. Feinstein FBA*
Prof of Economic History (Oxford)

Rt Revd Rowan Williams FBA*
Bishop of Monmouth

Lord Wedderburn of Charlton QC FBA* — 1997
Prof of Commercial Law (London) 1964-92

Prof Sir Andrew Wiles FRS*
Prof of Mathematics (Princeton)

Sir Richard Wilson KCB* — 1998
Cabinet Secretary,
Head of the Home Civil Service

His Excellency F.H. Cardoso Hon LLD*
President of Brazil

Source: *The Clare Association Annual*, 1999–2000.

The following members of the 23 Club (1960) each subscribed £100 to fund the launch of the project:

Geoffrey Alderson	Christopher Castleman	David Lloyd
Michael Armstrong	John Fletcher	Julian Platt
Nicholas Bosanquet	Mark St Giles	Tony Roberts
Anthony Bowring (and his father, Edgar)	Christopher Greening	Peter Tett
Adam Brand	Timothy Jenkins	Sam Wilson
Anthony Carey	David Lankester	Benjamin Wrey

In memoriam: *Anthony Gaitskell* and *Peter Nash*

The following subscribed in advance to ensure the project's success:

Peter Abbott	1963	Ian Baharie	1979	A.E. Binney	1992
The Rt Hon. Lord Ackner	1938	Christopher Bailey	1961	Ian Birch	1976
Paul Ackroyd	1968	P.D. Bailey	1933	Kenneth Bird	1958
Professor David K. Adams OBE	1951	Graham & Anne-Marie Baker	1986	Gordon L Black	1961
Isabelle Adams	2000	Dr Peter Baker FRC Psych	1940	Christopher Blackstone	1960
D.G. Airey	1950	Dr Peter Baldwin	1994	Michael Blair QC	1959
Kenneth E. Alder	1968	Roger Ball	1962	R.F. Blanchard	1957
Christopher Alderson	1959	Stephen Ball	1998	Jim & Lilo Bleasdale	1997
E.H. Alderson	1986	Howard Bamforth	1968	R.P. Boggon	1954
Ralph Aldwinckle	1958	Jacqueline Barbet	1997	Elly Bohme	
Dr S.C. Allcock	1980	Kevin Barbet	1999	Doctor Jason Boland	1994
Billie & Peter Allinson		Chris Barker	1967	John Boot	1954
Mr Simon A. Alterman	1976	John Barker	1958	Helen Bould	1999
Mohammed Amin	1969	Dr Amanda J. Barnes	1980	Professor Malcolm Bowie	1969
Tony Amor	1964	Geoffrey Barnett	1961	Dr M.G. Bown	1946
David R. Anderson	1973	Roger Barnett	1957	Fiona Boyd	1998
Roger Anderson	1964	J.M. Barr CBE	1948	Mr John L. Boyd	1954
Tim Anderson	1944	James Mark Barraclough	1955	Stephen A.C. Boyd	1962
A.T. Andrew	1943	Sir Kenneth J.B. Barraclough	1925	Grahame Boyes	1957
Heather Andrew	1979	Anthony M. Barrett	1948	James Boyes	1943
Daisy Andrewes	1999	Stuart Barriball	1998	Sarah Bramley	1998
Neville M. Andrews	1954	Peter Barron		R.S. Brealy	1944
John A. Anning	1957	Deborah Bartlett RIBA	1973	Eric L.P. Brentini	1939
M.A. Nova Araújo	1992	Tony Batty	1965	Jennifer Brentnall	2000
Nicholas Argyris	1962	Randolph Beard	1944	Victoria Brentnall	1997
Lindsey Arrick	1999	S.N. Beare	1957	Alan J. Bridgman	1950
Robert Ash	1960	Dr Roger Beck	1968	David P. Briggs	1998
Richard Atherton	1957	Bob Bell	1952	Dr P.D. Bristowe	1999
James Atkins	1987	Dr Wynne Bell	1995	Iain Brooksbank	1996
David Attenborough	1945	John Bellak	1949	Andrew Anand Brown	1996
Michael Aubrey	1961	Harvey Bennett	1986	Dr Barry Brown	1956
Brian Austin	1958	Leon Bennun	1981	C.W. Brown	1953
E.H.C. Avery	1996	Christopher Bentley-Phillips	1960	Chris F.A. Brown	1999
Tony Baden	1970	Dr Tara Bharucha	1992	Gemma L.M. Brown	1999
Heinrich Baelz	1997	Peter Bibby	1966	Ian Brown	1981
Dr Claude Baesens	1996	Dr R.J. Biggs	1975	J. M. Brown	1954

264

Professor P.J. Brown	1958	R.S. Coltart	1998	Jonathan K. Dormand	1996
Miss Tanya Brown	1993	Brian Colvin	1963	Garth Doubleday	1932
Amy E. Brownhill	1998	Dr Neville R. Comins	1967	Kate Doulton	1999
Mr Grant Buck	1939	Genevieve Connors	1966	Edward and Jean Dowding	1999
Dr Anthony Buckley	1939	Peter Cooch	1961	B.D. Dowker	1951
Brian Buckroyd	1951	Frances Cooke (nee Jackson)	1975	Nick Down	1983
Alison J. Budd	1973	Ria Mishaal Cooke	1999	Bob Downey	1954
Alice and Stephen Bull	1991	Eric H. Cooley	1945	Michael Downward	1960
Friedrich Wenzel Bulst	1996	Deann Cooper		Gordon B. Drummond	1963
B. Burch OBE	1956	J.S. Cooper	1947	Peter Drury	1971
Peter Burgess	1931	Dr David Cope	1966	Simon & Patricia Dudley	1999
Dr Bernard Burgoyne	1961	David Cope	1962	Dr S. Dukes	1966
Denis Burrell CBE DL	1950	Mrs Sue Cossey	1978	Guy Duncan	1953
Chloe R.V. Burrows	1999	Anthony Costello MD	1953	Kate Dunham	1988
Cassandra Burt	1992	John C. Cotman	1963	David Dunnett	1980
John C. Busby	1930	Christian P. Coulson	1997	Dr P. Dunstan	1975
Donald Bush	1952	Michael A. Covington	1977	Denis Dunstone	1956
David Bushill	1955	Neil S. Cox	1988	Dr D.J. Dunthorn	1961
Anthony Butler	1961	Mary Coxe	1971	Ian J. Eastwood	1943
Revd Canon Michael W. Butler	1957	Giles P.V. Creagh	1945	Simon R. Eccles	1969
Michael J. Butterfield	1967	David Cregan	1952	Mr Lawrence Edbrooke	1947
Abby Caine	1995	P.N.O. Crick	1959	Professor Richard J. Eden OBE	1951
Andrew Cainey	1982	Malcolm Crockford	1962	P.B. Edgley	1945
Michelle Calvert		A.P. Crook	1979	Robert B. Edwards	1976
David R. Campbell MD	1967	Jeremy Cross	1984	Tom Edwards	1986
Neil Campbell	1996	J. Anthony Cross	1987	Vincent Edwards	1966
A.L. Canham	1951	Jonathan Crossfield	1992	David Elder-Vass	1976
Gavin Canham	1985	Robert Crossley	1991	W. H. Elias	1946
William B. Carruthers	1949	P. Crowther	1967	Andrew Elkington	1954
Paul Cartledge	1981	Sir Josias Cunningham	1953	George Elkington	1982
Robert A. Cartlidge	1997	Michael Cunningham	1958	Kevin Elliker	1998
Stephen Cassell	1980	Louise Curran	1998	N. E. Elliott	1946
Georgina Maria Castiglione	1996	A.C. Currie	1974	Mark Ellison	1970
Christopher Castleman	1960	Philip Curtis	1940	John Elwick	1952
Tom Chamberlain	1996	Sarah Cutmore	1990	Mrs C.H.A. Emery	
Alastair Channing	1962	Tim Dallosso	1987	James F. English Jr.	1949
Andrew Charman	1985	Toby Damek	1996	Dr I.C. Eperon	1977
C.P.G. Chavasse	1949	Mr R.M. Damms	1984	Antony G. Evans	1998
Patrick Chavasse	1956	P.R. Daniels	1989	David J. Evans	1997
Paul Cherrington	1930	J.C. Dare	1952	Donald Evans	1944
Riccardo Chieppa		J. Davenport	1936	Simon Everard	1949
Dr John Chilton	1947	John K. Davenport DFC	1941	Derek Ewart	1967
William W. Chip	1971	Carolyne Davidson	1997	Harry M. Fairhurst	1943
Andrew Chisholm	1983	Josephine Davies	1999	Helen Worsfold	1972
Gavin Choyce	1961	Dr and Mrs J. Davies	1997	Dr Saul N. Faust	1987
David Maughan Churchill	1961	W.J. Davies	1979	T.P.N. Fawcett	1962
Richard Citron	1971	Dr Mark Davis	1991	Charles Feinstein	1963
D. Clapperton	1999	Mr and Mrs J.A. Davison and Family	1996	Peter R.K. Fender	1949
John A. Clare	1963	Richard W. Daw	1986	Rachel Fentem	1998
Revd David Clark	1949	Jack and Clare Dawe	1979	Miss Shehani Fernando	1997
Kirstin S. Clark	1991	Gervase Dawidek	1974	Eleanor Ferris	1991
John M. Clarke	1954	Norman W.F. Dawson	1966	Robert W. Field	1970
Chris Clausen-Sternwald	1969	Hugh Day	1948	Seumas V. Finn	1954
Natalie Clegg	1998	Niccolo McLeod de Masi	1998	Alan Flack	1983
A. Cliffe	1999	P.H. de Rougemont	1950	Jack Frederick Flatau	1950
Freddy & Maggi Clifford	1998	Chris Denison & Clare Coyne	1993	Terence Fleming	1975
Andrew Clive	1959	Carolyn E. Dewey	1999	Roger Fletcher	1949
Dr Ross Coles	1946	Robert Diamond	1950	Ian M Flowers	1948
L.A. Collett	1997	Dr Gerard Dickinson	1966	Julian Floyd	1981
Amy Collins	1998	Dick Doidge-Harrison	1962	Tony Flynn	1967

The Hon. Sir Alastair Forbes	1927
Dr M.J. Forbes	1964
Philip Ford	1981
Dr R.M.M. Fordham	1952
Dr W.A. Foster	1976
Daphne Fowler	1979
Will Fowler	1957
Laurie Friday (nee Barnes)	1974
Valerie Friend	1975
N.R. Frith	1952
Andrew J. Froggatt	1997
A. Michael Froomkin	1982
Dr James S. Frost	1988
Mary Ann M. Fuhry	1992
Geraint Fuller	1977
James Furner	1997
Anthony W. Furse	1944
Eva M. Götz (Miss)	1997
David Galliford	1942
Regan and Andrew Gambier	1989
Andrew Garety	1968
Robert R. Garnett	1926
Neil Garrard	1958
His Honour Judge Gaskell	1966
Colin Geary	1949
Peter George	1979
Dr Laurence Gerlis	1968
Anthony Gershuny	1972
C.J.M. Getty FRCS	1965
Dr Andrew Giddy	1984
Mark Giles	1991
Anton Gill	1967
Ronald Townley Gill	1934
Linda, Ian and Stuart Gill	1998
Dr Alan R. Gillespie	1969
Professor Alan Gillett	1950
Sir Paul Girvan	1967
Richard L. Gladstone	1941
Mark Glanville	1997
Barry Glaspell	1997
Clare P. Glover	1987
Malcolm Goddard	1975
Revd Canon John Goodchild	1961
Simon Goodchild	1999
Brian W. Goodman	1952
Mark Goodman	1982
Professor Stuart Goodwin	1951
John Gowenlock	1975
Philip Graf	1965
Michele Graham	1999
Dr Richard Grange	1943
Malcolm Grant	1991
Evan Gray	1971
Derek Grayson	1948
Clare V.L. Green	2000
David R. Green	1967
Professor Richard Green	1985
Canon Roger Greenacre	1949
Andrew Greenwood	1972
Claire Greenwood	1999

Maxwell Grender-Jones	1999
Ken Griffiths	1957
Mrs David Charles Grimes	
Dr Guy L. Gronquist	1980
Mr Russell Grosch	1954
Alison Grove	1984
Simon F. Guest	1995
Edward J. Gummow	1997
Dr Stephen Gutowski	1970
Philip Habershon	1952
Hugh R.B. Hack	1945
Richard & Jenny Hackworth	1997
D.B. Hadley	1967
E.A. Hadow	1938
David Hague	1957
Nicholas J. Hale	1965
Helen and Richard Hall	1973
Nick A. Hall	1983
Mr Geoff Halls	1972
Ben Halsted	1996
T.C. Hammarton	1992
Professor N.G.L. Hammond DSO FBA	1930
Dr Christopher Hand	1965
David Handforth	1955
Michael Hanmer	1955
Mr Roger Hardwick	2000
John Hardy	1953
Rt Revd R.M. Hardy	1957
Barney Harford	1991
Adrian Laurence Hargrave	1998
Dr Barry and Dr Gabriella Hargrave	
Neville Hargreaves	1980
Tim Harle	1972
Angie Harlock-Wilkinson	1974
Bill Harris	1997
Dr Judy E. Harrison	1980
Jon Hart	1990
Dr David Hartley	1956
John J. Hartley	1953
Derek Harvey-Piper	1940
Arwa Hassan	1991
Charles Hastings	1966
James Hawkins	1999
D. Stuart Hay	1952
M. G. Hayes	1975
Rose Serena Head	1999
Dr John A. Heap CMG	1957
Richard L. Heap	1980
Mr C.J. Heath	
David Hebden	1967
Colin Heggie	1964
Nigel Heggie	1967
Professor V. Heine	1960
Andrew E. Henderson	1996
Damian Charles Henderson	1997
Kenneth Henderson	1954
Alex Hewitson	1996
Charles A. Hicks	1965
Jeremy Hicks	1982
V.C-T. Higgs	1997

Dr M.A. & Dr H.K. Higton	1989
Ian R. Hill	1966
Bill Hill	1951
Christopher Hindle	1962
Guy Hitchings	1945
Christopher Hix	1975
Dale Hoak	1967
Mr Raymond & Mrs Irene Hodges	
Joe Hoffman	1999
Dr John Hoggett QC	1958
David Hollander	1997
Elizabeth Holman	1988
Andrew B. Holmes	1973
David Holmes	1972
John Holmes	1953
R.G.L. Holmes	1951
Ken and Eileen Hori	1987
Dr J.U.M. Horne	1967
Olivia Horsfall Turner	1998
Niall Hoskin	1972
E.W. Hoult	1952
Susanna Howard	1997
Richard Hoy	1950
John M. Hoyle	1957
T.C.E. Hughes	1931
Stephen Humphrey	1971
Dr Brian L. Hunt	1958
Katherine Hunter	1985
W.R.P. Hunter	1987
Vanessa Huntly	1997
Sir Michael Hutchison	1952
Roger Hyde	1945
John Irvine	1954
Mr and Dr W. Isalski	1998
Dr P.J. Islip	1955
Matthew Isotta	1984
Bruce J. Jack	1946
S.W. Jackman	1961
Barry Jackson	1949
Dr Catherine M. Jackson	1982
Peter A.D. Jackson	1969
Stephen Jackson	1970
Dr Thomas S. Jacques	1989
Michael Jaeger	1953
Hubertus F. Jahn	2000
Clair Jaquiss for Cranstoun Gill	1976
Faiz A.A. Jasdanwalla	1946
Stephen Jefferson	1972
Ian M.E. Jeffery	1952
Charles Jenkins	1989
Stewart M.F. Jennings	1967
Yvonne Jerrold	1974
M.J.S. Jessop	1989
Alan Johansson	1948
Bridget Johnson	1977
K.W. Johnson	1951
W. Johnson	1945
M. Elaine Johnston	1977
Arfon Jones	1962
Revd Douglas Jones	1942

266

Name	Year	Name	Year	Name	Year
Dr G.A. Jones	1954	Dr Antony Lloyd	1957	Ian McFarlane	1985
Glyn Jones	1973	David A. Lloyd	1960	Frank McGown	1933
Helen E. Jones	1997	John S. Lloyd	1946	Francis McKenzie	1997
Peter N. Jones	1971	Nigel Lloyd	1970	J.W. McKimm	1989
Peter & Alison Jones	1999	Ian S Lockhart	1959	Simon McTighe	1968
Linda Jotham	1978	James Loudon	1996	Philip Medcalf	2000
Katy Joubert	2000	Mr W.G.G. Loughridge	1956	Mr Ajatshatru Mehta	1998
The Very Revd Peter Judd	1976	Gordon Loveless	1949	Mrs J. Mela	
Simon Judge & Jane Cox	1978	D.J. Lowe	1999	Jonathan G. Midgley	1996
Dr Victor Kateck	1999	D.F. Lowther	1951	K.M.H. Millar	1953
W. Ken Keag	1969	John Lascalles Lucas	1950	Robin Millar	1967
Catherine Kearns	1999	Christopher A. Luckhurst	1998	Professor David Miller	1949
Nicholas Keen	1963	Anthony C. Lunn Sc.D	1964	Barry Millington	1971
Dr Alison Keightley	1972	Sarah Louise Lynam	1998	B. Mirosevic-Sorgo	1944
G.D. Kemp	1953	Martin Lyth	1937	Jacqui Mitchell	1991
Dr John Kempster	1950	Alan Macgregor	1952	Jessica Mnatzaganian	1991
Alastair Kennedy	1964	D.E. Mackie	1962	Kenneth Mobbs	1943
Ian H. Kerr	1945	Ian Mackrill	1937	D.E. Moggridge	1967
John Kibble	1943	David MacMillan	1965	Dr Anissa Mohamed	1988
G.S. Kidd	1945	Hugh MacMillan	1961	John Mollison	1935
James Killick	1990	Dr Elaine Maddock	1977	Jo Mooney	1995
Helen Kilsby (nee Atkinson)	1987	Dr & Mrs D.B. Magee	1999	Philip W. Moore	1979
Dr J.C. King	1975	Deborah Manning	1980	Richard Moore	1965
Peter King, School Teacher Fellow	1984	Kevin Mansell	1997	Timothy W. Moore	1998
Paul A.R. Kirby	1999	Hazel Mansfield	1997	Dr David F. Morgan	1962
A.H.M. Kirk-Greene	1947	Yannis Manuelides	1983	Christopher Morley	1999
Dr L.J. Kirsch	1965	Dr Kenneth Mao	1969	Peter Morley	1997
Matthew Kirshen	1999	Dr and Mrs B. Maraschin		Professor and Mrs Stephen Morley	1997
Mark Kissin	1969	R.G. Margetts	1972	P.C. Mornement	1949
Ms Amy Klohr	1975	Christos N. Markides	1997	Robin Morrall	1959
Dr Peter Knewstubb	1950	J.G. Marks	1950	C.E.H Morris	1925
Mr and Mrs C.J. Knight	1997	Professor B.P. Marmion AO	1953	Dr Roger Morris	1952
Mr Martin J. Knott	1957	N.F. Marsh CBE	1925	David B. Morton	1977
Andrzej Kowalski	1977	Michael C. Marshall	1999	Professor C.F.D. Moule	1944
Christian A. Kramer	1999	Helen Mary Martin	1999	Lea A. Muhlstein	1999
W. Christopher Kurowski	2000	Helen Martin	1997	Mr Oleg Mukovsky	1990
Dr Günter Kuscher and Mrs Astrid Kuscher		Jon Martin	1950	John Mulvaney	1951
Chi Lok Eddy Lai	1999	R. Michael Martin	1948	Jamie Mure	1981
Dr Roger Lane	1925	James Massy	1949	Caroline E. Musgrave	1998
J.S. Lang	1950	Meryl & Nigel Masterton	1997	Daniel Nabarro	1966
Carol Langendoen	1992	Arthur Mathisen	1957	C. John Naylor OBE	1962
Jon Lansman	1976	Stephanie Mathisen	1989	Jeff Neate CASM	1996
Michael Lapidge	1990	Keith Mattocks	1967	Rory Neeson	1999
Christopher Latham	1952	A.D. Maunder	1956	Annabel Newall	1990
Kate Lawrence	1998	H. Bernard Mayer	1942	Dr P.E. Newley	1969
John Lawton	1969	Christian Mayo	1989	Christopher Roger Newman	1997
Tom Lawton	1998	Miss Claire Roisin McAleer	1999	P. Newton	2000
M. Le Q. Herbert	1957	Mr & Mrs Patrick Kennedy Curran		David Nicholls	1975
Corinne Lee		Bruce McAlpine	1965	Dr Graham Nicholson	1966
Mr J.G. Lee	1985	Ian M. McAlpine	1961	Dr Eni G. Njoku	1969
Joff Lee	1997	Christopher C. McCann	1966	Peter Noll	1962
Richard Lees-Jones	1953	Stuart McCarthy	1993	Billy Normington	1955
George A. Lefroy	1964	Michael McCooe	1997	Nigel A.M. North	1969
Michael Leggatt	1951	Andrew McCormick	1998	Kingsley Norton	1970
H.K. Leventis	1960	Lieutenant Commander		Pat Nuttall	1952
James Geoffrey Levine	1998	Duncan McCue Royal Navy	1987	Donough O'Brien	1941
Alexandra Lewin	1992	Dr C. Behan McCullagh	1959	Adrienne A. O'Cofaigh	1999
Mrs Kate Littlechild, Chapel Secretary		Julie McCulloch (nee Bradshaw)	1990	Helen O'Hara (nee Smith)	1984
Timothy Lewis Lloyd	1955	Dr E. Lawson McDonald	1937	Professor Paul O'Higgins	1957
Bing Li	2000	Dr Ian McDonald	1951	John O'Neill	1956

267

268

Andrew J. Smith	1971
Caroline N.J. Smith	1998
David H.C. Smith	1981
Dr John D. Smith	1942
Martin Smith	1965
Martyn Smith	1978
Madeleine Smout	1981
Chris Smyth	1960
William J. Smyth	1987
David Henry Snowden	1998
Dr Peter Sole	1941
William Sommerville	1958
John Speed	1967
H.J. Spencer	1941
R.C.H. Spencer	1949
Clare Spottiswoode and Oliver Richards	1972
Dr Kumar Sriskandan	1976
The Revd Victor Standing	1967
Jacqui Stanford	1995
Nuna Staniaszek	1979
Christopher J. Stanley	1997
David Steeds	1967
Graham Steel	1995
Bob and Barbara Steiner	1972
The Revd Prof W.P. Stephens	1952
Mark Stephenson	1977
John A. Stevenson	1936
Mr Robin Steward	1954
Anita and Peter Stewart	1990
Brigadier Nigel M. Still CBE	1954
Mr H. Stockley	
Mark Stockton	1999
Andrew Stott	1973
Dr Wolfgang Strassl	1983
Mrs Corinne Stubbs	1977
T.J. Sullivan	1943
Prem. C. Sundaram	1988
Peter J. Sutton	1961
Susan Grimes Sweetland	
Lucy Swierczynski	1996
Richard Swift	1962
Sir Hugh Sykes DL	1952
Nigel Symington	1966
Cindy Tam	1983
Dr Francis S.K. Tan	1971
Drs Pat Tate and Richard Dyball	1977
A.E. Tattershall	1998
David Taylor CBE	1954
Peter J. Taylor	1977
Richard T. Taylor	1953
T. Paul A. Taylor	1975
Professor George Teeling Smith	1948
A.M. Telford	1959
Liz Tennant	1992
Diana Terry (Nee Streeten)	1979
Dr D.G. Thomas	1962
Eddie Thomas	1964
Dr Benjamin Thompson	1981
Jeremy Thompson	1971
Miss Keara Thompson	2000

Neil Thompson	1974
Jim Tiller	1960
John Tilley MA(Hons Chem.) MB B Chir	
(London. Hosp)	1935
Mrs Jan Tobin, College Nurse	
Wallace E. Tobin	1959
Dr Richard Tomiak	1975
A. Tovell	1986
Frankie Towers	1999
J.H.N. Towers	1958
Simon B. Towl	1997
Dr Steve Travis	1987
Joanna Treasure	1979
Donald Truman	1956
Dr Barbara C. Shepherd	1983
Brian Turnbull	1962
Nicholas Turner	1960
Stephen Turner	1952
Colin Turpin	1961
Dr Stephen Unwin	1973
M.I. Valtonen	1990
H.M. Vann	1998
P.H. Vaughan	1959
James E. Vigus	1998
Penelope Vincent-Sweet	1976
George Joseph Vining	1959
J.P. Visman	1953
Annan Astrid Voskuil	1996
Miss Nadine C. Waddington	1986
Jenny Wakeling	1989
Christopher Walbank	1978
Robert Walker	1969
David Wall	1963
O.R.D. and E.C. Wallis	
G.J.O. and J.H. Wallis	
Zoe H.V. Wallis	1999
H. Catherine Walter	1994
Peter M. Ward	1942
Michael Ware	1951
Douglas Warner	1998
Keith Warner	1952
Dr Madhuri V. Warren (nee Shembekar)	1985
Nigel S. Waters	1970
Alan Watson	1944
Alan R. Watson	
Victor H. Watson	1948
Jillian C. Watt	1999
Barry Weatherill	1959
David H. Weber	1972
Nigel Weiss	1954
Joanne Welch	1981
Simon Weller	1992
Colin Brown	1944
R.G. West	1948
Miles Weston	1965
Sally Weston	1981
Canon John Westwood	1974
M.J.M. Westwood	1966
Adrian Wheeler	1968
Michael Wheeler	1945

Margaret Faultless	1980
A.G.D. White OAM	1956
Eric White	1974
Lucie White	1996
Robert Whitfield	1964
Simon Whiting	1972
Peter Whitlock	1935
Simon Whitmore	1953
Dr Adam Whybrew	1989
David H. Whyte	1934
Stephen K. Wicken	2000
The Revd Mark Wigglesworth	1979
Anissa Wigham	1997
Hazel Wigham	
J. David Wigham	
Dr John Wigley	1993
Nigel Wildish	1966
Richard Wildman	1965
The Revd Prof M.F. Wiles	1959
Eric Wilkinson	1940
G.M.B. Wilkinson	1954
Richard Willets	1987
Dr C.R. Williams	1971
E.D.G. Williams	1954
Huw Richard Williams	1980
Revd Julian Williams	1984
Laura Katherine Williams	1998
Dr Richard H. Williams MCD MRTPI	
Mrs E.B. Williams Dunelm	
Tim Williams	1963
David Wilson	1967
H.W. Wilson	1936
Lin Wilson	1954
Robert M. Wilson	1957
John Winders	1954
W.R. Winfield	1965
Aino Lea Winther-Pedersen	1989
Anna Woerndl	1995
Helen J. Wood	1998
Helen M. Wood (nee Stoddart)	1975
Isabel Woodman	1998
Dr Charles J. Woodrow	1987
Duncan Woods	1993
Colin Woodward	1977
Emma Roisin Woodward	1991
Rachel Woolrych	1989
Sarah L. Wormald	1996
Ben Wrey	1960
Charles S.W. Wright FRCOG	1962
Dr Gordon H. Wright	1958
Claire Wring	1999
Dr & Mrs Sam Chak-Ming Yeung	
Mr Trevor Ming-Yee Yeung	1998
Robert A. Yorke	1963
Paul Young	1974
Peter Young	1959

272

Credits
Unless an acknowledgment appears below, the illustrations in this volume have been provided by Clare College, Cambridge. Every effort has been made to contact the copyright holders of all works reproduced in this book. However, if acknowledgements have been omitted, the publishers ask those concerned to contact Third Millennium Publishing.

Grateful acknowledgement is made to reprint from the following:

Extracts from *The Old Century and Seven More Years* and 'The Last Meeting' by Siegfried Sassoon, copyright Siegfried Sassoon by kind permission of George Sassoon; 'Untitled' and 'May Song' from *Eighteen Poems* by Thomas Merton ©1977,1985 by The Trustees of the Merton Legacy Trust, reprinted by permission of New Directions Publishing Corp. 'The Flight into Egypt' from *The Collected Poems of Thomas Merton* copyright ©1944 by Our Lady of Gethsemani Monastery, reprinted by permission of New Directions Publishing Corp; *Elected Silence* by Thomas Merton (Birchall & Sons, London 1949, repr. Burns and Oates) ©Our Lady of Gethsemani Monastery; Extracts from *Cambridge and Clare* by Sir Harry Godwin 1985, reproduced by permission of Cambridge University Press; 'Away', 'Transit' and 'Compline' from *The Collected Poems of John Berryman*, 1989, reproduced by permission of Faber and Faber; Extracts from *The House of Dr Dee* by Peter Ackroyd (Hamish Hamilton 1993), ©Peter Ackroyd, reproduced with permission of Penguin Books Limited; 'Punting into Clare' by Barbara Peck reproduced with permission from *The Guardian*, ©Guardian Newspapers.

Picture credits:

Arup Associates, 97, 98, 204; Tim Brown, 250, 251; Peter Barron, 38, 58, 95, 96, 237, 252; John Batten, 18, 69, 72 (all), 138, 187, 188, 255; By kind permission of 'The Cambridge Evening News,' 52; Beverley Carter 110, 111 with grateful acknowledgements; David M. Churchill, 146; Clare College Archive, 169; Teresa Livonian Cole, 228; Charlie Colmer, 12, 25, 60, 50, 61, 65, 195 (right), 196, 200, 202, 207–11, 236, 238, 239 (left), 241 (right), 252; Celia Duff, 224 (both); Richard Eden, 151, 153; Roy Fox, 22, 24, 39, 48, 54, 56, 81, 115, 142, 145, 149, 195 (left), 198, 199; Dona Haycraft, 11, 17, 239 (right), 241 (left), 243, 253, 256; The Hutlton Getty Picture Collection, 65; Peter Knewstubb 67, 99, 161, 220; Roger Morris, 186, 190; Everest Expedition Team taken by John Noel ©The John Noel Photographic Collection, 124; Andrew Norman, 69, 89, 74, 75, 76, 77, 160, 161, 162 (both), 165, 172, 173, 176 (both), 178, 179, 182, 183, 184, 185 (both), 189, 198, 229, 234; Nigel North, 228; Mallory and Irvine leaving Camp IV for the summit taken by Noel Odell, by permission of Peter Odell, 124; Alice Rawsthorn, 225; Nancy-Jane Rucker, 233; Photograph on page 141 taken from Plate 40 of *A Concise History of the University of Cambridge*, by Elizabeth Leedham-Green, (Cambridge University Press 1996).